The Handbook of Artificial Intelligence

The Handbook of Artificial Intelligence

Volume I

Edited by

Avron Barr and Edward A. Feigenbaum

Department of Computer Science
Stanford University

Pitman

PITMAN BOOKS LIMITED

39 Parker Street, London WC2B 5PB

Copyright © 1981 by William Kaufmann, Inc.
For further information, write to:
Permissions, William Kaufmann, Inc.,
One First Street, Los Altos, California 94022.

First published in Great Britain 1981

ISBN 0 273 08540 9

Printed in the United States of America

To the graduate students

CONTENTS OF VOLUME I

LIST OF CONTRIBUTORS

The following people have made the *Handbook* a reality. Together, over the last five years, they have combed the entire literature of AI and have attempted to make a coherent presentation of this very diverse field. These researchers and students, from Stanford and other AI centers, have contributed to Volumes I and II or are now engaged in preparing Volume III (being edited by Paul R. Cohen).

Chapter Editors

Janice Aikins
James S. Bennett
Victor Ciesielski (Rutgers U)
William J. Clancey
Paul R. Cohen
James E. Davidson
Thomas Dietterich

Robert Elschlager
Lawrence Fagan
Anne v.d.L. Gardner
Takeo Kanade (CMU)
Jorge Phillips
Steve Tappel
Stephen Westfold

Contributors

Robert Anderson (Rand)
Douglas Appelt
David Arnold
Michael Ballantyne (U Texas)
David Barstow (Schlumberger)
Peter Biesel (Rutgers U)
Lee Blaine (IMSSS)
W. W. Bledsoe (U Texas)
Rodney Brooks
Bruce Buchanan
Richard Chestek
Kenneth Clarkson
Randall Davis (MIT)
Gerard Dechen
Johan de Kleer (Xerox)

Jon Doyle
R. Geoff Dromey (U Wollongong)
Richard Duda (Fairchild)
Robert Engelmore
Ramez El-Masri (Honeywell)
Susan Epstein (Rutgers U)
Robert Filman (Indiana U)
Fritz Fisher
Christian Freksa (UC Berkeley)
Peter Friedland
Richard Gabriel
Michael Genesereth
Neil Goldman (ISI)
Ira Goldstein (Xerox)
George Heidorn (IBM)

Douglas Hofstadter (Indiana U)
Elaine Kant (CMU)
William Laaser (Xerox)
Douglas Lenat
William Long (MIT)
Robert London
Pamela McCorduck
Robert Moore (SRI)
Richard Pattis
Neil C. Rowe
Gregory Ruth (MIT)
Daniel Sagalowicz (SRI)
Behrokh Samadi

William Scherlis (CMU)
Andrew Silverman
Donald Smith (Rutgers U)
Phillip Smith (U Waterloo)
Reid G. Smith (Canadian DREA)
William Swartout (MIT)
William van Melle
Richard Waldinger (SRI)
Richard Waters (MIT)
Sholom Weiss (Rutgers U)
David Wilkins (SRI)
Terry Winograd

Reviewers

Harold Abelson (MIT)
Saul Amarel (Rutgers U)
Robert Balzer (ISI)
Harry Barrow (Fairchild)
Thomas Binford
Daniel Bobrow (Xerox)
John Seely Brown (Xerox)
Richard Burton (Xerox)
Lewis Creary
Andrea diSessa (MIT)
Daniel Dolata (UC Santa Cruz)
Lee Erman (ISI)
Adele Goldberg (Xerox)
Cordell Green (SCI)
Norman Haas (SRI)
Kenneth Kahn (MIT)

Jonathan King
Casimir Kulikowski (Rutgers U)
Brian P. McCune (AI&DS)
Donald Michie (U Edinburgh)
Nils Nilsson (SRI)
Glen Ouchi (UC Santa Cruz)
Ira Pohl (UC Santa Cruz)
Herbert Simon (CMU)
David E. Smith
Dennis Smith
Mark Stefik (Xerox)
Albert Stevens (BBN)
Allan Terry
Perry Thorndyke (Rand)
Donald Walker (SRI)
Keith Wescourt (Rand)

Production

Lester Ernest
Marion Hazen
David Fuchs
Dianne Kanerva

Roy Nordblom
Thomas Rindfleisch
Ellen Smith
Helen Tognetti

PREFACE

ARTIFICIAL INTELLIGENCE is of growing interdisciplinary interest and practical importance. People with widely varying backgrounds and professions are discovering new ideas and new tools in this young science. Theory-minded psychologists have developed new models of the mind based on the fundamental concepts of AI—symbol systems and information processing. Linguists are also interested in these basic notions, as well as in AI work in computational linguistics, aimed at producing programs that actually understand language. And philosophers, in considering the progress, problems, and potential of this work toward nonhuman intelligence, have sometimes found new perspectives on the age-old problems of the nature of mind and knowledge.

In other spheres of activity, people often first come across AI in the form of some "expert" system that is being applied experimentally in their own area—chemical data interpretation, symbolic integration, infectious disease diagnosis, DNA sequencing, computer systems debugging, structural engineering, computer-chip design, and so on. As the cost of computation continues to fall, many new computer applications become viable. Since, for many of these, there are no mathematical "cores" to structure the calculational use of the computer, such areas will inevitably be served by symbolic models and symbolic inference techniques. Yet those who understand symbolic computation have been speaking largely to themselves for the first 25 years of AI's history. We feel that it is urgent for AI to "go public" in the manner intended by this three-volume *Handbook of Artificial Intelligence*.

Since the *Handbook* project began in 1975, dozens of researchers have labored to produce short, jargon-free explanations of AI programming techniques and concepts. With these volumes, we have tried to build bridges to be crossed by engineers, by professionals and scientists in other fields, and by our own colleagues in computer science. We have tried to cover the breadth and depth of AI, presenting general overviews of the scientific issues, as well as detailed discussions of particular techniques and exemplary computer systems. And, most important, we have presented the key concepts—search, divide-and-conquer, semantic nets, means-ends analysis, hierarchical planning, ATNs, procedural knowledge, blackboard architecture, scripts and frames, goal-directed and data-driven processing, learning, and many more—in the context of their actual application in AI. If they were presented more abstractly, the unique perspective afforded by AI research on these universal ideas would be lost. Throughout, we have tried to keep in mind the reader who is not a specialist in AI.

In short, we have tried to present a survey of AI research that is motivated historically and scientifically, without attempting to present a new synthesis of this young, multifaceted, rapidly changing field. One can view these *Handbook* volumes as an encyclopedia of AI programming techniques, their successful applications, some of their limitations, and the computational concepts that have been used to describe them. Readers from different fields will interpret these data in different ways—we hope that many of you will find useful new ideas and new perspectives.

The *Handbook* contains several different kinds of articles. Key AI concepts and techniques are described in core articles (e.g., heuristic search, semantic nets). Important individual AI programs (e.g., SHRDLU, MACSYMA, PROSPECTOR) are presented in separate articles that indicate, among other things, the designer's goals, the techniques employed, and the reasons why the program is important. The problems and approaches in each major area are discussed in overview articles, which should be particularly useful to those who seek a summary of the underlying issues that motivate AI research.

We intend that the *Handbook of Artificial Intelligence* be a living and changing reference work. In particular, we hope that our colleagues will take time to alert us to errors we have made, of omission or commission, and that we have an opportunity to correct these in future editions.

Acknowledgments

Many people have contributed to the *Handbook* project. On pages ix–x is an alphabetical list of those who have been involved so far, including article contributors, reviewers, and the chapter editors who have spent months working the individual chapters into coherent presentations of a particular AI subarea. The following is as accurate a reconstruction as possible of the contributions to this first volume over the last five years.

The "Search" chapter was written by Anne Gardner, starting from some articles prepared for a problem seminar in the spring of 1975. Background material was made available by Nils Nilsson, who also read earlier drafts, as did Bruce Buchanan, Lewis Creary, James Davidson, Ira Pohl, Reid Smith, Mark Stefik, and David Wilkins.

"Representation of Knowledge" was edited by Avron Barr and James Davidson. The article on logic was written by Robert Filman, semantic nets by Douglas Appelt, semantic primitives by Anne Gardner, and frames by James Bennett. Mark Stefik carefully reviewed an early draft of this chapter.

Anne Gardner, James Davidson, and Avron Barr edited "Understanding Natural Language." Articles were worked on by Janice Aikins, Rodney Brooks, William Clancey, Paul Cohen, Gerard Dechen, Richard Gabriel, Norman Haas, Douglas Hofstadter, Andrew Silverman, Phillip Smith, Reid Smith, William van Melle, and David Wilkins. Neil Goldman reviewed an early draft of the chapter. Terry Winograd made background material available and also reviewed an early draft.

"Understanding Spoken Language" was prepared by Lawrence Fagan, Paul Cohen, and Avron Barr, with helpful comments from James Bennett, Lee Erman, and Donald Walker.

The professional editor responsible for the form of the final copy, including electronic typesetting and page design, was Dianne Kanerva. Earlier in the project's history, professional editing on several chapters was done by Helen Tognetti. Ellen Smith also assisted in this important work.

The book was set in Computer Modern fonts (Knuth, 1979) and was produced directly on a computer-driven phototypesetting device. Publisher William Kaufmann and his staff have been patient and helpful throughout this process.

The Advanced Research Projects Agency of the Department of Defense and the Biotechnology Resources Program of the National Institutes of Health supported the *Handbook* project as part of their long-standing and continuing efforts to develop and disseminate the science and technology of AI.   Earlier versions of *Handbook* material were distributed as technical reports of the Stanford Computer Science Department. The electronic text-preparation facilities available to Stanford computer scientists on the SAIL, SCORE, and SUMEX computers were used.

We wish specially to acknowledge Anne Gardner, whose scholarship during the early years of the *Handbook* project was invaluable, and inspirational.

Finally, let us not forget that many of the programs described herein as landmark events in the history of AI were labored over single-handedly by graduate students trying to implement their thesis ideas. These AI systems have consistently been among the most complex and innovative computer programs of their day.   They stand as a tribute to the caliber and creativity of those who have been drawn to AI research.

Chapter I

Introduction

CHAPTER I: INTRODUCTION

A. ARTIFICIAL INTELLIGENCE

ARTIFICIAL INTELLIGENCE (AI) is the part of computer science concerned with designing intelligent computer systems, that is, systems that exhibit the characteristics we associate with intelligence in human behavior—understanding language, learning, reasoning, solving problems, and so on. Many believe that insights into the nature of the mind can be gained by studying the operation of such programs. Since the field first evolved in the mid–1950s, AI researchers have invented dozens of programming techniques that support some sort of intelligent behavior. The *Handbook of Artificial Intelligence* is an encyclopedia of the major developments of the field's first 25 years—programs, programming techniques, and the computational concepts used to describe them.

Whether or not they lead to a better understanding of the mind, there is every evidence that these developments will lead to a new, *intelligent technology* that may have dramatic effects on our society. Experimental AI systems have already generated interest and enthusiasm in industry and are being developed commercially. These experimental systems include programs that

1. solve some hard problems in chemistry, biology, geology, engineering, and medicine at human-expert levels of performance,
2. manipulate robotic devices to perform some useful, repetitive, sensory-motor tasks, and
3. answer questions posed in simple dialects of English (or French, Japanese, or any other natural language, as they are called).

There is every indication that useful AI programs will play an important part in the evolving role of computers in our lives—a role that has changed, in our lifetimes, from remote to commonplace and that, if current expectations about computing cost and power are correct, is likely to evolve further from useful to essential.

The *Handbook* is composed of short articles about AI concepts, techniques, and systems, grouped into chapters that correspond to the major subdivisions of the field. This first article of the *Handbook* discusses what we mean by "artificial intelligence," both in terms of the interests and methods of the people doing AI research and in terms of the kinds of intelligent programs they have studied. We hope that this brief introduction will elucidate not only the potentially dramatic impact of intelligent technology on society, but also the possibilities that AI research affords for new insights into the puzzle that human intelligence is. The other two articles in this introductory chapter are meant as study guides: One describes the *Handbook* itself—its organization, what is in it and what is not—while the second offers guides for finding relevant material in the literature.

The Origins of Artificial Intelligence

> Scientific fields emerge as the concerns of scientists congeal around various phenomena. Sciences are not defined, they are recognized. (Newell, 1973a, p. 1)

The intellectual currents of the times help direct scientists to the study of certain phenomena. For the evolution of AI, the two most important forces in the intellectual environment of the 1930s and 1940s were *mathematical logic,* which had been under rapid development since the end of the 19th century, and new ideas about *computation.* The logical systems of Frege, Whitehead and Russell, Tarski, and others showed that some aspects of reasoning could be formalized in a relatively simple framework. Mathematical logic has continued to be an active area of investigation in AI, in part because logico-deductive systems have been successfully implemented on computers. But even before there were computers, the mathematical formalization of logical reasoning shaped people's conception of the relation between computation and intelligence.

Ideas about the nature of computation, due to Church, Turing, and others, provided the link between the notion of formalization of reasoning and the computing machines about to be invented. What was essential in this work was the abstract conception of computation as *symbol processing.* The first computers were numerical calculators that appeared to embody little, if any, real intelligence. But before these machines were even designed, Church and Turing had seen that numbers were an inessential aspect of computation—they were just one way of interpreting the internal states of the machine. Turing, who has been called the Father of AI, not only invented a simple, universal, and nonnumerical model of computation, but also argued directly for the possibility that computational mechanisms could behave in a way that would be perceived as intelligent. Douglas Hofstadter's book *Gödel, Escher, Bach: an Eternal Golden Braid* (1979) gives a thorough and fascinating account of the development of these ideas about logic and computation and of their relation to AI.

As Allen Newell and Herbert Simon point out in the "Historical Addendum" to their classic work *Human Problem Solving* (1972), there were other strong intellectual currents from several directions that converged in the middle of this century in the people who founded the science of Artificial Intelligence. The concepts of cybernetics and self-organizing systems of Wiener, McCulloch, and others focused on the macroscopic behavior of "locally simple" systems. The cyberneticists influenced many fields because their thinking spanned many fields, linking ideas about the workings of the nervous system with information theory and control theory, as well as with logic and computation. The ideas of the cyberneticists were part of the Zeitgeist, and in many cases they influenced the early workers in AI directly as their teachers.

What eventually connected these diverse ideas was, of course, the development of the computing machines themselves, guided by Babbage, Turing, von Neumann, and others. It was not long after the machines became available that people began to try to write programs to solve puzzles, play chess, and translate texts from one language to another—the first AI programs. What was it about computers that triggered the development of AI? Many ideas about computing relevant to AI emerged in the early designs—ideas about memories and processors, about systems and control, and about levels of languages and programs. But the single attribute of the new machines that brought about the emergence of a new science was their very *complexity*, encouraging the development of new and more direct ways of describing complex processes—in terms of complicated data structures and procedures with hundreds of different steps.

Computers, Complexity, and Intelligence

As Pamela McCorduck notes in her entertaining historical study of AI, *Machines Who Think* (1979), there has been a long-standing connection between the idea of complex mechanical devices and intelligence. Starting with the fabulously intricate clocks and mechanical automata of past centuries, people have made an intuitive link between the *complexity* of a machine's operation and some aspects of their own mental life. Over the last few centuries, new technologies have resulted in a dramatic increase in the complexity we can achieve in the things we build. Modern computers are orders of magnitude more complex than anything man has built before.

The first work on computers in this century focused on the kinds of numerical computations that had previously been performed collaboratively by teams of hundreds of clerks, organized so that each did one small subcalculation and passed his results on to the clerk at the next desk. Not long after the dramatic success demonstrated by the first digital computers with these elaborate calculations, people began to explore the possibility of more generally intelligent mechanical behavior—could machines play chess, prove theorems, or translate languages?

They could, but not very well. The computer performs its calculations following the step-by-step instructions it is given—the method must be specified *in complete detail.* Most computer scientists are concerned with designing new algorithms, new languages, and new machines for performing tasks like solving equations and alphabetizing lists—tasks that people perform with methods they can explicate. However, people cannot specify how they decide which move to make in a chess game or how they determine that two sentences "mean the same thing."

The realization that the detailed steps of almost all intelligent human activity were unknown marked the beginning of Artificial Intelligence as a separate part of computer science. AI researchers investigate different kinds of computation and different ways of describing computation in an effort not just to create intelligent artifacts, but also to understand what intelligence is. Their basic tenet is that human intellectual capacity will be best described in the terms that we invent to describe AI programs. However, we are just beginning to learn enough about those programs to know how to describe them. The computational ideas discussed in this book have been used in programs that perform many different tasks, sometimes at the level of human performance, often much worse. Most of these methods are obviously not the same ones that people use to perform the tasks—some of them might be.

Consider, for example, computer programs that play chess. Current programs are quite proficient—the best experimental systems play at the human "expert" level, but not as well as human chess "masters." The programs work by searching through a space of possible moves, that is, considering the alternative moves and their consequences several steps ahead in the game, just as human players do. Computers can search through thousands of moves in the same time it takes human players to search through a dozen or so, and techniques for efficient searching constitute some of the core ideas of AI. The reason that computers cannot beat the best human players is that looking ahead is not all there is to chess—since there are too many possible moves to search exhaustively, alternatives must be evaluated without knowing for sure which will lead to a winning game, and this is one of those abilities that human experts cannot explicate. Psychological studies have shown that chess masters have learned to "see" thousands of meaningful configurations of pieces when they look at a chess position, which presumably helps them decide on the best move, but no one has yet designed a computer program that can identify these configurations.

The Status of Artificial Intelligence

Within most scientific disciplines there are several distinct areas of research, each with its own specific interests, research techniques, and terminology. In AI, these specializations include research on language understanding, vision systems, problem solving, AI tools and programming languages, automatic programming, and several others. As is apparent from its chapter headings, the *Handbook* is organized around the different subareas, as are most reviews of progress in AI. (See, e.g., Nilsson's thorough, and surprisingly current, survey of AI research, written in 1974.) The following discussion of the status of AI attempts to cut across the subfields, identifying some aspects of intelligent behavior and indicating the state of relevant AI research.

There is an important philosophical point here that we will sidestep. Doing arithmetic or learning the capitals of all the countries of the world, for example, are certainly activities that *indicate* intelligence in humans. The issue here is whether a computer system that can perform these tasks can be said to *know* or *understand* anything. This point has been discussed at length (see, e.g., Searle, 1980, and appended commentary), and we will avoid it here by describing the *behaviors* as intelligent and not concerning ourselves with how to describe the machines that produce them. Many intelligent activities besides numerical calculation and information retrieval have been accomplished by programs. Many key thought processes—like recognizing people's faces and reasoning by analogy—are still puzzles; they are performed so "unconsciously" by people that adequate computational mechanisms have not been postulated for them.

One word of caution. Like the different subfields of AI, the different behaviors discussed here are not at all independent. Separating them out is just a convenient way of indicating what current AI programs can do and what they can't do. Most AI research projects are concerned with many, if not all, of these aspects of intelligence.

Problem solving. The first big "successes" in AI were programs that could solve puzzles and play games like chess. Techniques like looking ahead several moves and dividing difficult problems into easier subproblems evolved into the fundamental AI techniques of *search* and *problem reduction.* Today's programs play championship-level checkers and backgammon, as well as very good chess. Another problem-solving program that integrates mathematical formulas symbolically has attained very high levels of performance and is being used by scientists and engineers across the country. Some programs can even improve their performance with experience.

As discussed above, the open questions in this area involve capabilities that human players have but cannot articulate, like the chess master's ability to see the board configuration in terms of meaningful patterns. Another basic open question involves the original conceptualization of a problem, called in AI the choice of problem representation. Humans often solve a problem by finding a way of thinking about it that makes the solution easy—AI programs, so far, must be told how to think about the problems they solve (i.e., the space in which to search for the solution).

Logical reasoning. Closely related to problem and puzzle solving was early work on logical deduction. Programs were developed that could "prove" assertions by manipulating a database of facts, each represented by discrete data structures just as they are represented by discrete formulas in mathematical logic. These methods, unlike many other AI techniques, could be shown to be complete and consistent. That is, so long as the original facts were correct, the programs could prove all theorems that followed from the facts, and only those theorems.

Logical reasoning has been one of the most persistently investigated subareas of AI research. Of particular interest are the problems of finding ways of focusing on only the relevant facts in a large database and of keeping track of the justifications for beliefs and updating them when new information arrives.

Language. The domain of language understanding was also investigated by early AI researchers and has consistently attracted interest. Programs have been written that answer questions posed in English from an internal database, that translate sentences from one language to another, that follow instructions given in English, and that acquire knowledge by reading textual material and building an internal database. Some programs have even achieved limited success in interpreting instructions spoken into a microphone instead of typed into the computer. Although these language systems are not nearly so good as people are at any of these tasks, they are adequate for some applications. Early successes with programs that answered simple queries and followed simple directions, and early failures at machine translation, have resulted in a sweeping change in the whole AI approach to language. The principal themes of current language-understanding research are the importance of vast amounts of general, commonsense *world knowledge* and the role of *expectations*, based on the subject matter and the conversational situation, in interpreting sentences.

The state of the art of practical language programs is represented by useful "front ends" to a variety of software systems. These programs accept input in some restricted form—they cannot handle some of the nuances of English grammar and are useful for interpreting sentences only within a relatively limited domain of discourse. There has been very limited success at translating AI results in language and speech understanding programs into ideas about the nature of human language processing.

Programming. Although perhaps not an obviously important aspect of human cognition, programming itself is an important area of research in AI. Work in this field, called *automatic programming,* has investigated systems that can write computer programs from a variety of descriptions of their purpose—examples of input/output pairs, high-level language descriptions, and even English descriptions of algorithms. Progress has been limited to a few, fully worked-out examples. Research on automatic programming may result not only in semiautomated software-development systems, but also in AI programs that learn (i.e., modify their behavior) by modifying their own code. Related work in the theory of programs is fundamental to all AI research.

Learning. Certainly one of the most salient and significant aspects of human intelligence is the ability to learn. This is a good example of cognitive behavior that is so poorly understood that very little progress has been made in achieving it in AI systems. There have been several interesting attempts, including programs that learn from examples, from their own performance, and from being told. But in general, learning is not noticeable in AI systems.

Expertise. Recently the area of expert systems, or "knowledge engineering," has emerged as a road to successful and useful applications of AI techniques. Typically, the user interacts with an expert system in a "consultation dialogue," just as he would interact with a human who had some type of expertise—explaining his problem, performing suggested tests, and asking questions about proposed solutions. Current experimental systems have achieved high levels of performance in consultation tasks like chemical and geological data analysis, computer system configuration, structural engineering, and even medical diagnosis. Expert systems can be viewed as intermediaries between human experts, who interact with the systems in "knowledge acquisition" mode, and human users who interact with the systems in "consultation mode." Furthermore, much research in this area of AI has focused on endowing these systems with the ability to *explain* their reasoning, both to make the consultation more acceptable to the user and to help the human expert find errors in the system's reasoning when they occur.

Current research deals with a variety of problems in the design of expert systems. These systems are built through the painstaking interaction of a domain expert, who may not be able to articulate all of his knowledge, and the systems designer; the knowledge-acquisition process is the big bottleneck in the construction of expert systems. Current systems are limited in scope and do not have the same sense as humans have about knowing when they might be wrong. New research involves using the systems to teach novices as well as to consult with practitioners.

Robotics and vision. Another part of AI research that is receiving increasing attention involves programs that manipulate robot devices. Research in this field has looked at everything from the optimal movement of robot arms to methods of planning a sequence of actions to achieve a robot's goals. Although more complex systems have been built, the thousands of robots that are being used today in industrial applications are simple devices that have been programmed to perform some repetitive task. Most industrial robots are "blind," but some see through a TV camera that transmits an array of information back to the computer. Processing visual information is another very active, and very difficult, area of AI research. Programs have been developed that can recognize objects and shadows in visual scenes, and even identify small changes from one picture to the next, for example, for aerial reconnaissance.

Systems and languages. In addition to work directly aimed at achieving intelligence, the development of new tools has always been an important aspect of AI research. Some of the most important contributions of AI to the world of computing have been in the form of spin-offs. Computer-systems ideas like time-sharing, list processing, and interactive debugging were developed in the AI research environment. Specialized programming languages and systems, with features designed to facilitate deduction, robot manipulation, cognitive modeling, and so on, have often been rich sources of new ideas. Most recently, several knowledge-representation languages—computer languages for encoding knowledge and reasoning methods as data structures and procedures—have been developed in the last five years to explore a variety of ideas about how to build reasoning programs. Terry Winograd's article "Beyond Programming Languages" (1979) discusses some of his ideas about the future of computing, inspired, in part, by his AI research.

Invitation

There has been much activity and progress in the 25-year history of AI. And there is more activity now than ever. AI is a relatively well-funded discipline, principally, in the United States, by the Defense Department's Advanced Research Projects Agency and other government agencies. There are active AI research groups in other countries, including Japan, Canada, Britain, France, Germany, Australia, Italy, and the USSR. Increasing research support is coming from the private sector, where interest in using and marketing AI programs is on the rise. The real shortage is people—there are only a few AI research groups in universities and corporate laboratories; in terms of the number of people involved, the field is still quite small.

So, let us end this introduction with an invitation to those of you who are not working in AI: to join us in this rapidly moving field. The excitement of creating a powerful new technology is coupled in AI, as perhaps in no other field these days, with the potential for stumbling upon new insights into one of the *big* questions: Physicists ask what kind of place this universe is and seek to characterize its behavior systematically. Biologists ask what it means for a physical system to be *living*. We in AI wonder what kind of information-processing system can ask such questions.

B. THE AI HANDBOOK

By the mid–1970s, the science and technology of Artificial Intelligence had matured to the point at which widespread and significant application appeared to be possible. The move to application, though deemed desirable by both researchers and supporters, was inhibited by two factors. First, there was no cadre of industrial scientists and engineers schooled in the principles and techniques of the field. This was a problem of education. Most scientists and engineers, though very knowledgeable about the "standard" computer methods (e.g., numerical and statistical methods, simulation methods), simply had never heard about symbolic computation or Artificial Intelligence. There were so few courses in so few places, and so little literature accessible to and comprehensible by newcomers, that ignorance of AI and how to use it was almost total. Second, too few new people were being trained in AI, partly as a result of the same lack of written material that could be easily taught and easily learned.

The project to write a *Handbook of Artificial Intelligence* was begun as an attempt to fill this void. Initially, the *Handbook* was conceived as a self-help encyclopedia to which the aspiring practitioner could turn for explanations of fundamental ideas, descriptions of methods, and discussions of well-known programs as case studies. (This early goal has not been completely satisfied—within the limits of our energy there always seemed to be a few loose threads and uncovered topics.) As work progressed, it became clear that the material would be of great use to the Computer Science student studying AI, as an adjunct to a course or under the guidance of a faculty member, and our focus shifted somewhat toward this important audience.

The *Handbook* has turned out to be the most comprehensive reference work ever produced of the material that constitutes the science and technology of AI. But it is not a synthesis of that material, and it is not a text.

A typical chapter of the *Handbook* represents, first, the efforts of Stanford graduate students in AI to collect relevant material and draft sections; second, the effort of a chapter editor to clarify, reorganize, often rewrite the draft material, and prepare useful overview sections; third, the efforts of the *Handbook* editors to ensure a certain homogeneity of style, completeness of material, correctness of material as checked by specialists they consulted, and of course comprehensibility;

and fourth, the effort of a professional book editor to add the final polish necessary for book form.

The *Handbook's* organization, printed on the inside covers, is not the only way to divide up the material of AI. Some topics belong in more than one place. Other topics do not fit comfortably under any of our categories. We hope the chosen structure will help the reader to find what he is looking for most of the time. When this fails, there are many cross-references in each article that will point the way, as well as an extensive index for each volume.

The literature references after each article are extensive but certainly not exhaustive. We reference those readings that we thought would be of most use to our intended audience. The field of Artificial Intelligence is young and its literature is not immense, so the references listed with each article should prove to be adequate indirect pointers to just about everything published on the subject.

C. THE AI LITERATURE

One of the goals of the *Handbook of Artificial Intelligence* is to assist researchers and students in finding relevant material in the literature. Artificial Intelligence is a relatively young discipline and does not have a vast bibliography. Nevertheless, it is becoming increasingly difficult to find and follow publications of interest, partly because of the diversity of the backgrounds of researchers and the variety of journals in which they publish. Throughout the *Handbook* there are extensive citations of the "best next things to read" on each of the topics covered. This article is an attempt to map out roughly the geography of the field's literature and to suggest further readings of general interest.

Early Work (Through 1965)

The early period of AI research, through the mid–1960s, is well represented in the collections of papers entitled *Computers and Thought* and *Semantic Information Processing*, which were edited by Feigenbaum and Feldman (1963) and Minsky (1968), respectively. Both collections contain papers about the history of AI ideas as well as republications of reports on important early AI systems, many of which were done by graduate students as part of their research for doctoral dissertations. *Human Problem Solving* by Newell and Simon (1972) also contains a "Historical Addendum," giving their view of the origins of the discipline. This classic book on information processing psychology summarizes and synthesizes their 15 years of pioneering research into computational models of human cognition.

The series of edited volumes entitled *Machine Intelligence* started publication in 1967 and now includes nine collections of papers by many of the most influential AI researchers. Finally, McCorduck (1979) gives an insightful history of the early days of AI, focusing on the researchers themselves, in her entertaining book *Machines Who Think*.

The Middle Period (1966–1975)

The publication of *Understanding Natural Language* by Winograd (1972) was a landmark in the period of extensive AI research in language processing. Other books describing related work of this period include the collections of papers entitled *Computer Models of Thought and Language* (Schank and Colby, 1973), *The Psychology of Computer Vision* (Winston, 1975), and *Representation and Understanding* (Bobrow and Collins, 1975). Several papers on knowledge representation in the last two volumes were especially influential and discuss topics of active interest.

Nilsson (1974) provides an excellent short survey of all of the different AI research areas in the early 1970s, showing their inter-relations and state of progress. Nilsson also wrote an influential text-book of Artificial Intelligence (1971), bringing together core ideas in search and theorem proving.

Textbooks and Other General Introductions

In recent years there have been several books discussing AI and related topics aimed at the nontechnical audience. These include *Artificial Intelligence and Natural Man* by Boden (1977) and the book by McCorduck (1979) mentioned above. Also of interest along these lines is Simon's short, but great, *Sciences of the Artificial* (1969). The book *Gödel, Escher, Bach: an Eternal Golden Braid*, by Hofstadter (1979), discusses the development of some important ideas about the formalization of reasoning and their relation to AI. These books try to explain what is important and interesting about AI and how research in AI progresses through its programs.

Although somewhat more technical, the books by Norman and Rumelhart (1975) and Schank and Abelson (1977) develop, from first principles, entire conceptual systems for building AI programs (especially systems for natural language understanding). In a similar vein, Anderson and Bower (1973) present a self-contained introduction to AI-related work in models of human cognition, specifically the modeling of human sentence-memory.

The general textbooks on AI available now include those by Jackson (1974), Raphael (1976), and Winston (1977), as well as a completely new text by Nilsson (1980). Winston's book, *Artificial Intelligence*, includes a useful introduction to programming in LISP, the language of preference for AI research. Nilsson's recent book attempts to present all of AI from a formal perspective, stressing the fundamental ideas of search, logic, and productions. Winograd's forthcoming *Language as a Cognitive Process* is an excellent introduction to AI research in understanding natural language and related work in the representation of knowledge.

Charniak, Riesbeck, and McDermott's *Artificial Intelligence Programming* (1980) is a thorough introduction to LISP programming techniques. Siklossy (1976) has written a good, elementary introduction to LISP programming, called *Let's Talk LISP*. A more technical treatment of LISP is *Anatomy of LISP* by Allen (1978).

Recent Technical Publications

Recent AI research is described in the collections of papers on inference systems edited by Waterman and Hayes–Roth (1978), on vision systems edited by Hanson and Riseman (1978a), on speech understanding edited by Lea (1980b), on knowledge representation edited by Findler (1979), and on a variety of MIT research projects edited by Winston and Brown (1979). These collections all contain some excellent research reports, although, of course, they don't exhaustively cover current work in the field. Also of interest is the research of Lehnert (1978) and Marcus (1980) on natural language understanding, Barstow (1979) on automatic programming, and Lindsay, Buchanan, Feigenbaum, and Lederberg (1980) and Davis and Lenat (in press) on expert systems.

Journals and Conferences

Current research typically appears first in technical reports from the AI laboratories at universities and private companies. These laboratories include those at the Massachusetts Institute of Technology, Carnegie-Mellon University, Stanford University, SRI International, Inc., the Rand Corporation, Bolt Beranek and Newman, Inc., XEROX Palo Alto Research Center, Yale University, Rutgers University, Edinburgh University, Rochester University, the University of Massachusetts, the University of Texas, the University of Maryland, and many others. Short papers on very current research, as well as longer review papers, can be found in the proceedings of the large AI conferences: the biennial International Joint Conference on AI (IJCAI) and the annual national meeting of the American Association for Artificial Intelligence (AAAI). Important AI papers can also often be found in the proceedings of the conference on Theoretical Issues in Natural Language Processing (TINLAP), the annual meetings of the Association for Computational Linguistics (ACL), and the Artificial Intelligence in Medicine workshops (AIM).

The refereed journals and periodicals publish high-quality, current research papers. These include the journal *Artificial Intelligence* and the journal of the Cognitive Science Society, entitled *Cognitive Science*. Also, the ACL publishes a journal, called the *American Journal of Computational Linguistics*. The *SIGART Newsletter,* published by the special interest group on artificial intelligence of the Association for Computing Machinery (ACM), and the European *AISB Newsletter*, contain news, book reviews, and short articles on current activity. Finally, the AAAI has started publication of a semitechnical *AI Magazine*.

Other periodical publications sometimes containing AI papers include the journals *Cognition, International Journal of Man–Machine Studies, Behavioral and Brain Sciences, Transactions on Pattern Recognition and Machine Intelligence* of the Institute of Electronic and Electrical Engineers (IEEE), *Communications* of the Association for Computing Machinery (CACM), the interdisciplinary newsletter *Cognition and Brain Theory*, and the popular magazine entitled *Robotics Age*.

Recommendations

Readings on specific areas of AI research are, of course, suggested after each article in the *Handbook*. Almost all of the books mentioned in this article contain some material that would be appropriate for, and of interest to, the general reader. Serious students of AI these days follow the various AI conference proceedings, the two journals *Artificial Intelligence* and *Cognitive Science,* the *SIGART* and *AISB* newletters, and the *AI Magazine*.

Chapter II

Search

CHAPTER II: SEARCH

A. OVERVIEW

IN ARTIFICIAL INTELLIGENCE, the terms *problem solving* and *search* refer to a large body of core ideas that deal with deduction, inference, planning, commonsense reasoning, theorem proving, and related processes. Applications of these general ideas are found in programs for natural language understanding, information retrieval, automatic programming, robotics, scene analysis, game playing, expert systems, and mathematical theorem proving. In this chapter we examine search as a tool for problem solving in a more limited area. Most of the examples to be considered in detail are problems that are relatively easy to formalize. Some typical problems are:

1. finding the solution to a puzzle,
2. finding a proof for a theorem in logic or mathematics,
3. finding the shortest path connecting a set of nonequidistant points (the traveling-salesman problem),
4. finding a sequence of moves that will win a game, or the best move to make at a given point in a game,
5. finding a sequence of transformations that will solve a symbolic integration problem.

Organization of the Chapter

This overview takes a general look at search in problem solving, indicating some connections with topics considered in other chapters. The articles in the next section, Section II.B, describe the problem representations that form the basis of search techniques. The detailed examples there of state-space and problem-reduction representations will clarify what is meant by words like *search* and *problem solving* in AI. Readers to whom the subject of search is new are encouraged to turn to those articles for more concrete presentations of the fundamental ideas. Section II.B also discusses game trees, which are a historically and conceptually important class of representations.

Section II.C deals with the algorithms that use these various problem representations. *Blind search* algorithms, which treat the search space syntactically, are contrasted with *heuristic* methods, which use information about the nature and structure of the problem domain to limit the search. Various search algorithms are presented in full.

Finally, Section II.D reviews some well-known early programs based on search. It also describes two programs, STRIPS and ABSTRIPS, that introduce the closely related topic of *planning* in problem solving. This general topic, however, is treated more fully in Chapter XVI, in Volume III.

Components of Search Systems

Problem-solving systems can usually be described in terms of three main components. The first of these is a *database*, which describes both the current task-domain situation and the goal. The database can consist of a variety of different kinds of data structures including arrays, lists, sets of predicate calculus expressions, property list structures, and semantic networks. In theorem proving, for example, the current task-domain situation consists of assertions representing axioms, lemmas, and theorems already proved; the goal is an assertion representing the theorem to be proved. In information-retrieval applications, the current situation consists of a set of facts, and the goal is the query to be answered. In robot problem solving, a current situation is a *world model* consisting of statements describing the physical surroundings of the robot, and the goal is a description that is to be made true by a sequence of robot actions.

The second component of problem-solving systems is a set of *operators* that are used to manipulate the database. Some examples of operators include:

1. in theorem proving, rules of inference such as modus ponens and resolution;

2. in chess, rules for moving chessmen;

3. in symbolic integration, rules for simplifying the forms to be integrated, such as integration by parts or trigonometric substitution.

Sometimes the set of operators consists of only a few general rules of inference that generate new assertions from existing ones. Usually it is more efficient to use a large number of very specialized operators that generate new assertions only from very specific existing ones.

The third component of a problem-solving system is a *control strategy* for deciding what to do next—in particular, what operator to apply and where to apply it. Sometimes control is highly centralized, in a separate control executive that decides how problem-solving resources should be expended. Sometimes control is diffusely spread among the operators themselves.

The choice of a control strategy affects the contents and organization of the database. In general, the object is to achieve the goal by applying an appropriate sequence of operators to an initial task-domain situation. Each application of an operator modifies the situation in some way. If several different operator sequences are worth considering, the representation often maintains data structures showing the effects on the task situation of each alternative sequence. Such a representation permits a control strategy that investigates various operator sequences in parallel or that alternates attention among a number of sequences that look relatively promising. This is the character of most of the algorithms considered in this chapter; they assume a database containing descriptions of multiple task-domain situations or *states* (see, e.g., Article II.C1). It may be, however, that the description of a task-domain situation is too large for multiple versions to be stored explicitly; in this case, a *backtracking* control strategy may be used (see Article VI.B3, in Vol. II). A third approach is possible in some types of problems such as theorem proving, where the application of operators can add new assertions to the description of the task-domain situation but never can require the deletion of existing assertions. In this case, the database can describe a single, incrementally changing task-domain situation; multiple or alternative descriptions are unnecessary. (See Chap. XII, in Vol. III.)

Reasoning Forward and Reasoning Backward

The application of operators to those structures in the database that describe the task-domain situation—to produce a modified situation—is often called *reasoning forward*. The object is to bring the situation, or problem state, forward from its initial configuration to one satisfying a goal condition. For example, an initial situation might be the placement of chessmen on the board at the beginning of the game; the desired goal, any board configuration that is a checkmate; and the operators, rules for the legal moves in chess.

An alternative strategy, *reasoning backward,* involves another type of operator, which is applied, not to a current task-domain situation, but to the goal. The goal statement, or problem statement, is converted to one or more subgoals that are (one hopes) easier to solve and whose solutions are sufficient to solve the original problem. These subgoals may in turn be reduced to sub-subgoals, and so on, until each of them is accepted to be a trivial problem or its subproblems have been solved. For example, given an initial goal of integrating $1/(\cos^2 x)\,dx$, and an operator permitting $1/(\cos x)$ to be rewritten as $\sec x$, one can work backward toward a restatement of the goal in a form whose solution is immediate: The integral of $\sec^2 x$ is $\tan x$.

The former approach is said to use *forward reasoning* and to be *data driven* or *bottom-up*. The latter uses *backward reasoning* and is *goal directed* or *top-down*. The distinction between forward and backward reasoning assumes that the current task-domain situation or state is distinct from the goal. If one chooses to say that a current state is the state of having a particular goal, the distinction naturally vanishes.

Much human problem-solving behavior is observed to involve reasoning backward, and many artificial intelligence programs are based on this general strategy. In addition, combinations of forward and backward reasoning are possible. One important AI technique involving forward and backward reasoning is called *means-ends analysis;* it involves comparing the current goal with a current task-domain situation to extract a *difference* between them. This difference is then used to index the (forward) operator most relevant to reducing the difference. If this especially relevant operator cannot be immediately applied to the present problem state, subgoals are set up to change the problem state so that the relevant operator can be applied. After these subgoals are solved, the relevant operator is applied and the resulting, modified situation becomes a new starting point from which to solve for the original goal. (See Articles II.D2 and II.D5.)

State Spaces and Problem Reduction

A problem-solving system that uses forward reasoning and whose operators each work by producing a single new object—a new state—in the database is said to represent problems in a *state-space representation* (see Article II.B1).

For backward reasoning, a distinction may be drawn between two cases. In one, each application of an operator to a problem yields exactly one new problem, whose size or difficulty is typically slightly less than that of the previous problem. Systems of this kind will also be referred to, in this chapter, as employing state-space representations. Two instances of such representations are presented later in the chapter. One example is the Logic Theorist program (Article II.D1); the other is the backward-reasoning part of Pohl's *bidirectional search* (Articles II.C1 and II.C3d).

A more complex kind of backward reasoning occurs if applying an operator may divide the problem into a set of subproblems, perhaps each significantly smaller than the original. An example would be an operator changing the problem of integrating $2/(x^2-1)\,dx$ into the three subproblems of integrating $1/(x-1)\,dx$, integrating $-1/(x+1)\,dx$, and adding the results. A system using this kind of backward reasoning, distinguished by the fact that its operators can change a single object into a conjunction of objects, will be said to employ a *problem-reduction representation*. The relation between problem-reduction and state-space representations is examined further at the end of Article II.B2.

There may or may not be constraints on the order in which the subproblems generated by a problem-reduction system can be solved. Suppose, for example, that the original problem is to integrate $(f(x)+g(x))\,dx$. Applying the obvious operator changes it to the new problem consisting of two integrations, $f(x)\,dx$ and $g(x)\,dx$. Depending on the representation, the new problem can be viewed as made up of either (a) two integration subproblems that can be solved in any order or (b) two integration subproblems plus the third subproblem of summing the integrals. In the latter case, the third task cannot be done until the first two have been completed.

Besides the state-space and problem-reduction approaches, other variations on problem representation are possible. One is used in game-playing problems, which differ from most other problems by virtue of the presence of adversary moves. A game-playing problem must be represented in a way that takes into account the opponent's possible moves as well as the player's own. The usual representation is a *game tree* (see Article II.B3), which shares many features of a problem-reduction representation. Another variation is relevant to theorem-proving systems, many of which use forward reasoning and operators (rules of inference) that act on conjunctions of objects in the database. Although the representations discussed here assume that each operator takes only a single object as input, it is possible to define a *theorem-proving representation* that provides for multiple-input, single-output operators (Kowalski, 1972; see also Chap. XII, in Vol. III).

Graph Representation

In either a state-space or a problem-reduction representation, achieving the desired goal can be equated with finding an appropriate finite sequence of applications of available operators. While what one is primarily interested in—the goal situation or the sequence that leads to it—may depend on the problem, the term *search* can always be understood, without misleading consequences, as referring to the search for an appropriate operator sequence.

Tree structures are commonly used in implementing control strategies for the search. In a state-space representation, a tree may be used to represent the set of problem states produced by operator applications. In such a representation, the root node of the tree represents the initial problem situation or state. Each of the new states that can be produced from this initial state by the application of just one operator is represented by a *successor node* of the root node. Subsequent operator applications produce successors of these nodes, and so on. Each operator application is represented by a directed *arc* of the tree. In general, the states are represented by a *graph* rather than by a tree, since there may be different paths from the root to any given node. Trees are an important special case, however, and it is usually easier to explain their use than that of graphs. (See Article II.B1.)

Besides these ordinary trees and graphs, which are used for state-space representations, there are also specialized ones called *AND/OR graphs* that are used with problem-solving methods involving problem reduction. For problems in which the goal can be reduced to sets of subgoals, AND/OR graphs provide a means for keeping track of which subgoals have been attempted and which combinations of subgoals are sufficient to achieve the original goal. (See Article II.B2.)

The Search Space

The problem of producing a state that satisfies a goal condition can now be formulated as the problem of searching a graph to find a node whose associated state description satisfies the goal. Similarly, search based on a problem-reduction representation can be formulated as the search of an AND/OR graph.

It should be noted that there is a distinction between the graph to be searched and the tree or graph that is constructed as the search proceeds. In the latter, nodes and arcs can be represented by explicit data structures; the only nodes included are those for which paths from the initial state have actually been discovered. This explicit graph, which grows as the search proceeds, will be referred to as a *search graph* or *search tree*.

In contrast, the graph to be searched is ordinarily not explicit. It may be thought of as having one node for every state to which there is a path from the root. It may even be thought of, less commonly, as having one node for every state that can be described, whether or not a path to it exists. The implicit graph will be called the *state space* or, if generalized to cover non-state-space representations such as AND/OR graphs or game trees, the *search space*. Clearly, many problem domains (such as theorem proving) have an infinite search space, and the search space in others, though finite, is unimaginably large. Estimates of search-space size may be based on the total number of nodes (however defined) or on other measures. In chess, for example, the number of different complete plays of the average-length game has been estimated at 10^{120} (Shannon, 1950, 1956), although the number of "good" games is much smaller (see Good, 1968). Even for checkers, the size of the search space has been estimated at 10^{40} (Samuel, 1963).

Searching now becomes a problem of making just enough of the search space explicit in a search graph to contain a solution of the original goal. If the search space is a general graph, the search graph may be a subgraph, a subgraph that is also a tree, or a tree obtained by representing distinct paths to one search space node with duplicate search graph nodes.

Limiting Search

The critical problem of search is the amount of time and space necessary to find a solution. As the chess and checkers estimates suggest, exhaustive search is rarely feasible for nontrivial problems. Examining all sequences of n moves, for example, would require operating in a search space in which the number of nodes grows exponentially with n. Such a phenomenon is called a *combinatorial explosion*.

There are several complementary approaches to reducing the number of nodes that a search must examine. One important way is to recast the problem so that the size of the search space is reduced. A dramatic, if well-known, example is the mutilated chessboard problem:

> Suppose two diagonally opposite corner squares are removed from a standard 8 by 8 square chessboard. Can 31 rectangular dominoes, each the size of exactly two squares, be so placed as to cover precisely the remaining board? (Raphael, 1976, p. 31)

If states are defined to be configurations of dominoes on the mutilated board, and an operator has the effect of placing a domino, the search space for this problem is very large. If, however, one observes that every domino placed must cover both a red square and a black one and that the squares removed are both of one color, the answer is immediate. Unfortunately, little theory exists about how to find good problem representations. Some of the sorts of things such a theory would need to take into account are explored by Amarel (1968), who gives a sequence of six representations for a single problem, each reducing the search-space size by redefining the states and operators.

A second aspect concerns search efficiency within a given search space. Several graph- and tree-searching methods have been developed, and these play an important role in the control of problem-solving processes. Of special interest are those graph-searching methods that use *heuristic knowledge* from the problem domain to help focus the search. In some types of problems, these *heuristic search* techniques can prevent a combinatorial explosion of possible solutions. Heuristic search is one of the key contributions of AI to efficient problem solving. Various theorems have been proved about the properties of search techniques, both those that do and those that do not use heuristic information. Briefly, it has been shown that certain types of search methods are guaranteed to find optimal solutions (when such exist). Some of these methods, under certain comparisons, have also been shown to find solutions with minimal search effort. Graph- and tree-searching algorithms, with and without the use of heuristic information, are discussed at length in Section II.C.

A third approach addresses the question: Given one representation of a search problem, can a problem-solving system be programmed to find a better representation automatically? The question differs from that of the first approach to limiting search in that here it is the program, not the program designer, that is asked to find the improved representation. One start on answering the question was made by the STRIPS program (Article II.D5). STRIPS augments its initial set of operators by discovering, generalizing, and remembering *macro-operators*, composed of sequences of primitive operators, as it gains problem-solving experience. Another idea was used in the ABSTRIPS program (Article II.D6), which implements the idea of *planning*, in the sense of defining and solving problems in a search space from which unimportant details have been omitted. The details of the solution are filled in (by smaller searches within the more detailed space) only after a satisfactory outline of a solution, or *plan,* has been found. Planning is a major topic itself; for further discussion, see Chapter XVI, in Volume III.

The Meaning of Heuristic and Heuristic Search

Although the term *heuristic* has long been a key word in AI, its meaning has varied both among authors and over time. In general, its usage is illustrated by example better than by definition, and several of the prime examples are included in the programs of Section II.D. However, a brief review of the ways *heuristic* and *heuristic search* have been used may provide a useful warning against taking any single definition too seriously.

As an adjective, the most frequently quoted dictionary definition for *heuristic* is "serving to discover." As a noun, referring to an obscure branch of philosophy, the word meant the study of the methods and rules of discovery and invention (see Polya, 1957, p. 112).

When the term came into use to describe AI techniques, some writers made a distinction between methods for discovering solutions and methods for producing them algorithmically. Thus, Newell, Shaw, and Simon stated in 1957: "A process that *may* solve a given problem, but offers no guarantees of doing so, is called a *heuristic* for that problem" (Newell, Shaw, and Simon, 1963b, p. 114). But this meaning was not universally accepted. Minsky, for example, said in a 1961 paper:

> The adjective "heuristic," as used here and widely in the literature, means *related to improving problem-solving performance;* as a noun it is also used in regard to any method or trick used to improve the efficiency of a problem-solving program. . . . But imperfect methods are not necessarily heuristic, nor vice versa. Hence "heuristic" should not be regarded as opposite to "foolproof"; this has caused some confusion in the literature. (Minsky, 1963, p. 407n.)

These two definitions refer, though vaguely, to two different sets— devices that improve efficiency and devices that are not guaranteed. Feigenbaum and Feldman (1963) apparently limit *heuristic* to devices with both properties:

> A *heuristic (heuristic rule, heuristic method)* is a rule of thumb, strategy, trick, simplification, or any other kind of device which drastically limits search for solutions in large problem spaces. Heuristics do not guarantee optimal solutions; in fact, they do not guarantee any solution at all; *all that can be said for a useful heuristic is that it offers solutions which are good enough most of the time.* (p. 6; italics in original)

Even this definition, however, does not always agree with common usage, because it lacks a historical dimension. A device originally introduced as a heuristic in Feigenbaum and Feldman's sense may later be shown to guarantee an optimal solution after all. When this happens, the label *heuristic* may or may not be dropped. It has not been dropped, for example, with respect to the A^* algorithm (Article II.C3b). Alpha-beta pruning (Article II.C5b), on the other hand, is no longer called a heuristic.

It should be noted that the definitions quoted above, ranging in time from 1957 to 1963, refer to heuristic rules, methods, and programs, but they do not use the term *heuristic search*. This composite term

appears to have been first introduced in 1965 in a paper by Newell and
Ernst, "The Search for Generality" (see Newell and Simon, 1972,
p. 888). The paper presented a framework for comparing the methods
used in problem-solving programs up to that time. The basic framework, there called heuristic search, was the one called *state-space search*
in the present chapter. Blind search methods were included in the
heuristic search paradigm.

A similar meaning for heuristic search appears in Newell and Simon
(1972, pp. 91–105). Again, no contrast is drawn between heuristic
search and blind search; rather, heuristic search is distinguished from a
problem-solving method called *generate and test*. The difference between
the two is that the latter simply generates elements of the search space
(i.e., states) and tests each in turn until it finds one satisfying the goal
condition; whereas in heuristic search the order of generation can depend
both on information gained in previous tests and on the characteristics
of the goal. But the Newell and Simon distinction is not a hard and
fast one. By the time of their 1976 Turing Lecture, they seem to have
collapsed the two methods into one:

> Heuristic Search. A second law of qualitative structure for AI is
> that symbol systems solve problems by generating potential
> solutions and testing them, that is, by searching. (Newell and
> Simon, 1976, p. 126)

In the present chapter, the meaning attached to *heuristic search*
stems not from Newell and Simon but from Nilsson, whose 1971 book
provides the most detailed and influential treatment of the subject that
has yet appeared. For Nilsson, the distinction between heuristic search
and blind search is the important one. Blind search corresponds
approximately to the systematic generation and testing of search-space
elements, but it operates within a formalism that leaves room for
additional information about the specific problem domain to be
introduced, rather than excluding it by definition. If such information,
going beyond that needed merely to formulate a class of problems as
search problems, is in fact introduced, it may be possible to restrict
search drastically. Whether or not the restriction is foolproof, the
search is then called heuristic rather than blind.

References

See Amarel (1968), Feigenbaum and Feldman (1963), Good (1968),
Jackson (1974), Kowalski (1972), Minsky (1963), Newell and Ernst
(1965), Newell, Shaw, and Simon (1963b), Newell and Simon (1972,

1976), Nilsson (1971), Polya (1957), Raphael (1976), Samuel (1963), Shannon (1950, 1956), and Vanderbrug and Minker (1975).

B. PROBLEM REPRESENTATION

B1. State-space Representation

A state-space representation of a problem employs two kinds of entities: *states,* which are data structures giving "snapshots" of the condition of the problem at each stage of its solution, and *operators,* which are means for transforming the problem from one state to another.

A straightforward example of state-space representation is the simple, well-known puzzle called the 8-puzzle. An 8-puzzle is a square tray containing eight square tiles of equal size, numbered 1 to 8. The space for the ninth tile is vacant (see Fig. B1-1).

2	1	6
4		8
7	5	3

Figure B1-1. An 8-puzzle.

A tile may be moved by sliding it vertically or horizontally into the empty square. The problem is to transform some particular tile configuration, say, that of Figure B1-1, into another given tile configuration, say, that of Figure B1-2.

1	2	3
8		4
7	6	5

Figure B1-2. A solution configuration of the 8-puzzle.

A state is a particular configuration of tiles; each state might be represented by a 3 × 3 matrix, similar to Figures B1-1 and B1-2. The operators, corresponding to possible moves, might be defined with separate operators for each of tiles 1 through 8. However, a more concise definition is made possible by viewing the empty square as the object to be moved and stating the operators in terms of the movements of this square. In this formulation, only four operators are used:

UP	Move the blank up one square,
DOWN	Move the blank down one square,
LEFT	Move the blank left one square,
RIGHT	Move the blank right one square.

An operator may be inapplicable in certain states, as when it would move the blank outside the tray of tiles.

The set of all attainable states of a problem is often called its *state space*. The 8-puzzle, for example, has a state space of size 9!/2—since there are 9! configurations of the tiles but only half this number can be reached from any given starting configuration. This comes to only 181,440 possible states. For comparison, see the discussion of chess and checkers in Article II.A.

The four operators defined for the 8-puzzle form a set of *partial functions* on the state space: Each operator, if it applies to a given state at all, returns exactly one new state as its result. In more complex problems, however, the operators often contain variables. If, for a particular state and operator, the variables can be instantiated in more than one way, then each instantiation yields one new state, and the operators of the problem, if they are to be considered as defining functions, are more accurately termed *operator schemata*.

The complete specification of a state-space problem has three components. One is a set O of operators or operator schemata. In addition, one must define a set S of one or more *initial states* and find a predicate defining a set G of *goal states*. A state-space problem is then the triple (S, O, G). A *solution* to the problem is a finite sequence of applications of operators that changes an initial state into a goal state.

A state space can be treated as a directed graph whose nodes are states and whose arcs are operators transforming one state to another. For example, if state 1 is a state to which any of three operators can be applied, transforming it to state 2, 3, or 4, then the corresponding graph would be as in Figure B1-3. Nodes 2, 3, and 4 are called the *successors* of node 1.

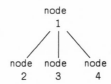

Figure B1-3.   Directed arcs.

In graph notation, a solution to a state-space problem is a path from an initial node to a goal node.   In Figure B1-4, one solution would be an application of operator B twice, followed by operator D, to reach the indicated goal node or final state.   There may be other final states and multiple ways to reach a particular final state.

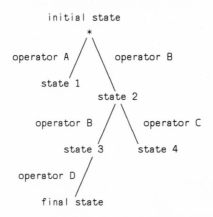

Figure B1-4.   A state-space graph.

A common variation on state-space problems requires finding not just any path but one of minimum cost between an initial node and a goal node.   In this case, each arc of the graph is labeled with its cost. An example is the traveling-salesman problem: Given a number of cities to be visited and the mileage between each pair of cities, find a minimum-mileage trip beginning and ending at city A that visits each of the other cities exactly once.   A sample mileage chart and the corresponding state-space graph are shown in Figure B1-5.   Because different paths to the same city represent distinct partial solutions, each state is identified not just as a city name but as a list of the cities visited so far.

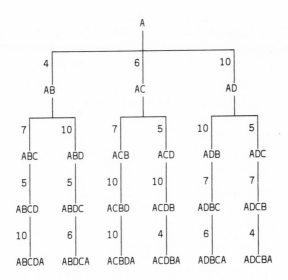

Figure B1-5.   The state-space graph for
a traveling-salesman problem.

The desired solution is *A–B–D–C–A,* or its reversal, with a total mileage of 25. (The two bottom levels of the graph could be omitted, since the mileage of each tour of *n* cities is determined by the first *n* – 1 cities chosen to be visited.)

Because the state-space graph is usually too large to represent explicitly, the problem of searching for a solution becomes one of generating just enough of the graph to contain the desired solution path. Search methods are discussed in Articles II.C1 and II.C3.

References
See Nilsson (1971).

B2. Problem-reduction Representation

Often distinguished from the state-space representation of problems is a technique called *problem-reduction representation*. In the problem-reduction approach, the principal data structures are problem descriptions or *goals*. An initial problem description is given; it is solved by a sequence of transformations that ultimately change it into a set of subproblems whose solutions are immediate. The transformations permitted are defined as *operators*. An operator may change a single problem into several subproblems; to solve the former, all the subproblems must be solved. In addition, several different operators may be applicable to a single problem, or the same operator may be applicable in several different ways. In this case, it suffices to solve the subproblems produced by any one of the operator applications. A problem whose solution is immediate is called a *primitive problem*. Thus, a problem representation using problem reduction is defined by a triple consisting of—

1. an initial problem description,
2. a set of operators for transforming problems to subproblems,
3. a set of primitive problem descriptions.

Reasoning proceeds backward from the initial goal.

An Example

An example that lends itself nicely to problem-reduction representation is the famous Tower of Hanoi puzzle. In one common version there are three disks, *A, B,* and *C,* of graduated sizes. There are also three pegs, 1, 2, and 3. Initially the disks are stacked on peg 1, with *A,* the smallest, on top and *C,* the largest, at the bottom. The problem is to transfer the stack to peg 3, as in Figure B2-1, given that (a) only one disk can be moved at a time and (b) no disk may be placed on top of a smaller disk.

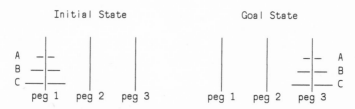

Figure B2-1. The Tower of Hanoi puzzle.

Only one operator need be used in the solution: Given distinct pegs i, j, and k, the problem of moving a stack of size $n > 1$ from peg i to peg k can be replaced by the three problems:

1. moving a stack of size $n - 1$ from i to j
2. moving a stack of size   1   from i to k
3. moving a stack of size $n - 1$ from j to k

The only primitive problem is that of moving a single disk from one peg to another, provided no smaller disk is on the receiving peg. If a smaller disk were present, this problem would be unsolvable (in view of the definition of the only available operator).

Each problem description can now be given by specifying the size n of the stack to be moved, the number of the sending peg, and the number of the receiving peg. The original problem, moving a stack of three disks from peg 1 to peg 3, would then be represented as ($n = 3$, 1 to 3), and the transformation of the original problem to primitive problems can be represented by a tree, as shown in Figure B2-2:

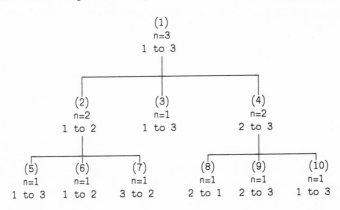

Figure B2-2. Solution of the Tower of Hanoi puzzle.

There happen to be two possible operator sequences that transform the original problem to primitive problems: Apply the operator to node 1, then node 2, and then node 4; or apply the operator to node 1, then node 4, and then node 2. Since node 3 is a primitive problem, it needs no further attention. Node 2 represents the subproblem of moving the top two disks on peg 1 to peg 2. This subproblem is solved by expanding it to the primitive problems at nodes 5, 6, and 7—which are solved by moving the smallest disk to peg 3, moving the middle disk to peg 2, and finally putting the small disk back on top of the middle one.

The sequence of operators to be applied should be distinguished from the sequence of actions to be taken to achieve the goal. In the Tower of Hanoi example, the actions are the actual movements of the disks. This sequence is given by the terminal nodes of the tree, read left to right. Whether or not it is considered important to assemble such a sequence of actions depends on the particular problem domain.

AND/OR Graphs

In the example above, a tree was used to display a problem-reduction solution to the Tower of Hanoi puzzle. The tree notation must be generalized if it is to represent the full variety of situations that may occur in problem reduction. This generalized notation for problem reduction is called an *AND/OR graph.*

According to one common formulation (Nilsson, 1971), an AND/OR graph is constructed according to the following rules:

1. Each node represents either a single problem or a set of problems to be solved. The graph contains a start node corresponding to the original problem.

2. A node representing a primitive problem, called a *terminal node,* has no descendants.

3. For each possible application of an operator to problem *P,* transforming it to a set of subproblems, there is a directed arc from *P* to a node representing the resulting subproblem set. For example, Figure B2-3 illustrates the reduction of *P* to three different subproblem sets: *A, B,* and *C.* Since *P* can be solved if any one of sets *A, B, or C* can be solved, *A, B,* and *C* are called *OR nodes.*

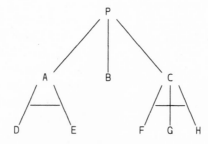

Figure B2-3.   An AND/OR tree.

4. Figure B2-3 illustrates further the composition of sets A, B, and C. Here, $A = \{D, E\}$, B consists of a single (unnamed) problem, and $C = \{F, G, H\}$. In general, for each node representing a set of two or more subproblems, there are directed arcs from the node for the set to individual nodes for each subproblem. Since a set of subproblems can be solved only if its members can *all* be solved, the subproblem nodes are called *AND nodes*. To distinguish them from OR nodes, the arcs leading to AND-node successors of a common parent are joined by a horizontal line.

5. A simplification of the graph produced by rules 3 and 4 may be made in the special case where only one application of an operator is possible for problem P and where this operator produces a set of more than one subproblem. As Figure B2-4 illustrates, the *intermediate OR node* representing the subproblem set may then be omitted. (Another example of this construction was given in Fig. B2-2.)

Figure B2-4.   An AND/OR tree with one
operator at problem P.

In the figures above, every node represents a distinct problem or set of problems. Since each node except the start node has just one parent, the graphs are in fact AND/OR *trees*. As a variation on Figure B2-3, assume that problem A is reducible to D and E; and problem C, to E, G, and H. Then E may be represented either by two distinct nodes, or by a single node as shown in Figure B2-5. The choice makes a difference in the search algorithms, which are discussed later in the chapter. For example, if node E is in turn reducible to C, the general graph representation simply adds another directed arc to Figure B2-5, but the corresponding tree becomes infinite.

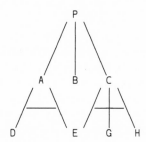

Figure B2-5. An AND/OR graph.

The constructions discussed so far concern graphs depicting the entire problem search space. To find a solution to the initial problem, one need only build enough of the graph to demonstrate that the start node can be solved. Such a subgraph is called a *solution graph* or, in the more restricted case of an AND/OR tree, a *solution tree*. The following rules apply:

A node is solvable if—

1. it is a terminal node (a primitive problem),
2. it is a nonterminal node whose successors are AND nodes that are all solvable, or
3. it is a nonterminal node whose successors are OR nodes and at least one of them is solvable.

Similarly, a node is unsolvable if—

1. it is a nonterminal node that has no successors (a nonprimitive problem to which no operator applies),
2. it is a nonterminal node whose successors are AND nodes and at least one of them is unsolvable, or
3. it is a nonterminal node whose successors are OR nodes and all of them are unsolvable.

Methods of searching an AND/OR graph for such a solution are discussed in Articles II.C2 and II.C4.

Relation Between Problem-reduction and State-space Representations

Some interesting general relationships can be found between problem-reduction and state-space representations. In the first place, although one representation often seems the more natural for a given problem, it is often possible to recast the problem definition so that it uses the other form. For example, the Tower of Hanoi puzzle can also be solved by a state-space search using operators that move a single disk and that represent all the legal moves in a given configuration. In comparison to the problem-reduction representation, which in fact gives an algorithm for solving the puzzle, the state-space representation would be a poor one since it leaves room for searching down unnecessarily long paths.

Second, it is possible to translate mechanically between state-space representations and problem-reduction representations without any fundamental shift in the way a problem is viewed. The ways of making such translations can provide helpful insight into many search programs in which the concepts of state-space and problem-reduction representation appear to be intermixed. Several translation schemes are described below. (Some readers may wish to skip the following material at first reading.)

State-space to problem-reduction representation. Two approaches suggest themselves for translating state-space representations to problem-reduction representations. In one, the state-space graph is understood as an AND/OR graph containing only OR nodes. Each state of the state-space version corresponds to the problem of getting from that state to a goal state, and a goal state of the state space becomes the primitive problem of getting from that goal state to itself. In other words, data structures representing states are simply reinterpreted as representing problem descriptions, where a problem consists of state information together with an implicit goal.

Alternately, there is a slight variation of the first approach that requires redefining the operators of the state-space representation. Each such operator, taking state i to state j, becomes an operator applicable to the problem of getting from state i to a goal state. Its effect is to reduce the problem to a pair of subproblems: (a) go from state i to state j (a primitive problem) and (b) go from state j to a goal state. Figure B2-6 illustrates this correspondence.

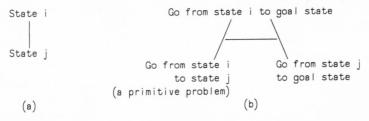

Figure B2-6.   (a) Part of a state-space tree; (b) the corresponding part of an AND/OR (problem-reduction) tree.

Problem-reduction to state-space representation. The translation from a problem-reduction representation to a state-space representation is a little more complex, assuming that the problem-reduction operators in fact produce AND nodes. The initial problem of the problem-reduction representation can be understood as having two components: (a) the description of the goal to be achieved, as discussed at the beginning of this article, and (b) the description of an initial state of the world. These components will be denoted g_0 and s_0, respectively. Some examples are

1. $g_0 = $ a theorem to be proved, and
    $s_0 = $ the axioms from which to prove it;
2. $g_0 = $ a configuration of objects to be achieved, and
    $s_0 = $ their existing configuration.

Each state S of the corresponding state-space representation is a pair consisting of a stack of goals $(g_i, \ldots, g_0)$ to be achieved and a current state s of the world. Thus, the initial state S_0 of the state-space representation is $S_0 = ((g_0), s_0)$. A final state is one in which the stack of goals to be achieved has been emptied.

For each problem-reduction operator, mapping a problem or goal g to a set of subgoals $\{g_m, \ldots, g_n\}$, the state-space representation has a corresponding operator mapping state S_1, where $S_1 = ((g_i, \ldots, g_0), s)$, to a state S_2 in which $\{g_m, \ldots, g_n\}$ have been added to the top of the goal stack (in the order in which they should be carried out, if relevant), and the state of the world s is unchanged; that is, $S_2 = ((g_m, \ldots, g_n, g_i, \ldots, g_0), s)$.

The state-space representation also needs a second type of operator, which becomes applicable whenever the goal on top of the stack represents a primitive problem. Its function is to remove that primitive problem from the stack and, at the same time, to change the state s to reflect its solution. In the Tower of Hanoi puzzle, for example, the new state would reflect the changed position of a single disk. In a theorem-proving problem, the new state would differ from the old one by the addition of one formula to those that had been given as axioms or established from having solved previous subproblems. A representation of this type is used explicitly in Fikes and Nilsson's STRIPS program, described in Article II.D5.

References

See Jackson (1974) and Nilsson (1971).

B3. Game Trees

Most games played by computer programs, including checkers, chess, Go, and tic-tac-toe, have several basic features in common. There are two players who alternate in making moves. At each turn, the rules define both what moves are legal and the effect that each possible move will have; there is no element of chance. In contrast to card games in which the players' hands are hidden, each player has complete information about his opponent's position, including the choices open to him and the moves he has made. The game begins from a specified state, often a configuration of men on a board. It ends in a win for one player and a loss for the other, or possibly in a draw.

A complete *game tree* is a representation of all possible plays of such a game. The root node is the initial state, in which it is the first player's turn to move. Its successors are the states he can reach in one move, their successors are the states resulting from the other player's possible replies, and so on. Terminal states are those representing a win, loss, or draw. Each path from the root node to a terminal node gives a different complete play of the game.

An important difference between a game tree and a state-space tree (Article II.B1) is that the game tree represents moves of two opposing players, say, A and B, whereas the arcs of a state-space tree are all "moves" of a single problem-solving agent. An AND/OR tree (Article II.B2), however, is sufficient to reflect this opposition. The game tree is ordinarily drawn to represent only one player's point of view. In a game tree drawn from A's standpoint, A's possible moves from a given position are represented by OR nodes since they are alternatives under his own control. The moves that B might make in return are AND nodes, since they represent sets of moves to which A must be able to respond. Because the players take turns, OR nodes and AND nodes appear at alternate levels of the tree. In the language of AND/OR graphs, the tree displays the search space for the problem of showing that A can win. A node representing a win for A corresponds to a primitive problem; a node representing a win for B or a draw, to an unsolvable problem. Unlike the usual AND/OR graph terminology, both of these kinds of nodes will be called *terminal nodes*.

As an example, Figure B3-1 shows a portion of the game tree for tic-tac-toe. The players are X and O, X has the first move, and the tree is drawn from X's standpoint. Positions are considered identical if one can be obtained from the other by rotation or reflection of the grid.

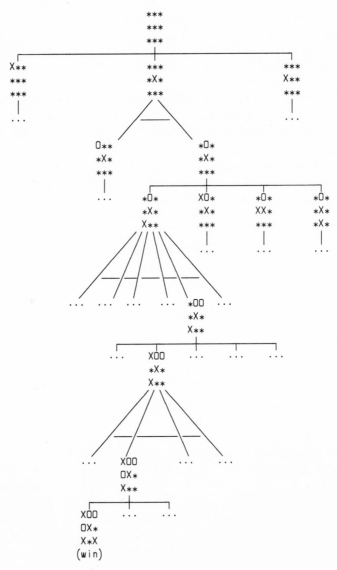

Figure B3-1. A game tree for Tic-tac-toe.

The tree could also be drawn from O's standpoint, even though X has the first move. In this case, the AND nodes would become OR nodes, and vice versa, and the labels "win" and "lose" would be reversed. An alternate formulation of game trees, not explicitly distinguishing between AND and OR nodes, is given in Article II.C5a.

Methods of searching a game tree for a winning strategy are

discussed in Section II.C5. As with search in other domains, the source of difficulty in challenging games is the unimaginably large search space. A complete game tree for checkers, for instance, which is harder than tic-tac-toe but far simpler than chess or Go, has been estimated as having about 10^{40} nonterminal nodes (Samuel, 1963). If one assumed that these nodes could be generated at the rate of 3 billion per second, generation of the whole tree would still require around 10^{21} centuries!

References

See Nilsson (1971) and Samuel (1963).

C. SEARCH METHODS

C1. Blind State-space Search

As discussed in Article II.B1, a problem in the state-space search paradigm is defined by a triple (S, O, G), where

> S is a set of one or more initial states,
> O is a set of operators on states, and
> G is a set of goal states.

The state space is commonly identified with a directed graph in which each node is a state and each arc represents the application of an operator transforming a state to a successor state. A solution is a path from a start state to a goal state. Goal states may be defined either explicitly or as the set of states satisfying a given predicate.

The search for a solution is conducted by making explicit just enough of the state-space graph to contain a solution path. If the order in which potential solution paths are considered is arbitrary, using no domain-specific information to judge where the solution is likely to lie, the search is called *blind search*. Although blind search is impracticable for nontrivial problems, because of the large proportion of the state space it may explore, it provides a useful foundation for the understanding of *heuristic search* techniques, discussed in Section II.C3.

Several blind-search methods are described below; they differ from one another mainly in the order in which nodes are examined. In each case, it is assumed that there is a procedure for finding all the *successors* of a given node—that is, all the states that can be reached from the current state by a single operator application. Such a procedure is said to *expand* the given node.

The first three algorithms also make two other assumptions:

1. The state-space graph is a tree. The implication is that there is only one start state (the root) and that the path from the start node to any other node is unique. Modifications to the search methods needed for a general directed graph are noted in Nilsson (1971) and in Article II.C3a.

2. Whenever a node is expanded, creating a node for each of its successors, the successor nodes contain pointers back to the parent node. When a goal node is finally generated, this feature makes it possible to trace the solution path.

Breadth-first Search

The breadth-first method expands nodes in order of their proximity to the start node, measured by the number of arcs between them. In other words, it considers every possible operator sequence of length n before any sequence of length $n + 1$. Thus, although the search may be an extremely long one, it is guaranteed eventually to find the shortest possible solution sequence if any solution exists.

Breadth-first search is described by the following algorithm:

1. Put the start node on a list, called OPEN, of unexpanded nodes. If the start node is a goal node, a solution has been found.
2. If OPEN is empty, no solution exists.
3. Remove the first node, n, from OPEN and place it in a list, called CLOSED, of expanded nodes.
4. Expand node n. If it has no successors, go to (2).
5. Place all successors of node n at the end of the OPEN list.
6. If any of the successors of node n is a goal node, a solution has been found. Otherwise, go to (2).

As an example of breadth-first search, consider a world consisting of a table and three toy blocks. The initial state of the world is that blocks 2 and 3 are on the table, and block 1 is on top of block 2 (see Fig. C1-1). We wish to reach a goal state in which the three blocks are stacked with block 1 on top, block 2 in the middle, and block 3 on the bottom.

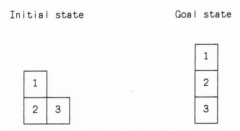

Figure C1-1. A sample problem for breadth-first search.

The only operator is MOVE X to Y, which moves object X onto another object, Y. As preconditions to applying the operator, it is required (a) that X, the object to be moved, be a block with nothing on top of it and (b) that if Y is a block, there must be nothing on Y. Finally, the operator is not to be used to generate the same state more than once. (This last condition can be checked from the lists of expanded and unexpanded nodes.)

Figure C1-2 shows the search tree generated by the breadth-first algorithm. The nodes are states S_0 through S_{10}; node S_1, for example, corresponds to the successor state of S_0 reached by "MOVE block 1 to the table." The nodes are generated and expanded in the order given by their numbers, that is, S_0, S_1, S_2, ..., S_{10}. When the algorithm terminates, finding S_{10} to be the goal, the list of expanded nodes contains S_0 through S_5, and the OPEN list still contains S_6 through S_{10}.

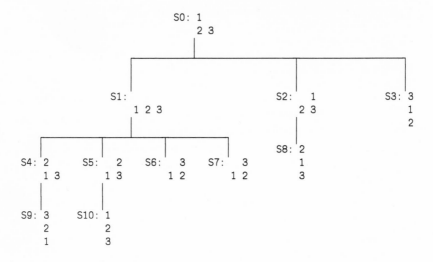

Figure C1-2.   The search tree for Figure C1-1.

Uniform-cost Search

The breadth-first algorithm can be generalized slightly to solve the problem of finding the cheapest path from the start state to a goal state. A nonnegative cost is associated with every arc joining two nodes; the cost of a solution path is then the sum of the arc costs along the path. The generalized algorithm is called a *uniform-cost search*. If all arcs have equal cost, the algorithm reduces to breadth-first search. The need for assigning costs to the arcs is illustrated by the traveling-salesman problem, described in Article II.B1, where the different distances between cities correspond to the arc costs and the problem is to minimize the total distance traveled.

In the uniform-cost algorithm given below, the cost of the arc from node i to node j is denoted by $c(i, j)$. The cost of a path from the start node to any node i is denoted $g(i)$.

1. Put the start node, s, on a list, called OPEN, of unexpanded nodes. If the start node is a goal node, a solution has been found. Otherwise, set $g(s) = 0$.
2. If OPEN is empty, no solution exists.
3. Select from OPEN a node i such that $g(i)$ is minimum. If several nodes qualify, choose node i to be a goal node if there is one; otherwise, choose among them arbitrarily. Move node i from OPEN to a list, CLOSED, of expanded nodes.
4. If node i is a goal node, a solution has been found.
5. Expand node i. If it has no successors, go to (2).
6. For each successor node j of node i, compute $g(j) = g(i) + c(i,j)$ and place all the successor nodes j in OPEN.
7. Go to (2).

Depth-first Search

Depth-first search is characterized by the expansion of the most recently generated, or deepest, node first. Formally, the *depth* of a node in a tree is defined as follows:

1. The depth of the start node is 0.
2. The depth of any other node is one more than the depth of its predecessor.

As a consequence of expanding the deepest node first, the search follows a single path through the state space downward from the start node; only if it reaches a state that has no successors does it consider an alternate path. Alternate paths systematically vary those previously tried, changing only the last n steps while keeping n as small as possible.

In many problems, of course, the state-space tree may be of infinite depth, or at least may be deeper than some known upper bound on the length of an acceptable solution sequence. To prevent consideration of paths that are too long, a maximum is often placed on the depth of nodes to be expanded, and any node at that depth is treated as if it had no successors. It should be noted that, even if such a *depth bound* is used, the solution path found is not necessarily the shortest one. The following algorithm describes depth-first search with a depth bound:

1. Put the start node on a list, OPEN, of unexpanded nodes. If it is a goal node, a solution has been found.
2. If OPEN is empty, no solution exists.
3. Move the first node, n, on OPEN to a list, CLOSED, of expanded nodes.
4. If the depth of node n is equal to the maximum depth, go to (2).

5. Expand node n. If it has no successors, go to (2).
6. Place all successors of node n at the beginning of OPEN.
7. If any of the successors of node n is a goal node, a solution has been found. Otherwise go to (2).

As an example, consider the following simple problem: A pawn is required to move through the matrix in Figure C1-3 from top to bottom. The pawn may enter the matrix anywhere in the top row. From a square containing 0, the pawn must move downward if the square below contains 0; otherwise, it must move horizontally. From a square containing 1, no further moves are possible. The goal is to reach a square containing 0 in the bottom row. A depth bound of 5 is assumed.

	1	2	3	4
1	1	0	0	0
2	0	0	1	0
3	0	1	0	0
4	1	0	0	0

Figure C1-3.   A sample problem for depth-first search.

The search tree generated by the depth-first algorithm is shown in Figure C1-4. At node S_0, the pawn has not yet entered the grid. At the other nodes, its position is given as a pair of the form (row number, column number). The numbering of nodes gives the order in which they are moved out of the OPEN list of unexpanded nodes. When the algorithm terminates, the OPEN list contains S_{17} (a goal node) and S_{18}; all other nodes are on the expanded list. The solution found, which is one move longer than the minimum, calls for the pawn to enter at $(1, 3)$, move one square right, and then go straight down to $(4, 4)$. Had no depth bound been used, the tree would have been one level deeper, since node S_{12} has a successor, $(4, 1)$. Since the algorithm treats the state space as a tree, not as a general graph, it does not discover that the distinct nodes S_2 and S_9 in fact represent the same state. Consequently, the search downward from S_9 duplicates the work already done from S_2.

$(3, 2)$

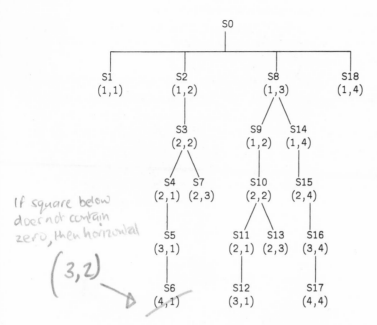

Figure C1-4. The search tree for Figure C1-3.

Bidirectional Search

Each of the algorithms given above uses *forward reasoning*, working from the start node of a state-space tree towards a goal node and using operators that each map a node i to a successor node j. In some cases, the search could equally well use *backward reasoning*, moving from the goal state to the start state. An example of this is the 8-puzzle, in which (a) the goal state can be fully described in advance and (b) it is easy to define inverse operators—each applicable operator mapping node j to a predecessor node i. Since backward search through a tree is trivial, it is assumed that node j can have more than one predecessor—that is, several inverse operators may apply at node j. For example, in the pawn-maze problem, Figure C1-4, position $(1, 2)$— at nodes S_2 and S_9—would have both nodes S_0 and S_8 as predecessors.

Forward and backward reasoning can be combined into a technique called *bidirectional search*. The idea is to replace a single search graph, which is likely to grow exponentially, by two smaller graphs—one starting from the initial state and one starting from the goal. The search terminates (roughly) when the two graphs intersect.

A bidirectional version of the uniform-cost algorithm, guaranteed to find the shortest solution path through a general state-space graph, is due to Pohl (1969, 1971). Empirical data for randomly generated graphs showed that Pohl's algorithm expanded only about one-fourth as many nodes as unidirectional search.

An algorithm for blind bidirectional search is given in detail below. A related algorithm for *heuristic* bidirectional search is discussed in Article II.C3d.

The following notation is used in the algorithm:

1. The start node is s; the goal or terminal node, t.
2. S–OPEN and S–CLOSED are lists of unexpanded and expanded nodes, respectively, generated from the start node.
3. T–OPEN and T–CLOSED are lists of unexpanded and expanded nodes, respectively, generated from the terminal node.
4. The cost associated with the arc from node n to node x is denoted $c\,(n,\,x)$.
5. For a node x generated from the start node, $gs(x)$ measures the shortest path found so far from s to x.
6. For a node x generated from the terminal node, $gt(x)$ measures the shortest path found so far from x to t.

The algorithm is as follows:

1. Put s in S–CLOSED, with $gs\,(s) = 0$. Expand node s, creating a node for each of its successors. For each successor node x, place x on S–OPEN, attach a pointer back to s, and set $gs(x)$ to $c\,(s,\,x)$. Correspondingly, put t in T–CLOSED, with $gt\,(t) = 0$. Expand node t, creating a node for each of its predecessors. For each predecessor node x, place x on T–OPEN, attach a pointer forward to t, and set $gt\,(x) = c\,(x,\,t)$.

2. Decide whether to go forward or backward. If forward, go to (3); if backward, to (4). (One way to implement this step is to alternate between forward and backward moves. Another way, which Pohl found to give better performance, is to move backward if T–OPEN contains fewer nodes than S–OPEN; otherwise, forward. It is assumed that a solution path does exist, so the chosen list will be nonempty.)

3. Select from S–OPEN a node n at which $gs(n)$ is minimum. Move n to S–CLOSED. If n is also in T–CLOSED, go to (5). Otherwise, for each successor x of n:
   a. If x is on neither S–OPEN nor S–CLOSED, then add it to S–OPEN. Attach a pointer back to n and the path cost $gs(x) = gs(n) + c\,(n,\,x)$.
   b. If x was already on S–OPEN, a shorter path to x may have just been found. Compare the previous path cost, $gs(x)$, with

the new cost $gs(n) + c(n, x)$. If the latter is smaller, set $gs(x)$ to the new path cost and point x back to n instead of its predecessor on the longer path.

c. If x was already on S–CLOSED, do nothing; although a new path to x has been found, its cost must be at least as great as the cost of the path already known. (For further consideration of this point, see Article II.C3b.)

Return to (2).

4. Select from T–OPEN a node n at which $gt(n)$ is minimum. Move n to T–CLOSED. If n is also in S–CLOSED, go to (5). Otherwise, for each predecessor x of n:

a. If x is on neither T–OPEN nor T–CLOSED, then add it to T–OPEN. Attach a pointer forward to n and the path cost $gt(x) = gt(n) + c(x, n)$.

b. If x was already on T–OPEN and a shorter path from x to t has just been found, reduce the stored value of $gt(x)$ and point x forward to n (instead of to its successor on the longer path).

c. If x was already on T–CLOSED, do nothing.

Return to (2).

5. Consider the set of nodes that are in both S–CLOSED and either T–CLOSED or T–OPEN. Select from this set a node n for which $gs(n) + gt(n)$ is minimum and exit with the solution path obtained by tracing the path from n back to s and forward to t.

References

See Nilsson (1971) and Pohl (1969, 1971).

C2. Blind AND/OR Graph Search

A problem to be solved using AND/OR-graph search can be defined by specifying a start node (representing an initial goal or problem description), a set of terminal nodes (descriptions of primitive problems), and a set of operators for reducing goals to subgoals. The rules for constructing an AND/OR graph, together with the use of such graphs for problem-reduction representation, were discussed in Article II.B2. To recapitulate briefly, each possible application of an operator at a node n (see Fig. C2-1) is represented by a directed arc from node n to a successor node; these successor nodes are called OR *nodes,* since only *one* of the operator applications will ever be needed to solve the problem that node n represents. Each OR node successor of node n represents a set of subproblems. If the set of subproblems represented by an OR node m has more than one element, then there are directed arcs from m to nodes representing the individual elements of the set. These successors are called AND *nodes,* because *all* of the elements of the set must be solved in order to solve the subproblem set represented by node m. To distinguish AND nodes visually from OR nodes, the arcs in the graph from m to its AND successors are joined by a horizontal line.

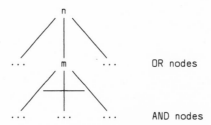

OR nodes

AND nodes

Figure C2-1. AND/OR graph notation.

Formally, a node or problem is said to be *solved* if one of the following conditions holds:

1. The node is in the set of terminal nodes (primitive problems). (In this case, the node has no successors.)
2. The node has AND nodes as successors and all these successors are solved.
3. The node has OR nodes as successors and any one of these successors is solved.

A solution to the original problem is given by a subgraph of the AND/OR graph sufficient to show that the start node is solved. In Figure C2-2, for example, assuming that nodes 5, 6, 8, 9, 10, and 11 are all terminal, there are three possible solution subgraphs: {1, 2, 4, 8, 9}, {1, 3, 5, 6, 7, 10}, and {1, 3, 5, 6, 7, 11}.

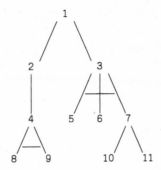

Figure C2-2. An AND/OR graph.

A node is said to be *unsolvable* if one of the following conditions is true:

1. The node has no successors and is not in the set of terminal nodes. That is, it is a nonprimitive problem to which no operator can be applied.
2. The node has AND nodes as successors and one or more of these successors are unsolvable.
3. The node has OR nodes as successors and all of these successors are unsolvable.

Again in Figure C2-2, node 1 would be unsolvable if all nodes in any of the following sets were unsolvable: {8, 5}, {8, 6}, {8, 10, 11}, {9, 5}, {9, 6}, {9, 10, 11}.

Two algorithms for the blind search of an AND/OR tree (breadth-first and depth-first) are given at the end of this article. They have several features in common with blind state-space search algorithms (Article II.C1): The operation of *expanding* a node is again present, and again the algorithms differ mainly in the order in which nodes are considered for expansion. It should be noted that the expansion of a node may differ slightly from the case of state-space search. In Figure C2-2, for example, two operators apply at node 1: One reduces it to a single equivalent problem (node 2) and the other to a set (node 3) of three subproblems (nodes 5, 6, and 7). In this case, nodes 2, 3, 5, 6, and 7 would all be generated in expanding node 1,

and each new node would be given a pointer to its immediate predecessor, but only nodes 2, 5, 6, and 7 would be placed on the list of
unexpanded nodes.

In contrast to the state-space search algorithms, most of which use
forward reasoning, the search algorithms below reason backward from
the initial goal. The algorithms described here make two important
simplifying assumptions: (a) The search space is an AND/OR tree and
not a general graph, and (b) when a problem is transformed to a set of
subproblems, the subproblems may be solved in any order. The first
assumption implies that identical subproblems may arise at different
nodes of the search tree and will need to be solved anew whenever one
of them is encountered. Modifications needed for searching a general
AND/OR graph are discussed in Nilsson (1971). A way of eliminating
the second assumption, that all subproblems are independent, is discussed in Article II.C4.

Breadth-first Search of an AND/OR Tree

The following algorithm describes the breadth-first search of an
AND/OR tree. If a solution tree exists, this algorithm finds a solution
tree of minimum depth, provided that intermediate OR nodes are ignored in calculating the depth of the tree. The start node is assumed
not to be a terminal node.

1. Put the start node on a list, OPEN, of unexpanded nodes.
2. Remove the first node, n, from OPEN.
3. Expand node n—generating all its immediate successors and, for
   each successor m, if m represents a set of more than one subproblem, generating successors of m corresponding to the individual subproblems. Attach, to each newly generated node, a
   pointer back to its immediate predecessor. Place all the new
   nodes that do not yet have descendants at the end of OPEN.
4. If no successors were generated in (3), then
   a. Label node n unsolvable.
   b. If the unsolvability of n makes any of its ancestors unsolv-
      able, label these ancestors unsolvable.
   c. If the start node is labeled unsolvable, exit with failure.
   d. Remove from OPEN any nodes with an unsolvable ancestor.
5. Otherwise, if any terminal nodes were generated in (3), then
   a. Label these terminal nodes solved.
   b. If the solution of these terminal nodes makes any of their
      ancestors solved, label these ancestors solved.

   c. If the start node is labeled solved, exit with success.
   d. Remove from OPEN any nodes that are labeled solved or
      that have a solved ancestor.
6. Go to (2).

Depth-first Search of an AND/OR Tree

   A bounded depth-first search can be obtained by changing only
step 3 of the breadth-first algorithm. The revised step 3 is as follows:

   3'. *If the depth of n is less than the depth bound, then:*
      Expand node *n*—generating all its immediate successors and, for
      each successor *m*, if *m* represents a set of more than one sub-
      problem, generating successors of *m* corresponding to the indi-
      vidual subproblems. Attach, to each newly generated node, a
      pointer back to its immediate predecessor. Place all the new
      nodes that do not yet have descendants at the *beginning* of
      OPEN.

The depth-first search will find a solution tree, provided one exists
within the depth bound. As with breadth-first search, the notion of
depth is more meaningful if intermediate OR nodes are not counted.
For this purpose one might add the following to the end of step 3':

      For each node *x* added to OPEN, set the depth of *x* to be the
      depth of node *n*, plus 1.

Given that the start node has depth 0, the depth of any node *x* will
then be the length of the operator sequence that must be applied to
reach node *x* from the start node.

References

   See Nilsson (1971).

C3. Heuristic State-space Search

C3a. Basic Concepts in Heuristic Search

In the blind search of a state-space (Article II.C1) or an AND/OR graph (Article II.C2), the number of nodes expanded before reaching a solution is likely to be prohibitively large. Because the order of expanding the nodes is purely arbitrary and does not use any properties of the problem being solved, one usually runs out of space or time (or both) in any but the simplest problems. This result is a manifestation of the *combinatorial explosion.*

Information about the particular problem domain can often be brought to bear to help reduce the search. In this section, it is assumed that the definitions of initial states, operators, and goal states all are fixed, thus determining a search space; the question, then, is how to search the given space efficiently. The techniques for doing so usually require additional information about the properties of the specific problem domain beyond that which is built into the state and operator definitions. Information of this sort will be called *heuristic information,* and a search method using it (whether or not the method is foolproof) will be called a *heuristic search method* (Nilsson, 1971).

The Importance of Heuristic Search Theory

Heuristic search methods were employed by nearly all early problem-solving programs. Most of these programs, though, were written to solve problems from a single domain, and the domain-specific information they used was closely intertwined with the techniques for using it. Thus, the heuristic techniques themselves were not easily accessible for study and adaptation to new problems, and there was some likelihood that substantially similar techniques would have to be reinvented repeatedly. Consequently, an interest arose in developing generalized heuristic search algorithms, whose properties could be studied independently of the particular programs that might use them. (See Newell and Ernst, 1965; Feigenbaum, 1969; Sandewall, 1971.) This task, in turn, required a way of describing problems that generalized across many different domains. Such generalized problem formulations have been discussed in Section II.B, in an approach generally following Nilsson (1971). Given a generalized problem representation, the most basic heuristic-search techniques can be studied as variations on blind search methods for the same type of problem representation.

The current state of heuristic search theory has been diversely judged. One of the best known students of the subject has remarked, "The problem of efficiently searching a graph has essentially been solved and thus no longer occupies AI researchers" (Nilsson, 1974, p. 787). Other work makes it clear, however, that the theory is far from complete (e.g., Simon and Kadane, 1975; Gaschnig, 1977). Its kinship with complexity theory now tends to be emphasized (see Pohl, 1977).

Ways of Using Heuristic Information

The points at which heuristic information can be applied in a search include—

1. deciding which node to expand next, instead of doing the expansions in a strictly breadth-first or depth-first order;
2. in the course of expanding a node, deciding which successor or successors to generate—instead of blindly generating all possible successors at one time; and
3. deciding that certain nodes should be discarded, or *pruned,* from the search tree.

A state-space search algorithm is presented below that uses heuristic information only at the first of these points, deciding which node to expand next, on the assumption that nodes are to be expanded fully or not at all. The general idea is always to expand the node that seems "most promising." A search that implements this idea is called an *ordered search* or *best-first search.* Ordered search has been the subject of considerable theoretical study, and several variations on the basic algorithm below are reviewed in Articles II.C3b through II.C3d (on ordered state-space search) and Article II.C4 (on ordered AND/OR graph search).

The other two uses of heuristic information can be discussed more briefly. Decisions of the second kind—determining which successors to generate—are often decisions of operator selection, determining which operator to apply next to a given node. A node to which some but not all applicable operators have been applied is said to have been *partially developed* or *partially expanded.* The use of heuristic information to develop nodes partially, reserving the possibility of fuller expansion at a later point in the search, has been investigated by Michie (1967) and by Michie and Ross (1970). Other applications of the idea of limiting the successors of a given node occur in game-playing programs (see Article II.C5c). Another important variant of the idea is *means-ends analysis,* which, instead of deciding on an applicable operator, chooses an operator most likely to advance the search whether or not it is immediately applicable. The problem of making the operator applicable, if necessary, is addressed secondarily. (See Articles II.D2 and II.D5.)

The third use of heuristic information, for *pruning*, amounts to deciding that some nodes should never be expanded. In some cases, it can be definitely determined that a node is not part of a solution, and the node may then be safely discarded, or pruned, from the search tree. In other cases, pruning may be desirable even though the nodes pruned cannot be guaranteed inessential to a solution. One reason, in conjunction with a best-first search, is simply to save the space that would be required to retain a large number of apparently unpromising nodes on a list of candidates for possible future expansion. For examples, see Doran (1967) and Harris's *bandwidth search* (Article II.C3c). Another reason for pruning is as a restriction on a search that is otherwise blind. For example, a breadth-first search could be modified to choose between expansion and pruning for each node it considers. This pruning to control the search is also very important for problems in which all solutions, rather than just a single solution, must be found: Finding all solutions implies an exhaustive exploration of all unpruned parts of the search space. An example of a search for all solutions is the DENDRAL program (see Article VII.C2, in Vol. II).

Ordered State-space Search

An *ordered* or *best-first search,* as mentioned above, is one that always selects the most promising node as the next node to expand. The choice is ordinarily assumed to be global, that is, to operate on the set of all nodes generated but not yet expanded. A local choice would also be possible, however; for example, an *ordered depth-first search* would be one that always expands the most promising successor of the node last expanded.

The promise of a node can be defined in various ways. One way, in a state-space problem, is to estimate its distance from a goal node; another is to assume that the solution path includes the node being evaluated and estimate the length or difficulty of the entire path. Along a different dimension, the evaluation may consider only certain predetermined features of the node in question, or it may determine the relevant features by comparing the given node with the goal. In all these cases, the measure by which the promise of a node is estimated is called an *evaluation function.*

A basic algorithm for ordered state-space search is given by Nilsson (1971). The evaluation function is f^*; it is defined so that the more promising a node is, the smaller is the value of f^*. The node selected for expansion is one at which f^* is minimum. The state space is assumed to be a general graph.

The algorithm is as follows:

1. Put the start node s on a list, called OPEN, of unexpanded nodes. Calculate $f^*(s)$ and associate its value with node s.
2. If OPEN is empty, exit with failure; no solution exists.
3. Select from OPEN a node i at which f^* is minimum. If several nodes qualify, choose a goal node if there is one, and otherwise choose among them arbitrarily.
4. Remove node i from OPEN and place it on a list, called CLOSED, of expanded nodes.
5. If i is a goal node, exit with success; a solution has been found.
6. Expand node i, creating nodes for all its successors. For every successor node j of i:
   a. Calculate $f^*(j)$.
   b. If j is neither in list OPEN nor in list CLOSED, then add it to OPEN, with its f^* value. Attach a pointer from j back to its predecessor i (in order to trace back a solution path once a goal node is found).
   c. If j was already on either OPEN or CLOSED, compare the f^* value just calculated for j with the value previously associated with the node. If the new value is lower, then
      i. Substitute it for the old value.
      ii. Point j back to i instead of to its previously found predecessor.
      iii. If node j was on the CLOSED list, move it back to OPEN.
7. Go to (2).

Step 6c is necessary for general graphs, in which a node can have more than one predecessor. The predecessor yielding the smaller value of $f^*(j)$ is chosen. For trees, in which a node has at most one predecessor, step 6c can be ignored. Note that even if the search space is a general graph, the subgraph that is made explicit is always a tree, since node j never records more than one predecessor at a time.

Breadth-first, uniform-cost, and depth-first search (Article II.C1) are all special cases of the ordered-search technique. For breadth-first search, we choose $f^*(i)$ to be the depth of node i. For uniform-cost search, $f^*(i)$ is the cost of the path from the start node to node i. A depth-first search (without a depth bound) can be obtained by taking $f^*(i)$ to be the negative of the depth of the node.

The purpose of ordered search, of course, is to reduce the number of nodes expanded as compared to blind-search algorithms. Its effectiveness in doing this depends directly on the choice of f^*, which should discriminate sharply between promising and unpromising nodes. If the discrimination is inaccurate, however, the ordered search may miss an optimal solution or all solutions. If no exact measure of promise is available, therefore, the choice of f^* involves a trade-off between time and space, on the one hand, and the guarantee of an optimal solution, or any solution, on the other.

Problem Types and the Choice of f^*

The measure of a node's promise—and consequently the appropriateness of a particular evaluation function—depends on the problem at hand. Several cases can be distinguished by the type of solution they require. In one, it is assumed that the state space contains multiple solution paths with different costs; the problem is to find the optimal (i.e., minimum cost) solution. This first case is well understood; see Article II.C3b on the A^* algorithm.

The second situation is similar to the first but with an added condition: The problem is hard enough that, if it is treated as an instance of the first case, the search will probably exceed bounds of time and space before finding a solution. The key questions for the second case are (a) how to find good (but not optimal) solutions with reasonable amounts of search effort and (b) how to bound both the search effort and the extent to which the solution produced is less than optimal.

A third kind of problem is one in which there is no concern for the optimality of the solution; perhaps only one solution exists, or any solution is as good as any other. The question in this third case is how to minimize the search effort—instead of, as in the second case, trying to minimize some combination of search effort and solution cost.

An example of the third case comes from theorem proving, where one may well be satisfied with the most easily found proof, however inelegant. A clear example of the second case is the traveling-salesman problem, in which finding some circuit through a set of cities is trivial, and the difficulty, which is very great, is entirely in finding a shortest or close-to-shortest path. Most treatments, however, do not clearly distinguish between the two cases. A popular test problem, the 8-puzzle, can be treated as being in either class. For further discussion of the second and third cases, see Article II.C3c.

References

See Doran (1967), Feigenbaum (1969), Gaschnig (1977), Michie (1967), Michie and Ross (1970), Newell and Ernst (1965), Newell and Simon (1972), Nilsson (1971, 1974), Pohl (1977), Sandewall (1971), and Simon and Kadane (1975).

C3b. A^*—Optimal Search for an Optimal Solution

The A^* algorithm, described by Hart, Nilsson, and Raphael (1968), addresses the problem of finding a minimal-cost path joining the start node and a goal node in a state-space graph. This problem subsumes the problem of finding the path between such nodes containing the smallest number of arcs. In the latter problem, each arc (representing the application of an operator) has cost 1; in the minimal-cost-path problem, the costs associated with arcs can be arbitrary. Historically, the predecessors of A^* include Dijkstra's algorithm (1959) and Moore's algorithm (1959). A class of algorithms similar to A^* is used in operations research under the name of *branch-and-bound* algorithms (see Hall, 1971; Hillier and Lieberman, 1974; Lawler and Wood, 1966; Reingold, Nievergelt, and Deo, 1977).

The algorithm used by A^* is an *ordered state-space search* (see Article II.C3a). Its distinctive feature is its definition of the *evaluation function, f^**. As in the usual ordered search, the node chosen for expansion is always one at which f^* is minimum.

Since f^* evaluates nodes in light of the need to find a minimal-cost solution, it considers the value of each node n as having two components: the cost of reaching n from the start node and the cost of reaching a goal from node n. Accordingly, f^* is defined by

$$f^*(n) = g^*(n) + h^*(n) \ ,$$

where g^* estimates the minimum cost of a path from the start node to node n, and h^* estimates the minimum cost from node n to a goal. The value $f^*(n)$ thus estimates the minimal cost of a solution path passing through node n. The actual costs, which f^*, g^*, and h^* only estimate, are denoted by f, g, and h, respectively. It is assumed that all arc costs are positive.

The function g^*, applied to a node n being considered for expansion, is calculated as the actual cost from the start node s to n along the cheapest path found so far by the algorithm. If the state space is a tree, then g^* gives a perfect estimate, since only one path from s to n exists. In a general state-space graph, g^* can err only in the direction of overestimating the minimal cost; its value is adjusted downward if a shorter path to n is found. Even in a general graph, there are certain conditions (mentioned below) under which $g^*(n)$ can be shown to be a perfect estimate by the time node n is chosen for expansion.

The function h^* is the carrier of *heuristic information* and can be defined in any way appropriate to the problem domain. For the interesting properties of the $A*$ algorithm to hold, however, $h*$ should be nonnegative, and it should never overestimate the cost of reaching a goal node from the node being evaluated. That is, for any such node n, it should always hold that $h*(n)$ is less than or equal to $h(n)$, the actual cost of an optimal path from n to a goal node. This last condition is called the *admissibility condition*.

Admissibility and Optimality of $A*$

It can be shown that if $h*$ satisfies the admissibility condition and if, in addition, all arc costs are positive and can be bounded from below by a positive number, then $A*$ is guaranteed to find a solution path of minimal cost if any solution path exists. This property is called the property of *admissibility*.

Although the admissibility condition requires $h*$ to be a lower bound on h, it is to be expected that the more nearly $h*$ approximates h, the better the algorithm will perform. If $h*$ were identically equal to h, an optimal solution path would be found without ever expanding a node off the path (assuming only one optimal solution exists). If $h*$ is identically zero, $A*$ reduces to the blind uniform-cost algorithm (Article II.C1). Two otherwise similar algorithms, say, A_1 and A_2, can be compared with respect to their choices of the $h*$ function, say, h_1* and h_2*. Algorithm A_1 is said to be *more informed than* A_2 if, whenever a node n (other than a goal node) is evaluated,

$$h_1*(n) > h_2*(n) .$$

On this basis an *optimality* result for $A*$ can be stated: If A and $A*$ are admissible algorithms such that $A*$ is more informed than A, then $A*$ never expands a node that is not also expanded by A. A proof (correcting the proof given in Nilsson, 1971) appears in Gelperin (1977).

Optimality and Heuristic Power

The sense in which $A*$ yields an optimal search has to do only with the number of nodes it expands in the course of finding a minimal-cost solution. But there are other relevant considerations. First, the difficulty of computing $h*$ also affects the total computational effort. Second, it may be less important to find a solution whose cost is absolutely minimum than to find a solution of reasonable cost within a search of moderate length. In such a case, one might prefer an $h*$ that evaluates nodes more accurately in most cases but sometimes overestimates the distance to a goal, thus yielding an inadmissible algorithm. (See Article

II.C3c.) The choice of h^* and the resulting *heuristic power* of the algorithm depend on a compromise among these considerations.

A final question one might consider is the number of node expansions, as opposed to the number of distinct nodes expanded by A^*. The two totals will be the same provided that whenever a node n is expanded (moved to the CLOSED list), an optimal path to n has already been found. This condition is always satisfied in a state-space tree, where $g^*(n) = g(n)$ necessarily. It will also be satisfied in a general state-space graph if a condition called the *consistency assumption* holds (see Hart, Nilsson, and Raphael, 1968). The general idea of the assumption is that a form of the triangle inequality holds throughout the search space. Specifically, the assumption is that for any nodes m and n, the estimated distance $h^*(m)$ from m to a goal should always be less than or equal to the actual distance from m to n plus the estimated remaining distance, $h^*(n)$, from n to a goal. For an h^* not satisfying the consistency assumption on a general state-space graph, Martelli (1977) has shown that A^* is not optimal with respect to the number of expansions and has given an algorithm that runs more efficiently under these circumstances.

References

See Dijkstra (1959), Gelperin (1977), Hall (1971), Hart, Nilsson, and Raphael (1968, 1972), Hillier and Lieberman (1974), Lawler and Wood (1966), Martelli (1977), Moore (1959), and Reingold, Nievergelt, and Deo (1977).

C3c. Relaxing the Optimality Requirement

The A^* algorithm (Article II.C3b) is an ordered state-space search using the evaluation function $f^* = g^* + h^*$. If the appropriate conditions are met, including most importantly the *admissibility condition* that the estimate $h^*(n)$ is always less than or equal to $h(n)$, then A^* is guaranteed to find an optimal solution path if one exists. Again under suitable conditions, the performance of A^* is optimal in comparison with other similarly defined admissible algorithms. Still, several questions remain:

1. One may be more concerned with minimizing search effort than with minimizing solution cost. Is $f^* = g^* + h^*$ an appropriate evaluation function in this case?
2. Even if solution cost is important, the combinatorics of the problem may be such that an admissible A^* cannot run to termination. Can speed be gained at the cost of a bounded decrease in solution quality?
3. It may be hard to find a good heuristic function h^* that satisfies the admissibility condition; with a poor but admissible heuristic function, A^* deteriorates into blind search. How is the search affected by an inadmissible heuristic function?

Minimizing Search Effort

An approach to the first question can be stated as follows. The reason for including g^* in the evaluation function is to add a breadth-first component to the search; without g^*, the evaluation function would estimate, at any node n, the remaining distance to a goal and would ignore the distance already covered in reaching n. If the object is to minimize search effort instead of solution cost, one might conclude that g^* should be omitted from the evaluation function. An early heuristic search algorithm that did just this was Doran and Michie's Graph Traverser (Doran and Michie, 1966; Doran, 1967); the evaluation function used was of the form $f^* = h^*$, and the object was to minimize total search effort in finding solutions to the 8-puzzle and other problems. A generalization covering the Graph Traverser algorithm, A^*, and others has been defined by Pohl (1969, 1970a, 1970b) as the Heuristic Path Algorithm (HPA). This algorithm gives an ordered state-space search with an evaluation function of the form

$$f^* = (1 - w)g^* + wh^*,$$

where w is a constant in $[0, 1]$ giving the relative importance to be attached to g and h. Choosing $w = 1$ gives the Graph Traverser algorithm, $w = 0$ gives breadth-first search, and $w = .5$ is equivalent to the A^* function $f^* = g^* + h^*$.

Pohl's results concerning HPA indicate that, at least in special cases, omitting g^* from the evaluation function is a mistake. One case is that in which h^* is the most accurate heuristic function possible: If $h^*(n) = h(n)$ at every node n, the evaluation function $f^* = h^*$ still expands no fewer nodes than $f^* = g^* + h^*$. The other case assumes a simplified state space, whose graph is an infinite m-ary tree, and assumes that the error in h^*—which may underestimate or overestimate h—is bounded by a nonnegative integer e. In this situation, it is shown that the maximum number of nodes expanded with $f^* = h^*$ is greater than the maximum number expanded with $f^* = g^* + h^*$, and that the difference between the maxima is exponential in the error bound e. This analysis by Pohl is one of the earliest applications of oracle or adversary analysis for discovering worst-case algorithmic efficiency. As such, it is an important precursor to work on NP (nondeterministic polynomial-time) complete problems and their attempted solution by heuristics. (For a general introduction to NP-completeness, see Aho, Hopcroft, and Ullman, 1974.)

The two functions $f^* = h^*$ and $f^* = g^* + h^*$ have not been analyzed with respect to their average-case, as opposed to worst-case, behavior. Pohl's empirical results suggest that ordered search may typically expand the fewest nodes, provided the h^* function is fairly good, if g^* is included but given less weight than h^*—that is, with w greater than .5 but less than 1. These results were obtained for the 15-puzzle, a task exactly like the 8-puzzle except that it uses 15 tiles in a 4×4 array.

For problems that differ from the 15-puzzle, in that some states lead to dead ends rather than only to longer solutions, a somewhat different approach has been taken recently by Simon and Kadane (1975). Whereas the evaluation functions $f^* = g^* + h^*$ and $f^* = h^*$ are based on the estimated solution cost at a given node, Simon and Kadane propose that the function should also take explicit account of the probability that the node is in fact on a solution path. With such a function, an expected long search with high probability of success could readily rate just as favorably as one that is potentially shorter but that has a higher chance of failing.

Solution Quality and Heuristic Error

The second question, of speed versus solution quality, has been studied by Pohl (1973, 1977) and Harris (1973, 1974). Harris's work concerns the third question (inadmissible heuristic functions) as well, as do Pohl's results, which were summarized above. Both Harris and Pohl consider the *traveling-salesman problem*, which is NP-complete (Karp, 1972).

Pohl's approach is a further generalization of the HPA evaluation function: Now $f^*(n) = g^*(n) + w(n)h^*(n)$. That is, the relative weight w to be attached to g^* and h^* is no longer constant; the function $w(n)$, which may be greater than or equal to 1, is defined to vary with the depth of node n. This approach is called *dynamic weighting*. With a definition of w that weights h^* less heavily as the search goes deeper, and with the assumption that h^* is a lower bound on h, Pohl shows that HPA will find a solution to the traveling-salesman problem whose cost is bounded by the ratio

$$\frac{\text{cost of tour found}}{\text{cost of optimal solution}} < 1 + e$$

where e is a constant in $[0, 1)$, which appears in the definition of w.

Dynamic weighting was tested on an instance of the traveling-salesman problem, known as the Croes problem, which involves 20 cities and has a known optimal-solution cost of 246. An admissible A^*— which produces an optimal solution if it produces any—had still not terminated after expanding 500 nodes. With dynamic weighting, however, together with an appropriate choice of e and the same h^* function, a solution with cost 260 was found by expanding only 53 nodes.

Harris's approach, called *bandwidth search*, is somewhat different from Pohl's. It assumes that no good h^* function satisfying the admissibility condition is available. In its place, he introduces the *bandwidth condition*, which requires that for all nongoal nodes n,

(1) $h^*(n) \leq h(n) + e$

and

(2) $h(n) - d \leq h^*(n)$.

It is assumed that h^* satisfies the *consistency assumption* (see Article II.C3b).

With respect to the first part of the condition, it can be shown that if h^* never overestimates the distance to a goal by more than e, the cost of a solution found by A^* will not exceed the cost of an optimal solution by more than e. With such an h^*, the algorithm is said to be *e-admissible;* and the goal it finds, *e-optimal.*

Once the bandwidth search finds some solution, a further application of condition (1) may show that the cost of the solution found is in fact closer than e to an optimal solution. This is possible because (a) the cost of the solution found is known and (b) a lower bound on the cost of every other solution is the minimum, over all nodes n remaining on the OPEN list, of $f^*(n) - e$. If the difference between these two quantities is too big, the search can be continued until it finds a solution that is acceptably close to the optimum.

The second part of the bandwidth condition, condition (2), can be used to save storage space by dropping nodes from the OPEN list, without any risk of dropping a node that is in fact on an optimal path to a goal. Let node q be a node that, having a minimum value of f^*, has been selected for expansion. Then any node m may safely be dropped from OPEN if $f^*(m)$ is hopelessly big compared to $f^*(q)$. Specifically, it can be shown that all nodes m can be dropped if there is a node q such that

$$f^*(m) - (e + d) > f^*(q) \ .$$

Harris notes that it may be difficult to find a heuristic function h^* that satisfies both parts of the bandwidth condition. One may instead define two heuristic functions, one to order the search and one to determine which nodes can be dropped. Such functions, say, h_1^* and h_2^*, should then satisfy

(1') $$h_1^*(n) \le h(n) + e$$

and

(2') $$h(n) - d \le h_2^*(n) \ .$$

Using two such heuristic functions, Harris tested the bandwidth search on several instances of the traveling-salesman problem, including the 20-city Croes problem mentioned above. Harris's results, including a comparison with A^* using an admissible heuristic function, are summarized in Figure C3-1. The OPEN list was limited to 500 nodes.

	BANDWIDTH SEARCH		ADMISSIBLE SEARCH	
No. of cities	Quality of solution	Nodes expanded	Quality of solution	Nodes expanded
6	5-optimal	6		
6	optimal	14	optimal	18
11	optimal	14	none	500 open nodes
20	4-optimal	42	none	500 open nodes

Figure C3-1. Comparison of bandwidth search and admissible search.

References

See Aho, Hopcroft, and Ullman (1974), Doran (1967), Doran and Michie (1966), Harris (1973, 1974), Karp (1972), Nilsson (1971), Pohl (1969, 1970a, 1970b, 1973, 1977), and Simon and Kadane (1975).

C3d. Bidirectional Search

Earlier articles in this chapter described (a) heuristic state-space search methods using forward reasoning and (b) a blind state-space search combining forward and backward reasoning into a *bidirectional* algorithm. The kinds of problems to which a bidirectional state-space method applies were considered in Article II.C1; in general, it must be possible in these problems to search either forward, from the initial state toward the goal, or backward, from the goal toward the initial state. A bidirectional search pursues both lines of reasoning in parallel, growing two search trees and terminating when they meet. The motivation is that, in many cases, the number of nodes in a search tree grows exponentially with its depth; if a solution can be found by using two trees of half the depth, the search effort should be reduced significantly. Blind bidirectional search was in fact found to expand far fewer nodes than its unidirectional counterpart. A natural next question is whether heuristic bidirectional search can give still greater improvements in efficiency.

This question was investigated by Pohl (1969, 1971). Whereas his blind bidirectional algorithm used forward and backward uniform-cost search, his heuristic algorithm used forward and backward *ordered search*. Otherwise, the two algorithms differed mainly in their termination conditions. In both cases, the termination condition was complicated by the fact that the algorithms were designed to find an *optimal* path between the start and goal nodes; they could be simplified if any path would do.

As *evaluation functions,* Pohl's heuristic bidirectional algorithm used functions parallel to those of A^*. For a node x in the forward search tree:

$gs(x)$ measured the shortest path found so far from the start node, s, to x;

$hs(x)$ estimated the minimum remaining distance from x to the terminal node, t; and

$fs(x) = gs(x) + hs(x)$ was the evaluation function.

Similarly, for a node x generated in the backward search:

$gt(x)$ measured the shortest path found so far from x to t;

$ht(x)$ estimated the minimum distance from s to x; and

$ft(x) = gt(x) + ht(x)$ was the evaluation function.

Constraints were placed on the heuristic functions hs and ht, corresponding to the admissibility condition and the consistency assumption of A^*, in order to guarantee the optimality of the solution.

Pohl's results, in experiments using bidirectional heuristic search on the 15-puzzle, were disappointing. It was hoped that the search trees rooted at the start and goal nodes would meet near the middle of the solution path. In blind search, this had happened necessarily because both trees were expanded breadth-first. (Recall that uniform-cost search is a generalization of the breadth-first algorithm.) In the heuristic case, however, the search in each direction was narrowed. Since each problem had many alternate solutions, the typical outcome was that both search trees grew to include nearly complete, but different, solution paths before intersecting.

Several ideas have been advanced for forcing the trees to meet earlier while retaining the benefit of heuristic information (Pohl, 1971, 1977; Kowalski, 1972; de Champeaux and Sint, 1977). One that has been tested is that of de Champeaux and Sint (1977), which redefines the heuristic functions hs and ht as follows:

> Let T-OPEN be the list of unexpanded nodes of the backward search tree. For a node x in the forward search tree, $hs(x)$ estimates the minimum distance from x to the goal t by way of some node y in T-OPEN. That is, $hs(x)$ is the minimum, over all nodes y on T-OPEN, of the estimated distance from x to y plus $gt(y)$, the length of the shortest known path from y to the goal.

The function ht is defined analogously. The authors reported, for the same problems Pohl had used, that the algorithm generally produced shorter solution paths, with fewer nodes expanded, and that the search graphs now did meet near the middle of the search space. Unfortunately, however, hs and ht were so expensive to compute—since for each node x to be expanded, its distance must be estimated to every node y on the opposite OPEN list—that the algorithm still ran much more slowly than unidirectional heuristic search.

References

See de Champeaux and Sint (1977), Kowalski (1972), and Pohl (1969, 1971, 1977).

C4. Heuristic Search of an AND/OR Graph

This article returns to the problem of searching an AND/OR graph, as opposed to an ordinary state-space graph. The distinction between the two is the presence of AND nodes, which add conceptual complications to the search problem. Each node of the AND/OR graph represents a goal to be achieved. It will be assumed throughout that reasoning is backward, from an initial goal (the root) toward an equivalent set of subgoals, all of which have immediate solutions. On this assumption, an AND/OR graph constitutes (in the terminology of this chapter) a *problem-reduction representation*. This identification gives another way of stating the distinction between problem-reduction and state-space representations: State-space operators always take exactly one input and produce exactly one output; a problem-reduction operator also takes a single input but may produce multiple outputs (see Sec. II.B).

To put the matter further into perspective, one may also conceive of searching an AND/OR graph in the forward direction—from the primitive problems, whose solutions are already known, toward the problem one actually wishes to solve. Just such a graph search is the one typically conducted by a resolution theorem-prover, as it brings together two or more axioms or previous conclusions and applies to them an operator yielding one new deduction as its result. (See Chap. XII, in Vol. III.) Forward reasoning in an AND/OR graph, then, would be distinguished from a state-space search by the presence of multiple-input, single-output operators. For further discussion, including an algorithm for bidirectional search of an AND/OR graph, see Kowalski (1972); see also Martelli and Montanari (1973).

The search of an AND/OR graph using backward reasoning raises numerous problems. Previous articles (II.B2 and II.C2) have considered—

1. what constitutes a solution subgraph of an AND/OR graph, and
2. blind-search algorithms for finding a solution subgraph.

This article considers three additional problems:

3. What might one mean by an optimal solution subgraph?
4. How can *heuristic information* be brought to bear on the search for an optimal solution?

5. What limitations are there on AND/OR graphs and the associated search algorithms as general tools for problem solving?

The Definition of an Optimal Solution

A solution of an AND/OR graph is a subgraph demonstrating that the start node is solved. As in a state-space search, one may ask for a solution of minimal cost. The cost of a solution tree can be defined in either of two ways (Nilsson, 1971):

1. The *sum cost* of a solution tree is the sum of all arc costs in the tree.

2. The *max cost* of a solution tree is the sum of arc costs along the most expensive path from the root to a terminal node.

For example, if every arc in the solution tree has cost 1, then the sum cost is the number of arcs in the tree and the max cost is the depth of the deepest node.

If the entire search space had been explored, then an optimal solution tree could be constructed and its cost measured as follows. Let $c(n, m)$ be the cost of the arc from node n to a successor node m. Define a function $h(n)$ by:

1. If n is a terminal node (a primitive problem), then $h(n) = 0$.

2. If n has OR successors, then $h(n)$ is the minimum, over all its successors m, of $c(n, m) + h(m)$.

3. If n has AND successors and sum costs are used, then $h(n)$ is the summation, over all successors m, of $c(n, m) + h(m)$.

4. If n has AND successors and max costs are used, then $h(n)$ is the maximum, over all successors m, of $c(n, m) + h(m)$.

5. If n is a nonterminal node with no successors, then $h(n)$ is infinite.

According to this definition, $h(n)$ is finite if and only if the problem represented by node n is solvable. For each solvable node n, $h(n)$ gives the cost of an optimal solution tree for the problem represented by node n. If s is the start node, then $h(s)$ is the cost of an optimal solution to the initial problem.

Consider, for example, the AND/OR tree of Figure C4-1, with arc costs as indicated. Each node without successors is marked t or u according to whether it is terminal or unsolvable.

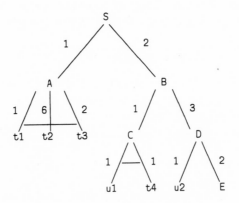

Figure C4-1. An AND/OR tree.

If *sum costs* are used, the values of h are as shown in Figure C4-2, and the optimal solution is the subgraph comprising nodes S, B, D, E, t_5, and t_6. The abbreviation *inf* denotes infinity.

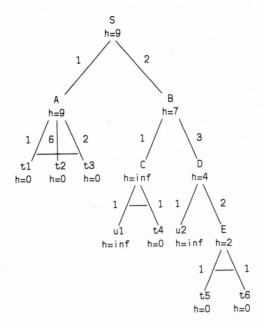

Figure C4-2. Sum costs.

If *max costs* are used, then the values of h are as shown in Figure C4-3, and the optimal solution is the subgraph comprising nodes S, A, t_1, t_2, and t_3.

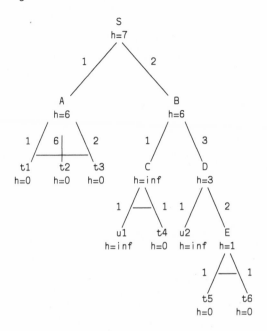

Figure C4-3. Max costs.

Ordered-search Algorithms for an AND/OR Graph

In an ordered state-space search, one may use an *evaluation function* f^* that, applied to node n, returns the estimated minimum cost of a solution path passing through node n. The next node expanded is always one at which f^* is minimum—that is, one extends the most promising potential solution path. The successors of node n are new nodes, but one could just as well think of them as new potential solution paths, each differing from a parent (potential solution path) by the inclusion of one more step.

In the extension of heuristic search to AND/OR graphs, there is no longer a one-to-one correspondence between the choice of a node to expand and the choice of a potential solution to be extended. Consider, for example, the search graph of Figure C4-4.

Figure C4-4.   An AND/OR graph containing
two potential solution trees.

Since C and D are OR nodes, an actual solution of node S will contain only one of them.   To expand node A is thus to extend two
potential solution trees,

Conversely, a decision to extend the potential solution tree on the left
can be carried out by expanding either node A or node C.   One must
be clear, therefore, about what kind of object the expansion process is
to apply to.   This decision will affect the definition of the evaluation
function.

Nilsson's algorithm.   An approach taken by Nilsson (1969, 1971)
selects individual nodes to expand by a two-step process: First, identify
the most promising potential solution tree; then, choose a node within
that tree for expansion.   To accomplish the first step, an evaluation
function h^* is defined at every node n of the tree that has not been
shown to be unsolvable.   This function is an estimate of $h(n)$; that is, it
estimates the cost of an optimal solution to the problem at node n.   If n
is known to be a terminal node, then by definition $h^*(n) = h(n) = 0$.
Otherwise, if n has not yet been expanded, then the estimate must be
based on whatever heuristic information is available from the problem
domain.   For example, in the search tree of Figure C4-4, h^* would
provide heuristic estimates of the cost of solving nodes A, C, and D.
The following rule then permits h^* to be computed for each node whose
successors have already been generated (and to be recomputed as the
search tree is expanded):

1. If n has OR successors m, then $h^*(n)$ is the minimum, over these successors, of $c(n, m) + h^*(m)$.

2. If n has AND successors m and sum costs are used, then $h^*(n)$ is the summation, over these successors, of $c(n, m) + h^*(m)$.

3. If n has AND successors m and max costs are used, then $h^*(n)$ is the maximum, over these successors, of $c(n, m) + h^*(m)$.

Finally, the most promising potential solution tree, T, is defined in terms of h^*:

1. The start node s is in T.

2. If the search tree (the part of the search space generated so far) contains a node n and AND successors of n, then all these successors are in T.

3. If the search tree contains a node n and OR successors m of n, then one successor m is in T such that $c(n, m) + h^*(m)$ is minimal.

The estimated cost of T is $h^*(s)$. If all the other potential solution trees for the same search tree were constructed, it would be found that T is one for which $h^*(s)$ is minimal. An ordered-search algorithm for an AND/OR tree can now be stated as follows:

1. Put the start node, s, on a list, OPEN, of unexpanded nodes.

2. From the search tree constructed so far (initially, just s), compute the most promising potential solution tree T.

3. Select a node n that is on OPEN and in T. Remove node n from OPEN and place it on a list called CLOSED.

4. If n is a terminal node, then
   a. Label node n solved.
   b. If the solution of n makes any of its ancestors solved, label these ancestors solved.
   c. If the start node is solved, exit with T as the solution tree.
   d. Remove from OPEN any nodes with a solved ancestor.

5. Otherwise, if node n has no successors (i.e., if no operator can be applied), then
   a. Label node n unsolvable.
   b. If the unsolvability of n makes any of its ancestors unsolvable, label all such ancestors unsolvable as well.
   c. If the start node is labeled unsolvable, exit with failure.
   d. Remove from OPEN any nodes with an unsolvable ancestor.

6. Otherwise, expand node n, generating all its immediate successors and, for each successor m representing a set of more than one subproblem, generating successors of m corresponding to the individual subproblems. Attach, to each newly generated

node, a pointer back to its immediate predecessor and compute
h^* for each newly generated node. Place all the new nodes
that do not yet have descendants on OPEN. Finally, recompute
$h^*(n)$ and h^* at each ancestor of n.

7. Go to (2).

The ordered-search algorithm can be shown to be *admissible*—that
is, it will find a minimum-cost solution tree if any solution exists—
provided that: (a) $h^*(n)$ is less than or equal to $h(n)$ for each open
node n and (b) all arc costs are greater than some small positive
number d. The efficiency of the algorithm, however, depends both on
the accuracy of h^* and on the implementation of step 3, in which,
having found the most promising potential solution tree to expand, one
must decide to expand a specific node within that tree. If the partial
tree T is in fact part of an optimum solution, the choice is immaterial.
If it is not, however, then the best node to expand would be the one
that will earliest reveal the error.

Chang and Slagle's algorithm. A different approach has been taken
by Chang and Slagle (1971). Here the objects expanded are potential
solution graphs. A *tip node* in such a graph is any node that does not
yet have successors. To expand the potential solution graph, one expands all its nonterminal tip nodes at once and then forms all the new
potential solution graphs that result. Each graph is represented on the
OPEN list by the conjunction of its tip nodes, representing a set of
subproblems to which the start node can be reduced.

For example, suppose that expansion of the initial graph, consisting
of only the start node S, shows that S can be reduced to problems A
and B or to problem C. The OPEN list then becomes $(A\&B, C)$.
Assume that $A\&B$ is selected for expansion, that A can be reduced to D
or E, and that B can be reduced to F or G. There are four new
potential solution trees, and the OPEN list is now $(D\&F, D\&G, E\&F,$
$E\&G, C)$. The search succeeds when it selects for expansion a potential
solution graph represented by a conjunction of nodes all of which are
terminal.

The Chang and Slagle approach assimilates AND/OR graph search to
the problem of state-space search. Each distinct conjunction of problems to be solved corresponds to a distinct state of a state-space graph.
The evaluation function used, f^*, is also parallel to the function used in
A^*: It is defined by $f^* = g^* + h^*$, where g^* measures the cheapest
way found so far to reduce the start node to a given conjunction of
subproblems and h^* estimates the minimum remaining cost of a graph
sufficient to solve all those subproblems.

The treatment of AND/OR graph search as an instance of state-space search has several consequences. One is that the search of a general AND/OR graph, as opposed to an AND/OR tree, now raises no special problems. Another is that the algorithm can be shown (Chang and Slagle, 1971), under appropriate conditions, to be not only admissible but also optimal with respect to the number of potential solution graphs expanded. It does not, however, appear to be optimal (in some reasonable sense of that term) in comparison with algorithms that expand only one node at a time (see Kowalski, 1972).

Interdependent Subproblems

The discussion so far has assumed that whenever the start node is reduced to a conjunction of subproblems, all subproblems can be solved independently, so that the solution to one has no effect on the solution to any other. This assumption is frequently unjustified, and much of Chapter XVI (in Vol. III) explores ways of dealing with interacting subproblems. Two kinds of examples, given by Levi and Sirovich (1975, 1976) with explicit reference to the AND/OR graph formalism, are: (a) problems requiring consistent binding of variables and (b) problems involving the expenditure of scarce resources.

An illustration of the former is the well-known problem of showing that there exists a fallible Greek, given that the entire search space is as follows (Fig. C4-5):

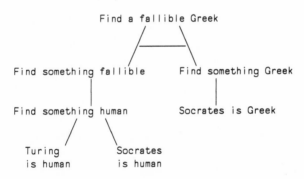

Figure C4-5. An AND/OR graph requiring consistent binding of the variable *something*.

An algorithm like Nilsson's fails here for two reasons. First, it has no mechanism for discovering that *Turing is human* and *Socrates is Greek* fail to constitute a solution. Second, even if such a mechanism were introduced, the algorithm has no means for undoing the solution to a subproblem once it has been solved. If *Turing is human* is the first problem found to be primitive, then *Find something human* and *Find something fallible* are marked solved; *Socrates is human* is removed from the OPEN list as no longer in need of consideration; and *Find something Greek,* using the previous value of *something,* then becomes unsolvable.

An example of the second type of problem is the following: Show that John can seduce the actress, given that seducing the actress can be reduced to getting a car and getting a yacht—and that John has $5,000, a car costs $5,000, and a yacht costs $5,000. Here, either of the algorithms given above would wrongly conclude that John can seduce the actress. A variant of the scarce-resource problem arises in robot planning tasks (such as those performed by STRIPS, Article II.D5), where application of an operator representing a robot action solving one subproblem may make inapplicable the operator needed to solve another subproblem.

To handle problems of these kinds, Levi and Sirovich define a *generalized AND/OR graph,* which differs most importantly from an ordinary AND/OR graph in that reduction operators are permitted to take two or more nodes as input. For example, let R be a resource that can be used only once. Then if, in the standard formulation, the original problem is to accomplish P_1 and P_2, the problem is reformulated as P_1 & P_2 & R. Suppose the following reduction operators are available (where "→" means *can be reduced to* and T denotes a trivial problem):

1. $S \rightarrow P_1$ & P_2 & R
2. P_1 & $R \rightarrow T$
3. $P_1 \rightarrow P_3$
4. P_2 & $R \rightarrow P_3$
5. $P_3 \rightarrow T$
6. $R \rightarrow T$

Then there is only one solution, which is achieved using operators 1, 3, 4, and 5.

In the ordered search of a generalized AND/OR graph, the objects placed on the OPEN list are potential solution graphs, not individual nodes. Expansion of a potential solution graph (PSG) consists of applying all possible operators to obtain a new set of PSGs, each differing from its parent by virtue of one additional operator application. If the same subproblem occurs more than once within a PSG, each occurrence is represented by a separate node. If the same PSG is generated more than once, later occurrences are simply discarded. Since distinct PSGs are retained, alternate solutions to the same subproblem are available.

As in the usual ordered search, the object chosen for expansion next is always one where the evaluation function is minimum. The evaluation function is $h*$; for each PSG, it is computed similarly to the $h*$ of Nilsson's algorithm. The value of each potential solution graph is then the evaluation of the start node, $h*(s)$, as computed for that graph. Both *admissibility* and *optimality*—the latter with respect to the number of PSGs expanded—can be shown.

References

See Chang and Slagle (1971), Kowalski (1972), Levi and Sirovich (1975, 1976), Martelli and Montanari (1973), and Nilsson (1969, 1971).

C5. Game Tree Search

C5a. Minimax Procedure

The Minimax Formalism

The minimax procedure is a technique for searching game trees (see Article II.B3). As a first example, Figure C5-1 gives a simple game tree to which the procedure may be applied. Each node represents a position in the game. Nonterminal nodes are labeled with the name of the player, *A* or *B*, who is to move from that position. It is *A*'s turn, and the problem is to find his best move from position 1. Exactly three moves remain in the game. Terminal nodes are marked with their value to player *A* by the words "win," "lose," or "draw."

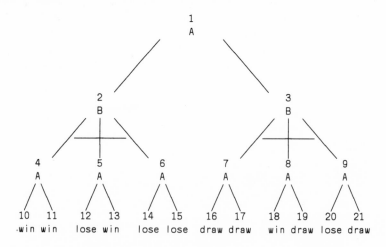

Figure C5-1.   A game tree from the standpoint of
player *A*, who is to move next.

According to the minimax technique, player *A* should move to whichever one of positions 2 or 3 has the greater value to him. Given the values of the terminal positions, the value of a nonterminal position is computed, by backing up from the terminals, as follows:

(1) The value to player A of a node with OR successors (a node from which A chooses the next move) is the maximum value of any of its successors.

The value to A of a node with AND successors (a node from which B chooses the next move) is the minimum value of any of its successors.

In the example, node 2 evaluates to a loss for A (since B can then force a loss by moving to node 6), and node 3 evaluates to a draw (since the best B can then do is move to node 7 or 9). It will be noted that the prediction of the opponent's behavior assumes he is also using minimax: In evaluating a node with AND successors, A must assume that B will make his best possible move. The technique ignores the possibility that B might overlook his chance for a sure win if A goes to node 2. Similarly, it supplies no basis on which B might choose to move to node 9 in preference to node 7.

Because of the way in which nodes are evaluated, player A (whose viewpoint the tree represents) is often called MAX, and player B, MIN. The names PLUS and MINUS are also sometimes used. If the tree of Figure C5-1 were to be evaluated from MIN's standpoint instead of MAX's, it would appear as in Figure C5-2. The AND and OR nodes are reversed, and the value of each node to MIN is the opposite of its value to MAX.

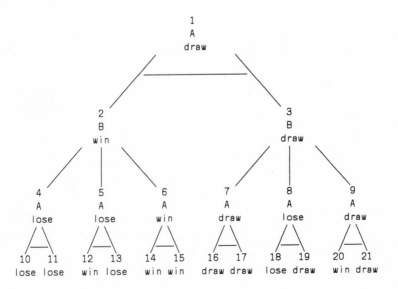

Figure C5-2. The game tree of Figure C5-1 from B's standpoint.

The Negmax Formalism

Knuth and Moore (1975) have given a game-tree representation that unifies Figures C5-1 and C5-2 and conveniently permits a single procedure to return optimal moves for both players A and B. In this representation, the value given each node is its value to the player whose turn it would be to move at that node. If n is a terminal node, its value is an integer denoted $f(n)$. (The value of n to the other player is $-f(n)$.) The value of every node is then returned by a function F defined as follows:

$F(n) = f(n)$, if n has no successors;

$F(n) = \max\{-F(n_1), \ldots, -F(n_k)\}$, if n has successors $n_1, \ldots, n_k$.

The best move for either player is then to a node with maximum value; that is, the player whose turn it is at node n should move from node n to a node n_i with $-F(n_i) = F(n)$. This formulation, which is equivalent to minimax, is called *negmax*. The tree it produces for the game of Figures C5-1 and C5-2 is shown in Figure C5-3. The numerical value of a win is assumed to be $+1$; of a loss, -1; and of a draw, 0.

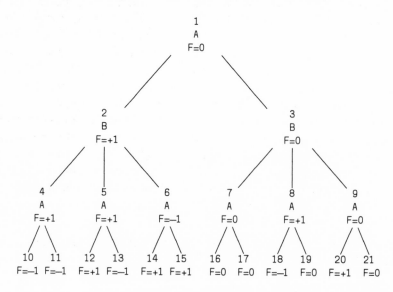

Figure C5-3. The game tree of Figure C5-1 in NEGMAX notation.

Searching a Partial Game Tree

In the above descriptions of the minimax and negmax algorithms, it was assumed that a complete game tree had already been generated. For most games, however, the tree of possibilities is far too large to be generated fully and searched backward from the terminal nodes for an optimal move. An alternative is to generate a reasonable portion of the tree, starting from the current position; make a move on the basis of this partial knowledge; let the opponent reply; and then repeat the process beginning from the new position. A "reasonable portion of the tree" might be taken to mean all legal moves within a fixed limit of depth, time, or storage, or it might be refined in various ways. For discussion of the refinements, see Article II.C5c.

Once the partial tree exists, minimaxing requires a means for estimating the value of its *tip nodes*, that is, the nodes of the partial tree without successors. A function assigning such a value is called a *static evaluation function;* it serves a purpose comparable to that of the heuristic function h^* used in Nilsson's ordered search of an AND/OR tree (Article II.C4). If the partial game tree contains any nodes that are terminal for the entire tree, the static evaluation function conventionally returns positive infinity for a win, negative infinity for a loss, and zero for a draw. At other tip nodes, the function has a finite value which, in the minimax formulation, is positive for positions favorable to MAX and negative at positions favorable to MIN. The minimax procedure then assigns *backed-up values* to the ancestors of the tip nodes in accordance with the rules given in condition (1) in the preceding discussion of the minimax formalism. It is assumed that the backed-up evaluations give a more accurate estimate of the true value of MAX's possible moves than would be obtained by applying the static evaluation function directly to those moves and not looking ahead to their consequences.

References

See Knuth and Moore (1975), Nilsson (1971), Slagle (1971), and Winston (1977).

C5b.   Alpha-Beta Pruning

The minimax procedure described in Article II.C5a decides on a best move from node n, in a full or partial game tree, by evaluating every node in the tree that descends from node n. Frequently, this exhaustive evaluation is a waste of time. Two examples are shown in Figures C5-4 and C5-5. Each node is marked with the name of the player who is to move from that position.

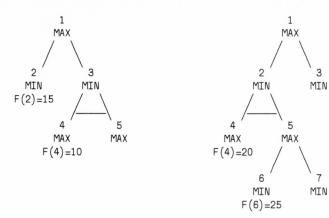

Figure C5-4.   An alpha cutoff.   Figure C5-5.   A beta cutoff.

In Figure C5-4, nodes 2 and 4 have been evaluated either by the static evaluation function or by backing up from descendants omitted from the figure. If MAX moves to node 2, he achieves a position whose estimated value is 15. If he moves to node 3, MIN can hold him to 10. Therefore, the value of node 3 is at most 10, so MAX should decide to move to node 2. The important point is that this decision can be made without evaluating node 5 or any of its possible descendants.

In Figure C5-5, node 4 has an estimated value to MAX of 20. When node 6 is evaluated at 25, it becomes clear that MIN should avoid moving to node 5. Node 2 can therefore be assigned a value of 20 without any need to evaluate node 7 or any of its descendants.

The *alpha-beta technique* for evaluating nodes of a game tree eliminates these unnecessary evaluations. If, as is usual, the generation of nodes is interleaved with their evaluation, then nodes such as the descendants of node 5 in Figure C5-4 and of node 7 in Figure C5-5 need never even be generated. The technique uses two parameters, *alpha* and *beta*. In Figure C5-4, the parameter *alpha* carries the lower bound of 15 on MAX's achievement from node 1; the elimination of node 5 is an *alpha cutoff*. In Figure C5-5, the parameter *beta* is set to 20 at node 4, representing an upper bound on the value to MAX of node 2; the elimination of node 7 is a *beta cutoff*. The procedure guarantees that the root node of the tree will have the same final value as if exhaustive minimaxing were employed.

A concise statement of the alpha-beta procedure has been given by Knuth and Moore (1975). It uses their *negmax* representation in which both players are treated as wishing to maximize (see Article II.C5a). Figure C5-6 shows how Figures C5-4 and C5-5 are transformed in the negmax representation.

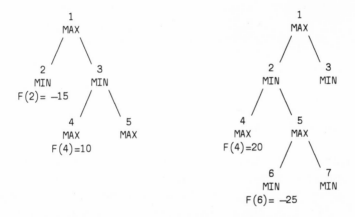

Figure C5-6.   The NEGMAX representation of Figures C5-4 and C5-5.

To evaluate node 1 of either tree, the procedure is called with the parameters POSITION = node 1, ALPHA = negative infinity, and BETA = positive infinity. The static evaluation function is called f. The procedure, here called VALUE, is as follows:

```
integer procedure VALUE (position p, integer alpha, integer beta):
  begin
      integer m, i, t, d;
      determine the successor positions p₁, p₂, . . ., p_d of position p;
      if d = 0 then VALUE := f(p) else
        begin m := alpha;
            for i := 1 step 1 until d do
              begin
                  t := -VALUE (p_i, -beta, -m);
                  if t > m then m := t;
                  if m ≥ beta then go to done;
              end;
          done: VALUE := m;
        end;
  end;
```

For an intuitively developed LISP version of the alpha-beta procedure, see Winston (1977). An excellent review of the historical development of the technique appears in Knuth and Moore (1975).

Ordering of Successors

The degree to which the alpha-beta procedure represents an improvement in efficiency over straight minimaxing varies with the order in which successor nodes are evaluated. For example, no cutoff would occur in Figure C5-4 if node 3 were considered before node 2.

In general, it is desirable that the best successor of each node be the first one evaluated—that is, that the first move MAX considers be his best move, and that the first reply considered for MIN be the move that is best for MIN and worst for MAX. Several schemes for ordering the successors of a node have been described to try to achieve this state of affairs. One possibility, an example of *fixed ordering*, is to apply the static evaluation function to the successors, taking the results of this preliminary evaluation as an approximation of their expected backed-up values. A method of this sort will result in depth-first generation and evaluation of the partial game tree, subject to the depth bound or other criteria for terminating generation. For some other possibilities, see Article II.C5c.

Efficiency in Uniform Game Trees

Since the alpha-beta procedure is more complicated than minimax-ing, although it yields the same result, one may inquire how great an increase it produces in search efficiency. Most theoretical results on this question deal with *uniform* game trees: A tree is said to be uniform if every tip node has depth d and every nontip node has exactly b successors. Here, b is called the *branching factor* or *degree* of the tree.

The results reviewed below come from Knuth and Moore (1975) and, for the best case, Slagle and Dixon (1969). For other related work, see Fuller, Gaschnig, and Gillogly (1973), Newborn (1977), and Baudet (1978).

The best case. A uniform game tree of depth d and degree b contains exactly b^d tip nodes, all of which must be examined by minimax. In the worst case, alpha-beta also must examine every tip node. In the best case, alpha-beta examines only about twice the square root of the number of tip nodes. More precisely, assuming the value of the root is not infinite, the number of tip nodes examined in the best case is

$$b^{[(d+1)/2]} + b^{[d/2]} - 1$$

(where square brackets represent the greatest integer function); and the nodes examined in the tree as a whole are precisely the *critical nodes*, defined as follows:

> *Type 1* critical nodes are the root node and all first successors of type 1 nodes.
>
> *Type 2* critical nodes are all further successors (except the first) of type 1 nodes and all successors of type 3 nodes.
>
> *Type 3* critical nodes are the first successors of type 2 nodes.

Figure C5-7 illustrates the distribution of critical nodes in a uniform tree of degree 3 and depth 3.

Knuth and Moore have shown that the best case occurs for a uniform tree if the best move is considered first at each critical node of types 1 and 2. Attempts to order the successors of type 3 positions contribute nothing to efficiency, since these successors are type 2 nodes, which must all be examined anyway.

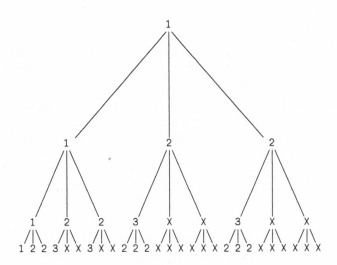

Figure C5-7.   Distribution of critical nodes.

Random uniform game trees. Knuth and Moore also show that the alpha-beta technique is optimal in the sense that no algorithm can evaluate any game tree by examining fewer nodes than alpha-beta does with an appropriate ordering of successors. Realistically, of course, one cannot expect to achieve the optimal successor ordering, since this would imply full knowledge of the game tree before it is generated. Assuming, therefore, that the tip nodes of the tree have distinct random values, Knuth and Moore show that the expected number of tip nodes examined, in evaluation of a uniform tree with branching factor b and depth d, has an asymptotic upper bound of

$$(b/(\log b))^d$$

as d goes to infinity.

Totally dependent, uniform game trees. One other type of tree considered by Knuth and Moore, perhaps more realistic than the one in which tip nodes have random values, corresponds to games in which each move is critical: If a poor move is ever chosen, there is no way to recoup. The model is a uniform game tree that is *totally dependent:* For any two successors of node p, these successors can be labeled q and r, so that every tip node descended from node q has greater value than any tip node descended from node r. In this type of tree, if the degree is at least 3, the expected number of tip positions examined is bounded by a constant (depending on the degree) multiplied by the number of tip nodes examined by the alpha-beta method in the best case.

References

See Baudet (1978), Fuller, Gaschnig, and Gillogly (1973), Knuth and Moore (1975), Newborn (1977), Nilsson (1971), Slagle (1971), Slagle and Dixon (1969), and Winston (1977).

C5c.   Heuristics in Game Tree Search

In the search of a game tree (Article II.B3), as in other kinds of search, there are various points at which heuristic information may be applied.   The parallel is not exact, however.   In one-person problem solving, the main uses for heuristic information are to decide which node to expand next, which operator to apply next, and, in some algorithms, which nodes to prune from the search tree (see Article II.C3a).   These questions are also present in game-playing programs, but with a shift in emphasis.   In addition, some new questions arise: When should the search be terminated?   How should a move be chosen on the basis of the search that has been made?

The simplest answers to these questions were described in Article II.C5a: Expand every node completely, in any convenient order and with no pruning, until every tip node represents a termination of the game.   Then, working back from the end of the game, use the minimax procedure to find a winning line of play (if one exists) and follow this line of play throughout the game.   Article II.C5b described an improvement on this approach that yields the same final result with greater efficiency.

A program using only these basic techniques would play a theoretically perfect game; its task would be like searching an AND/OR tree for a solution to a one-person problem.   For a simple game like tic-tac-toe (see Article II.B3), such a program would no doubt be feasible.   For complex games, however, it has been recognized from the beginning that searching from the start of the game to its end would be impossible.   In chess, for example, with around 30 legal moves from each position and about 40 moves for each player in a typical game, there are some $(30^2)^{40}$ or 10^{120} different plays of the game (Shannon, 1950).

Because of the magnitude of the search space in chess, checkers, and other nontrivial games, there is a major difference between programs that play such games and programs that use the methods of this chapter to solve nonadversary problems.   The latter either find a solution or fail, having run out of time or space; much of the research assumes that some solution can be found and deals with how to guarantee that it is optimal or nearly optimal (see Sec. II.C3).   The question for a chess program, in contrast, is how to play a good game even though it has not found a solution to the problem of winning.   Repeatedly the program must become committed to its next move long before the end of the game comes into view.   Whether the move chosen is in fact part of a winning strategy is unknown until later in the game.

For a nontrivial game-playing program, then, the issues listed at the beginning of this article are all aspects of a broader question: Can the basic search techniques, designed for seeking a guaranteed win, be successfully adapted to the problem of simply choosing the next move? In addition, one might well ask whether there are alternatives to search as the basis for move selection. Most of the work exploring these questions has been done in the specific domain of chess. In general, the discussion below is limited to chess programs and Samuel's checkers program (1963, 1967).

Alternatives to Search

An example of choosing a move on a basis other than search is the use of "book moves" in the opening of a chess game (see Frey, 1977, pp. 77–79). More generally, there is an emphasis in the recent computer-chess literature on treating the problem of move choice as a problem of recognizing patterns on the board and associating appropriate playing methods with each pattern (e.g., Charness, 1977, p. 52; Bratko, Kopec, and Michie, 1978; Wilkins, 1979).

It is not expected, however, that search can be eliminated entirely from chess programs; even human players do some searching. Rather, the choice-of-move problem is seen as involving a trade-off between the amount of specialized chess knowledge a program has and the amount of search it needs to do. (See, e.g., Berliner, 1977c; Michie, 1977.) And there are limits on the amount of knowledge a program can be given: The combinatorics of chess preclude storing an exhaustive representation of the game, and even the knowledge possessed by chess masters, which greatly restricts search in human play, also remains very far from complete formalization.

The last section of this article reviews several programs that attempt to use human-like knowledge to eliminate most searching. The sections preceding it concern techniques used in programs in which search rather than knowledge is predominant.

Search-based Programs

The most successful game-playing programs so far have made search rather than knowledge their main ingredient. These include, among the earlier programs, Samuel's checkers program (1963, 1967), which came close to expert play, and Greenblatt's chess program (1967), which was the first to compete in tournaments and which earned a rating of 1400–1450, making it a Class C player. (Current classes of the United States Chess Federation are E through A, Expert, Master, and Senior

Master; see Hearst, 1977, p. 171.) Notable later programs include the Soviet program KAISSA (Adelson–Velskiy, Arlazarov, and Donskoy, 1975), which won the first world computer-chess championship in 1974, and Slate and Atkin's CHESS 4.5 (1977), whose current standing is mentioned below under "Iterative deepening." (For general reviews of computer-chess competition, see Newborn, 1975; Mittman, 1977; Berliner, 1978a.)

All the programs referred to above follow the basic search paradigm formulated by Shannon in 1950. In its simplest form, which was called a Type A program, Shannon's paradigm made just two changes to the procedure mentioned above that calls for searching exhaustively all the way to the end of the game. First, the game tree was to be generated only to a fixed depth. Second, since the nodes at the depth limit would normally be nonterminal, a means of estimating the promise of these nodes was required. The estimate was to be given by a *static evaluation function,* whose values could then be backed up by minimaxing to determine the next move. After this move was made and the opponent had replied, the search process would be repeated beginning from the new position.

Shannon noted that a simple Type A program would play chess both badly and slowly. He suggested two directions for improvement in a Type A program, with which the program would become Type B. The general objectives were, first, to let the exploration of a line of play continue to a reasonable stopping point instead of invariably cutting it off at an arbitrary depth and, second, to provide some selectivity about the lines of play considered, so that more time could be spent investigating strong moves and less on pointless ones.

Even a Type B program, Shannon concluded, seemed to rely too much on brute-force calculation rather than on knowledgeable analysis of the situation to choose a move. Nevertheless, his proposals established a framework that most competitive game-playing programs have adopted. The framework raises a large number of interrelated issues, which are discussed in the following sections.

Static Evaluation

A *static evaluation function,* by definition, is one that estimates the value of a board position without looking at any of that position's successors. An ideal function would be one that reports whether the position leads to a win, a loss, or a draw (provided neither side makes a mistake). Even more informatively, the function might report the number of moves required to win, with an arbitrarily large value if no win is possible. But functions that can distinguish between winning and losing positions are known only for simple games; an example of such a function for the game Nim is given in Shannon (1950).

Where perfect evaluation functions are unavailable, the actual static evaluator must return an estimate. Unlike the evaluation function used in an ordinary state-space or AND/OR graph search (see Articles II.C3a and II.C4), the static evaluation function of a game-playing program does not normally attempt directly to estimate the distance to a win from the position evaluated. (For a proposal that the function should do just this, see Harris, 1974.) Instead, the function is usually a linear polynomial whose terms represent various features of the position, high values being given for features favorable to the program and low ones for those favoring the opponent. In chess, the most important feature is material; the corresponding term of the evaluation function might be computed by assigning a numerical value to each kind of piece and finding the difference between the total values of the two players' pieces on the board. Other typical features, familiar to chess players, include king safety, mobility, center control, and pawn structure.

The most extended treatment of evaluation functions in the literature is provided by Samuel (1963, 1967). For checkers, he concluded that the optimal number of features to be used in the evaluation function was between 20 and 30 (1967, p. 611). Samuel's main interest was in machine learning; one approach he took was to provide his checkers program with a large set of features for possible use in the evaluation function and to let the program determine, as it gained playing experience, both which of these features should be included and what their relative weights should be. In a later version of the program, the emphasis was shifted to taking the interactions among features into account in evaluating positions. With this change, the evaluation function became nonlinear, and considerable improvement was reported in its quality as measured by the correlation with moves chosen in master play (Samuel, 1967; see also Griffith, 1974). For further discussion of Samuel's work, see Chapter XV, in Volume III.

Reasonably accurate static evaluation, then, requires a rather complex function. But there is an important limit on the complexity that is feasible, especially for a program that plays in tournaments, under time limitations. As the total number of tip nodes in the search tree increases, the time available for evaluating any single tip node goes down. Thus Gillogly's chess program TECH (1972), which was intended as an experiment in how much could be accomplished on advanced machines by simple brute-force search, and which generates up to 500,000 tip nodes even with alpha-beta pruning, uses material as the only factor in its static evaluations.

Backed-up Evaluation

The Shannon paradigm assumes that the step between static evaluation and the choice of a move is simply minimaxing: The program moves to any position with the best backed-up minimax value. This step is indeed very commonly used. But it is worth noting that, since the static evaluation function may be wrong, the minimax procedure no longer serves its original purpose of defining and identifying a move that is theoretically correct. Instead, minimaxing has itself become a heuristic for the choice of move. Several programs have therefore experimented with varying or supplementing the minimax procedure. Slagle and Dixon (1970), for example, in experiments with the game of Kalah, compute the backed-up value of a node by taking into account not only the value of its best successor but also whether the node has several good successors or just one. Gillogly's TECH (1972), having computed minimax values on the basis of an extremely simple static evaluation, breaks ties between moves with equal minimax values by an analysis of features not considered by the evaluation function. Newell, Shaw, and Simon (1963a) set a value in advance that the search is expected to achieve; the first move found that meets this standard is made, and only if no move is good enough is the best minimax value used to determine the move (see also Newell and Simon, 1972).

Depth of Search

If perfect evaluation functions were available, a game-playing program could proceed at each turn by generating all legal moves, evaluating each of the resulting positions, and choosing the move leading to the best value. The reason for looking farther ahead is to compensate for errors in the static evaluation. The assumption is that, since static evaluation has a predictive aspect, there will be less room for mistaken prediction if a deep tree is generated before the evaluation function is applied.

The controlling fact about search depth is the combinatorial explosion. If the average number of legal moves from a position, the *branching factor*, is b, the game tree will have about b^d nodes at depth d. According to Shannon's estimate for chess, a complete tree carried to depth 6—three moves for each player—would already have about one billion tip nodes. At the same time, Shannon noted, a world champion may occasionally look ahead, along a single line of play, to a depth as great as 15 or 20. More recently, Hans Berliner, a former World Correspondence Chess Champion, has said he finds it necessary at least once in a game to look ahead to a depth of 14 or more (1974,

p. I–8). The question, then, is how to get the needed depth, in the right places, without succumbing to the combinatorial explosion. An alternative question would be how to avoid the need for so deep a search. The remainder of this article concerns attempts to solve or at least alleviate these problems. First, however, experience with the use of depth bounds as such will be reviewed.

Fixed-depth search with extensions for quiescence. The simplest look-ahead procedure, which was called for by Shannon's Type A strategy, is to set a fixed depth, or *ply*, to which the game tree is to be generated and to apply the static evaluation function only to nodes at this depth. Thus a four-ply search would statically evaluate the positions reached after exactly two turns for each player. There are serious drawbacks in this procedure, as Shannon observed, and it was used only in very early programs (Kister et al., 1957; Bernstein et al., 1959). For example, a chess evaluation function based mainly on material cannot return a realistic value if, at the depth limit, the players happen to be halfway through an exchange of pieces. The concept of a *quiescent,* or *dead,* position was introduced to get around such difficulties (Shannon, 1950; see also Turing, 1953): Search would be extended beyond the normal limit, from nonquiescent positions only, until all tip nodes were relatively stable or perhaps until some absolute depth-bound had been reached.

This introduction of a quiescence search was one of the two features that changed a program, in Shannon's terminology, from Type A to Type B. On Shannon's suggested definition, a position was considered nonquiescent if "any piece is attacked by a piece of lower value, or by more pieces than defences or if any check exists on a square controlled by opponent" (1950, p. 271). Many programs have adopted a similar definition, with the result that the only moves examined beyond the normal limit are checks and immediate captures (e.g., Gillogly, 1972; Adelson–Velskiy et al., 1975; Slate and Atkin, 1977). If such a quiescence search is combined with considering all legal moves down to the normal depth limit, the program is still called Type A in current terminology (e.g., Berliner, 1978b).

The horizon effect. Searching to an arbitrarily limited depth, even with extensions for checks and captures, creates a phenomenon that Berliner (1973, 1974) has called the *horizon effect.* Berliner's general observation is that, whenever search is terminated (short of the end of the game) and a static evaluation function is applied, the program's "reality exists in terms of the output of the static evaluation function, and anything that is not detectable at evaluation time does not exist as far as the program is concerned" (1974, p. I–1).

Two kinds of errors ensue. The first is called the negative horizon effect: The program manipulates the timing of moves to force certain positions to appear at the search horizon, and it thus may conclude that it has avoided some undesirable effect when in fact the effect has only been delayed to a point beyond the horizon. A second kind of error, the positive horizon effect, involves reaching for a desirable consequence: Either the program wrongly concludes that the consequence is achievable or it fails to realize that the same consequence could also be achieved later in the game in a more effective form. This last problem, Berliner believes, can be met only by finding ways to represent and use more chess knowledge than traditional programs have included (1974, p. I–7).

For most of the errors coming from the horizon effect, however, the diagnosis is that the typical definitions of quiescence are highly oversimplified. Ideally, a position would be considered quiescent only when the static evaluation function, applied to that position, could return a realistic value, that is, when the value of every term included in the function had become stable. A quiescence search that pursues only sequences of captures and checking moves, however, seeks stability only in the material term. The material term itself, moreover, usually reflects only the presence of the pieces on the board; its value will be unchanged by a move that guarantees a capture later instead of making a capture now.

To get around the problems arising from inadequate quiescence analysis, a first approach called *secondary search* was developed by Greenblatt (1967): Whenever a move seemed, on the basis of the regular search (including quiescence), to be the best move considered so far, the predicted line of play was extended by searching another two ply (plus quiescence) to test the evaluation. Berliner points out, however: "The horizon effect cannot be dealt with adequately by merely shifting the horizon" (1974, p. I–4). One direction in current work, therefore, is toward a much fuller quiescence analysis as a substitute for arbitrary depth bounds. (See Harris, 1975, 1977a; Slate and Atkin, 1977, pp. 115–117; and, for an early example, Newell and Simon, 1972, pp. 678–698.) Berliner (1977c, 1978a), meanwhile, is developing a general algorithm, not limited to chess, for causing tree search to terminate with a best move, even though no depth limit has been set and no full path to a win has been found.

Iterative deepening. Despite its drawbacks, most current programs still use a fixed-depth search, extended for checks and capture sequences. A variation used by CHESS 4.5 (Slate and Atkin, 1977) is called *iterative deepening:* A complete search, investigating all legal moves (subject to alpha-beta pruning), is done to depth 2, returning a move. The search is then redone to depth 3, again to depth 4, and so on, until a preset time limit is exceeded. For efficiency, information from earlier iterations is saved for use in later ones. Running on the very fast CDC Cyber 176 computer, the program searches to an average depth of six plies in tournament play, with search trees averaging 500,000 nodes (Newborn, 1978). It is the first program to have achieved an Expert rating in human play. In the fall of 1978 a new version, CHESS 4.7, was reportedly rated 2160 (Levy, 1979); Master ratings begin at 2200. It remains an open question how much stronger the program can become.

Ordering of Search

The Shannon paradigm did not specify any particular order in which the nodes of the search tree were to be explored or any order in which moves from a given node were to be considered. For efficient use of space, the order of node expansion is usually depth-first; a depth-first algorithm needs to store explicitly only those nodes on the path it is currently investigating and not the parts of the tree in which search has been completed.

With the invention of alpha-beta pruning, the order of considering moves within a depth-first search became highly significant. If the order is ideal, then in a tree with branching factor b, the number of nodes that must be examined at depth d is reduced from b^d to only about $2b^{d/2}$ (see Article II.C5b). For example, Shannon's estimated 10^9 chess positions at depth 6 would be reduced to around 50,000. It also follows that, for a constant number of tip nodes examined, correct ordering of the moves for alpha-beta cutoffs would allow the search depth to be roughly doubled. In general, the desired ordering is one in which the first move considered at a position is the best move for the player whose turn it is. Usually, of course, there is no method guaranteed to achieve this ordering, for if there were, it would enable moves to be chosen with no search at all. Several heuristics have been used, however, to try to approximate optimal ordering.

Perhaps the simplest idea for move ordering is the *fixed-ordering* method mentioned in Article II.C5b: For each move from a node, generate a new node for the resulting position, apply the static evaluation function to the position, and order the nodes according to this preliminary estimate. For greater efficiency, several programs have used a separate function for move ordering, which applies to the move itself instead of to the position that results from it (Greenblatt, 1967;

Berliner, 1974, p. II–16; Adelson–Velskiy et al., 1975). In either case, the game tree is explored by an *ordered depth-first search* (Article II.C3a).

A fuller basis for choosing which move to consider first is provided by Slate and Atkin's iterative deepening technique, which makes repeated depth-first searches. Each iteration constructs a line of play, down to its depth limit, consisting of apparently best moves. The following iteration, going one ply deeper, thus has available an estimated best move from each position along this line of play. (See Slate and Atkin, 1977, pp. 102–103.)

A further approach to move ordering makes explicit the idea of a *refutation move:* For each move that is not a best move, it should be shown as quickly as possible that the move is bad. To do this, strong replies should be considered first, which may refute the move proposed. Typical implementations consider all capturing moves first and then consider *killer moves*. The idea here, called the *killer heuristic*, is that if a move has served as a refutation in some previously examined position that is similar to the current one, it is likely to be a refutation in the current position, too. For more on the killer heuristic and other refutation techniques, see Gillogly (1972), Adelson–Velskiy et al. (1975), Frey (1977, pp. 54–81), and Slate and Atkin (1977).

Once the moves have been ordered at a given node and the search has moved downward, following the move that seemed best, it may turn out that this move is actually a very bad one for reasons that were not apparent earlier. Since accurate move-ordering is important to maximizing alpha-beta cutoffs, it might be worthwhile at this point to go back, reorder the moves, and start again with a different estimated best move. Such a procedure, called *dynamic ordering*, was investigated by Slagle and Dixon (1969), using the game of Kalah. They reported a modest improvement over fixed ordering for trees of depth at least 6. On the other hand, Berliner's chess program experienced a serious increase in running time when dynamic ordering was used (1974, p. IV–14). A procedure somewhat similar to dynamic ordering was also used by Samuel (1967).

If dynamic ordering is carried to its limit, so that reordering is considered every time a node is expanded instead of only under more limited conditions, the search procedure in effect changes from depth-first to *best-first.* That is, the move considered next (or the position to which it leads) is on some estimate the most promising in the entire search tree generated so far, subject to whatever depth limit exists. Nilsson (1969, 1971) implements this idea by adapting his algorithm for best-first

AND/OR-tree search (Article II.C4) to game trees. Harris (1975, 1977a) suggests another adaptation in which the motivation of maximizing alpha-beta pruning no longer plays a role and instead the objective is to expand the most active positions first, applying a thorough quiescence analysis rather than a depth limit as the criterion for search termination.

Width of Search

The techniques discussed so far are consistent with the idea that all legal moves from a position must be examined, at least sufficiently to establish that they can be safely pruned by the alpha-beta method. This consideration of all legal moves is referred to as *full-width searching*. Some of the earliest programs used a full-width search for simplicity; in programs strong by current standards, it is used because of the great difficulty in determining, without search, which moves can be safely ignored (Turing, 1953; Kister et al., 1957; Gillogly, 1972; Adelson–Velskiy et al., 1975; Slate and Atkin, 1977). The problem, of course, is that an excellent move may look very poor at first sight.

Yet the average number of legal moves from a chess position is at least 30, and even with a maximum of alpha-beta pruning, the tree grows exponentially. Making the search more selective was Shannon's second requirement to change a program from Type A to Type B. Many people have been convinced that such selectivity is essential to a strong chess program, both to increase search depth and to permit more sophisticated evaluation of the nodes remaining in the search tree. Berliner, for example, has advocated reducing the total search tree size to at most 5,000 nodes, with a branching factor of less than 1.9 (1974, p. I–16). Although some reconsideration of these ideas has been prompted by the success of CHESS 4.7 with full-width search, it appears that that program is still weak at long end-game sequences (see Berliner, 1978b; Michie and Bratko, 1978). Moreover, there are other games for which it is even clearer that full-width search is not the answer. For the game of Go, for example, the average branching factor has been estimated at perhaps 200 (Thorp and Walden, 1970), and for backgammon, where legal moves depend on the throw of the dice as well as the board position, the factor is over 800 (Berliner, 1977a).

Various devices have been tried in the effort to increase the selectivity of the search without missing good moves. Some are conceptually simple, introducing little or no new chess-specific knowledge into the program. Others attempt to formulate and use chess concepts as sophisticated as those a chess master might employ. The remainder of this section reviews chiefly the earlier search-controlling devices. The following section mentions work, some of which moves outside the Shannon paradigm, in which the effort to capture expert chess knowledge becomes primary.

Forward pruning. One way of limiting the number of moves to be considered introduces no new complications: Simply generate all legal moves at a position, use a fixed-ordering scheme to sort them according to their apparent goodness, or *plausibility,* and then discard all but the best few moves. Such a technique, called *plausible-move generation* or *forward pruning,* was used by Kotok (1962) and Greenblatt, Eastlake, and Crocker (1967); see also Samuel (1967). A further feature of these programs, sometimes called *tapered forward pruning,* was that the number of moves retained was a function of the depth at which they were generated. For example, Greenblatt's program in tournament play retained 15 moves from a position at either of the top two levels of the tree, 9 moves at the next two levels, and 7 moves thereafter. These figures could be increased in special cases—for example, to be sure that moves of more than a single piece were considered.

Another form of forward pruning, distinct from plausible-move generation, operates not at the time when moves are originally generated but later, when one of these moves (or the position to which it leads) is being selected for further exploration. At this point, a preliminary estimate of the value of the move or position may already have been made by the move-ordering scheme. If this estimate is outside the limits *alpha* and *beta,* the currently known bounds on the outcome of the entire search (see Article II.C5b), the node is pruned without further investigation. It is possible, of course, that the actual backed-up value of the node would have turned out to be between *alpha* and *beta.* In that case, a good move may have been missed. (See Samuel, 1967; Berliner, 1974, p. IV–13.)

Still another basis for forward pruning has been explored by Adelson–Velskiy et al. (1975). They observe that KAISSA's search trees include many lines of play that a human would consider absurd, not necessarily because the moves are bad a priori but because the human player has already considered and rejected the same moves in an analogous position. The proposal, then, is to remember moves that have been found to be absurd (on some definition) and to reject them in other positions, too, unless there has been an appropriate change of circumstances. In effect, this *method of analogies* involves trying to establish conditions under which a refutation is guaranteed to be effective.

Then the line of play constituting the refutation would not need to be explored separately every time it is applicable. (See Frey, 1977, p. 68.)

Goal-directed move generation. Returning to the initial generation of moves, there is another kind of plausible-move generator that comes closer to mimicking the way that humans might decide which moves are worth considering. Instead of generating all legal moves and discarding some, this approach does not generate moves at all unless they seem relevant to some *goal.* The earliest step in this direction was Bernstein's program (1959), which contained a sequence of board features to be tested for and a procedure for generating moves in response to each feature that was present. The first few tests in the sequence were, first, whether the king is in check; second, whether material can be gained, lost, or exchanged; and, third, whether castling is possible. A maximum of seven plausible moves was returned. Questions later in the sequence were not asked if earlier questions caused the maximum to be reached. Searching to a fixed depth of four ply, the program generated trees with about 2,400 tip nodes.

More explicitly goal-directed move-generation was included in Newell, Shaw, and Simon's 1958 chess program (Newell, Shaw, and Simon, 1963a; Newell and Simon, 1972). Indeed, the entire program was organized in terms of goals, although only three—material, center control, and piece development—were actually implemented. At each turn, the program began by making a preliminary analysis to decide which of the goals were relevant to the situation; these were entered, in order of importance, on a current goal-list. It was intended, in a more fully developed program, that as the game progressed, the goals of center control and development would drop out, since they are important mainly in the opening, and would be replaced by others more appropriate to later phases of the game.

Each active goal in the Newell, Shaw, and Simon program was responsible for generating relevant moves at the first level of the tree. In addition, each goal contained its own separate generator for moves at deeper levels, its own criteria for whether a position was dead, and its own static evaluation function. The search proceeded, in a highly selective manner, until the tip nodes were dead with respect to all active goals. Static evaluations with respect to the various goals were combined lexicographically, so that the highest priority goal was dominant and the others served only as tiebreakers. Newell and Simon (1972, p. 694) report that the program's average search tree contained only 13 nodes—with no apparent loss in playing power compared to other programs up to that time.

Knowledge-based Programs

The Bernstein program and the Newell, Shaw, and Simon program were early efforts to introduce significant chess knowledge, organized in human terms, to limit brute-force search. The actual knowledge was very sketchy; apparently neither program ever won a game (see Newell and Simon, 1972, pp. 677, 690).

An attempt at fuller use of chess knowledge was made in Berliner's program, CAPS-II (1974, 1977b). Much of the work involved developing a representation suitable for use in selectively generating moves, making preliminary evaluations of the moves so proposed, and describing the actual consequences discovered when a move was tried. The moves generated depend on the current goal state, which may be King in Check, Aggressive, Preventive Defense, Nominal Defense, Dynamic Defense, or Strategy. In contrast to the Newell, Shaw, and Simon program, the goal states are mutually exclusive, and state transitions take place dynamically as the tree is searched, in accordance with a complex flowchart. An important feature of the program, the Causality Facility, relates to both move generation and move ordering, as well as to pruning in some cases. The problem it attacks is a general one in tree searching: When a path has been explored and found unsatisfactory, most programs have no way to diagnose what went wrong or to use this information in deciding where to search next.

The basic search algorithm in CAPS-II is depth-first, with minimaxing and alpha-beta pruning. The Causality Facility operates as a refinement on this search. A first new feature is that, whenever a value is backed up in the search tree as a tentative minimax value, certain information is accumulated about the consequences of the move or moves that produced the value. The data structure in which the information is stored is called a Refutation Description. As the basis for making use of the Refutation Description, the program uses a variable representing the expected value of the position at the root of the search tree; this value, which may be updated during the search, lies somewhere. between the bounds given by *alpha* and *beta*. Now, the tentative value newly backed up to a node can be compared with the expected value. If the comparison is unsatisfactory, the Causality Facility uses the Refutation Description to decide whether the last move tried from the node could have been responsible. It generates a list of alternative moves from the node, with the aim of avoiding the unsatisfactory result. These moves are compared with the list of moves from the node that had been generated earlier but that have not yet been tried. The comparison is used to reorder moves already on the untried list and, depending on the state the program is in, to add new moves to the list and to prune old ones.

Whereas Berliner's program plays the full game of chess, there are several other recent programs that, in their emphasis on representing chess knowledge, limit their task to solving problems involving only selected aspects of the game. Two of these are the programs by Pitrat (1977) and Wilkins (1979). In each, the task is to find a line of play that wins material, beginning from a given middle-game position. The approach in both programs is to work backward from the goal of winning material to a structure of subgoals that constitutes a *plan* (see Chap. XVI, in Vol. III). Wilkins's program, PARADISE, for example, has as a main theme the expression of chess concepts, like making a square safe for a piece or safely capturing a piece, in terms that can be used as subgoals and eventually reduced to specific moves. Initially, a plan is based not on search but on an extensive analysis of the originally given position; it may contain conditional branches depending on general categories of moves with which the opponent might reply. The general plan is then used to guide search, generating a very small tree. Moves considered for the program to make are only those relevant to the current subgoal; for the simulated opponent, all reasonable defensive moves are considered. If search shows that the plan has failed, a causality facility similar to Berliner's is used to analyze the difficulty and suggest a new plan.

Both the Pitrat and the Wilkins programs have succeeded in solving problems where the winning line of play goes to a depth of around 20 ply. Pitrat reports, for a set of 11 problems, that search-tree sizes ranged from about 200 to 22,000 nodes; computation time varied from under 3 seconds to about 7.5 minutes. Wilkins's PARADISE generates smaller trees but uses more time; for 89 problems solved, the number of nodes in the search tree ran from a minimum of 3 to a maximum of 215, and time to find the solution varied from 19 seconds to 33 minutes. Wilkins also reports a good success rate compared to previous programs tested on the same set of problems, including Berliner's program, Gillogly's TECH, and an earlier version of CHESS 4.5. The programs other than PARADISE, however, were tested with a time limit of only 5 minutes per problem.

A final example of the use of chess knowledge to solve a class of problems is the work of Donald Michie and his colleagues on chess endgames (e.g., Bratko, Kopec, and Michie, 1978; Michie and Bratko, 1978). Here each combination of pieces with which the end game may be played is treated as posing a separate problem. One problem, denoted KNKR, is to defend with king and knight against king and rook, starting from any of some 3 million legal positions involving only those pieces. The objective is to provide the program with enough knowledge about this specific class of chess problems to achieve theoretically correct play, even in situations where chess masters sometimes err, and to accomplish this with only a moderate amount of search.

The program's knowledge is encoded in a data structure called an Advice Table, within which patterns occurring on the board may be described. Each pattern has an associated list of goals, or "pieces of advice," in the order in which they should be attempted. The object then becomes to find a solution—in the sense of a solution subtree of an AND/OR tree (Article II.C2)—to the problem of satisfying one of the goals. Unlike a standard AND/OR tree search, however, the "advice" includes not only a definition of when tip nodes should be considered terminal but also constraints that every intermediate node in the solution tree must satisfy.

The amount of search required to find a solution using an Advice Table depends on how much knowledge the table contains. If the only goal provided were avoidance of checkmate, a search to the impossible depth of 85 ply would be needed to find the best defense from some positions. With the additional advice not to lose the knight and to keep king and knight together, search to about 10 ply is sufficient. With the further refinements included in the actual Advice Table, the program is reported to play the KNKR end game at master level with only a four-ply search.

References

See Adelson–Velskiy, Arlazarov, and Donskoy (1975), Berliner (1973, 1974, 1977a, 1977b, 1977c, 1978a, 1978b), Bernstein et al. (1959), Bratko, Kopec, and Michie (1978), Charness (1977), Frey (1977), Gillogly (1972), Greenblatt, Eastlake, and Crocker (1967), Griffith (1974), Harris (1974, 1975, 1977a), Hearst (1977), Kister et al. (1957), Kotok (1962), Levy (1979), Michie (1977), Michie and Bratko (1978), Mittman (1977), Newborn (1975, 1978), Newell, Shaw, and Simon (1963a), Newell and Simon (1972), Nilsson (1969, 1971), Pitrat (1977), Samuel (1963, 1967), Shannon (1950), Slagle and Dixon (1969, 1970), Slate and Atkin (1977), Thorp and Walden (1970), Turing (1953), and Wilkins (1979).

D. SAMPLE SEARCH PROGRAMS

D1. Logic Theorist

The Logic Theorist (LT) was a program written by Allen Newell, J. C. Shaw, and H. A. Simon in 1956, as a joint project of the RAND Corporation and the Carnegie Institute of Technology. It was one of the earliest programs to investigate the use of heuristics in problem solving. The term *heuristics*, as used by Newell, Shaw, and Simon (1963b, p. 109), referred to "the complex processes . . . that are effective in problem-solving." They stated,

> We are not interested in methods that guarantee solutions, but which require vast amounts of computation. Rather, we wish to understand how a mathematician, for example, is able to prove a theorem even though he does not know when he starts how, or if, he is going to succeed. (p. 109)

Heuristics were thus identified with processes "that may solve a given problem, but offer no guarantee of doing so" (p. 114; see also Article II.A).

In descriptions of the Logic Theorist program, the heuristics discussed by Newell, Shaw, and Simon relate principally to limiting the search space by means of an apt problem formulation. Within the defined space, the search was blind except for some minor selectivity in the choice of operators (see Article II.C3a).

The problem domain of the Logic Theorist is the proof of theorems in the propositional calculus (see Article III.C1). The basis is Whitehead and Russell's *Principia Mathematica,* from which both axioms and theorems to be proved were taken. There are five axioms, as follows:

1. $(p \lor p) \supset p$
2. $p \supset (q \lor p)$
3. $(p \lor q) \supset (q \lor p)$
4. $[p \lor (q \lor r)] \supset [q \lor (p \lor r)]$
5. $(p \supset q) \supset [(r \lor p) \supset (r \lor q)]$

Some typical theorems that LT was given to prove include:

2.01. $(p \supset \neg p) \supset \neg p$

2.45. $\neg(p \lor q) \supset \neg p$

2.31. $[p \lor (q \lor r)] \supset [(p \lor q) \lor r]$

The numbering of the theorems is taken from Whitehead and Russell. In some cases, the data given the program included not only the axioms but also previously proved theorems from that work. When all earlier theorems were included with the axioms, the program succeeded in proving 38 of the first 52 theorems in Chapter 2 of *Principia Mathematica*, in the sequence given there.

The program operates by *reasoning backward* from the theorem to be established to the axioms and given theorems. Three operators were provided for reducing the theorem to be proved, let us say X, to an axiom or theorem. These operators were:

Detachment: To show X, find an axiom or theorem of the form $A \supset X$ and transform the problem to the problem of showing A.

Forward chaining: To show X where X has the form $A \supset C$, find an axiom or theorem of the form $A \supset B$ and transform the problem to the problem of showing $B \supset C$.

Backward chaining: To show X where X has the form $A \supset C$, find an axiom or theorem of the form $B \supset C$ and transform the problem to the problem of showing $A \supset B$.

Since the axioms and given theorems contain variables, consideration must be given to the means for deciding whether a problem has in fact been reduced to something known. The question is whether a current problem expression X is an instance of an axiom or known theorem. The test, called the Substitution Test, uses two rules of inference distinct from those reflected in the operators:

Substitution: A variable in a theorem may be replaced, in all its occurrences throughout the theorem, by an expression. For example, substituting the expression $p \lor q$ for the variable p transforms

$$p \supset (q \lor p)$$

into

$$(p \lor q) \supset [q \lor (p \lor q)] \;.$$

Replacement: The connective "$\supset$" is interchangeable with its definition. That is, if p and q are expressions, then

$$p \supset q$$

can be replaced by

$$\neg p \lor q$$

and vice versa.

As well as being used to determine whether a proof is complete, the Substitution Test is also essential for determining what applications of the three operators are possible with respect to a given problem expression.

The general algorithm used by the Logic Theorist is a blind, breadth-first, state-space search using backward reasoning. The initial state corresponds to the original theorem to be proved. To test whether an expression has been proved, the program applies the Substitution Test, pairing the problem expression with each axiom and assumed theorem, in turn. If substitution fails, the expression is placed on a list of open problems; problems are selected from this list to become the current problem in first-in, first-out order.

To a problem selected from the list, each of the three operators is applied, in fixed order and in all possible ways, to generate new open problems. The search terminates with success as soon as a single problem is generated that passes the substitution test, since this means that a path has been completed between an axiom and the original problem. The search fails if it exceeds time or space limits or if it runs out of open problems.

An example of a case in which the latter occurs is the attempted proof of the theorem

$$p \text{ or } \neg\neg\neg p .$$

To succeed with this proof, LT would have needed more powerful operators; this particular problem required the ability, which LT lacked, to transform a problem to a set of subproblems, or conjunctive subgoals, that *all* had to be solved in order to solve the original problem.

There are some qualifications to the preceding general description of LT. One concerns the statement that each operator is applied to the current problem in every possible way, that is, that the current problem expression is matched against every axiom and assumed theorem to determine the applicability of any of the operators to that expression-axiom pair. In fact, the program attempted a match for the purpose of discovering an appropriate substitution only if the pair had passed a test indicating equality of certain gross features, such as the number of distinct variables in each. This test for similarity occasionally rejected a pair for which a substitution in fact would have been possible, thus excluding a proof the program would otherwise have found. Overall, the utility of this similarity test was considered rather marginal.

Some other additions, apparently made in a later version of the program (see Newell and Simon, 1972, pp. 125–128), included (a) ordering the open problems, taking up those involving simpler expressions first instead of proceeding in a strictly breadth-first order, and (b) rejecting some subproblems entirely as too complicated or apparently unprovable. In the implementation of these features, the latter appeared to be the more effective measure in reducing search effort. There was also experimentation, as mentioned previously, with the number of theorems that could be assumed as given in addition to the basic axioms. The conclusion on this point was that "a problem solver may be encumbered by too much information, just as he may be handicapped by too little" (p. 127).

References

See Newell, Shaw, and Simon (1963b), Newell and Simon (1972), and Whitehead and Russell (1925).

D2. General Problem Solver

The General Problem Solver (GPS) was developed by Newell, Shaw, and Simon beginning in 1957. The research had a dual intention: It was aimed at getting machines to solve problems requiring intelligence and at developing a theory of how human beings solve such problems. GPS was the successor of the authors' earlier Logic Theorist program (Article II.D1), whose methods had only a slight resemblance to those used by humans working on similar problems. Development of GPS continued through at least 10 years and numerous versions of the program. The final version, described in detail in Ernst and Newell (1969), was concerned with extending the generality of the program, not with the psychological theory.

The name "General Problem Solver" came from the fact that GPS was the first problem-solving program to separate its general problem-solving methods from knowledge specific to the type of task at hand. That is, the problem-solving part of the system gave no information about the kind of task being worked on; task-dependent knowledge was collected in data structures forming a *task environment*. Among the data structures were *objects* and *operators* for transforming the objects. A task was normally given to GPS as an initial object and a desired object, into which the initial object was to be transformed. GPS objects and operators were similar to the states and operators of a state-space problem representation (Article II.B1).

The general problem-solving technique introduced by GPS, however, does not fit neatly into either the state-space or the problem-reduction representation formalisms. It differs from a standard state-space search (e.g., Article II.C1) in the way it decides what path to try next. This technique, called *means-ends analysis*, is a major theoretical contribution of the program. It assumes that the *differences* between a current object and a desired object can be defined and classified into types and that the operators can be classified according to the kinds of differences they might reduce. At each stage, GPS selects a single relevant operator to try to apply to the current object. The search for a successful operator sequence proceeds depth first as long as the chosen operators are applicable and the path shows promise. Backup is possible if the current path becomes unpromising—for example, if eliminating one difference has introduced a new one that is harder to get rid of.

An important feature of means-ends analysis is that the operator selected as relevant to reducing a difference may actually be inapplicable to the current object. Rather than rejecting the operator for this reason, GPS attempts to change the current object into an object appropriate as input to the chosen operator. The result of this strategy is a recursive, goal-directed program that records the search history in an AND/OR graph (Article II.B2) with partial development of nodes (Article II.C3a).

Goals and Methods

The most important data structure used by GPS is the *goal.* The goal is an encoding of the current situation (an object or list of objects), the desired situation, and a history of the attempts so far to change the current situation into the desired one. Three main types of goals are provided:

1. *Transform* object A into object B.
2. *Reduce* a difference between object A and object B by modifying object A.
3. *Apply* operator Q to object A.

Associated with the goal types are *methods,* or procedures, for achieving them. These methods, shown in a simplified version in Figure D2-1, can be understood as problem-reduction operators that give rise either to AND nodes, in the case of *transform* or *apply,* or to OR nodes, in the case of a *reduce* goal.

The initial task presented to GPS is represented as a *transform* goal, in which A is the initial object and B the desired object. The recursion stops if the goal is primitive—that is, for a *transform* goal, if there is no difference between A and B, and for an *apply* goal, if the operator Q is immediately applicable. For a *reduce* goal, the recursion may stop, with failure, when all relevant operators have been tried and have failed.

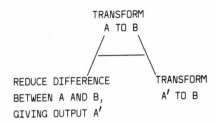

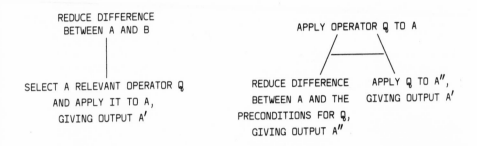

Figure D2-1.   The three GPS methods for problem reduction.

Selection of Operators

In trying to transform object *A* into object *B*, the *transform* method uses a matching process to discover the differences between the two objects. The possible types of differences are predefined and ordered by estimated difficulty, for each kind of task. The most difficult difference found is the one chosen for reduction. A domain-dependent data structure called the Table of Connections lists the operators relevant to reducing each difference type.

Depth Bounds

Several heuristics are provided to prevent GPS from following a false path indefinitely. Some of the bases for determining whether a current goal should be abandoned, at least temporarily, are the following:

1. Each goal should be easier than its parent goal.
2. Of a pair of AND nodes representing subgoals generated by *transform* or *apply*, the second subgoal attempted should be easier than the first.

3. A newly generated object should not be much larger than the objects occurring in the topmost goal.

4. Once a goal has been generated, the identical goal should not be generated again.

An Example

The first task environment to which GPS was applied was the domain of the Logic Theorist: proving theorems in the propositional calculus. The initial and desired objects were expressions, one to be transformed into the other by means of operators representing rules of inference. There were 12 operators altogether, including the following rules. (An arrow means that the expression may be rewritten in the direction of the arrow head.)

$$\text{Rule 1.} \quad A \lor B \;\to\; B \lor A$$
$$A \land B \;\to\; B \land A$$
$$\ldots$$
$$\text{Rule 5.} \quad A \lor B \;\leftrightarrow\; \neg(\neg A \land \neg B)$$
$$\text{Rule 6.} \quad A \supset B \;\leftrightarrow\; \neg A \lor B$$

Six possible difference types were recognized:

1. occurrence of a variable in one expression but not the other,
2. occurrence of a variable a different number of times in the two expressions,
3. difference in sign,
4. difference in binary connective,
5. difference in grouping, and
6. difference in position of components.

The list just given is in decreasing order of assumed difficulty. Every difference between main expressions, however, was considered more difficult than any difference between subexpressions.

With this background, a trace (slightly simplified) of GPS's performance on a simple example can be given. The problem is to transform the initial expression

$$R \land (\neg P \supset Q) \,,$$

denoted L_1, into the desired expression

$$(Q \lor P) \land R \,,$$

denoted L_0. The trace is shown below.

Goal 1: Transform L_1 into L_0.

    Goal 2: Reduce positional difference between L_1 and L_0.

        Goal 3: Apply Rule 1 to L_1.

        Return L_2: $(\neg P \supset Q) \wedge R$

    Goal 4: Transform L_2 into L_0.

        Goal 5: Reduce difference in connective between left subexpressions of L_2 and L_0.

            Goal 6: Apply Rule 5 to left part of L_2.

                Goal 7: Reduce difference in connective between left part of L_2 and precondition for Rule 5.

                Reject goal 7 as no easier than goal 5.

            Goal 8: Apply Rule 6 to left part of L_2.

            Return L_3: $(P \vee Q) \wedge R$

        Goal 9: Transform L_3 into L_0.

            Goal 10: Reduce positional difference between left parts of L_3 and L_0.

                Goal 11: Apply Rule 1 to left part of L_3.

                Return L_4: $(Q \vee P) \wedge R$

            Goal 12: Transform L_4 to L_0.

            No difference exists, so problem is solved.

The Problem of Generality

GPS was intended to model generality in problem solving through use of the broadly applicable techniques of heuristic search, and the strategy of means-ends analysis in particular. The implementation of these techniques was dependent on the internal representation of objects and operators. These representations, in early versions of GPS, were nicely suited to logic tasks like the example above. But they were inadequate for many other kinds of heuristic search problems. Before Ernst's extensions to the program (Ernst and Newell, 1969), GPS had in fact solved only two problems outside the logic domain.

The object of Ernst's work was to extend the number of kinds of problems that GPS could handle while holding its power at a constant level. One of his generalizations was in the representation of objects. Earlier, a desired object had had to be specified by giving its exact form. Forms containing variables and lists of forms could be used if necessary. But these, too, were inadequate for representing symbolic integration problems, in which the desired object is any form whatever that does not contain an integral sign. Hence, the description of a desired object by a list of constraints was introduced.

Another change was in the representation of operators, originally specified by giving the form of the input object and the form of the resulting output object. For some kinds of problems, it was desirable to have other tests of applicability besides the form of the input object and to be able to describe the output object as a function of the input. A third change allowed GPS to deal with unordered sets of symbols, eliminating the need for special operators to permute their elements.

The generalized program succeeded in solving problems of 11 different kinds, including symbolic integration, resolution theorem proving, and a variety of puzzles. Each generalization, however, entailed changes in the ways the problem representations could be processed, and these led in turn to deterioriation with respect to the kinds of differences that could be detected. The only representable differences became "local" ones. An example of a global difference, which GPS could no longer recognize, was the total number of times a variable occurred in a logic formula. Consequently, theorem proving in the propositional calculus was not among the 11 tasks that the final version of GPS could do.

In the task domains in which GPS did succeed, it could solve only simple problems; and those, less efficiently than special-purpose problem solvers. If a long search was required, it ran out of memory space, and even easy problems, if they needed objects as complex as a chess position, quickly exhausted memory on a machine with 65K words. But GPS was not expected to be a performance program. What it yielded, in its authors' view, was "a series of lessons that give a more perfect view of the nature of problem solving and what is required to construct processes that accomplish it" (Ernst and Newell, 1969, p. 2). Although additional generalizations, such as game playing, were considered feasible, the authors concluded that GPS needed no further programming accretions and recommended that it be laid to rest.

References

See Ernst and Newell (1969), Newell and Ernst (1965), Newell, Shaw, and Simon (1960), and Newell and Simon (1963, 1972).

D3. Gelernter's Geometry Theorem-proving Machine

Herbert Gelernter's geometry theorem-proving machine was a program written in 1959 at the IBM Research Center in New York. The program was written in an extended FORTRAN, the FORTRAN List Processing Language, and implemented on an IBM 704 computer. The purpose of the program was to solve problems taken from high-school textbooks and final examinations in plane geometry. As with Newell, Shaw, and Simon's Logic Theorist, which proved theorems in the propositional calculus, the fact that there were algorithms for solving problems in these domains was considered irrelevant, since the object was to explore the use of heuristic methods in problem solving.

The formal system within which the geometry program worked contained axioms on parallel lines, congruence, and equality of segments and angles. This set of axioms, which was not meant to be either complete or nonredundant, was along the lines of an elementary textbook. The axioms played the role of *problem-reduction* operators. Some examples are:

1. In order to show that two line segments are equal, show that they are corresponding elements of congruent triangles;

2. In order to show that two angles are equal, show that they are both right angles;

3. In order to show that two triangles are congruent, show the equality of a side and two angles in corresponding positions or of an angle and two sides.

The operators for establishing congruence split the problem into three subproblems, each to be solved separately by showing equality for one pair of elements. Newell and Simon (1972, p. 138) indicate that the geometry machine was the first program that was able to handle *conjunctive subgoals*. The program works backward from the theorem to be proved, recording its progress in what amounted to an AND/OR tree (Article II.B2).

Some examples of problems solved by the program were the following:

1. Given that angle *ABD* equals angle *DBC,* that segment *AD* is perpendicular to segment *AB*, and that segment *DC* is perpendicular to segment *BC,* show that *AD* equals *CD.* (See Fig. D3-1.)

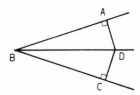

Figure D3-1. Diagram for problem 1.

2. Given that *ABCD* is a quadrilateral, with segment *BC* parallel to segment *AD* and with *BC* equal to *AD*, show that segment *AB* equals segment *CD*. (See Fig. D3-2.)

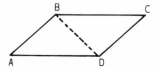

Figure D3-2. Diagram for problem 2.

A problem was given to the program in the form of a statement describing the premises and the goal. A proof was a sequence of statements giving the reduction of the goal to trivial goals—ordinarily, goals to establish an already established formula. One feature used to reduce the search effort needed to find a proof was the recognition of *syntactic symmetry*. Some examples of symmetric pairs of goals are the following:

1. If $d(x, y)$ is the distance from point x to point y, then $d(A, B) = d(C, D)$ is symmetric with $d(D, C) = d(A, B)$.

2. If *ABCD* is a parallelogram and point *E* is the intersection of its diagonals *AC* and *BD*, then $d(A, E) = d(E, C)$ is symmetric with $d(B, E) = d(E, D)$.

The recognition of symmetry was used in two ways. First, if a given goal was ever reduced to a subgoal symmetric with it, the subgoal could be rejected as representing circular reasoning. Second, if parallel goals *A* and *B* were syntactically symmetric and goal *A* had been established, then goal *B* could be established by symmetry—in effect by saying, for the second half of the proof, "Similarly, *B*."

The most notable feature of the program, however, was an additional part of the problem statement used to avoid attempting proofs by blind syntactic manipulation alone. This input was a diagram, similar to Figures D3-1 and D3-2 (although specified by lists of coordinates), of the points and line segments mentioned in the theorem. The particular input figure was chosen to avoid spurious coincidences and reflect the greatest possible generality. Whenever a subgoal was generated, it was checked for consistency with the diagram. If false in the diagram, the subgoal could not possibly be a theorem and therefore could be *pruned* from the search tree. A slight qualification is that finite precision arithmetic, applied to the diagram, occasionally caused a provable subgoal to be pruned erroneously; but it was reported that the program had found other paths to the solution in such cases. It was estimated that the use of a diagram, together with the discard of subgoals representing circular reasoning, eliminated about 995 out of every 1,000 subgoals.

The diagram also served a second purpose: It provided an additional criterion by which a problem could be considered *primitive*. For example, a rigorous proof of the theorem in problem 1 would require showing that DB is a line segment and that BCD and BAD are triangles. The axioms needed would have been (a) if X and Y are distinct points, then XY is a line segment, and (b) if X, Y, and Z are three distinct noncollinear points, then XYZ is a triangle. For a limited class of such properties, the program did not require formal proof but rather considered them established if they were true in the diagram. It recorded explicitly the assumptions that had been made based on the diagram.

The central loop of the program repeatedly selected the next goal to try. Two heuristics were included for goal selection. One gave highest priority to classes of goals, such as identities, that could usually be established in one step. The second assigned a "distance" between the goal statement and the set of premise statements; after the one-step goals had been developed, the remaining goals were selected in order of increasing distance from the premise set.

Once a goal was chosen for development, the action taken depended on its status. Ordinarily, it would be reduced to subgoals, and the subgoals, if consistent with the diagram but not sufficient to establish the current goal immediately, would be added to the list of goals to try. If no new acceptable subgoals were generated, the program checked whether a *construction* was possible—a construction being the addition to the premises of the problem of a line segment between two existing but previously unconnected points. The new segment would be extended to its intersections with other segments in the figure. New points could be added to the premises only if generated by such intersections.

A goal for which a construction was found possible was saved—to be tried again later if all goals not requiring construction should be exhausted. If the goal was later selected for a second try, a construction would be made and the problem started over with an expanded premise set. An example of the use of this technique occurs in problem 2, where in considering the goal $AB = CD$, the program generated a subgoal of showing that triangles ABD and CDB were congruent. The subgoal makes sense only if a line segment BD exists, so the segment is constructed, and the proof eventually succeeds.

References

See Elcock (1977), Gelernter (1959, 1963), Gelernter, Hansen, and Gerberich (1960), Gelernter, Hansen, and Loveland (1963), Gelernter and Rochester (1958), and Gilmore (1970).

D4. Symbolic Integration Programs

Slagle's SAINT

James Slagle's SAINT program (Symbolic Automatic INTegrator) was written as a 1961 doctoral dissertation at M.I.T. The program solves elementary symbolic integration problems—mainly indefinite integration—at about the level of a good college freshman. SAINT was written in LISP and run interpretively on the IBM 7090 computer.

The kinds of questions Slagle intended his thesis to address were some of the earliest questions for AI. They included, for example, "Can a computer recognize the kinds of patterns that occur in symbolic expressions? Just how important is pattern recognition? . . . Can intelligent problem solving behavior really be manifested by a machine?" (Slagle, 1961, p. 9). The domain of symbolic integration was chosen as a source of well-defined, familiar, but nontrivial problems requiring the manipulation of symbolic rather than numerical expressions.

The integration problems that SAINT could handle could have only elementary functions as integrands. These functions were defined recursively to comprise the following:

1. Constant functions;
2. The identity function;
3. Sum, product, and power of elementary functions;
4. Trigonometric, logarithmic, and inverse trigonometric functions of elementary functions.

Three kinds of operations on an integrand were available:

1. Recognize the integrand as an instance of a standard form, thus obtaining the result immediately by substitution. Twenty-six such standard forms were used. A typical one indicated that if the integrand has the form $c^v\, dv$, the form of the solution is $(c^v)/(\ln c)$.

2. Apply an "algorithm-like transformation" to the integral—that is, a transformation that is almost guaranteed to be helpful whenever it can be applied. Eight such transformations were provided, including (a) factoring out a constant and (b) decomposing the integral of a sum into a sum of integrals.

3. Apply a "heuristic transformation"—that is, a transformation carrying significant risk such that, although applicable, it might not be the best next step. The 10 heuristic transformations

included certain substitutions and the technique of integration by parts. One technique that was not implemented was the method of partial fractions.

The program starts with the original problem as a goal, specified as an integrand and a variable of integration. For any particular goal, the strategy is first to try for an immediate solution by substitution into a standard form; failing that, to transform it by any applicable algorithm-like transformation; and, finally, to apply each applicable heuristic transformation in turn. Both the algorithm-like and the heuristic transformations, however, generate new goals, to which the same strategy may be applied. The result is an AND/OR graph of goals (Article II.B2).

The order in which goals are pursued by SAINT depends heavily on what operations can be applied to them. At the level of heuristic transformations, the algorithm is an *ordered search*: A list, called the Heuristic Goal List, keeps track of goals on which progress can be made only by applying heuristic transformations—that is, integrands that are not of standard form nor amenable to any algorithm-like transformation. To each goal on this list is attached an estimate of the difficulty of achieving it. The measure of difficulty used is the maximum level of function composition in the integrand. Other characteristics of the goal, such as whether it is a rational function, an algebraic function, a rational function of sines and cosines, and the like, are also stored as an aid to determining which heuristic transformations will in fact apply. The outer loop of the program repeatedly selects the goal that looks the easiest from the Heuristic Goal List, expands it by applying all applicable heuristic transformations, and possibly, as a result of the expansion, adds new elements to the Heuristic Goal List. The program terminates with failure if it runs out of heuristic goals to work on or if it exceeds a preset amount of working space.

An important qualification to this process concerns the use of standard forms and algorithm-like transformations. As soon as any new goal is generated (or the original goal read in), an immediate solution of it is attempted. The attempt consists of, first, checking whether the integrand is a standard form; if it is not, checking whether an algorithm-like transformation applies; and if one does, applying it and calling the immediate solution procedure recursively on each goal resulting from that transformation. When the recursion terminates, either the generated goal has been achieved or there is a set of goals—the generated goal itself or some of its subgoals—to be added to the Heuristic Goal List. During expansion of a node (one iteration of the outer loop), new heuristic goals are accumulated in a temporary goal list; only after expansion is complete are their characteristics computed and the additions made to the Heuristic Goal List.

Whenever a goal is achieved, the implications of its achievement are immediately checked. If it is the original goal, the program terminates successfully. Otherwise, if it was achieved by substitution into a standard form, it may cause the achievement of one or more parent goals as well. If it was achieved by solution of a sufficient number of its subproblems, it not only may cause its parent or parents to be achieved in turn, but also may make others of its subproblems, which have not yet been solved, superfluous. These checks are implemented in a recursive process, referred to as "pruning the goal tree," that is initiated as soon as any goal is achieved. Thus a heuristic goal can be achieved without having been fully expanded.

Moses's SIN

A second important symbolic integration program, SIN (Symbolic INtegrator), was written by Joel Moses in 1967, also as a doctoral dissertation at M.I.T. Its motivation and its strategy as an AI effort were quite different from those of SAINT. Whereas Slagle had compared the behavior of SAINT to that of freshman calculus students, Moses aimed at behavior comparable to expert human performance. He viewed SAINT as emphasizing generality in that it examined mechanisms, like heuristic search, that are useful in many diverse problem domains. SIN, in contrast, was to emphasize expertise in a particular, complex domain. To do this, it concentrated on problem analysis, using more knowledge about integration than SAINT had employed, to minimize the need for search. In fact, Moses did not view SIN as a heuristic search program. Hence, the program will be described only briefly here, and a second part of Moses's dissertation—a differential equation solver called SOLDIER—will not be described.

SIN worked in three stages, each stage capable of solving harder problems than the stage before. Stage 1 corresponded roughly to Slagle's immediate solution procedure but was more powerful. It used a table of standard forms, two of Slagle's algorithm-like transformations, and, most importantly, a method similar to one of Slagle's heuristic transformations, referred to as the derivative-divides method. The idea behind this grouping of methods was that they alone would be sufficient to solve the most commonly occurring problems, without invoking the computationally more expensive machinery of the later stages.

A problem that stage 1 could not solve was passed on to stage 2. This stage consisted of a central routine, called FORM, and 11 highly specific methods of integration. (One of these methods was a program for integrating rational functions that had been written by Manove, Bloom, and Engelman, of the MITRE Corporation, in 1964.) In general, the task of FORM was to form a hypothesis, usually based on local clues in the integrand, about which method, if any, was applicable to the problem. Only rarely did more than one method apply. The routine chosen first tried to verify its applicability; if it could not, it returned to let FORM try again. If the routine did verify the hypothesis, however, SIN then became committed to solving the problem by that method or not at all. The method chosen either solved the problem using mechanisms internal to it or transformed the problem and called SIN recursively to solve the transformed problem.

Stage 3 of SIN was invoked, as a last resort, only if no stage 2 method was applicable. Two general methods were programmed here. One method was integration by parts, which used blind search, subject to certain constraints, to find the appropriate way to factor the integrand. The other was a nontraditional method based on the Liouville theory of integration and called the EDGE (EDucated GuEss) heuristic. This method involved guessing the form of the integral. The EDGE heuristic was characterized as using a technique similar to *means-ends analysis*, if its guess did not lead directly to a solution.

Performance of SAINT and SIN

SAINT was tested on a total of 86 problems, 54 of them chosen from M.I.T. final examinations in freshman calculus. It succeeded in solving all but two. The most difficult problem it solved, in terms of both time and the number of heuristic transformations occurring in the solution tree (four), was the integral of

$$\frac{\sec^2 t}{1 + (\sec^2 t) - 3(\tan t)} \, dt \ .$$

Slagle proposed additional transformations that would have handled the two failures, which were the integrals of

$$x(1 + x)^{1/2} \, dx \quad \text{and} \quad \cos(x^{1/2}) \, dx \ .$$

SIN, in contrast, was intended to model the behavior of an expert human integrator. The results of running SIN on all of Slagle's test problems were that more than half were solved in stage 1, and all but two of the rest (both of which used integration by parts) were solved in stage 2. After adjusting for the facts that SAINT and SIN ran on different machines and that one was interpreted and the other compiled, and for other factors making the programs difficult to compare, Moses estimated that SIN would run on the average about three times faster than SAINT. Taking into account a test on more difficult problems as well, he expressed the opinion that SIN was "capable of solving integration problems as difficult as ones found in the largest tables" (p. 140) and that it was fast and powerful enough for use in "a practical on-line algebraic manipulation system" (p. 6). For later developments in this direction, see Article VII.D1, in Volume II.

References

See Manove, Bloom, and Engelman (1968), Moses (1967), and Slagle (1961, 1963).

D5. STRIPS

STRIPS is a problem-solving program written by Richard Fikes and Nils Nilsson (1971) at SRI International. Each problem for STRIPS is a goal to be achieved by a robot operating in a simple world of rooms, doors, and boxes. The solution is a sequence of operators, called a *plan*, for achieving the goal. (For a review of the various senses of the word *plan*, see Chap. XVI, in Vol. III.) The robot's actual execution of the plan is carried out by a separate program, distinct from STRIPS. A later (1972) addition to the basic STRIPS system permits plans to be generalized and used again, giving the system some capacity for *learning*.

The Basic STRIPS System

The world model. The world in which the STRIPS robot works consists of several rooms connected by doors, along with some boxes and other objects that the robot can manipulate. STRIPS represents this world by a set of well-formed formulas in the first-order predicate calculus (see Article III.C1). Some formulas in the world model are static facts, such as which objects are pushable and which rooms are connected. Other facts, such as the current location of objects, must be changed to reflect the actions of the robot.

Operators. The actions available to the robot for affecting the world are described, for the purpose of finding a plan of action, by *operators.* Typical operators describe actions of going somewhere and pushing an object somewhere, the locations being given as parameters. Each operator has *preconditions* to its applicability; to push a box, for example, the robot must first be next to the box. The application of an operator is realized by making changes in the world model. The appropriate changes are given by a *delete list* and an *add list*, specifying the formulas to be removed from and added to the world model as a result of the operation. Thus, each operator explicitly describes what it changes in the world model.

A typical operator is GOTOB, which denotes the robot's going up to an object in the same room:

```
GOTOB (bx)  "go to object bx"
     Preconditions:  TYPE (bx, OBJECT) and
             THERE EXISTS (rx) such that
                       [INROOM (bx, rx) and INROOM (ROBOT, rx)]
     Delete list:   AT (ROBOT, *, *), NEXTTO (ROBOT, *)
     Add list:   NEXTTO (ROBOT, bx)
```

The precondition statement requires that bx be an object and that both bx and the robot be in the same room, rx. The asterisks in the delete list represent arguments with any values whatever.

Method of operation. STRIPS operates by searching a space of world models to find one in which the given goal is achieved. It uses a *state-space representation* in which each state is a pair (world model, list of goals to be achieved). The initial state is $(M_0, (G_0))$, where M_0 is the initial world model and G_0 the given goal. A terminal state gives a world model in which no unsatisfied goals remain.

Given a goal G (stated as a formula in the predicate calculus), STRIPS first tries to prove that G is satisfied by the current world model. To do this, the program uses a modified version of the resolution-based theorem prover QA3 (Garvey and Kling, 1969). Typically the proof fails, within a prespecified resource limit, because no more resolvents can be formed (see Article XII.B, in Vol. III). At this point, STRIPS needs to find a different world model that the robot can achieve and that satisfies the goal. Because this task is complicated for a simple theorem prover, the system switches to a *means-ends analysis* similar to that of GPS (Article II.D2).

To do the means-ends analysis, the program extracts a *difference* between the goal and the current model and selects a relevant operator to reduce the difference. The difference consists of any formulas from the goal that remain outstanding when the proof attempt is abandoned (pruned, if this set is large). A relevant operator is one whose add list contains formulas that would remove some part of the difference, thereby allowing the proof to continue.

If the operator is applicable, the program applies it and tries to achieve the goal in the resulting model; otherwise, the operator's precondition becomes a new subgoal to be achieved. Since there may be several relevant operators at each step, this procedure generates a tree of models and subgoals. STRIPS uses a number of heuristics to control the search through this tree.

An Example of the Basic System's Performance

As a simple example, suppose the robot is in ROOM1 and the goal is for it to be next to BOX1, which is in adjacent ROOM2. The initial world model M_0 contains such clauses as

```
INROOM (ROBOT, ROOM1),
INROOM (BOX1, ROOM2),
TYPE (BOX1, OBJECT),
CONNECTS (DOOR12, ROOM1, ROOM2),
STATUS (DOOR12, OPEN), . . .
```

and the goal G_0 is

```
G0 = NEXTTO (ROBOT, BOX1)  .
```

G_0 is not satisfied, and the difference between it and the initial model is $\neg$ NEXTTO (ROBOT, BOX1). STRIPS determines that GOTOB (bx), defined above, is a relevant operator, with bx instantiated as BOX1. The operator instance GOTOB (BOX1), denoted OP_1, is not immediately applicable (because the robot is in the wrong room), so its precondition G_1,

```
G1 = TYPE (BOX1, OBJECT) and
     THERE EXISTS (rx) [INROOM (BOX1, rx) and INROOM (ROBOT, rx)]
```

becomes a new subgoal. Relevant operators for reducing the difference between G_1 and the initial model M_0 are: OP_2 = GOTHRUDOOR $(dx, \text{ROOM2})$ and OP_3 = PUSHTHRUDOOR (BOX1, dx, ROOM1) (i.e., move the robot to the room with the box, or move the box to the room with the robot). If the former course (the better one, obviously) is selected, the precondition

```
G2 = STATUS (dx, OPEN) and  NEXTTO (ROBOT, dx) and
     THERE EXISTS (rx) [INROOM (ROBOT, rx) and CONNECTS (dx, rx, ROOM2)]
```

is the new subgoal. The difference $\neg$ NEXTTO (ROBOT, DOOR12) can be reduced by the operator OP_4 = GOTODOOR (DOOR12), which is applicable immediately. Applying OP_4 adds the clause NEXTTO (ROBOT, DOOR12) to the model, creating a new world model M_1. G_2 is now satisfied with dx = DOOR12, so OP_2 can be instantiated as GOTHRUDOOR (DOOR12, ROOM2) and applied. This deletes the clause INROOM (ROBOT, ROOM1) and adds INROOM (ROBOT, ROOM2). G_1 is now satisfied, so OP_1 is applied, deleting NEXTTO (ROBOT, DOOR12) and adding NEXTTO (ROBOT, BOX1), the desired goal. The final plan is thus:

```
OP4:    GOTODOOR (DOOR12)
OP2:    GOTHRUDOOR (DOOR12, ROOM2)
OP1:    GOTOB (BOX1)
```

The corresponding solution path through the state space tree is as follows:

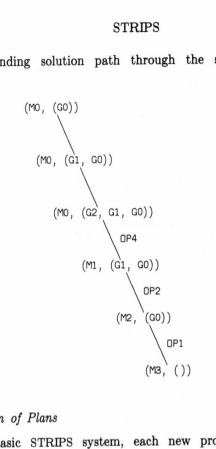

Generalization of Plans

In the basic STRIPS system, each new problem was solved from scratch. Even if the system had produced a plan for solving a similar problem previously, it was not able to make any use of this fact. A later version of STRIPS provided for generalizing plans and saving them, to assist both in the solution of subsequent problems and also in the intelligent monitoring of the robot's execution of the particular plan.

Triangle tables. A specific plan to be generalized, say, $(OP_1, OP_2, \ldots, OP_n)$, is first stored in a data structure called a *triangle table*. This is a lower triangular array representing the preconditions for and effects of each operator in the plan. Some of its properties are the following:

1. Cell $(i, 0)$ contains clauses from the original model that are still true when operator i is to be applied and that are preconditions for operator i, OP_i.

2. Marked (starred) clauses elsewhere in row i are preconditions for operator i added to the model by previous operators.

3. The effects of applying operator i are shown in row $i + 1$. The operator's add list appears in cell $(i + 1, i)$. For each

previous operator, say, operator j, clauses added by operator j and not yet deleted are copied into cell $(i + 1, j)$.

4. The add list for a sequence of operators 1 through i, taken as a whole, is given by the clauses in row $i + 1$ (excluding column 0).

5. The preconditions for a sequence of operators i through n, taken as a whole, are given by the marked clauses in the rectangular subarray containing row i and cell $(n + 1, 0)$. This rectangle is called the i-th *kernel* of the plan.

The triangle table for the previous example is shown in Figure D5-1. Operators have been renumbered in the order of their use.

	0	1	2	3
1	*INROOM(ROBOT, ROOM1) *CONNECTS(D12, ROOM1,ROOM2)	OP1 GOTODOOR(D12)		
2	*INROOM(ROBOT, ROOM1) *CONNECTS(D12, ROOM1,ROOM2) *STATUS (D12, OPEN)	*NEXTTO (ROBOT,D12)	OP2 GOTHRUDOOR (D12,ROOM2)	
3	*INROOM(BOX1, ROOM2) *TYPE(BOX1, OBJECT)	NEXTTO (ROBOT,D12)	*INROOM (ROBOT,ROOM2)	OP3 GOTOB(BOX1)
4			INROOM (ROBOT,ROOM2)	NEXTTO (ROBOT,BOX1)

Figure D5-1. A triangle table.

Method of generalization. The plan is generalized by replacing all constants in each of the clauses in column 0 by distinct parameters and the rest of the table with clauses that assume that no argument to an operator has been instantiated. The result may be too general, so the proof of the preconditions for each operator is run again, noting any substitutions for parameters that constrain the generality of the plan. Some further corrections are made for remaining overgeneralization, which might make the plan either inconsistent or inefficient in use. Finally, the generalized plan, termed a MACROP, is stored away for future use.

In the example above, the generalized plan would be

GOTODOOR (dx)
GOTHRUDOOR (dx, rx1)
GOTOB (bx)

with preconditions:

INROOM (ROBOT, rx2)
CONNECTS (dx, rx2, rx1)
STATUS (dx, OPEN)
INROOM (bx, rx1)
TYPE (bx, OBJECT)

and add list:

NEXTTO (ROBOT, bx)
INROOM (ROBOT, rx1)

That is, the generalized plan sends the robot from any room through a connecting door to an object in the adjacent room.

Using the MACROP to guide execution. When STRIPS produces a detailed plan to achieve a goal, it does not necessarily follow that the robot should execute the plan exactly as given. One possibility is that some action fails to achieve its expected effect, so that the corresponding step of the plan needs to be repeated. Another is that the plan found is less than optimal and would be improved by omitting some steps entirely. The necessary flexibility during execution is provided by using the MACROP rather than the detailed plan in monitoring the robot's actions.

At the beginning of execution, the parameters of the MACROP are partially instantiated to the case at hand. The robot then attempts, at each stage, to execute the highest numbered step of the plan whose preconditions are satisfied. This procedure omits unnecessary steps and allows repeated execution, possibly with changed parameters, of a step that has failed. If there is no step whose preconditions are satisfied, replanning occurs. Determining which step can be done next is accomplished by a scan that exploits the design of the triangle table.

Using MACROPs in planning. When STRIPS is given a new problem, the time it takes to produce an answer can be reduced very considerably if there is a MACROP that can be incorporated into its solution. The MACROP given above, for example, could be used as the first part of a plan to fetch a box from an adjacent room. The part of the MACROP consisting of its first two suboperators, if used alone, would also give a ready-made solution to the problem "Go to an adjacent room," or it could be used repeatedly in solving "Go to a distant room."

The triangle table provides the means of determining whether a relevant macro operator exists. To determine whether the sequence of operators 1 through i of the MACROP is relevant, STRIPS checks the add list of this sequence as given by the $(i + 1)$st row of the table. Once a MACROP is selected, irrelevant operators are edited out by a straightforward algorithm, leaving an economical, possibly parameterized operator for achieving the desired add list. The operator's preconditions are taken from the appropriate cells of column 0. Thus, almost any sub-sequence of operators from a MACROP can become a macro operator in a new plan. To keep new MACROPs from producing an overwhelming number of different operators that must be considered during planning, the system contains provisions for preventing consideration of redundant parts of overlapping MACROPs and for deleting MACROPs that have been completely subsumed by new ones.

In a sequence of problems given to STRIPS, the use of MACROPs in some cases reduced planning time by as much as two-thirds. The longest plan so formed, consisting of 11 primitive operations, took the robot from one room to a second room, opened a door leading to a third room, took the robot through the third room to a fourth room, and then pushed two pairs of boxes together. One drawback noted by the authors was that, however long the solution sequence, STRIPS at each stage of its search dealt with every operation in complete detail. A later program, Sacerdoti's ABSTRIPS (Article II.D6), provides the mechanism for deferring the details of the solution until after its main outline has been completed.

References

See Fikes, Hart, and Nilsson (1972), Fikes and Nilsson (1971), and Garvey and Kling (1969).

D6. ABSTRIPS

A combinatorial explosion faces all problem solvers that attempt to use heuristic search in a sufficiently complex problem domain. A technique called *hierarchical search* or *hierarchical planning*, implemented in Earl Sacerdoti's ABSTRIPS (1974), is an attempt to reduce the combinatorial problem. The idea is to use an approach to problem solving that can recognize the most significant features of a problem, develop an outline of a solution in terms of those features, and deal with the less important details of the problem only after the outline has proved adequate.

The implementation of this approach involves using distinct levels of problem representation. A simplified version of the problem, from which details have been omitted, occurs in a *higher level problem space* or *abstraction space;* the detailed version, in a *ground space.* By a slight extension, providing for several levels of detail instead of just two, a hierarchy of problem spaces is obtained. In general, each space in the hierarchy serves both as an abstraction space for the more detailed space just below it and as a ground space with respect to the less detailed space just above it.

Background—The STRIPS System

ABSTRIPS is a modification of the STRIPS system, described in Article II.D5. The problem domain for both programs is a world of robot planning. In both, the program is given an initial state of the world, or *world model*, consisting of a set of formulas that describe the floor plan of a group of rooms and other facts such as the location of the robot and other objects within these rooms. The goal state to be achieved is also given. The elements of a solution sequence are *operators* representing robot actions; examples are operators for going up to an object, pushing an object, and going through a door. The definition of each operator contains three kinds of formulas: (a) its *preconditions*, representing statements that must be true of a world model in order for the operator to be applicable; (b) its *add list*, a list of formulas that will become true and should be added to the world model when the operator is applied; and (c) its *delete list*, a corresponding list of formulas to be deleted from the model upon application of the operator. The search for a sequence of operators producing the desired world model is guided by a *means-ends analysis* similar to that of GPS (Article II.D2).

Abstraction Spaces

Given the world models and operator descriptions of the basic STRIPS system, the first question is how to define the "details" that are to be ignored in the first pass at a solution. Sacerdoti's answer was to treat as details certain parts of the operator preconditions. At all levels of abstraction, the world models and the add and delete lists of operators remain exactly the same. Such a definition of "details" was found to be strong enough to produce real improvements in problem-solving efficiency, while keeping a desirable simplicity in the relationship between each abstraction space and its adjacent ground space.

The preconditions for an operator are stated as a list of predications, or *literals*, concerning the world model to which the operator is to be applied. The relative importance of literals is indicated by attaching to each a number called its *criticality value*. The hierarchy of problem spaces is then defined in terms of levels of criticality: In the space of criticality n, all operator preconditions with criticality less than n are ignored.

The assignment of criticality values is done just once for a given definition of the problem domain. The general ideas to be reflected in the assignment are the following:

1. If the truth value of a literal cannot be changed by any operator in the problem domain, it should have the highest criticality.

2. If the preconditions for an operator include a literal L that can be readily achieved once other preconditions for the same operator are satisfied, then L should be less critical than those other preconditions.

3. If the possibility of satisfying literal L depends on additional preconditions besides those referred to in (2), then L should have high but less than maximum criticality.

The actual assignment of criticalities is done by a combination of manual and automatic means. First, the programmer supplies a partial ordering of all predicates that can appear in operator preconditions. The partial ordering serves two purposes: It supplies a tentative criticality value for all instances of each predicate, and it governs the order in which the program will consider literals for possible increases (but not decreases) in criticality.

As an example, consider an operator TURN-ON-LAMP (x), with preconditions

```
TYPE (x, LAMP) and THERE EXISTS (r) [INROOM (ROBOT, r) and
    INROOM (x, r) and PLUGGED-IN (x) and NEXTTO (ROBOT, x)]   .
```

The partial ordering of predicates, reflecting an intuitive view of their relative importance, might be as follows (Fig. D6-1):

Predicate	Rank
TYPE	4
INROOM	3
PLUGGED—IN	2
NEXTTO	1

Figure D6-1. Initial ranking of predicates.

The assignment algorithm, whose output is summarized in Figure D6-2, would first find that the truth of TYPE (x, LAMP) is beyond the power of any operator to change and therefore would set its criticality to the maximum; in this case, 6. Then it would find that TYPE (x, LAMP) is an insufficient basis for achieving INROOM (ROBOT, r) or INROOM (x, r); so these two literals would have their criticality raised to the next highest value, 5. Next, PLUGGED-IN (x) is considered, and a plan to achieve PLUGGED-IN (x) is found using only the literals already processed as a starting point. Hence, the PLUGGED-IN literal retains its tentative criticality of 2, and, similarly, NEXTTO (ROBOT, x) is given criticality 1. The result, after similar processing of the preconditions of the other operators in the domain, is a hierarchy of at least four, and possibly six, distinct problem spaces.

Literal	Criticality Value
TYPE (x, LAMP)	6
INROOM (ROBOT, r)	5
INROOM (x, r)	5
PLUGGED—IN (x)	2
NEXTTO (ROBOT, x)	1

Figure D6-2. Final criticality of literals.

Control Structure

A problem statement for ABSTRIPS, as for STRIPS, consists of a description of the state of the world to be achieved. A solution is a plan, or sequence of operators, for achieving it. ABSTRIPS proceeds by forming a crude plan at the highest level of abstraction and successively refining it. The executive is a recursive program taking two parameters: the current level of criticality, defining the abstraction space in which planning is to take place, and a list of nodes representing the plan to be refined. Before the initial call, criticality is set to the maximum, and the skeleton plan is initialized to a single operator—a dummy—whose preconditions are precisely the goal to be achieved. ABSTRIPS computes the difference between the preconditions and the current world model, finds operators relevant to reducing the difference, and, if necessary, pursues subgoals of satisfying the preconditions of the selected operators. During this process, any preconditions of less than the current criticality are ignored. A search tree is built from which, if the process succeeds, a fuller operator sequence leading from the initial world model to the goal can be reconstructed. This new skeleton plan, together with the next lower criticality level, are passed recursively to the executive for the next round of planning.

The search strategy used by ABSTRIPS can be called *length-first*, in that the executive forms a complete plan for reaching the goal in each abstraction space before considering plans in any lower level space. This approach has the advantage that it permits early recognition of dead ends, thus reducing the work wasted in extending the search tree along fruitless paths involving detailed preconditions. If a subproblem in any particular space cannot be solved, control is returned to its abstraction space, and the search tree is restored to its previous state in that space. The node that caused the failure in the lower level space is eliminated from consideration and the search is continued in the higher level space. This mechanism, an example of *backtracking*, suffers from the problem that no information is available at the higher level on what caused the plan to fail.

Because backtracking can be inefficient and also because each operator in an abstraction space may be expanded to several operators in the ground space, it is important for ABSTRIPS to produce good plans at the highest level. Two modifications to STRIPS were made to try to ensure that it would do so.

First, whereas a STRIPS search tended to be *depth-first* and therefore sometimes found nonoptimal solutions, ABSTRIPS makes the order of expanding nodes in the search tree dependent on the level of abstraction. At the highest level it uses an *evaluation function* that may increase the search effort but that ensures that the shortest possible solution sequence will be found. (See Article II.C3b on A^*.)

The second change relates to the instantiation of operator parameters, in cases where two or more choices seem equally good. While STRIPS made a choice arbitrarily, ABSTRIPS defers the choice until a greater level of detail indicates one to be preferable. Backtracking can still take place should the choice be mistaken.

Performance

ABSTRIPS and STRIPS were compared on a sequence of problems. One of the longest, needing 11 operators for its solution, required the robot to open a door, go through the adjacent room to another room, push two boxes together, and then go through two more doors to reach the room where it was to stop. The basic STRIPS system required over 30 minutes of computer time to find the solution; ABSTRIPS used 5:28 minutes and generated only half the number of search-tree nodes. It was noted that by the time ABSTRIPS reached the most detailed level, it had in effect replaced the original large problem by a sequence of seven easy subproblems.

References

See Sacerdoti (1974).

Chapter III

Representation of Knowledge

CHAPTER III: REPRESENTATION OF KNOWLEDGE

A. OVERVIEW

ARTIFICIAL INTELLIGENCE research involves building computer systems capable of performing tasks like talking, planning, playing chess, and analyzing molecular structure. When we talk about people who do these things, we always talk about what they have to *know* in order to do them. In other words, we describe someone's ability to behave with intelligence in terms of his or her *knowledge*. Similarly, we say that a computer program *knows* how to play cards, or understand spoken English, or manipulate a robot. We *ascribe* knowledge to programs in the same manner as we ascribe it to each other—based on observing certain behavior; we say that a program knows about objects in its domain, about events that have taken place, or about how to perform specific tasks.

The nature of knowledge and intelligence has been pondered by psychologists, philosophers, linguists, educators, and sociologists for hundreds of years. Since AI research methodology involves the design of programs that exhibit intelligent behavior, AI researchers have often taken a rather pragmatic approach to the subject of knowledge, focusing on improving the behavior of their programs. (In AI, a *representation of knowledge* is a combination of data structures and interpretive procedures that, if used in the right way in a program, will lead to "knowledgeable" behavior.) Work on knowledge representation in AI has involved the design of several classes of data structures for storing information in computer programs, as well as the development of procedures that allow "intelligent" manipulation of these data structures to make. inferences.

Keep in mind that a data structure is not knowledge, any more than an encyclopedia is knowledge. We can say, metaphorically, that a book is a source of knowledge, but without a reader, the book is just ink on paper. Similarly, we often talk of the list-and-pointer data structures in an AI database as knowledge per se, when we really mean that they represent facts or rules when used by a certain program to behave in a knowledgeable way. (This point is expanded in Article III.C5.)

Techniques and theories about knowledge representation have undergone rapid change and development in the last five years. The articles in this chapter try to give a general review of the different representation schemes that researchers have thought up—what they can do well and what they cannot do. Our understanding of these matters is still incomplete; knowledge representation is the most active area of AI research at the present time.

This introductory article should help guide the reader's understanding of the various formalisms described in the articles that follow. After briefly discussing the kinds of knowledge that need to be represented in AI systems, we introduce some issues that will serve as a vocabulary for talking about and comparing different representation methods—terms like *scope, understandability,* and *modularity.* The second article in the chapter is a brief survey of the most important representation formalisms, intended to give an overview of the kinds of systems we are talking about. The remaining articles describe, in more detail, the mechanics of the various representation schemes, their historical development, and some of the current research problems.

Knowledge

What kinds of knowledge are needed to behave knowledgeably? What things do we know "about"? To approach these questions, consider the following list of types of knowledge that might need to be represented in AI systems:

Objects: Typically, we think of knowledge in terms of *facts* about objects in the world around us. *Birds have wings. Robins are birds. Snow is white.* So, of course, there should be some way to represent objects, classes or categories of objects, and descriptions of objects.

Events: We also know about actions and events in the world. *Bob kissed Mary behind the barn. The sky will fall tomorrow.* In addition to encoding the events themselves, a representation formalism may need to indicate the time course of a sequence of events and their cause-and-effect relations.

Performance: A behavior like riding a bicycle involves knowledge beyond that of objects and events—knowledge about *how* to do things, the performance of skills. Like bike riding, most cognitive behaviors—for example, composing sentences and proving theorems—involve performance knowledge, and it is often hard to draw the line between performance knowledge and object knowledge. (Beware: Pushing too hard on this point leads right back to the fundamental philosophical issue of what knowledge is!)

Meta-knowledge: We also use *knowledge about what we know,* called *meta-knowledge.* For example, we often know about the extent and origin of our knowledge of a particular subject, about the

reliability of certain information, or about the relative importance of specific facts about the world. Meta-knowledge also
includes what we know about our own performance as cognitive
processors: our strengths, weaknesses, confusability, levels of
expertise in different domains, and feelings of progress during
problem solving. For example, Bobrow (1975) describes a robot
who is planning a trip; its knowledge that it can read the
street signs to find out where it is along the way illustrates
meta-knowledge.

The questions of whether these kinds of knowledge are distin-
guishable and whether there are also other varieties of knowledge are
interesting psychological issues. For now, however, we will ignore the
psychological aspects of the problem of knowledge. In this article we
discuss some of the features of the AI knowledge representation schemes
that make it possible, sometimes, for computer programs to exhibit
behaviors indicating these four different types of knowledge.

Using Knowledge

The most important consideration in examining and comparing
knowledge representation schemes is the eventual *use* of the knowledge.
The goals of AI systems can be described in terms of cognitive tasks
like recognizing objects, answering questions, and manipulating robotic
devices. But the actual use of the knowledge in these programs involves three stages: (a) acquiring more knowledge, (b) retrieving facts
from the knowledge base relevant to the problem at hand, and (c)
reasoning about these facts in search of a solution.

Acquisition. We usually think of *learning* as the accumulation of
knowledge, but it involves more than the addition of new facts to our
brains. Indeed, *knowledge acquisition* involves relating something new to
what we already know in a psychologically complex way; see, for
example, Piaget's theory of human *adaptation by assimilation and
accommodation* (Flavell, 1977, pp. 6–11). AI systems often *classify* a
new data structure before it is added to the database, so that it can be
retrieved later when it is relevant. Also, in many kinds of systems, new
structures can *interact* with old, sometimes resulting in interference with
tasks that had previously been performed properly. Finally, some
representation schemes are concerned with acquiring knowledge in a form
that is *natural* to humans, who serve as the source of new knowledge
(see Article VII.B, in Vol. II). If these integrative processes did not take
place during acquisition, the system would accumulate new facts or data
structures without really improving its knowledgeable behavior.

Retrieval. Determining what knowledge is relevant to a given problem becomes crucial when the system "knows" many different things. Humans are incredibly proficient at this task, and many representation schemes that have been directly concerned with this issue have been based on ideas about human memory (see Articles III.C3 and III.C7, and Chap. XI, in Vol. III, on the use of AI methods in building psychological models). The fundamental ideas about retrieval that have been developed in AI systems might be termed *linking* and *lumping:* If it is known that one data structure is going to entail another in an expected reasoning task, an explicit link is put in between the two; if several data structures are typically going to be used together, they are grouped into a larger structure.

Reasoning. When the system is required to do something that it has not been explicitly told how to do, it must *reason*—it must figure out what it needs to know from what it already knows. For instance, suppose an information retrieval program "knows" only that *Robins are birds* and that *All birds have wings.* Keep in mind that for a system to know these facts means only that it contains data structures and procedures that would allow it to answer the questions:

<pre>
Are Robins birds?   Yes
Do all birds have wings?   Yes
</pre>

If we then ask it, *Do robins have wings?* the program must *reason* to answer the query. In problems of any complexity, the ability to do this becomes increasingly important. The system must be able to deduce and verify a multitude of new facts beyond those it has been told explicitly.

For a given knowledge representation scheme, we must ask, "What kind of reasoning is possible, easy, natural, and so on, in this formalism?" There are many different kinds of reasoning one might imagine:

Formal reasoning involves the syntactic manipulation of data structures to deduce new ones following prespecified *rules of inference.* Mathematical logic is the archetypical formal representation (see Article III.C1).

Procedural reasoning uses simulation to answer questions and solve problems. When we use a program to answer *What is the sum of 3 and 4?* it uses, or "runs," a procedural model of arithmetic (Article III.C2).

Reasoning by analogy seems to be a very natural mode of thought for humans but, so far, difficult to accomplish in AI programs. The idea is that when you ask the question *Can robins fly?* the system might reason that "robins are like sparrows, and I know that sparrows can fly, so robins probably can fly."

Generalization and *abstraction* are also natural reasoning processes for humans that are difficult to pin down well enough to implement in a program. If one knows that *Robins have wings*, that *Sparrows have wings*, and that *Blue jays have wings*, eventually one will believe that *All birds have wings*. This capability may be at the core of most human learning, but it has not yet become a useful technique in AI (however, see Chaps. XI and XV, in Vol. III, for current research).

Meta-level reasoning is demonstrated by the way one answers the question *What is Paul Newman's telephone number?* You might reason that "if I knew Paul Newman's number, I would know that I knew it, because it is a notable fact." This involves using "knowledge about what you know," in particular, about the extent of your knowledge and about the importance of certain facts. Recent research in psychology and AI indicates that meta-level reasoning may play a central role in human cognitive processing (Gentner and Collins, in press; Flavell, 1979); some work on implementing this kind of inference mechanism in AI systems has begun (Davis, in press; Bobrow and Winograd, 1977b; Brachman, 1978).

Two things need to be said about the uses of knowledge described here. First, they are *interrelated:* When acquiring new knowledge, the system must be concerned with how that knowledge will be retrieved and used later in reasoning. Second, for most AI research, *efficacy* is the primary consideration in designing knowledge-based AI systems. Although there is serious concern among AI researchers about the psychological validity of the various representation schemes, it is not yet possible to prove that one scheme captures some aspect of human memory better than another. There is no *theory of knowledge representation*. We don't yet know why some schemes are good for certain tasks and others not. But each scheme has been successfully used in a variety of programs that do exhibit intelligent behavior.

We will now discuss some of the characteristics of representation schemes that have been used to describe and compare different formalisms.

Scope and Grain Size

What portion of the external world can be represented in a system? In what detail are objects and events represented? And how much of this detail is actually needed by the reasoning mechanisms? Questions like these, concerning the *scope* and *grain size* of a representation scheme, can help determine the suitability of a given formalism for the solution of a particular problem, but they are not easy to answer.

For one thing, of course, the answers depend totally on the particular application intended. A knowledge representation based on *logic*, for instance, might be an extremely fine-grain representation in a mathematical reasoning program but might result in a coarse simplification for a vision program. Exactly how much detail is needed depends on the performance desired (see McCarthy and Hayes, 1969). In general, uniformity of detail across the objects and events seems desirable for a given reasoning task (Bobrow, 1975).

If one asks, "Can everything that the system must know be represented in the formalism?" the answer is almost always, "Yes, but some things are more easily represented than others." Getting a feeling for what it means to be "represented more easily"—which involves the representation, the domain, and the reasoning strategies—is, at present, part of the art of doing AI research; there is no formal metric for the appropriateness of a representation scheme. Bobrow refers to the process of *mapping* the objects and events in the world into some internal encoding; then one can ask if the mapping in a given situation is easy, natural, psychologically valid, and the like.

Indeterminacy and Semantic Primitives

In any representation formalism—logic, semantic nets, procedures, and so forth—the choice of the primitive attributes of the domain that are used to build up facts in the database strongly affects the expressive power of the knowledge representation scheme. One particular problem affected by the choice of *semantic primitives* is the multiplicity of ways in which a particular fact or event might be encoded. For instance, the fact that robins have wings could be represented in either of the sample semantic nets below (see Article III.C3):

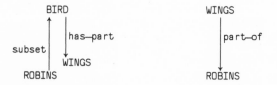

The first is interpreted as *All robins are birds, and all birds have wings,* while the second states directly that *Wings are a part of all robins.* Although this inherent *indeterminacy* might be used to great advantage, allowing redundant storage of information with an eye to future relevance, for example, it generally gives rise to confusion and expense, since the system doesn't know exactly what structures to look for when it comes time to retrieve a given fact.

One particular task in which the problem of nonspecificity of representation was critical was the *paraphrase* task popular in *natural language understanding* research (see Chap. IV). Problems encountered in trying to build programs that could rephrase an input sentence, check whether two sentences have the same meaning, or translate a sentence from one language into another led researchers like Norman and Rumelhart (1975), Schank and Abelson (1977), and Wilks (1977b) to try using canonical internal representations based on semantic primitives. Thus, in Schank's MARGIE system and Wilks's machine translation system, all representation structures are built from a set of primitives in such a way that two structures that mean the same thing reduce to the same network of primitive nodes (see Articles IV.F2 and IV.F5). The selection of primitive elements for the expression of knowledge in a given domain is a basic problem in all representation schemes, whether the primitives are represented as nodes in a *semantic net,* predicates in *logic* formulas, or slots in a *frame.* (The status of semantic primitives in knowledge representation research is discussed in Article III.C6.)

Modularity and Understandability

If one thinks of the data structures in a program as pieces of knowledge, then adding new data structures is like adding knowledge to the system. One characteristic that is often used to compare representation schemes is *modularity,* which refers to the ability to add, modify, or delete individual data structures more or less independently of the remainder of the database, that is, with clearly circumscribed effects on what the system "knows."

In general, humans find modular or decomposable systems easier to understand and work with (Simon, 1969). To illustrate the difficulty encountered in nonmodular systems, consider the complicated interdependence of procedures in a large computer program such as an operating system. The following situation will be familiar to readers who have helped write and maintain large programs: A large system is composed of many procedures that call each other in a complex way that becomes increasingly hard to follow as the system grows. Often modification of procedure X, so that it will work properly when called by procedure A, interferes with the proper functioning of X when it is called by procedure B. In other words, in order to modify a large system successfully, the programmer must understand the interactions of all of its pieces, which can become an impossibly difficult task.

In general terms, the problem with nonmodular systems is that the meaning of data structures in the knowledge base depends on the *context* in which the knowledge is being used. (Computer programs themselves illustrate a notoriously nonmodular representation scheme called *procedural representation*—see Article III.C2.) Context dependence, in turn, dramatically affects the *modifiability* of the knowledge base; modification is much easier if the meaning of a fact can be specified when the fact is entered or removed, independent of the rest of the system.

On the other hand, some human knowledge seems inherently nonmodular and is very difficult for people to express as *independent* rules or facts. Winograd (1974) made the generalization that in modular systems the facts are easy to recognize but the reasoning process may be quite opaque, and the opposite is often true in procedural representations. The degree to which the system is *understandable* by humans is important in several phases of its development and performance: design and implementation, acquisition of knowledge from human experts, performance of the task, and interaction with and explanations for the eventual user.

In some representation schemes the data structures (e.g., production rules, logic formulas) seem less inherently intertwined, but the control of the interaction of the various database entries is a very important characteristic of all representation schemes. Winograd (1975) suggests that no system is completely modular—in all systems there is some degree of interaction between the data structures that form the knowledge base—but some formalisms are more inherently modular than others.

Explicit Knowledge and Flexibility

Another issue to keep in mind when examining various representation schemes is what part of the system's knowledge is *explicit*. By this we mean, to what knowledge do the programmer and the system have direct, manipulatory access, and what knowledge is built-in? For example, an operating system has an explicit representation of its priority queues, but its full knowledge about scheduling jobs (deciding which of several users to serve first) is typically hidden deep in voluminous code. The knowledge is there, of course, since the system behaves in a knowledgeable way, but it is *implicit* in the system's program (Winograd, 1980b, p. 228).

One particular advantage of explicit representation schemes is that, because the facts are in a form that allows a global interpretation, the same fact can be used for multiple purposes. In some large systems this feature has been a significant advantage. For example, in MYCIN (see Article VIII.B1, in Vol. II), the production rules that form the system's knowledge about how to diagnose the possible causes of infectious diseases are used not only by the diagnosis module itself, but also by the routines that *explain* the diagnosis module's reasoning to the consulting physician and that *acquire* new rules from expert physicians (Davis and Buchanan, 1977).

Declarative versus Procedural Representations

On a closely related subject, the dispute about the relative merits of *declarative* versus *procedural* knowledge representations is a historically important battle from which much of current representation theory was painfully developed (Winograd, 1975). Many of the issues discussed in this article were identified during the declarative-procedural debate. The declarative systems were typified by resolution-based *theorem provers* (see Article III.C1 on logic and Chap. XII, in Vol. III) and the procedural systems by Winograd's PLANNER-based SHRDLU (Article IV.F4). The Declarativists talked about the *flexibility* and *economy* of their representation schemes, about their *completeness* and the *certainty* of the deductions, and about the *modifiability* of the systems. The Proceduralists stressed the *directness* of the line of inference (using *domain-specific heuristics* to avoid irrelevant or unnatural lines of reasoning) and the *ease of coding* and *understandability* of the reasoning process itself.

Although in retrospect these positions seem somewhat arbitrarily chosen over the space of possible features of representation schemes, the declarative-procedural battle was an important one in AI. It dissolved, rather than being resolved, and the result was a much greater respect for the importance of knowledge representation in current AI work.

Final Remarks

This article has not been about representation formalisms per se, but rather about the pragmatics of *epistemology*, the study of the nature of knowledge. The intention has been to lay the groundwork for an appreciation of the problems inherent in representing knowledge in AI programs. The discussion may also guide a critical comparison of the representation methods described in the articles to follow.

There are many open questions, indeed serious problems, in knowledge representation research. For example, *quantification*, the ability to specify properties of arbitrarily defined sets, is an area of active theoretical research. Other current problems include how to represent people's beliefs (which may or may not be true), degrees of certainty, mass nouns, time and tense information, and processes that consist of sequenced actions taking place over time.

The following article is a quick summary of the knowledge representation schemes used in AI. The articles in Section III.C go into substantial detail about individual representation schemes, discussing their development, their technical features, their use in AI systems, and their shortcomings.

References

The best recent review of knowledge representation research in AI is Winograd (in press). Earlier excellent discussions include the papers in Bobrow and Collins (1975), especially Bobrow (1975) and Winograd (1975). Other recent general discussions of knowledge representation are found in Boden (1977) and Findler (1979). Brachman and Smith (1980) report on a survey of knowledge representation researchers, showing the wide diversity of goals and approaches among workers in the field.

B. SURVEY OF REPRESENTATION TECHNIQUES

As stated in the preceding article, AI research deals in *experimental epistemology;* to create programs that exhibit intelligent behavior, researchers in AI develop schemes for incorporating knowledge about the world into their programs. These *knowledge representation* techniques involve routines for manipulating specialized data structures to make intelligent inferences. Although some aspects of each knowledge representation technique are incidental and will seem unmotivated, in its way each scheme touches on concerns central to the study of cognition and intelligence.

This survey article presents sketches of the representation schemes that have been used in AI programs that play chess, converse in English, operate robots, and so forth. Seeing simple examples of the major techniques will perhaps help the reader get a clearer idea of what a knowledge representation is. Most of this research assumes that *what* needs to be represented is known, a priori; the AI researcher's job is just figuring out *how* to encode the information in the system's data structures and procedures.

State-space Search

Perhaps the earliest representation formalism used extensively in AI programs was the state-space representation, developed for problem-solving and game-playing programs. The search space is not a representation of knowledge, per se: What it represents is the structure of a problem in terms of the *alternatives* available at each possible state of the problem, for example, the alternative moves available on each turn of a game. The basic idea is that from a given state in a problem, all possible next states can be determined with a small set of rules, called *transition operators* (or *legal-move generators* in game-playing programs). For example, in a chess game, the original state is the board position at the beginning of the game. The legal-move generators correspond to the rules for moving each piece. So all of the next states of the game (i.e., the board configurations after each of White's possible first moves) can be generated by applying the move generators to the original positions of the pieces. Similarly, all of the possible states after Black's first response can be generated.

One rather straightforward way to find the winning move is to try all of the alternative moves, then try all of the opponent's responses to these moves, and then try all of the possible responses to those, until all of the possible continuations of the game have been exhausted and it is clear which was optimal. The problem with this solution is that, for interesting problems like chess, there are far too many possible combinations of moves to try in a reasonable amount of time on a machine of conceivable computational power. This problem, called the *combinatorial explosion*, is an important general difficulty for AI systems in all applications (see Chap. II).

The solution adopted in AI research is to limit the number of alternatives searched at each stage of the look-ahead process to the *best* possibilities. And in order to determine which alternatives are best, programs must *reason* from large amounts knowledge about the world, encoded within the program in some *knowledge representation*. Whatever domain the systems deal with, chess or organic chemistry or pizza parlor scenarios, the goal of research in knowledge representation is to allow AI programs to behave as if they *knew* something about the problems they solve.

Logic

The classical approach to representing the knowledge about the world contained in sentences like

All birds have wings.

is formal logic, developed by philosophers and mathematicians as a calculus of the process of making inferences from facts. The example about birds' wings would be translated into the mathematical formula

$$\forall \ x. \ \text{Bird} \ (x) \ \rightarrow \ \text{HasWings} \ (x) \ ,$$

which reads, *For any object x in the world, if x is a bird, then x has wings.* The advantage of formal representation is that there is a set of rules, called the *rules of inference* in logic, by which facts that are known to be true can be used to derive other facts that *must* also be true. Furthermore, the truth of any new statement can be checked, in a well-specified manner, against the facts that are already known to be true.

For example, suppose we add another fact to our database,

$$\forall \ x. \ \text{Robin} \ (x) \ \rightarrow \ \text{Bird} \ (x) \ ,$$

which reads, *For any object x in the world, if x is a Robin, then x is a Bird.* Then from these two facts, we can conclude, using the rules of inference, that the following fact *must* be true:

$$\forall \ x. \ \text{Robin} \ (x) \ \rightarrow \ \text{HasWings} \ (x) \ ;$$

that is, that *All robins have wings*. Note that there is a specific rule of inference that allows this deduction based on the superficial structure, or *syntax*, of the first two formulas, independent of whether they dealt with birds or battleships, and that new facts derived through application of the rules of inference are always true so long as the original facts were true.

The most important feature of logic and related formal systems is that deductions are guaranteed correct to an extent that other representation schemes have not yet reached. The semantic *entailment* of a set of logic statements (i.e., the set of inferences or conclusions that can be drawn from those statements) is completely specified by the rules of inference. Theoretically, the database can be kept logically consistent and all conclusions can be guaranteed correct. Other representation schemes are still striving for such a definition and guarantee of logical consistency.

One reason that logic-based representations have been so popular in AI research is that the derivation of new facts from old can be mechanized. Using automated versions of *theorem proving* techniques, programs have been written to determine automatically the validity of a new statement in a logic database by attempting to *prove* it from the existing statements (see Chap. XII, in Vol. III). Although mechanistic theorem provers of this sort have been used with some success in programs with relatively small databases (Green, 1969), when the number of facts becomes large, there is a combinatorial explosion in the possibilities of which rules to apply to which facts at each step of the proof. More knowledge about what facts are relevant to what situations is needed, and, again, incorporating additional knowledge is the goal of continuing work in representation theory.

Procedural Representation

The idea of procedural representation of knowledge first appeared as an attempt to encode some explicit control of the theorem-proving process within a logic-based system. (This refers to research on the PLANNER programming language; see Article VI.C2, in Vol. II.) In a procedural representation, knowledge about the world is contained in procedures—small programs that know how to do specific things, how to proceed in well-specified situations. For instance, in a parser for a natural language understanding system, the knowledge that a *noun phrase* may contain articles, adjectives, and nouns is represented in the program by calls (within the NP procedure) to routines that know how to process articles, nouns, and adjectives.

The underlying knowledge, the permissible grammar for a noun phrase in our example, is not stated explicitly and thus is not typically extractable in a form that humans can easily understand. The consequent difficulty that humans have in verifying and changing procedural representations is the major flaw of these systems. Nevertheless, all AI systems use a procedural representation at some level of their operation, and general consensus gives a legitimate role for procedural representation in AI programs (Winograd, 1975). The advantages and disadvantages of procedural knowledge representation are discussed fully in Article III.C2. Recent work has emphasized *procedural attachment* in frame-based systems (Article III.C7).

Semantic Nets

The semantic net, developed by Quillian (1968) and others, was invented as an explicitly psychological model of human associative memory. A net consists of *nodes,* representing objects, concepts, and events, and *links* between the nodes, representing their interrelations. Consider, for example, the simple net:

where BIRD and WINGS are nodes representing sets or concepts and HAS-PART is the name of the link specifying their relationship. Among the many possible interpretations of this net fragment is the statement

All birds have wings.

As illustrated earlier, statements of this sort also have a natural representation in logic-based representation systems. One key feature of the semantic net representation is that important associations can be made explicitly and succinctly: Relevant facts about an object or concept can be inferred from the nodes to which they are directly linked, without a search through a large database.

The ability to point directly to relevant facts is particularly salient with respect to ISA and SUBSET links, which establish a *property inheritance hierarchy* in the net. For example, the net segment

might be interpreted to mean that since robins are birds, and birds have wings, then robins have wings. The interpretation (semantics) of net structures, however, depends solely on the program that manipulates them; there are no conventions about their meaning. Therefore, inferences drawn by manipulation of the net are not assuredly *valid*, in the sense that they are assured to be valid in a logic-based representation scheme.

Production Systems

Production systems, developed by Newell and Simon (1972) for their models of human cognition (see Chap. XI, in Vol. III), are a *modular* knowledge representation scheme that is finding increasing popularity in large AI programs. The basic idea of these systems is that the database consists of rules, called *productions*, in the form of condition-action pairs: "If this condition occurs, then do this action." For example,

IF *stoplight is red* AND *you have stopped* THEN *right turn* OK.

The utility of the formalism comes from the fact that the conditions in which each rule is applicable are made *explicit* and, in theory at least, the interactions between rules are minimized (one rule doesn't "call" another).

Production systems have been found useful as a mechanism for controlling the interaction between statements of declarative and procedural knowledge. Because they facilitate human understanding and modification of systems with large amounts of knowledge, productions have been used in several recent large applications systems like DENDRAL, MYCIN, PROSPECTOR, and AM (see Chap. VII, in Vol. II). Current work on production systems has emphasized the control aspects of the formalism and the ability to develop self-modifying (learning) systems.

Special-purpose Representation Techniques

Some of the domains that AI researchers work in seem to suggest natural representations for the knowledge required to solve problems. For example, a visual scene from a robot's camera is often encoded as an array representing a grid over the scene: The values of the elements of the array represent the average brightness over the corresponding area of the scene (see Chap. XIII, in Vol. III). This *direct representation* is useful for some tasks, like finding the boundaries of the objects in the scene, but is clumsy for other tasks, like counting the number of objects. In the latter case, a list—each element of which represents one object indicating its location, orientation, and size—might be a more useful representation. (See the discussion in Bobrow, 1975.)

This example illustrates a very important principle to realize when comparing representation techniques. In some sense, these two (and all other) knowledge representation methods are interchangeable: If we know one representation in enough detail, we could for the most part construct the other one. It is the intended *use* of the knowledge about the scene that recommends one representation scheme over another. In a big AI system, like the *speech understanding* programs, multiple representations of the same information may be used simultaneously for different purposes.

Other special-purpose representation schemes of particular interest are those used in the early natural language understanding programs, like SAD–SAM and SIR (see Article IV.F1), and the *discrimination net* used in the EPAM program (Article XI.D, in Vol. III).

Frames

The most recently developed AI knowledge-representation scheme is the *frame*, still in its early development stage. Researchers have different ideas about exactly what a frame is, but basically, a frame is a data structure that includes declarative and procedural information in predefined internal relations. Thus, a generic frame for a dog might have knowledge hooks, or *slots,* for facts that are typically known about dogs, like the BREED, OWNER, NAME, and an "attached procedure" for finding out who the owner is if that is not known. In the frame-like language KRL (Bobrow and Winograd, 1977b), a dog-frame might look like this:

```
Generic DOG Frame
        Self:    an ANIMAL; a PET
        Breed:
        Owner:   a PERSON
                 (If-Needed: find a PERSON with pet=myself)
        Name:    a PROPER NAME (DEFAULT=Rover)


DOG-NEXT-DOOR Frame
        Self:    a DOG
        Breed:   mutt
        Owner:   Jimmy
        Name:    Fido
```

The semantics of this example, as well as the ideas being developed in frame-based formalisms, is discussed in Article III.C7.

An interesting, much discussed feature of frame-based processing is the ability of a frame to determine whether it is applicable in a given situation. The idea is that a likely frame is selected to aid in the process of understanding the current situation (dialogue, scene, problem) and this frame in turn tries to match itself to the data it discovers. If it finds that it is not applicable, it could transfer control to a more appropriate frame (Minsky, 1975). Although many issues about the possible implementations of frame-based systems are unresolved, and others may not have surfaced yet, the basic idea of frame-like structuring of knowledge appears promising.

Conclusion

This brief summary of knowledge representation indicates the variety of techniques being used in AI projects. The remaining articles in this chapter go into most of these schemes in greater detail. Many researchers feel that the representation of knowledge is the key issue at this point in the development of AI. Knowledge representation is also one area in which AI and cognitive psychology share fundamental concerns, for the brain's operation is sometimes best described by one representation formalism, sometimes by another, and sometimes not very well by any we have thought up. The interested reader should peruse Chapter XI, in Volume III.

References

The best current survey of knowledge representation in AI is in Winograd (in press). References on each of the schemes are given after the corresponding article in the following.

C. REPRESENTATION SCHEMES

C1. Logic

Philosophers have been grappling with the nature of reasoning and knowledge since the time of the ancient Greeks. This tradition, formalized in the last half of the 19th century with the work of Boole, Frege, and Russell and expanded and amplified in the current century by philosophers like Quine, Carnap, and Tarski, is an important part of Western intellectual history and has developed into the philosophical and mathematical study of *logic*.

This article is about logic—about how the formal treatment of knowledge and thought, as developed in philosophy, has been applied to the development of computer programs that can reason. The first two sections of the article, dealing with the *propositional* and *predicate calculi*, are an introduction to formal logic. This particular introduction has been written with the AI applications of logic in mind. It is followed by an illustration of the way that a simple problem, the famous *Tower of Hanoi puzzle*, might be formalized in the predicate calculus. Then, after a survey of some of the important AI systems that have used logic for a representation, we discuss the advantages and problems of this representational formalism in AI.

The Propositional Calculus

Logic, which was one of the first representation schemes used in AI, has two important and interlocking branches. The first is consideration of *what can be said*—what relations and implications one can formalize, the *axioms* of a system. The second is the deductive structure—the *rules of inference* that determine what can be inferred if certain axioms are taken to be true. Logic is quite literally a formal endeavor: It is concerned with the form, or *syntax*, of statements and with the determination of truth by *syntactic* manipulation of formulas. The expressive power of a logic-based representational system results from building. One starts with a simple notion (like that of truth and falsehood) and, by inclusion of additional notions (like conjunction and predication), develops a more expressive logic—one in which more subtle ideas can be represented.

The most fundamental notion in logic is that of *truth*. A properly formed statement, or *proposition,* has one of two different possible *truth values,* TRUE or FALSE. Typical propositions are *Bob's car is blue, Seven plus six equals twelve,* and *John is Mary's uncle.* Note that each of the sentences is a proposition, not to be broken down into its constituent parts. Thus, we could assign the truth value TRUE to the proposition *John is Mary's uncle,* with no regard for the *meaning* of *John is Mary's uncle,* that is, that John is the brother of one of Mary's parents. Propositions are those things that we can call true or false. Terms such as *Mary's uncle* and *seven plus four* would not be propositions, as we cannot assign a truth value to them.

Pure, disjoint propositions aren't very interesting. Many more of the things we say and think about can be represented in propositions that use *sentential connectives* to combine simple propositions. There are five commonly employed connectives:

And	$\wedge$ or &
Or	$\vee$
Not	$\neg$
Implies	$\rightarrow$ or $\supset$
Equivalent	$\equiv$

The use of the sentential connectives in the syntax of propositions brings us to the simplest logic, the *propositional calculus,* in which we can express statements like *The book is on the table or it is on the chair* and *If Socrates is a man, then he is mortal.* In fact, the meanings of the sentential connectives are intended to keep their *natural* interpretations, so that if X and Y are any two propositions,

$X \wedge Y$ is TRUE if X is TRUE *and* Y is TRUE; otherwise $X \wedge Y$ is FALSE.

$X \vee Y$ is TRUE if either X is TRUE *or* Y is TRUE *or* both.

$\neg X$ is TRUE if X is FALSE, and FALSE if X is TRUE.

$X \rightarrow Y$ is meant to be the propositional calculus rendition of the notion *If we assume that X is true, then Y must be so;* that is, the truth of X *implies* that Y is true. We use this concept in everyday speech with statements like *If Jenny is nine months old, then she can't do calculus.* The truth value of X $\rightarrow$ Y is defined to be TRUE if Y is TRUE or X is FALSE.

$X \equiv Y$ is TRUE if both X and Y are TRUE, or both X and Y are FALSE; $X \equiv Y$ is FALSE if X and Y have different truth values.

The following table, a compressed *truth table*, summarizes these definitions.

X	Y	X∧Y	X∨Y	X→Y	¬X	X≡Y
T	T	T	T	T	F	T
T	F	F	T	F	F	F
F	T	F	T	T	T	F
F	F	F	F	T	T	T

From syntactic combinations of variables and connectives, we can build sentences of propositional logic, just like the expressions of mathematics. Parentheses are used here just as in ordinary algebra. Typical sentences are:

(1) $(X \rightarrow (Y \land Z)) \equiv ((X \rightarrow Y) \land (X \rightarrow Z))$

(2) $\neg(X \lor Y) \equiv \neg(\neg Y \land \neg X)$

(3) $(X \land Y) \lor (\neg Y \land Z)$

Sentence 1 is a *tautology;* it states, "Saying X implies Y and Z is the same as saying that X implies Y and X implies Z." This is a tautology because it is true no matter what propositions are substituted for the *sentential constants X, Y,* and *Z.* Sentence 2 is a *fallacy* or contradiction. No matter what assignment of values is used, the sentence is always false. (It states, "Saying X or Y is false is the same as saying that 'X is false and Y is false' is false.") Sentence 3 is neither a tautology nor a fallacy. Its truth value depends on what propositions are substituted for X, Y, and Z.

In the propositional calculus, we also encounter the first *rules of inference.* An inference rule allows the deduction of a new sentence from previously given sentences. The power of logic lies in the fact that the new sentence is assured to be true if the original sentences were true. The best known inference rule is *modus ponens.* It states that if we know that two sentences of the form X and $X \rightarrow Y$ are true, then we can *infer* that the sentence Y is true. For example, if we know that the sentence *John is an uncle* is true and we also know that *If John is an uncle, then John is male* is true, then we can conclude that *John is male* is true. More formally, the *modus ponens* rule would be expressed as:

$$(X \land (X \rightarrow Y)) \rightarrow Y \,.$$

Note that if we think of X and $X \to Y$ as two entries in a database, the *modus ponens* rule allows us to replace them with the single statement, Y, thus *eliminating* one occurrence of the connective "$\to$." In what are called *natural deduction* systems of logic, there are typically two rules of inference for each connective, one that *introduces* it into expressions and one that eliminates it. *Modus ponens* is therefore called the "$\to$"-*elimination* rule.

The Predicate Calculus

For the purposes of AI, propositional logic is not very useful. In order to capture adequately in a formalism our knowledge of the world, we need not only to be able to express true or false propositions, but also to be able to speak of objects, to postulate relationships between these objects, and to generalize these relationships over classes of objects. We turn to the *predicate calculus* to accomplish these objectives.

The predicate calculus is an extension of the notions of the propositional calculus. The meanings of the connectives ($\wedge$, $\vee$, $\to$, $\neg$, and $\equiv$) are retained, but the focus of the logic is changed. Instead of looking at sentences that are of interest merely for their truth value, predicate calculus is used to represent statements about specific objects, or *individuals*. Examples of individuals are *you, this sheet of paper, the number 1, the queen of hearts, Socrates,* and *that coke can.*

Predicates. Statements about individuals, both by themselves and in relation to other individuals, are called *predicates*. A predicate is applied to a specific number of arguments and has a value of either TRUE or FALSE when individuals are used as the arguments. An example of a predicate of one argument is the predicate *is-red.* Of the individuals mentioned in the previous paragraph, the predicate *is-red* has the value TRUE when applied to the individuals *the queen of hearts* and *that coke can* and FALSE when the individual *this paper* is used as the argument. Other examples of predicates are *less-than-zero, Greek, mortal,* and *made-of-paper.*

Predicates can have more than one argument. An example of a two-place predicate from mathematics is *is-greater-than,* for example, *is-greater-than* (7, 4). Physical objects could be compared by the two-place predicate *is-lighter-than.* A three-place predicate from geometry might be *Pythagorean,* which takes three line-segments as arguments and is TRUE whenever two are the sides of a right triangle with the third as its hypotenuse. One very important two-place predicate is *equals.*

Each one-place predicate defines what is called a *set* or *sort.* That is, for any one-place predicate P, all individuals X can be sorted into two disjoint groups, with those objects that *satisfy* P (for which $P(X)$ is TRUE) forming one group and those that don't satisfy P in the other. Some sorts include other sorts; for example, all men are animals, and all knaves are playing-cards.

Quantifiers. We shall often have occasion to refer to facts that we know to be true of all or some of the members of a sort. For this, we introduce two new notions, those of *variable* and *quantifier*. A variable is a place holder, one that is to be filled in by some constant, as X has been used in this article. There are two quantifiers, $\forall$, meaning *for all ...*, and $\exists$, meaning *there exists ...* The English-language sentence *All men are mortal* is thus expressed in predicate calculus, using the variable X, as

$$\forall X. \text{Man } (X) \rightarrow \text{Mortal } (X) \text{ ,}$$

which is loosely rendered, "For all individuals X, if X is a man (i.e., Man(X) is true), then X is mortal." The English sentence *There is a playing card that is red and is a knave* becomes the predicate calculus statement

$$\exists X. \text{Playing-card } (X) \wedge \text{Knave } (X) \wedge \text{Is-red } (X) \text{ .}$$

More complicated expressions, or *well-formed formulas* (WFFs), are created with syntactically allowed combinations of the connectives, predicates, constants, variables, and quantifiers.

Inference rules for quantifiers. In a typical natural deduction system, use of the quantifiers implies the introduction of four more *inference rules,* one for the introduction and elimination of each of the two quantifiers. For example, the $\forall$-elimination, or *universal specialization,* rule states that, for any well-formed expression Φ that mentions a variable X, if we have

$$\forall X. \Phi(X) \text{ ,}$$

we can conclude

$$\Phi(A)$$

for any individual A. In other words, if we know, for example,

$$\forall X. \text{Man } (X) \rightarrow \text{Mortal } (X) \text{ ,}$$

we can apply this to the individual Socrates, using the $\forall$-elimination rule, to get:

Man (Socrates) → Mortal (Socrates).

The rules of the propositional calculus, extended by predicates, quantification, and the inference rules for quantifiers, result in the *predicate calculus*.

First-order logic. Predicate calculus, as we've described it, is very general, and often quite clumsy. Two other additions to the logic will make some things easier to say, without really extending the range of what can be expressed. The first of these is the the notion of operators, or *functions*. Functions, like predicates, have a fixed number of arguments; but functions are different from predicates in that they do not just have the values TRUE or FALSE, but they "return" objects related to their arguments. For example, the function *uncle-of* when applied to the individual *Mary* would return the value *John*. Other examples of functions are *absolute-value, plus,* and *left-arm-of.* Each of the arguments of a function can be a variable, a constant, or a function (with its arguments). Functions can, of course, be combined; we can speak of the *father-of (father-of (John))*, who would, of course, be John's paternal grandfather.

The second important addition is that of the predicate *equals.* Two individuals X and Y are equal if and only if they are indistinguishable under all predicates and functions. More formally, $X = Y$ if and only if, for all predicates P, $P(X) \equiv P(Y)$, and also for all functions F, $F(X) = F(Y)$. What we arrive at with these additions is no longer pure predicate calculus; it is a variety of *first-order logic.* (A logic is of first order if it permits quantification over individuals but *not* over predicates and functions. For example, a statement like *All predicates have only one argument* cannot be expressed in a first-order theory.) First-order logic is both *sound* (it is impossible to prove a false statement) and *complete* (any true statement has a proof). The utility of these properties in AI systems will be discussed after we present the *axiomatization* of a sample problem, that is, its formal expression in sentences of first-order logic.

A Sample Axiomatic System

So far, we have sketched the language of logic, its parts of speech, and its grammar. We have not talked about how to express a problem to be solved in this language. Deciding how to express the notions he or she needs is up to the user of logic, just as a programmer must construct programs from the elements presented in the programming language manual. However, a good programming manual ought to present sample programs; we present a sample *axiomatization* of the famous

Tower of Hanoi problem (see Article II.B2). One common version of this puzzle involves three pegs—1, 2, and 3—and three disks of graduated sizes—*A, B,* and *C.* Initially the disks are stacked on peg 1, with *A,* the smallest, on top and *C,* the largest, at the bottom. The problem is to transfer the stack to peg 3, as in Figure C1-1, given that (a) only one disk can be moved at a time, and it must be free, that is, have no other disks on top of it, and (b) no disk may ever be placed on top of a smaller disk.

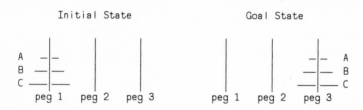

Figure C1-1.   The Tower of Hanoi puzzle.

The expression and solution of problems in logic have several parts. We must first specify the vocabulary of our domain—what the variables, constants, predicates, and functions are. Second, we define *axioms*— expressions that we assert state the necessary relationships between the objects needed to model our domain.

Obvious objects (constants) for this axiomatization are the disks, *A, B,* and *C,* and the pegs, 1, 2, and 3; obvious predicates are the *sorts,* DISK and PEG. DISK (A) is TRUE, since *A* is a disk; PEG (C) is FALSE.

We need also to be able to compare disk size; for that, we have a binary predicate, SMALLER. We define SMALLER (A, B) to be TRUE if and only if disk *A* is smaller than disk *B.* If we have variables *X, Y,* and *Z* denoting disks, we can have our first axiom express the transitivity of SMALLER:

$$\forall\, X\, Y\, Z.\; (\text{SMALLER}\,(X,\, Y)\; \wedge\; \text{SMALLER}\,(Y,\, Z)) \;\rightarrow\; \text{SMALLER}\,(X,\, Z)\,.$$

In other words, *If disk X is smaller than Y, and Y is smaller than Z, then X is smaller than Z.* The given size relationships between the disks are stated by the premise

$$\text{SMALLER}\;(A,\, B)\; \wedge\; \text{SMALLER}\;(B,\, C)\,.$$

Note that by using the preceding two expressions, we can establish, or *prove,* SMALLER $(A,\, C)$.

We need also to be able to talk about the status of our problem solving as we work through a solution and to be able to compare the status after a series of moves. A common strategy to deal with this difficulty is that of introducing a *situational* constant. A situation is a "snapshot" of where things are at any given point. Thus, in the Tower of Hanoi problem, we might have disk C under disk A at some point called, say, situation SIT12.

The vertical relationships of the disks and the pegs are, after all, the primary predicate of this problem. Hence, we need a three-place predicate ON (X, Y, S), which asserts that disk X is on disk (or peg) Y in situation S. The axiomatization of the fact that a disk is free (i.e., has no other disk on it) in a situation S becomes:

$$\forall\ X\ S.\ \text{FREE}\ (X, S)\ \equiv\ \neg\exists\ Y.\ (\text{ON}\ (Y, X, S))\ ,$$

which is read, "For all disks X and situations S, X is free in situation S if and only if there does not exist a disk Y such that Y is ON X in situation S." Notice how specific and concise the formal statement of these relations can be.

To describe the idea that moving a disk, X, onto Y is "legal" in a given situation only if both X and Y are free and Y is bigger, we create the predicate LEGAL:

$$\forall\ X\ Y\ S.\ \text{LEGAL}\ (X, Y, S)$$
$$\equiv\ (\text{FREE}\ (X, S)\ \wedge\ \text{FREE}\ (Y, S)\ \wedge\ \text{DISK}\ (X)\ \wedge\ \text{SMALLER}\ (X, Y)).$$

Now all we lack is a way of generating new situations. The *function* MOVE, defined on two objects and a situation, produces a new situation in which the first object is on top of the second. And what does this new situation, S', look like? Well, X is on Y, and nothing else has changed:

$$\forall\ S\ S'\ X\ Y.$$
$$S' = \text{MOVE}\ (X, Y, S)\ \rightarrow\ (\text{ON}\ (X, Y, S'))$$
$$\wedge\ \forall\ Z\ Z_1.\ ((\neg Z = X\ \wedge\ \neg Z_1 = Y)$$
$$\rightarrow\ (\text{ON}\ (Z, Z_1, S)\ \equiv\ \text{ON}\ (Z, Z_1, S')))$$
$$\wedge\ \forall\ Z.\ (\text{ON}\ (X, Z, S)\ \rightarrow\ \text{FREE}\ (Z, S'))\ .$$

S' will be a SITUATION if that MOVE is LEGAL:

$$\forall\ X\ Y\ S.\ \text{LEGAL}\ (X, Y, S)\ \equiv\ \text{SITUATION}\ (\text{MOVE}\ (X, Y, S))\ .$$

This example gives an idea of how to express in first-order logic the notions involved in the Tower of Hanoi problem. The solution of the problem involves *proving* that the goal state can be reached from the original state. More precisely, one proves a theorem that states that, given the problem's premises expressed like the ones above, such a goal state exists. There are very general methods for automated *theorem proving* in first-order logic, involving programs that manipulate internally stored logical expressions using rules of inference supplied as procedures. The details of this process are discussed in Chapter XII, in Volume III. The AI systems described in the next section all use some kind of theorem prover to make deductions based on facts expressed as logic formulas.

Applications of Logic to Artificial Intelligence

In this section we shall survey various AI systems that use logic to represent knowledge. We shall also mention the different processes they use to make deductions, since this is an equally important aspect of the system, but we will not describe the various alternatives in detail.

QA3 (Green, 1969) was a general-purpose, *question-answering* system that solved simple problems in a number of domains. Deductions were performed by the *resolution method* of inference, with simple general heuristics for control. The system could solve problems in chemistry, robot movement, puzzles (like the Tower of Hanoi), and automatic programming. For example, given the following chemical facts (among others) about ferrous sulfide (FeS)

FeS is a sulfide, it is a dark-gray compound, and it is brittle.

represented as the first-order logic formula

sulfide (FeS) $\wedge$ *compound (FeS)* $\wedge$ *darkgray (FeS)* $\wedge$ *brittle (FeS)* ,

QA3 could then answer questions like "Is it true that no dark-gray thing is a sulfide?"—that is,

$$\neg\ \exists\, X.\ darkgray\ (X)\ \wedge\ sulfide\ (X)\ ?$$

Despite its generality and its success on simple problems, QA3 could not handle really difficult problems. The fault lay in the method of deduction, resolution theorem proving, which became impossibly slow as the number of facts it knew about a particular domain increased beyond just a few. In AI terminology, as the number of facts in the database increases, there is a combinatorial explosion in the number of ways to combine facts to make inferences (see Article II.A), and the resolution method of proving theorems was too indiscriminate in which combinations it tried. Although unrestricted resolution is *complete,* in the sense that it will always return an answer if one exists, it is too *indirect* for nontrivial problems. Even the use of *heuristic* rules to suggest which alternatives might be most profitably followed at various points of the proof did not constrain the search sufficiently to make

QA3's approach feasible for large databases (see, however, Chap. XII, in Vol. III, for current research on more sophisticated theorem provers).

STRIPS, the Stanford Research Institute Problem Solver, was designed to solve the *planning* problems faced by a robot in rearranging objects and navigating in a cluttered environment (Fikes, Hart, and Nilsson, 1972). Since the representation of the world must include a large number of facts dealing with the position of the robot, objects, open spaces, and the like, simpler methods often used for puzzles or games would not suffice. The representation scheme chosen for STRIPS was again the first-order predicate calculus.

A simple problem was:

> Given a robot at point A and boxes at points B, C, and D, gather the boxes together.

The current situation is described as

$$\text{ATR } (A)$$
$$\text{AT (BOX1, } B)$$
$$\text{AT (BOX2, } C)$$
$$\text{AT (BOX3, } D)$$

and the goal as

$$\exists X. \text{ AT (BOX1, } X) \wedge \text{ AT (BOX2, } X) \wedge \text{ AT (BOX3, } X) ,$$

that is, *Get all the boxes together at some place, X.* Problem solving in a robot domain such as this involves two types of processes: (a) deduction in a particular world model, to find out whether a certain fact is true, and (b) searching through a space of world models, to find one in which the given condition is satisfied (e.g., How can we get the three blocks together?).

The former process is usually called *question answering;* the latter, *planning.* STRIPS applied different methods to solve these two kinds of problems. Question answering was done with resolution theorem proving, as in Green's QA3 system; planning was performed with *means-ends analysis,* as in the GPS system of Newell and Simon (1972). This dual approach allowed world models that were more complex and general than in GPS and provided more powerful search heuristics than those found in theorem-proving programs. GPS, STRIPS, and its successor ABSTRIPS are described in detail in Chapter II.

FOL (Filman and Weyhrauch, 1976) is, among other things, a very flexible proof checker for proofs stated in first-order logic. Deduction is done with the *natural deduction* system of Prawitz (1965), which includes the *introduction* and *elimination* rules of inference discussed above. FOL can more properly be viewed as a sophisticated, interactive environment for using logic to study epistemological questions (see Weyhrauch, 1978).

Logic and Representation

First-order logic, as we have described it, demands a clean syntax, clear semantics, and, above all, the notions of *truth* and *inference*. Clarity about what is being expressed and about the consequences of, or possible inferences from, a set of facts is perhaps the most important quality of this formalism.

In a classic paper, McCarthy and Hayes (1969) differentiate two parts of the AI problem. The *epistemological* part was defined as determining "what kinds of facts about the world are available to an observer with given opportunities to observe, how these facts can be represented in the memory of a computer, and what rules permit legitimate conclusions to be drawn from these facts" (McCarthy, 1977). The issue of processing, of using the knowledge once it is represented (what McCarthy and Hayes called the *heuristic* part of the AI problem), was separated from the representation issue. Given this distinction, there are several reasons that logic can be a useful means for exploring the epistemological problems.

1. Logic often seems a *natural* way to express certain notions. As McCarthy (1977) and Filman (1979) pointed out, the expression of a problem in logic often corresponds to our intuitive understanding of the domain. Green (1969) also indicated that a logical representation was easier to reformulate; thus, experimentation is made easier.

2. Logic is *precise*. There are standard methods of determining the *meaning* of an expression in a logical formalism. Hayes (1977a) presents a complete discussion on this issue and argues for the advantages of logic over other representation systems on these grounds.

3. Logic is *flexible*. Since logic makes no commitment to the kinds of processes that will actually make deductions, a particular fact can be represented in a single way, without having to consider its possible use.

4. Logic is *modular*. Logical assertions can be entered in a database independently of each other; knowledge can grow incrementally, as new facts are discovered and added. In other representational systems, the addition of a new fact might sometimes adversely affect the kinds of deductions that can be made.

The major disadvantage of logic stems also from the separation of *representation* and *processing*. The difficulty with most current AI systems lies in the heuristic part of the system, that is, in determining how to use the facts stored in the system's data structures, not in deciding how to store them (e.g., QA3's failure with large databases). Thus, separating the two aspects and concentrating on epistemological questions merely postpone addressing the problem. Work on *procedural representation* schemes, such as PLANNER (Article III.C2), and on *frame-based* schemes (Article III.C7) are attempts to incorporate the heuristic aspect into the epistemological; systems like GOLUX (Hayes, 1977b) and FOL (Weyhrauch, 1978) are attempts to formalize control of processing while retaining the logical precision.

References

Nilsson (1971) gives a brief, elementary introduction to the use of logic in AI in Chapters 6 and 7, including an introduction to automated theorem proving techniques. More thorough discussions can be found in any of the introductory logic texts, like Manna (1973) and Suppes (1957).

C2.   Procedural Representations

The distinction between *declarative* and *procedural* representations of knowledge has had a key role in the historical development of AI ideas. Declarative representations stress the static aspects of knowledge—facts about objects, events, and their relations and about states of the world. The proponents of procedural representations pointed out that AI systems had to *know how to use* their knowledge—how to find relevant facts, make inferences, and so on—and that this aspect of knowledgeable behavior was best captured in procedures. (Hayes, 1977a, discusses the different kinds of knowledge amenable to different kinds of representation schemes.)

As a simple example of what it means to represent knowledge procedurally, consider what a typical alphabetization program could be said to know about its task. The knowledge that "A comes before B in the alphabet" is represented *implicitly* in the body of the alphabetization procedure, which really does an integer comparison of the computer codes for A and B. All computer programs incorporate procedural knowledge of this sort. What the proceduralists pointed out was that, while the knowledge about alphabetical order was implicit in such a system, the knowledge about *how to alphabetize* was represented *explicitly* in the alphabetization procedure. On the other hand, in a declarative system, where knowledge about alphabetical order might be explicitly represented as facts like *A comes before B, B comes before C,* and so on, the knowledge about how to alphabetize is implicit in the programs that manipulate those facts (theorem prover, production system interpreter, etc.).

Before the advent of proceduralism, workers in AI focused on determining what kinds of knowledge could be represented adequately in formalisms like *logic* and *semantic nets*. Questions about how the data structures involved could be manipulated effectively as the databases grew larger were considered a secondary concern. The proceduralists took exception to this view. They argued that the useful knowledge of a domain is intrinsically bound up with the specialized knowledge about how it is to be used (Hewitt, 1975). Through an evolving series of new systems and *AI programming languages*, the proponents of procedural knowledge representation brought concerns about the relevance and utility of knowledge into the center of knowledge-representation research.

Early Procedural Systems

The first AI systems that might be called procedural were not extreme in their stance: Their factual knowledge was stored in a database similar to those used by the then-popular theorem-proving programs, but their *reasoning* was structured in a new way. (See Winograd, 1972, for a discussion of the development of proceduralist ideas.)

Such an approach was used in Raphael's (1968) early *question answering* system, SIR (see Article IV.F1). SIR could answer questions about simple logical relationships, such as *Is a finger part of a person?* Its knowledge was stored in two forms: Facts about the parts of things were represented as properties linked to the nodes representing the objects, and the inference-making mechanism was represented as specialized procedures. Thus, to answer the question about a finger, SIR would use two stored facts, that a finger is part of a hand and that a hand is part of a person, and one procedure, a specialized induction procedure that traced PART-OF links between nodes. The inference routines were specialized in that they had to be custom-built for each new type of inference and link in the database.

However, the most characteristically procedural quality of the SIR system was that the *meaning* of an input sentence or question, the final result of SIR's *parsing* stage, was a procedure. When executed, this routine performed the desired action—either adding to the database or printing information found therein. In other words, when the sentence *A finger is part of a hand* was entered into the system, SIR produced and immediately executed a procedure that added a PART-OF link to the database between the FINGER node and the HAND node.

Woods (1968) implemented the most sophisticated of the early procedural systems. His program handled questions about airline flight schedules. The questions were translated into functions that, when run over the system's database, produced the correct response. For example, the question *What American Airlines flights go from Boston to Chicago?* would be translated into the query language as:

```
(FOR-EVERY X1/FLIGHT;
        EQUAL (OWNER(X1), AMERICAN-AIRLINES)
                AND CONNECT (X1, BOSTON, CHICAGO);
        LIST(X1))
```

This expression of the question is a function (in the LISP programming language) built from other specialized-knowledge procedures like FOR-EVERY and CONNECT. When evaluated, this function would retrieve a list of all of the flights in the database, then find out which of those were owned by American Airlines and went from Boston to Chicago, and finally print the resulting list.

Representing How to Use Knowledge

The great advantage of the early procedural systems was that they were *directed* in their problem-solving activity in the sense that they did not use irrelevant knowledge or follow unnatural lines of reasoning. These inefficient behaviors, characteristic of the early declarative systems that blindly tried to apply anything they knew to the problem at hand until something worked, were eliminated by the specialized inference procedures. But this solution created problems of its own. In general, as procedural systems become very complex, they become very hard for people to understand and modify.

Thus, in the late 1960s there was an attempt to merge the two types of representation, seeking the ease of modification of the declarative systems (especially *logic*) and the directedness of the earlier procedural systems. The essence of this approach was to represent declarative knowledge of the kind typically encoded in logic expressions along with *instructions for its use*. The thrust of the later work in procedural representations was to try to find better ways of expressing this *control* information.

Information about how to use a piece of knowledge might concern various aspects of processing. One form of control is to indicate the *direction* in which an implication can be used. For example, to encode the idea that to prove that something flies you might want to show that it is a bird, from which the desired conclusion follows, one might write something like this:

```
(IF-NEEDED    FLIES (X)
 TRY-SHOWING  BIRD (X))
```

Thus, if we are trying to prove that Clyde can fly, this *heuristic* tells us to try first to prove that he is a bird. Note that the knowledge that *All birds can fly,* as represented here, is not usable in the other direction—if we learn that Fred is a bird, we will not be able immediately to conclude anything about Fred being able to fly.

Another use of procedural knowledge is in trying to specify what knowledge will be relevant to achieving a specific goal. For example, if we expect that we might want to prove that something is a bird, and that two facts called, say, THEOREM1 and THEOREM2 might be useful in proving birdhood, we could write:

```
(GOAL BIRD (TRY-USING THEOREM1 THEOREM2)) .
```

In essence, what has been done here is to embellish the straight-forward deduction provided by *resolution* or *natural deduction* theorem proving in a logic-based representation. The inferences here are *controlled;* we have told the system how and when it can use the knowledge that it has. Three major methods of specifying control information have been tried:

1. Specify control by the way in which one states the facts; this is the approach of the examples above and of PLANNER, discussed below.

2. Encode the representation language at a lower level, so that the user has access to the set of mechanisms for specifying the reasoning process. This is the approach taken in the CONNIVER programming language (see Sussman and McDermott, 1972, and Article VI.C2, in Vol. II).

3. Define an additional language, for expressing control information, that works together with the representation language. This idea was the foundation for the GOLUX project (Hayes, 1973) and for Kowalski's (1974) predicate calculus programming.

Of the three approaches, the work on PLANNER was the most widely used and was seminal for later work on procedural representations.

PLANNER: Guided Inference and Extended Logic

PLANNER (Hewitt, 1972) was an *AI programming language* designed to implement both representational and control information. The features of the language are described in Article VI.C2 (in Vol. II), and we discuss here only those aspects relevant to knowledge representation. The specific concern of the PLANNER research was not to facilitate the class of inferences that were logically *possible,* as would be the focus in *theorem proving* work, but to expedite the inferences that were *expected* to be actually needed. This approach created its own problems; there are some quite straightforward deductions that PLANNER is unable to make, as will be discussed later.

The relevant features of the PLANNER language include being able to specify whether theorems should be used in a forward or backward direction and to recommend the use of specific theorems in given situations, as described in the preceding section. In fact, the ability to recommend pieces of knowledge was somewhat more general than indicated previously. Besides recommending possibly useful theorems by name, general *classes* of theorems could be suggested by the use of *filters*. For example, the following PLANNER expression states that using theorems about zoology might be a useful way to prove that something is a bird:

(GOAL BIRD (FILTER ABOUT-ZOOLOGY)) .

The implementation of these *inference guiding* control features did not change the nature of the possible inferences themselves. However, other procedural knowledge implemented in PLANNER did allow inferences beyond those found in classical logical systems, particularly the various forms of *default reasoning* (Reiter, 1978). One form of default, as implemented in PLANNER, is the THNOT primitive. For example, the expression

(THNOT OSTRICH (X) ASSUME FLIES (X))

refers to all birds, *X*, and means that unless it can be shown that *X* is an ostrich, assume that it can fly.

The primitive THNOT can function correctly only if certain aspects of our knowledge are *complete*. In the above example, we assume that, if *X* were an ostrich, we would either know that fact or have some way to deduce it. If the knowledge base is not complete in this sense, the system might make incorrect inferences. This is not necessarily a serious problem; there might be times that we want the system to "jump to conclusions." This will be discussed later.

THNOT and similar functions take us beyond the realm of ordinary logic, since they violate the property of *monotonicity*. Monotonicity states that if a conclusion is derivable from a certain collection of facts, the same conclusion remains derivable if more facts are added. Thus, procedural and declarative systems implement *different logics* (Reiter, 1978). As Hewitt (1972) points out, the logic of PLANNER is a combination of classical logic, intuitionistic logic, and recursive function theory. Winograd (1980a) outlines a taxonomy of *extended inference modes* that are outside the provision of ordinary logic.

PLANNER thus serves as a programming language in which knowledge about both the problem to be solved and the methods of solution can be stated in a modular, flexible style reminiscent of logic. The intent is that the user be able to state as much or as little *domain-specific knowledge* as required. The most extensive use of PLANNER was in Winograd's (1972) SHRDLU system (see Article IV.F4). A number of AI programming language projects followed PLANNER, including CONNIVER (Sussman and McDermott, 1972), QA4 (Rulifson, Derkson, and Waldinger, 1972), POPLER (Davies, 1972), and QLISP (Reboh et al., 1976). For further discussion of many of these languages, see Chapter VI, in Volume II.

Advantages and Disadvantages of Procedural Representations

Chief among the advantages of using procedures to represent knowledge is their facility for representing *heuristic* knowledge, especially domain-specific information that might permit more *directed* deduction processes. This includes information about whether a theorem should be used in a backward or a forward direction, about what knowledge should be applied in a given situation, and about which subgoals should be tried first. The most important result of this ability to encode heuristic knowledge is the *directedness* realized by such systems, which, of course, is crucial in large systems that would get bogged down if the problem solving were not efficient. Efficiency in this sense was the motivation behind most of the work on procedural representations.

A related advantage is the ability to perform *extended-logical* inferences, like the default reasoning described in the preceding section. There are attempts to achieve this kind of informal or *plausible reasoning* in more formal logical systems (McCarthy, 1977). Winograd (1980a) discusses this issue further, arguing that these types of inferences are necessary in a system that attempts to model human reasoning.

Procedural representation may also be at an advantage with regard to what is called *modeling,* particularly in relation to the *frame problem* as identified by McCarthy and Hayes (1969). This difficulty, common to all representation formalisms, is their inability to model *side effects* of actions taken in the world by making corresponding modifications in the database representing the state of the world. (Note that the *frame problem* has nothing to do with the *frame* as a representation formalism, discussed in Article III.C7.) For example, suppose we are reasoning about a robot, with a key, moving from ROOM-1 to ROOM-2 to find and unlock a safe. The initial situation, S_0, might be represented in the database with assertions like:

```
1. IN (ROOM-1, ROBOT, S0)
2. IN (ROOM-1, KEY, S0)
3. IN (ROOM-2, SAFE, S0)
```

After the robot has moved from ROOM-1 to ROOM-2, the system must somehow know that assertions 1 and 2 are now false, while assertion 3 is still true.

In a large system with many facts, keeping track of these changes—especially the side effects of actions, like the moving of the key to the safe—can be very tricky. The propagation of those facts that have not changed is sometimes much easier in a procedural system: The procedure that *performs* the actions can update the database immediately. (See also the discussion of a similar way of dealing with the the frame problem in a *direct representation,* Article III.C5.)

Two problems of the procedural approach in relation to more formal representational schemes concern *completeness* and *consistency*. Many procedural systems are not complete, meaning that there are cases in which a system like PLANNER could know all the facts required to reach a certain conclusion but not be powerful enough to make the required deductions (Moore, 1975). Of course, completeness is not necessarily always desirable. There are cases when we might want the system to work quickly and not spend a long time finding a particular answer or concluding that it cannot find the answer.

A deductive system is consistent if all its deductions are correct— that is, if the conclusion necessarily follows from the premises. Again, most theorem-proving systems have this property, but procedural systems often do not. For example, the use of default reasoning can introduce inconsistency in the presence of incomplete knowledge. Thus, if we use the fact that *Fred is a bird* to conclude that he can fly and later discover that he is an ostrich, we will have inconsistency. Hewitt (1975) refers to this as the "Garbage In—Garbage Out" principle.

Like completeness, consistency is not necessarily always desirable. McDermott and Doyle (in press) argue that much of our reasoning is done by revising our beliefs in the presence of new information. Similarly, Hewitt points out that most of our knowledge is not absolute; we regularly accept caveats and exceptions. If we control the reasoning sufficiently tightly in the presence of inconsistency, the Garbage In— Garbage Out effect can be avoided.

Another drawback of procedural representations in their current form is that the control information sometimes gets in the way. For example, if we want to prove that both statements A and B are true, PLANNER allows us to express this as a goal: (THAND A B). But this expression really means, "Prove A and then prove B"—there is no way to state the goal without including some control information.

Another feature that is sacrificed in the procedural approach is the *modularity* of knowledge in the database that was so advantageous in logic and other declarative schemes. In a procedural representation, the interaction between various facts is unavoidable because of the heuristic information itself. Therefore, a change in or addition to the knowledge base might have more far-reaching effects than a similar change in a base of logic assertions. In essence, this is the price that is paid for the greater degree of control permitted using procedures.

Two specific criticisms have been directed at PLANNER's method of specifying control. First, it is too *local:* PLANNER is unable to consider the overall shape of the problem's solution and therefore can make only local problem-solving decisions. Second, PLANNER cannot reason about its control information; ideally, it should be able to make decisions on the basis of facts about control, as it can now make decisions on the basis of facts about the world.

Conclusions

The consensus among AI researchers is that there should be ways to embed control in a deductive system, but that the methods tried thus far have many flaws in them (see, e.g., Moore, 1975, Chap. 5). Current research, especially on frame systems (Article III.C7), emphasizes a somewhat different approach to the problem of organizing knowledge with special regard to its expected use, called *procedural attachment*.

References

The most readable discussion of the issues involved in procedural knowledge representation is Winograd (1975). Hayes (1977a) presents these issues from the perspective of a declarativist. The original statement of what procedural representation was all about is Hewitt (1972) and, more readably, Winograd (1972). Winograd (in press) offers a recent study of knowledge representation in which procedural ideas are fully discussed.

C3. Semantic Networks

Many of the recent systems developed in AI research use a class of knowledge representation formalisms that are called *semantic networks*. These representation formalisms are grouped together because they share a common notation, consisting of *nodes* (drawn as dots, circles, or boxes in illustrations) and *arcs* (or *links;* drawn as arrows) connecting the nodes. Both the nodes and the arcs can have labels. Nodes usually represent *objects, concepts,* or *situations* in the domain, and the arcs represent the *relations* between them.

The superficial similarity of this notation is all that some semantic network systems have in common. For example, researchers in psychology, such as Quillian (1968), Norman and Rumelhart (1975), and Anderson and Bower (1973), have developed semantic network systems primarily as psychological models of human memory. Researchers in computer science have been more concerned with developing functional representations for the variety of types of knowledge needed in their systems. Because of these diverse goals, there is no simple set of unifying principles to apply across all semantic network systems. This article, however, will attempt to characterize some of the most common network schemes. We will present a description of how simple concepts are represented in semantic networks and then review some AI systems that use semantic networks. Finally, some more difficult problems in semantic net representation will be mentioned and some of the proposed solutions reviewed.

A Basic Description of the Representation Scheme

Suppose we wish to represent a simple fact like *All robins are birds* in a semantic network. We might do this by creating two nodes to designaté *robins* and *birds* with a link connecting them, as follows:

If Clyde were a particular individual who we wished to assert is a robin, we could add a node for Clyde to the network as follows:

Notice that in this example we have not only represented the two facts we initially intended to represent, but we have also made it very easy to deduce a third fact, namely, that Clyde is a bird, simply by following the ISA links: *Clyde is a robin. Robins are birds. So, Clyde is a bird.* The ease with which it is possible to make deductions about *inheritance hierarchies* such as this is one reason for the popularity of semantic networks as a knowledge representation. In a domain where much of the reasoning is based on a very complicated *taxonomy*, a semantic network is a natural representation scheme (see, e.g., the PROSPECTOR system, Article F2).

Besides their taxonomic classification, one usually needs to represent knowledge about the properties of objects. For example, one might wish to express the fact *Birds have wings* in the network. We could do this as follows:

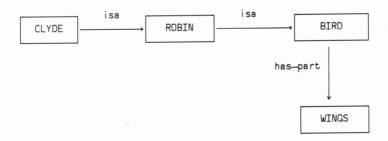

As in the previous example, our choice of representation has made it very easy to write a procedure to make the deductions that robins have wings and that Clyde has wings. All that is necessary is to trace up the ISA-hierarchy, assuming any facts asserted about higher nodes on the hierarchy can be considered assertions about the lower ones also, without having to represent these assertions explicitly in the net. In AI terminology, this kind of reasoning is called *property inheritance,* and the ISA link is often referred to as a *property inheritance link.*

Suppose we wish to represent the fact *Clyde owns a nest.* Our first impulse may be to encode this fact using an ownership link to a node representing Clyde's nest:

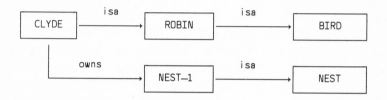

In the above example, NEST-1 is the nest that Clyde owns. It is an *instance* of NEST; that is, the NEST node represents a general class of objects of which the NEST-1 node represents an example. The above representation may be adequate for some purposes, but it has short-comings. Suppose one wanted to encode the additional information that Clyde owned NEST-1 from spring until fall. This is impossible to do in the current network because the ownership relation is encoded as a link, and links, by their nature, can encode only binary relations. What is needed is the semantic-net equivalent of a four-place *predicate* in logic, which would note the start-time and end-time of the ownership relation, as well as the owner and the object owned.

A solution to this problem was proposed by Simmons and Slocum (1972) and later adopted in many semantic net systems: to allow nodes to represent situations and actions, as well as objects and sets of objects. Each situation node can have a set of outgoing arcs, called a *case frame,* which specifies the various arguments to the situation predicate. For example, using a situation node with case arcs, the network representation of the fact *Clyde owned a nest from spring until fall* becomes

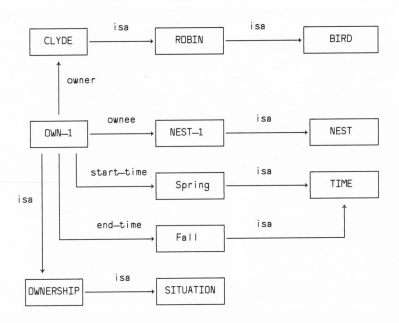

The node NEST-1 is created to represent Clyde's nest, which, of course, ISA nest, as shown. The OWN-1 node represents a particular instance of OWNERSHIP, namely, Clyde owning his nest. And like all nodes that are instances of OWNERSHIP, OWN-1 *inherits* case arcs to OWNER, OWNEE, START-TIME, and END-TIME nodes. Many semantic network systems use sets of case arcs motivated by linguistic considerations, for example, general case structures for agent and object (see Article IV.C4). One important use of the case-frame structure for nodes is the possibility of allowing instance nodes, like OWN-1, to inherit *expectations* about, and even *default values* for, certain of their attributes (see Article III.C7 for a discussion of inheritance in *frame* systems).

One more thing to note about the representation scheme described above is that it lends itself to the expression of states and actions in terms of a small number of primitive concepts. For example, FLYING might be considered a type of MOTION and could be represented by a FLYING node having an ISA arc to the MOTION node and case arcs that describe how flying is a *specialization* of moving. The use of a small number of *semantic primitives* as the basis of a system's knowledge representation has both advantages and disadvantages, and it is discussed fully in Article III.C6.

There are still some serious problems with our semantic net representation as it has been developed so far. Suppose one wished to make the assertion *The robin is an endangered species.* The simplest thing to do would be to create the following representation for this fact in our net structure:

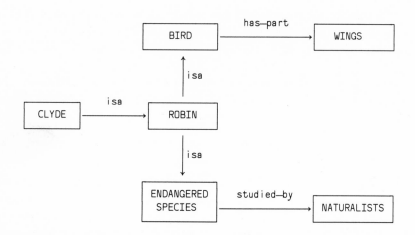

This structure indicates that ROBINS are an ENDANGERED SPECIES, and that ENDANGERED SPECIES are studied by NATURALISTS. The problem that is illustrated in this simple example involves inheritance. Since the reasoning procedures, as they have been defined, treat the ISA link as a property inheritance link, the instance node CLYDE inherits all the properties of ENDANGERED SPECIES, just as it inherits the property of *having wings* from the BIRD node. In this way, one might conclude from the fact that *Naturalists study endangered species* that *Naturalists study Clyde*, which may or may not be true.

The source of the problem is that that there is as yet no distinction in our network formalism between an *individual* and a *class* of individuals. Furthermore, some things said about a class are meant to be true of all members of a class, like *Robins are birds,* while some refer to the class itself, for example, *Robins are an endangered species.* Recent semantic net research has explored various ways of making the *semantics* of network structures more precise and of specifying different property inheritance strategies (Woods, 1975b; Hendrix, 1976; Brachman, 1979; Stefik, 1980).

A Brief History of Semantic-network-based Systems

The node-and-link formalism of semantic networks has found use in many AI systems in different application domains. It is impossible to mention every one of these systems here, but we will try to note the highlights and point out where in the AI literature these and related systems are described more fully.

Ross Quillian (1968) designed two early semantic-network-based systems that were intended primarily as psychological models of associative memory. Quillian was the first to make use of the node-and-link formalism, but his networks were simpler than those in the bird's nest example above: They consisted of a number of groups of nodes, called *planes*. Each plane encoded knowledge about a particular concept through interconnections of nodes representing other concepts in the system. These interconnecting links allowed a few simple ways of combining concepts: conjunction, disjunction, and the modification of one concept by another.

Quillian wrote procedures that manipulated the network to make inferences about a pair of concepts by finding connections between the nodes that represented them. The method, called *spreading activation*, started from the two nodes and "activated" all the nodes connected to each of them. Then all of the nodes connected to each of those were in turn activated, forming an expanding sphere of activation around each of the original concepts. When some concept was activated simultaneously from two directions, a connection had been found. The program then tried to describe the connecting route through the net in a stylized version of English (see Article IV.E for an example).

Quillian's second system, called the Teachable Language Comprehender (1969), attempted to solve some of the problems with the original system, like the lack of *directedness* in the net search, and was a bit more complex. Other semantic-network-based computer programs that were designed as psychological models of memory, including the HAM program (Anderson and Bower, 1973) and the Active Structural Network system (Norman and Rumelhart, 1975), are described fully in Chapter XI, in Volume III.

Bertram Raphael's (1968) early AI system, SIR, mentioned earlier in Article III.C2, was one of the first programs to use semantic network techniques. SIR could *answer questions* requiring a variety of simple reasoning tasks, such as *A finger is part of a hand; a hand is part of an arm; therefore a finger is part of an arm.* Although he did not claim to use a node-and-link formalism, Raphael's use of binary predicates, such as PART-OF (FINGER, HAND), and reasoning procedures was much like the early semantic net systems and faced many of the same problems that these systems faced. (SIR is described in Article IV.F1 on early natural language understanding systems.)

In the early 1970s, Robert Simmons designed a semantic network representation for use in his research on natural language understanding. As mentioned in the previous section, Simmons's system used a linguistically motivated *case frame* approach for choosing arc types. The system could *parse* sentences (with an ATN grammar), translate their meaning into network structures, and finally generate answers to questions using the semantic network (Simmons and Slocum, 1972; Simmons, 1973).

Around the same time, Jaime Carbonell used a semantic network as the basis of his tutoring program, SCHOLAR, which answered questions about the geographical information stored in the net. In a *mixed initiative* dialogue on the subject of South American geography, SCHOLAR answered questions posed by the student and also generated appropriate questions on its own initiative, giving timely hints when necessary (Carbonell, 1970; Carbonell and Collins, 1974; SCHOLAR is described fully in Article IX.C1, in Vol. II).

Two of the AI *speech understanding* systems, the systems developed at Bolt, Beranek and Newman (Woods et al., 1976) and SRI International (Walker, 1976), used semantic networks to represent knowledge about their subject domains (see Chap. V). In connection with the SRI speech understanding research, Hendrix (1976) developed the idea of *network partitioning*, which provides a mechanism for dealing with a variety of difficult representation problems including representing logical connectives, quantification, and hypothetical worlds.

Recent network research involves structuring of the nodes and links in the network and is related to the work on *frame* systems described in Article III.C7. For example, Myopolous and his associates (1975) designed a system for grouping related parts of a semantic network into units called *scenarios*. The network was used by the TORUS system, a program to provide natural-language access to a database management system. Hayes (1977b) also designed a system that incorporates higher level structures similar to scenarios, which he calls *depictions*.

Reasoning with Semantic Networks

In semantic network representations, there is no *formal semantics,* no agreed-upon notion of what a given representational structure means, as there is in *logic,* for instance. Meaning is assigned to a network structure only by the nature of the procedures that manipulate the network. A wide variety of network-based systems have been designed that use totally different procedures for making inferences.

One example of a network reasoning procedure was Quillian's *spreading activation* model of human memory, described above. However, the reasoning mechanism used by most semantic network systems is based on *matching* network structures: A *network fragment* is constructed, representing a sought-for object or a query, and then matched against the network database to see if such an object exists. Variable nodes in the fragment are *bound* in the matching process to the values they must have to make the match perfect. For example, suppose we use the following network as a database

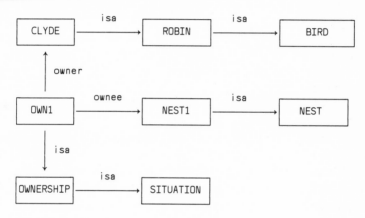

and suppose we wish to answer the question *What does Clyde own?* We might construct the fragment

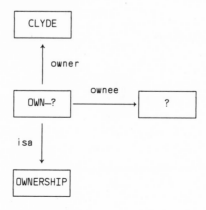

which represents an *instance* of OWNERSHIP in which Clyde is the owner. This fragment is then matched against the network database looking for an OWN node that has an OWNER link to CLYDE. When it is found, the node that the OWNEE link points to is bound in the partial match and is the answer to the question. Had no match been found, the answer would have been, of course, *Clyde doesn't own anything.*

The matcher can make *inferences* during the matching process to create network structure that is not explicitly present in the network. For example, suppose we wish to answer the question *Is there a bird who owns a nest?* We could translate that question into the following network fragment:

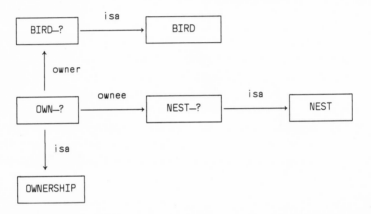

Here, the BIRD-?, NEST-?, and OWN-? nodes represent the yet to be determined bird-owning-nest relation. Notice that the query network fragment does not match the knowledge database exactly. The deduction procedure would have to construct an ISA link from CLYDE to BIRD to make the match possible. The matcher would bind BIRD-? to the node CLYDE, OWN-? to OWN-1, and NEST-? to NEST-1, and the answer to the question would be *Yes, Clyde,* since the CLYDE node was bound to BIRD-? in order to match the query fragment to the database.

A good example of a network deduction system constructed around this matching paradigm is the SNIFFER system (Fikes and Hendrix, 1977). SNIFFER has the general power of a *theorem prover* for making deductions from the network database. It is also capable of taking advantage of *heuristic* knowledge embedded in procedures called *selector functions,* which provide advice about which network elements should be matched first and about how to match the selected element. These heuristics allow the system to proceed in a *direct* and sensible way when the amount of information in the database becomes very large and blind retrieval strategies, like spreading activation or systematic matching, are useless because they take too long to retrieve an answer.

Status of Network Representations

Semantic networks are a very popular representation scheme in AI. Node-and-link structure captures something essential about symbols and pointers in symbolic computation and about association in the psychology of memory. Most current work on the representation of knowledge involves elaboration of the semantic net idea, in particular, work on aggregate network structures called *frames*. But like most of the efforts to deal with knowledge in AI, the simple idea of having nodes that stand for things in the world and links that represent the relations between things can't be pushed too far. Besides computational problems that arise when network databases become large enough to represent nontrivial amounts of knowledge, there are many, more subtle problems involving the semantics of the network structures. What does a node really mean? Is there a unique way to represent an idea? How is the passage of time to be represented? How does one represent things that are not facts about the world but rather ideas or beliefs? What are the rules about inheritance of properties in networks? Current research on network-representation schemes attempts to deal with these and similar concerns.

References

Introductory discussions of semantic networks can be found in Simmons (1973), Anderson and Bower (1973), Norman and Rumelhart (1975), and Winograd (in press). Current semantic network research is surveyed in the articles in Findler (1979).

C4. Production Systems

Production systems were first proposed by Post (1943) but have since undergone such theoretical and application-oriented development in AI that the current systems have little in common with Post's formulation. In fact, just as the term *semantic net* refers to several different knowledge-representation schemes based on the node-and-link formalism, so the term *production system* is used to describe several different systems based on one very general, underlying idea—the notion of condition-action pairs, called *production rules*, or just *productions*. In this article we illustrate the basics of a production system (PS) with an elementary example and discuss some of the design decisions that give rise to the variety of production system architectures. We also describe some of the important AI systems that have been built with PS architectures and discuss current issues in PS design.

A Sample Production System

A production system consists of three parts: (a) a *rule base* composed of a set of production rules; (b) a special, buffer-like data structure, which we shall call the *context;* and (c) an *interpreter*, which controls the system's activity. After briefly describing each of these components, we'll go step by step through an example to show how a production system works.

A *production rule* is a statement cast in the form "If this *condition* holds, then this *action* is appropriate." For example, the rule

Always punt on fourth down with long yardage required

might be encoded as the production rule

IF *it is fourth down* AND *long yardage is required* THEN *punt.*

The IF part of the productions, called the *condition part* or *left-hand side*, states the conditions that must be present for the production to be applicable, and the THEN part, called the *action part* or *right-hand side,* is the appropriate action to take. During the execution of the production system, a production whose condition part is satisfied can *fire,* that is, can have its action part executed by the interpreter. Although there are only a few productions in the rule base of our example below, typical AI systems nowadays contain hundreds of productions in their rule bases.

The *context,* which is sometimes called the *data* or *short-term memory buffer,* is the focus of attention of the production rules. The left-hand side of each production in the rule base represents a condition that must be present *in the context data structure* before the production can fire. For example, the sample production above requires that the facts *it's fourth down* and *long yardage required* be in the context. The actions of the production rules can change the *context,* so that other rules will have their condition parts satisfied. The context data structure may be a simple list, a very large array, or, more typically, a medium-sized buffer with some internal structure of its own.

Finally there is the *interpreter,* which, like the interpreters in all computer systems, is a program whose job is to decide what to do next. In a production system, the interpreter has the special task of deciding which production to fire next.

Consider a production system that might be used to identify food items, given a few hints, by a process similar to that used in the game of Twenty Questions. The context data structure for this system is a simple list of symbols, called a context list (CL). "On-CL *X*" means that the symbol *X* is currently in the context. The system has the following rule base and interpreter.

PRODUCTIONS:

P1. IF On-CL *green* THEN Put-On-CL *produce*

P2. IF On-CL *packed in small container* THEN Put-On-CL *delicacy*

P3. IF On-CL *refrigerated* OR On-CL *produce* THEN Put-On-CL *perishable*

P4. IF On-CL *weighs 15 lbs* AND On-CL *inexpensive* AND NOT On-CL *perishable* THEN Put-On-CL *staple*

P5. IF On-CL *perishable* AND On-CL *weighs 15 lbs* THEN Put-On-CL *turkey*

P6. IF On-CL *weighs 15 lbs* AND On-CL *produce* THEN Put-On-CL *watermelon*

INTERPRETER:

1. Find all productions whose condition parts are TRUE and make them applicable.

2. If more than one production is applicable, then deactivate any production whose action adds a duplicate symbol to the CL.

3. Execute the action of the lowest numbered (or only) applicable production. If no productions are applicable, then quit.

4. Reset the applicability of all productions and return to S1.

The condition part of each of the productions corresponds to a question one might ask in the Twenty Questions game: Is the item green? does it come in a small container? and so on. The action parts of the productions represent additions to our knowledge about the unknown item.

Production systems operate in cycles. In each cycle, the productions are examined in a manner specified by the interpreter to see which are appropriate and could fire. Then, if more than one is found appropriate, a single production is selected from among them. Finally, the production is fired. These three *phases* of each cycle are called *matching, conflict resolution,* and *action.*

Suppose the original knowledge about the mystery food item is that it is green and weighs 15 pounds; in other words, the value of the context list before the beginning of the first cycle is:

$$CL = (green,\ weighs\ 15\ lbs)\ .$$

The cycle starts with step 1 of the interpreter algorithm: finding all the applicable productions by testing their condition parts. Since only P1 is applicable, step 2 is not necessary, and step 3 causes the action part of P1 to be executed. This adds the symbol *produce* to the context list, representing a new fact about the unknown food item:

$$CL = (produce,\ green,\ weighs\ 15\ lbs)\ .$$

Step 4 ends the first cycle and brings us back to step 1—finding all the applicable productions. In the second cycle, productions P1, P3, and P6 are all applicable. So in step 2 we must check if any of these three adds a duplicate symbol to the context list. P1 adds *produce,* which is a duplication, so it is eliminated. Then in step 3 we select P3 to be executed (because it has a lower number than P6), resulting in:

$$CL = (perishable,\ produce,\ green,\ weighs\ 15\ lbs)\ .$$

In the third cycle, we find that productions P1, P3, P5, and P6 are applicable. Checking, in step 2, for redundant entries, we eliminate P1 and P3 from consideration. In step 3, we decide to execute P5, once again because it comes before P6. This results in the context list

$$CL = (turkey,\ perishable,\ produce,\ green,\ weighs\ 15\ lbs)\ .$$

Clearly this last step was a mistake—we wouldn't want to ascribe to something that we know is *green produce* the attribute *turkey.*

In its next two cycles of execution, our sample production system will finish. In cycle 4, the symbol *watermelon* is added to the context list, and in the last cycle, finding no nonredundant productions to fire, the interpreter finally quits, leaving the context list

CL = *(watermelon, turkey, perishable, produce, green, weighs 15 lbs)* .
If we define the system's answer to be the first symbol on the context
list, we can ignore the suspicious attribute *turkey.* The reader can
probably think of more satisfying ways to "fix up" the rule base, or the
interpreter, such as changing the productions (particularly adding conditions to the condition part of P5), switching the order of the productions in the rule base around, adding new productions, and so on. This
feeling of *manageability* of the rule base is perhaps one of the strongest
attractions of production systems as a knowledge-representation scheme.

Advantages and Disadvantages of Production Systems

Production systems have most often been used in AI programs to
represent a body of knowledge about how people do a specific, real-
world task, like speech understanding, medical diagnosis, or mineral exploration. In psychology, production systems have also been a popular
tool for modeling human behavior, perhaps because of the stimulus-
response character of production rules (Anderson and Bower, 1973;
Newell, 1973b). These psychological models are described in Chapter XI,
in Volume III. The AI systems based on productions have been quite
diverse in most respects, but there are some features of the production-
system formalism, both good and bad, that can be generalized.

Modularity. One obvious quality of production systems is that the
individual productions in the rule base can be added, deleted, or
changed independently. They behave much like independent *pieces of
knowledge.* Changing one rule, although it may change the performance
of the system, can be accomplished without having to worry about
direct effects on the other rules, since rules communicate only by means
of the context data structure (looking to see if their conditions are
satisfied in the context and then modifying the context); they don't *call*
each other directly. This relative *modularity* of the rules is important in
building the large rule bases of current AI systems—knowing what a
proposed rule will mean, in whatever situation it is used, makes the
creation of the database much easier. There are indications, however,
that modularity is harder to maintain as one moves to larger systems
(Rychener, 1976), and, even if modularity can be preserved, strongly
constraining interaction between rules leads to *inefficiencies* that might
become important problems in large systems (see below).

Uniformity. Another general attribute of production systems is the
uniform structure imposed on the knowledge in the rule base. Since all

information must be encoded within the rigid structure of production rules, it can often be more easily understood, by another person, or by another part of the system itself, than would be possible in the relatively free form of *semantic net* or *procedural* representation schemes, for example. Production systems that examine and automatically modify their own rules are exemplified by those of Waterman, Davis, and Anderson (see below).

Naturalness. A further advantage of the production-system formalism is the ease with which one can express certain important kinds of knowledge. In particular, statements about *what to do* in predetermined *situations* are naturally encoded into production rules. Furthermore, it is these kinds of statements that are most frequently used by human experts to explain how they do their jobs.

Inefficiency. There are, however, significant disadvantages inherent in the production-system formalism. One of these is *inefficiency* of program execution. The strong modularity and uniformity of the productions result in high overhead in their use in problem solving. For example, since production systems perform *every* action by means of the match-action cycle and convey all information by means of the *context* data structure, it is difficult to make them efficiently responsive to predetermined *sequences* of situations or to take *larger steps* in their reasoning when the situation demands it (see Barstow, 1979). Lenat and McDermott (1977) propose solutions to this type of problem, sacrificing some of the advantages of production systems.

Opacity. A second disadvantage of the production-system formalism is that it is hard to follow the flow of control in problem solving—*algorithms* are less apparent than they would be if they were expressed in a programming language. In other words, although situation-action knowledge can be expressed naturally in production systems, algorithmic knowledge is not expressed naturally. Two factors that contribute to this problem are the isolation of productions (they don't *call* each other) and the uniform *size* of productions (there is nothing like a *subroutine hierarchy* in which one production can be composed of several subproductions). Function calls and subroutines, common features of all programming languages, would help to make the *flow of control* easier to follow.

Appropriate Domains for Production Systems

The features of production systems described in the previous section can be seen as having both good and bad consequences. A more fruitful way to evaluate the utility of production systems is to characterize the domains for which production rules might be a useful knowledge-representation scheme. Davis and King (1977) proposed as appropriate—

1. domains in which the knowledge is diffuse, consisting of many facts (e.g., clinical medicine), as opposed to domains in which there is a concise, unified theory (physics);

2. domains in which processes can be represented as a set of independent actions (a medical patient-monitoring system), as opposed to domains with dependent subprocesses (a payroll program);

3. domains in which knowledge can be easily separated from the manner in which it is to be used (a classificatory taxonomy, like those used in biology), as opposed to cases in which representation and control are merged (a recipe).

Rychener (1976) rephrased this characterization of appropriate domains in AI terms: If we can view the task at hand as a sequence of transitions from one state to another in a *problem space* (see Article II.A), we can model this behavior with production systems, since each transition can be effectively represented by one or more production firings. The following examples of important AI production systems may help demonstrate their utility.

Waterman (1970) implemented an *adaptive production system* to play the game of draw poker (see Article XV.D3, in Vol. III). The program was adaptive in that it automatically changed the productions in its rule base—it started with a set of fairly simple heuristics for playing poker (when to raise, when to bluff, etc.) and extended and improved these rules as it gained experience in actually playing the game. The fact that knowledge in production systems is represented in a constrained, modular fashion facilitated the learning aspect of the system, since the program needed to analyze and manipulate its own representation. Other examples of production systems that model human learning are those of Hedrick (1976), Vere (1977), and Anderson, Kline, and Beasley (1979).

The MYCIN system (Shortliffe, 1976; Davis, Buchanan, and Shortliffe, 1977) acts as a medical consultant, aiding in the diagnosis and selection of therapy for patients with bacteremia or meningitis infections (see Article VIII.B1, in Vol. II). It carries on an interactive dialogue with a physician and is capable of *explaining* its reasoning. It also includes a *knowledge acquisition* subsystem, TEIRESIAS, which helps expert physicians expand or modify the rule base (Article VII.B, in Vol. II). MYCIN's rule base contains several hundred production rules representing human-expert-level knowledge about the domain. The system is distinguished by its use of a *backward chaining* control structure (see below) and *inexact reasoning*, involving confidence factors that are attached to the conclusion part of each production to help determine the relative strengths of alternative diagnoses.

Lenat (in press) modeled the process of *discovery* in mathematics, viewed as heuristic search, in his AM production system (see Article VII.D2, in Vol. II). AM started with a minimal knowledge of mathematical concepts and used heuristics, represented as production rules, to expand its knowledge about these concepts and *learn* new ones. In the course of its operation, AM discovered a large number of important mathematical concepts, such as prime numbers and the arithmetic functions, and also two mathematical concepts that had not been discovered before. AM is especially important because of its sophisticated data structures and control mechanisms.

Rychener (1976) built several production systems to reimplement a number of AI systems that had been developed previously with other techniques, including Bobrow's STUDENT, Newell and Simon's GPS, Feigenbaum's EPAM, Winograd's SHRDLU, and Berliner's CAPS. Rychener's intent was to show that the production-system formalism was a natural one for programming. His primary problem was the difficulty of building very complex control structures (Rychener, 1977).

Current Issues in the Design of Production Systems

Complexity of left- and right-hand sides. The structure of the two sides of the productions in the rule base has been progressively extended as the size and complexity of systems have increased, so that in many current systems the left-hand side (LHS) is a LISP function that can evaluate an arbitrarily complex condition. In some systems, the testing of the LHS can even have *side effects*, so that the rule can alter the context or change the control sequence without ever being fired. Similarly, the form of the right-hand side (RHS) has been extended to include *variables*, whose values are bound during the test phase of the cycle, and to allow arbitrary programs to be run rather than just making changes in the context. These programs usually specify actions in terms of a set of domain-specific conceptual primitives. In some systems (Riesbeck, 1975; Rychener, 1976) these actions could include activation or deactivation of sets of other productions. Again, this represents a radical extension of the original production-system formalism.

Structure of the rule base and context. Of the three phases of each production-system cycle—matching, conflict resolution, and action—the matching process uses by far the most computational resources. As production systems have become bigger and more complex, questions of efficiency have necessitated making both the rule base and the context into more complex data structures. For example, to allow rapid determination of which productions are applicable in a given situation without checking through all of the rule base, the productions are often *indexed* or *partitioned* according to conditions that will make them fire (see Davis, in press; Lenat and McDermott, 1977). The *context* data structure has increased in internal complexity both to make it more efficient and to allow it to represent more complicated situations. MYCIN's *context tree* (Shortliffe, 1976), HEARSAY's *blackboard* (Erman and Lesser, 1975), and PROSPECTOR's *semantic net* (Duda et al., 1978) are examples of complex context data structures. A good example of the work in organizing the rule base and database is that of McDermott, Newell, and Moore (1978).

Conflict resolution. In practice, it is often the case that more than one rule could fire in each cycle of the operation of a typical large production system; the system is required to choose one rule from among this set (called the *conflict set*). This *conflict resolution* phase of each cycle is where basic cognitive traits like action sequencing, attention focusing, interruptibility, and control of instability are realized. Several different approaches to conflict resolution have been tried, including choosing—

1. the *first* rule that matches the context, where "first" is defined in terms of some explicit linear order of the rule base;

2. the highest *priority* rule, where "priority" is defined by the programmer according to the demands and characteristics of the task (as in DENDRAL);

3. the most *specific* rule, that is, the one with the most detailed condition part that matches the current context;

4. the rule that refers to the element most *recently* added to the context;

5. a *new* rule, that is, a rule-binding instantiation that has not occurred previously;

6. a rule *arbitrarily;*

7. not to choose—exploring *all* the applicable rules in parallel (as in MYCIN).

Different systems use different combinations of these simple conflict-resolution methods, some of which become quite complicated *scheduling algorithms* (see, e.g., AM and HEARSAY). Good discussions of conflict resolution can be found in Davis and King (1977). Also, McDermott and Forgy (1978) discuss the way conflict-resolution strategies affect two important characteristics for production systems: *sensitivity*, the ability to respond quickly to changes in the environment, and *stability*, the ability to carry out relatively long sequences of actions. They conclude that no simple conflict-resolution strategy can be completely satisfactory.

Direction of inference. Research on deductive inference has recognized two fundamentally different ways that people reason. Sometimes we work in a *data driven, event driven,* or *bottom-up* direction, starting from the available information as it comes in and trying to draw conclusions that are appropriate to our goals. This is how our sample production system worked, for example. In production-system research this is called a *forward chaining* method of inference. We sometimes work the other way, however, starting from a *goal* or *expectation* of what is to happen and working backwards, looking for evidence that supports or contradicts our hunch. This is called *goal driven, expectation driven,* or *top-down* thinking, and in production systems it is referred to as *backward chaining*, since it requires looking at the action parts of rules to find ones that would *conclude* the current goal, then looking at the left-hand sides of those rules to find out what conditions would make them fire, then finding other rules whose action parts conclude these conditions, and so on. MYCIN's use of backward chaining is described fully in Article VIII.B1, in Volume II.

Primitive vocabulary. As the complexity of the condition and action parts of the productions in the rule base increases, there has been greater concern about the nature of the expressions allowed—the kinds of conditions and actions that can be expressed. A significant aspect of the representation language issue concerns the choice of vocabulary or *semantic primitives*, that is, the functions or predicates in terms of which the rules and context elements are expressed (see Article III.C6). Different systems will define their vocabulary at higher or lower levels, depending upon the task to be accomplished.

Conclusion

Perhaps the final word on production systems is that they capture in a *manageable* representation scheme a certain type of problem-solving knowledge—knowledge about what to do in a specific situation. Although this kind of knowledge is basically *procedural*, the production-system formalism has many of the advantages of declarative representation schemes, most importantly, *modularity* of the rules. Furthermore, the way that the productions themselves are structured is very similar to the way that people *talk* about how they solve problems.

For this reason, production systems have been used as the backbone of expert AI systems like DENDRAL, MYCIN, and PROSPECTOR (see Chaps. VII, VIII, and IX, in Vol. II). Research on these knowledge-based expert systems, called *knowledge engineering* (Feigenbaum, 1977; Bernstein, 1977) is concerned not only with expert-level performance but also with the *interactive transfer of expertise*—acquisition of knowledge from human experts and explanation of reasoning to human users (Davis, in press).

References

Winston (1977) gives a basic introduction to production systems with examples. An excellent review of production systems and the issues involved in their design was prepared by Davis and King (1977). Current research in production-system design and applications is reported in the collection of papers edited by Waterman and Hayes–Roth (1978).

C5. Direct (Analogical) Representations

There is a class of representation schemes, called analogical or *direct* representations—like maps, models, diagrams, and sheet music—that can represent knowledge about certain aspects of the world in especially natural ways. This type of knowledge representation is central to many AI tasks but seems at first quite different from the usual *propositional* representation schemes like logic and semantic nets. Understanding the sense in which direct and propositional representations are the same may help clarify the meaning of concepts like *representation, data structure,* and *interpretative procedure.*

Direct representations have been defined as schemes in which "properties of and relations between parts of the representing configuration represent properties and relations of parts in a complex represented configuration, so that the structure of the representation gives information about the structure of what is represented" (Sloman, 1971). The significant point here is the requirement of correspondence between the relations in the representational data structures and the relations in the represented situation. For example, a street map is a *direct* representation of a city in the sense that the distance between two points on the map must *correspond* to the distance between the places they represent in the city. Hayes (1974) calls this form of connection between the representation and the situation one of *homomorphism* (structural similarity) rather than just *denotation.*

Direct representations may be contrasted with the more prevalent *propositional* or *Fregean* forms (so called after Gottlob Frege, who invented the *predicate calculus*), which do not require this homomorphic correspondence between relations in the representation and relations in the situation. Proximity of assertions in the database of a *logic* system, for instance, indicates nothing about the location of objects in the world. Note that the propositional and direct representations may actually use the same data structures but differ in *how* they use them— which properties of the data structures are used in what way by the routines that operate on the representation to make inferences. Continuing with the map example, if a routine for examining a map retrieved all distances from an internal table, rather than looking at the map, it would be pointless to say that the map was *direct* with respect to distance.

Thus, it is the combination of the data structures and the *semantic interpretation function* (SIF) manipulating them that should be referred to as direct, and only with respect to certain properties (Pylyshyn, 1975, 1978). For example, a map (with a reasonable semantic interpretation function) is direct with respect to location and hence distance, but not, usually, with respect to elevation. For some problems, direct representation has significant advantages. In particular, the problem of *updating* the representation to reflect changes in the world is simpler. For example, if we add a new city to a map, we need only put it in the right place. It is not necessary to state explicitly its distance from all the old cities, since the distance on the map accurately represents the distance in the world. See the discussion in Article III.C2 of the *frame problem* (McCarthy and Hayes, 1969).

The distinction between direct and propositional representations has also been the subject of discussions in psychology concerning the character of human memory, which seems to have properties of both types (Pylyshyn, 1973). The next section of this article presents some AI systems that use direct representations. The final section returns to a discussion of their advantages and disadvantages.

Systems Using Analogical Representations

The *Geometry Theorem Prover* (Gelernter, 1963) was one of the earliest automated theorem provers and was distinguished by its reliance on a *diagram* to guide the proof. The system proved simple, high-school-level theorems in Euclidean geometry like the following:

Given: Angle ABD equals angle DBC.
         Segment AD perpendicular segment AB.
         Segment DC perpendicular segment BC.

Prove: Segment AD equals segment CD.

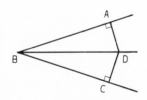

Using *problem reduction* techniques, the system worked backward from the goal to be proved.

In Gelernter's system, which is described fully in Article II.D3, the problem diagram was used in two ways. The more important of these was the *pruning heuristic:* "Reject as false any hypothesis (goal) that is not true in the diagram." In other words, those subgoals that were obviously false in the diagram were not pursued through the formal proof methods. This use of the diagram to guide the solution search resulted in the pruning of about 995 out of every 1,000 subgoals at each level of search.

The other use of the diagram was to establish obvious facts concerning, for example, the order in which points fall on a given line and the intersection properties of lines in a plane. Many of these are self-evident from the diagram but would be tiresome to prove from fundamental axioms. In certain such circumstances, the program would assume the fact to be true if it were true in the diagram, while explicitly noting that it had made such an assumption. The program was also able to add lines to the diagram, when necessary, to facilitate the proof.

Work on the *General Space Planner* (Eastman, 1970, 1973) addressed the task of arranging things in a space (e.g., furniture in a room) subject to given *constraints* that must be satisfied (e.g., room for walkways and no overlapping). A simple problem is the following:

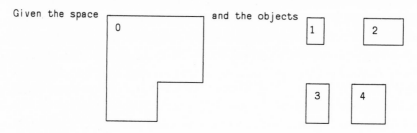

and the constraints

    (3) must be adjacent to (4)
    (2) must be adjacent to (3)
    (1) must be visible from (3)
    (1) must not be adjacent to any other objects,

one solution is:

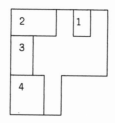

The system used a direct representation, called a *variable domain array*, which was a specialization of the sort of two-dimensional diagram used by Gelernter. Since the structure of the representation reflected the structure of the space, with respect to the properties of size, shape, and position, the system could be described as analogical for those properties. Space was partitioned into a set of rectangles, and in addition to the above properties, two others that are particularly important for the space-planning task were easily detectable from the variable-domain array representation: (a) filled versus empty space and (b) overlapping objects.

The system solved the problems by means of a *depth-first search* algorithm, finding locations for successive objects and *backing up* when it couldn't proceed without violating some constraint.   The search was facilitated by a *constraint graph* that represented, by restrictions on the amount of area left, the effects of constraints between pairs of objects. Thus, by attacking the most restrictive constraint first, the search was relatively efficient. This method has been called *constraint structured planning*.

Note that Eastman's work is in one sense the reverse of Gelernter's. Gelernter's system performed search in a propositional space (sets of formal statements) using an analogical representation (the diagram) for guidance.   Eastman's system performed search in an analogical space (the diagrammatic array) using a propositional form for heuristic guidance (the constraint graph).

WHISPER (Funt, 1976, 1977) was a system designed to reason exclusively by the analogical representation.   WHISPER operated in a simplified blocks-world environment, solving problems like the following:

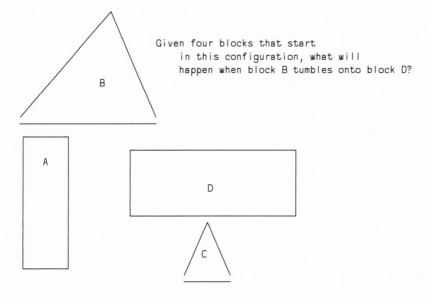

Given four blocks that start
in this configuration, what will
happen when block B tumbles onto block D?

The system had three components:

1. *Diagram:* An array that represented the two-dimensional scene in the obvious way, as shown above;

2. *Retina:* A set of parallel receptors arranged in concentric circles, with each receptor viewing a small part of the diagram;

3. *High-level reasoner:* The domain-dependent part of the system that contained qualitative physical knowledge (in this case, it employed information regarding the behavior of rigid bodies when acted upon by gravity).

The significance of the diagram to WHISPER lay in the fact that there were two types of analogues present—analogues between static states of the diagram and the world and also between dynamic behavior of objects in the diagram and of objects in the world.

The correspondences between the diagram and the world were simple and well defined; no complicated processes were required to map from one to the other. A number of properties, such as position, orientation, and size of blocks, were represented analogically. For these properties, it was not necessary to perform complicated deductions, since the desired information "fell out" of the diagrams. For example, as in Eastman's space planner, to test whether or not a particular area of the world was empty (i.e., not occupied by any block), the system had only to look at the corresponding area of the diagram. With most propositional representations, it would be necessary to examine each block individually, testing whether or not that block overlapped the space in question (see, e.g., Fahlman, 1974). The retina also provided a number of *perceptual primitives*, including center of area, contact finding, and similarity testing. The high-level reasoner never looked at the diagram directly. Note that certain properties (color and weight) were not represented in the analogue. To reason about these, normal inference-making processes would be necessary.

Baker (1973) had earlier suggested a similar representational formalism. Like Funt, he envisioned a two-dimensional array to represent the diagram; however, he also discussed the possibility of retaining spatial smoothing information *within* each cell of the array, to remove some of the error caused by the coarseness of the array. Both Funt and Baker suggested that the *parallelism* of their systems, pursuing several goals simultaneously, coupled well with the analogical representations. Individual elements of their processors (in Funt's case, the *retina*) could operate autonomously, with connections only to their (spatially) neighboring cells. In this sort of network, arbitrary transformations, through combinations of translation and rotation, could be represented.

Issues Concerning Direct Representations

The work done to date on direct representations raises a number of questions. First, following Sloman (1975), we should clarify some common misconceptions about direct representations. Analogical representations need not be continuous, nor need they be two-dimensional; an ordered list of numbers, for example, can be analogical with respect to size. Also, like propositional representations, analogical ones may have a *grammar* that defines what data structures are well formed, or "legal." The difference between the two types of representation schemes lies in the nature of the correspondence between aspects of the structure of the representation and the structure of the represented situation.

One of the advantages of analogical representations over their propositional counterparts relates to the difference between *observation* and *deduction.* In some situations, the former can be accomplished relatively cheaply in terms of the computation involved, and direct representations often facilitate observation since important properties are "directly observable" (Funt, 1976). For example, determining whether three points are collinear might be much easier using a direct representation (a diagram) than it would be to calculate analytically using their coornates. As another example, Filman (1979) implemented a chess reasoning system that relied on both inference (searching several moves ahead) and observation (looking at a *semantic model* of the current state of the chess board).

Funt (1976) relates a more abstract justification for the use of analogical representations. A propositional representation of a situation—for example, a set of statements in the predicate calculus—will often admit to several *models.* In other words, there might be many situations of the world that would be represented by the same statements, since they are distinguished in aspects that are not captured in the representation. Direct representations, on the other hand, are usually more exhaustive and specific, admitting fewer models and, in turn, making for more efficient problem solving.

In addition, as illustrated by Gelernter's work, the use of analogical representations can facilitate search. Constraints in the problem situation are represented by constraints on the types of transformations applied to the representation, so that impossible strategies are rejected immediately.

There are, however, some disadvantages to the use of these direct representations. First, the tendency toward more specific inference schemes mentioned earlier has its drawbacks—as Sloman (1975) points out, there are times when generality is needed. For example, consider the problem "If I start in room *A* and then move back and forth between room *A* and room *B*, which room will I be in after exactly 377 moves?" For this case, the best approach is not to simulate the action, but to generalize the effects of odd and even numbers of moves.

Second, Funt notes that some features of the analogue may not hold in the actual situation, and we might not know which ones these are. This is related to the general problem of knowing the limits of the representation.

Third, analogical representations become unwieldy for certain kinds of incomplete information. That is, if a new city is added to a map, its distance from other cities is obtained easily. But suppose that its location is known only indirectly, for example, that it is equidistant from cities *Y* and *Z*. Then the distance to other cities must be represented as equations, and the power of the analogue has been lost.

To conclude, direct representations are *analogous with respect to some properties* to the situation being represented. Some properties (especially physical ones) may be relatively easily represented analogically, resulting in significant savings in computation for certain types of inferences.

References

General discussions of the research on direct representations in AI are Funt (1976) and Sloman (1971, 1975). Related psychological concerns are discussed by Pylyshyn (1975, 1978).

C6. Semantic Primitives

The knowledge representation formalisms described in this chapter—logic, procedures, semantic nets, productions, direct representations, and frames—are all ways of expressing the kinds of things we express in English, that is, the kinds of things we know. Having chosen a representation technique, another major question in the design of an AI system concerns the vocabulary to be used within that formalism. In a logic-based representation, for example, what predicates are to be used? In a semantic net, what node and link types should be provided? Research on *semantic primitives* is concerned with this problem of establishing the representational vocabulary. This article, then, is not about a knowledge representation technique per se, but rather about a representational issue that concerns all of the techniques used in AI.

The term *semantic primitive* has no clear-cut definition. As a starting point, one may think of a primitive as any symbol that is used but not defined within the system. The term is so used by Wilks, for example, who accordingly concludes that "primitives are to be found in all natural language understanding systems—even those . . . that argue vigorously against them" (Wilks, 1977c). A second and narrower usage takes semantic primitives to be elements of meaning into which the meanings of words and sentences can be broken down; examples of such work come from linguistics (e.g., Jackendoff, 1975, 1976) and psychology (Miller, 1975; Miller and Johnson–Laird, 1976; Norman and Rumelhart, 1975), as well as from AI.

Additional issues have arisen as to what primitives really are, how they may be used in reasoning, and what alternatives there are to using primitives. Winograd (1978) provides a general survey and analysis of such questions. Some of these are illustrated in the following discussion of the two major AI systems for natural language understanding that are characterized by their authors as using semantic primitives.

Wilks's System

Yorick Wilks, now of the University of Essex, has been developing a natural language system for machine translation since 1968 (described fully in Article IV.F2). The system accepts paragraphs of English text, producing from them an internal representation that is a data structure composed of nodes representing semantic primitives. From this structure, a French translation of the input is generated. The translation serves as a test of whether the English has been understood, which is a more objective test than just inspection of the internal representation. The translation task also has the advantage, Wilks suggests, that correct translation of the input may often require a shallower understanding than would the ability to answer arbitrary questions about it. Consistent with these reasons for the choice of translation as a task, most of the effort in Wilks's system is spent in converting the English input to the internal representation.

The first major problem that Wilks addressed was the resolution of *word-sense ambiguity,* for this was the problem on which earlier attempts at machine translation had foundered (see Article IV.B). For example, in the sentence *The old salt was damp,* it is necessary to determine from the surrounding context whether *salt* means a chemical compound or a sailor. Wilks's system also addressed problems involving other kinds of ambiguity and extended word senses, as for the word *drink* in *My car drinks gas.*

The general idea of Wilks's approach, which he calls *preference semantics,* is to use knowledge of possible word meanings to disambiguate other words. For example, part of the meaning of *drink* is that it prefers a fluid object, and part of the meanings of *wine* and *gas* is that they are fluids. If the best fit among possible word senses does not satisfy all preferences (such as the preference of *drink* for an animate subject), then an extended word sense can be accepted. The formalism within which preferences are expressed, Wilks suggests, is closer to a *frame* representation than to a *semantic net.*

As the description above should make clear, a central requirement in Wilks's system is a dictionary distinguishing among the various senses of words that can appear in the input text. Definitions in the dictionary use a vocabulary of *semantic primitives,* grouped into five classes. Examples from each class are given below:

```
Entities

        MAN     . a human
        STUFF     a substance
        PART      a part of an entity


Actions

        CAUSE     causing something to happen
        BE        being as equivalence or predication
        FLOW      moving as liquids do
```

```
Cases

        TO      direction toward something
        IN      containment

Qualifiers

        GOOD    morally correct or approved
        MUCH    much, applied to a substance

Type indicators

        HOW     being a type of action—for adverbial constructions
        KIND    being a quality—for adjectival constructions
```

In addition to the primitive elements, of which there are currently over 80, Wilks uses several elements, distinguished by names beginning with an asterisk, that are defined as equivalent to a class of primitives. For example, *ANI (animate) encompasses MAN, FOLK (a human group), BEAST (a nonhuman animal), and certain others. A typical definition using the primitives is the following definition for one sense of the word *break:*

```
(BREAK:  (*HUM SUBJ)
         (*PHYSOB OBJE)
         ((((NOTWHOLE KIND) BE) CAUSE) GOAL)
         (THING INST)
         STRIK)
```

This says roughly that *break* means a STRIKing, done preferably by a HUMan SUBJect and preferably with an INSTrument that is a THING, with the GOAL of CAUSing a PHYSical OBject to BE NOT WHOLE. Words other than verbs are also defined by such structured formulas. A detailed description of the syntax of such word-sense definitions, or *semantic formulas,* is given in Wilks (1977c).

The completed representation of a text is a structure made up of such word-sense formulas. At a level corresponding to the clause or simple sentence, formulas are arranged into triples, or *templates,* standing for an agent, an action, and an object; any of the three may itself be qualified by other formulas. For example, *Small men sometimes father big sons* would be structured as follows:

```
    [man]  ←——→  [father]  ←——→  [sons]
      ↑             ↑              ↑
      |             |              |
   [small]     [sometimes]      [big]
```

Here the bracketed English words should be imagined as being replaced by the semantic formulas representing their appropriate sense. Relations among templates are indicated at a still higher level of structure.

What is the status of the primitive vocabulary in Wilks's system? First, he argues, primitives are not essentially different from natural-language words. A semantic description in terms of primitives is just a description in "a reduced micro-language, with all the normal weaknesses and vagueness of a natural language" (Wilks, 1977c). The justification for using a language of primitives, then, is that it provides "a useful organizing hypothesis ... for an AI natural language system."

Second, Wilks claims that individual primitives have their meaning in the same way that English words do: neither by direct reference to things, nor by correspondence to nonlinguistic psychological entities, but only by their function within the overall language.

Third, in light of the nature of primitives, there is no one correct vocabulary for a primitive language, any more than there is a correct vocabulary for English. The test of the adequacy of a particular set of primitives is an operational one—the success or failure of the linguistic computations that use it. As suggestive evidence that Wilks's own set of primitives will indeed turn out to be adequate, he observes that it is very similar to the 80 words that occur most frequently in definitions in Webster's dictionary.

Finally, there are some general considerations in choosing a set of primitives. Wilks (1977c) identifies the following properties as desirable:

1. *Finitude.* The number of primitives should be finite and should be smaller than the number of words whose meanings the representation scheme is to encode.

2. *Comprehensiveness.* The set should be adequate to express and distinguish among the senses of the word set whose meanings it is to encode.

3. *Independence.* No primitive should be definable in terms of other primitives.

4. *Noncircularity.* No two primitives should be definable in terms of each other.

5. *Primitiveness.* No subset of the primitives should be replacable by a smaller set.

A qualification should be noted concerning the property of comprehensiveness: The definition in primitives of a word sense is not required to be exhaustive of meaning. Wilks cites *hammer, mallet,* and *axe* as terms among which a representation in primitives cannot be expected to distinguish. In addition, the definition of a term is not expected to say everything; Wilks distinguishes between the meanings of words, which definitions express, and facts about things. The definition of *water,* for example, might say that water is a liquid substance, but not that water freezes into ice. Facts of the latter sort are expressed in Wilks's system as commonsense inference rules, which are separate from the dictionary and are used only as a last resort in disambiguation.

Schank's Conceptual Dependency Theory

The conceptual dependency theory of Roger Schank, now of Yale University, has been under development since 1969. Its most distinctive feature, the attempt to provide a representation of all actions using a small number of primitives, was first introduced in 1972. (See Articles IV.F5 and IV.F6 on Schank's natural language understanding systems.)

There are significant differences between the systems of Schank and Wilks, both in the general outline of their systems and in their views of primitives. Wilks's system, for example, is oriented toward the task of machine translation, whereas conceptual dependency theory makes broader claims. First, Schank emphasizes task independence. The theory has been used, in fact, as the basis for programs that, among other things, can *paraphrase* an input text, *translate* it to another language, draw *inferences* from it, or *answer questions* about it. Second, the theory is offered not only as a basis for computer programs that understand language, but also as an intuitive theory of human language processing.

Consistent with these claims, Schank holds that it is the business of an adequate representation of natural-language utterances to capture their underlying conceptual structure. A first requirement is that the representation be unambiguous, even though the input may contain syntactic ambiguity, as in *I saw the Grand Canyon flying to New York,* or semantic ambiguity, as in *The old man's glasses were filled with sherry.* The speaker of an ambiguous sentence usually intends an unambiguous meaning, so the representation is expected to reflect only the most likely version of what was intended.

A second requirement is that the representation be unique—that is, that distinct sentences with the same conceptual content should have the same representation. Some examples of groups of sentences that are all represented the same way are

> *I want a book.*
> *I want to get a book.*
> *I want to have a book.*

and

> *Don't let John out of the room.*
> *Prevent John from getting out of the room.*

The principle of uniqueness of representation has been characterized as the basic axiom of the system. It has also been identified as accounting for human abilities to paraphrase and translate text. The problem of paraphrase—"how sentences which were constructed differently lexically could be identical in meaning"—is a major theme throughout Schank's work (Schank, 1975c).

To obtain unique, unambiguous representations of meaning, Schank's system relies principally on a set of 11 primitive ACTs (Schank, 1975a; Schank and Abelson, 1977):

```
Physical acts

    PROPEL   apply a force to a physical object
    MOVE     move a body part
    INGEST   take something to the inside of an animate object
    EXPEL    force something out from inside an animate object
    GRASP    grasp an object physically

Acts characterized by resulting state changes

    PTRANS   change the location of a physical object
    ATRANS   change an abstract relationship, such as
             possession or ownership, with respect to an object

Acts used mainly as instruments for other acts

    SPEAK    produce a sound
    ATTEND   direct a sense organ toward a stimulus

Mental acts

    MTRANS   transfer information
    MBUILD   construct new information from old information
```

There are several other categories, or concept types, besides the primitive ACTs in the representational system. They are:

> *Picture Producers* (PPs), which are physical objects. Some special cases among the PPs are natural forces like wind and three postulated divisions of human memory: the Conceptual Processor (where conscious thought takes place), the Intermediate Memory, and the Long Term Memory.
>
> *Picture Aiders* (PAs), which are attributes of objects.
>
> *Times.*
>
> *Locations.*
>
> *Action Aiders* (AAs), which are attributes of ACTs.

Only a little work has been done on reducing these latter categories to a primitive set; see Russell (1972) and Lehnert (1978) on the analysis of picture producers and Schank (1975a) on the treatment of picture aiders as attribute-value pairs.

Detailed rules are provided for the ways that elements of these categories can be combined into representations of meaning. There are two basic kinds of combinations, or *conceptualizations.* One involves an actor (a picture producer—PP) doing a primitive ACT; the other involves an object (again, a PP) and a description of its state (a picture aider—PA). Conceptualizations can be tied together by relations of instrumentality or causation, among others.

The primitive elements that occur in conceptualizations are not words, according to Schank, but concepts; they reflect a level of thought underlying language rather than language itself. Consequently, representations of text in conceptual dependency are said to be language-free. The task of translation, then, becomes only one task among many; it is accomplished by parsing from one language into conceptual dependency and then generating text in the second language from the conceptual dependency representation.

The notion of language-free primitive concepts requires explication. For Schank, as for Wilks, the justification for using primitives is functional. Schank differs from Wilks, however, in his choice of the sort of function to be optimized, as well as in his view of primitives as language-free and psychologically plausible. Schank particularly emphasizes the computational advantages, to both programs and people, of storing propositions in a canonical form (Schank, 1975b). This requires, in Schank's view, that information implicit in a sentence be made explicit (Schank, 1975a; Schank and Abelson, 1977). Obtaining the implicit information in turn requires inferring, and it is as an aid to making inferences that the use of primitives receives its most important justification:

> Rather than stating that if you see something then you know it and if you hear something then you know it and if you read something then you know it and so on, we simply state that whenever an MTRANS exists, a likely inference is that the MTRANSed information is in the mental location LTM [Long Term Memory] (our representation for "know"). This is a tremendous savings of time and space. (Schank, 1975b, p. 40)

Each primitive ACT, then, entails its own set of inferences. As a fuller example, the following are the main inferences from the fact that X PTRANSed Y from W to Z:

1. Y is now located at Z.
2. Y is no longer at location W.

3. If $Z = X$, or Z is human and requested the PTRANS, then Z will probably do whatever one ordinarily does with Y. Moreover, Z probably will become pleased by doing this. (Schank, 1975a, p. 71)

Such inferences provide both the criterion for choosing a set of primitives and the definition of what primitives are. The primitive ACTs, Schank and Abelson (1977) state, are no more than the sets of inferences to which they give rise. Moreover:

The theoretical decision for what constitutes a primitive ACT is based on whether the proposed new ACT carries with it a set of inferences not already accounted for by an ACT that is already in use. Similarly, a primitive ACT is dropped when we find that its inferences are already handled by another ACT. (Schank, 1975b, p. 40)

In his earlier work, Schank (1973a) claimed that the primitive ACTs of conceptual dependency, together with some set of possible states of objects, were sufficient to represent the meaning of any English verb. It soon became clear, however, that additional mechanisms would be needed for a general-purpose language-understanding system. For example, there are problems of quantification and of metaphor, which have not yet been addressed (Schank and Abelson, 1977). There are problems raised by the fact that natural-language communications often presuppose a great deal of background knowledge, some of which has to do with the typical course of events in commonplace situations like eating in a restaurant or taking a bus (see Article III.C7 on *frame* systems). Finally, of particular importance with respect to the use of primitives, there are problems arising from the fact that conceptual dependency generally expresses the meaning of an action verb only in terms of its physical realization. One example is the reduction of *kiss* to MOVE *lips to lips* (Schank and Abelson, 1977). The inadequacy of this representation becomes especially apparent in light of the claim that no information is lost by the use of primitive ACTs to represent actions.

Recently Schank has added several new devices to his representational system to reflect the purposive aspects of actions as well as their physical descriptions. These include *goals*, which can be realized by appropriate sequences of acts; *scripts*, which provide such sequences in simple stereotyped situations; *plans*, which provide a more flexible way of specifying the appropriate action sequences, including the treatment of a whole set of alternative sub-sequences as a single subgoal; and *themes*, which include people's occupations (e.g., lawyer), their relationships with others (e.g., love), and their general aims (e.g., getting rich) and which are offered as the source of their goals. The representation of a piece of text is thus extended to try to take into account not only what caused what, but also what was intended to cause what and why the actor might have had such an intention in the first place. In addition, Schank has recently supplemented the primitive ACTs with several social ACTs—AUTHORIZE, ORDER, DISPUTE, and PETITION—in order to represent yet another dimension of human actions more readily. None of these devices, however, is characterized as introducing a new set of primitives.

References

The best descriptions of the two systems using semantic primitives in AI discussed here are Wilks (1975c) and Schank and Abelson (1977). Norman and Rumelhart (1975) describe a computer model of human memory, MEMOD, and discuss the psychological basis of the semantic primitives used in their model (see also Article XI.E4, in Vol. III). See Wilks (1977a, 1977c) and Winograd (1978) for further discussions of the issue of semantic primitives.

C7. Frames and Scripts

There is abundant psychological evidence that people use a large, well-coordinated body of knowledge from previous experiences to interpret new situations in their everyday cognitive activity (Bartlett, 1932). For example, when we visit a restaurant where we have never been before, we have an extensive array of *expectations* based on experience in other restaurants about what we will find: menus, tables, waiters, and so forth. In addition to these expectations about the *objects* in a typical restaurant, we have strong expectations about the *sequences of events* that are likely to take place. Representing knowledge about the objects and events *typical* to specific situations has been the focus of the AI knowledge-representation ideas called *frames* and *scripts*. Frames were originally proposed by Minsky (1975) as a basis for understanding visual perception, natural-language dialogues, and other complex behaviors. Scripts—frame-like structures specifically designed for representing sequences of events—have been developed by Schank and Abelson (1977) and their colleagues. Both refer to methods of *organizing* the knowledge representation in a way that directs attention and facilitates recall and inference.

Organizing Knowledge and Expectations

Frames provide a structure, a framework, within which new data are interpreted in terms of concepts acquired through previous experience. Furthermore, the organization of this knowledge facilitates *expectation-driven processing,* looking for things that are expected based on the context one thinks one is in. The representational mechanism that makes possible this kind of reasoning is the *slot,* the place where knowledge fits within the larger context created by the frame. For example, a simple frame for the generic concept of chair might have slots for number of legs and style of back. A frame for a particular chair has the same slots—they are *inherited* from the CHAIR frame—but the contents of the slots are more fully specified:

```
CHAIR Frame

          Specialization-of:  FURNITURE
          Number-of-legs:     an integer (DEFAULT=4)
          Style-of-back:      straight, cushioned, . . .
          Number-of-arms:     0, 1, or 2
```

```
JOHN'S-CHAIR Frame
        Specialization-of:  CHAIR
        Number-of-legs:     4
        Style-of-back:      cushioned
        Number-of-arms:     0
```

By supplying a place for knowledge, and thus creating the possibility of missing or incompletely specified knowledge, the slot mechanism permits reasoning based on seeking confirmation of expectations—"filling in slots."

To illustrate some of the current ideas about slots and frames and how they might be used by a frame-based reasoning system, consider the following example of a Restaurant Frame. The terminology used for this example is intended only to give a sense of the structure of knowledge in a frame and does not follow any of the varied formalisms developed by the different researchers in this area (e.g., Minsky, 1975; Bobrow and Winograd, 1977b; Schank and Abelson, 1977; Szolovitz, Hawkinson, and Martin, 1977; Goldstein and Roberts, 1977; Brachman, 1978; Aikins, 1979; Stefik, 1980).

```
Generic RESTAURANT Frame
        Specialization-of:  Business-Establishment
        Types:
                range:     (Cafeteria, Seat-Yourself, Wait-To-Be-Seated)
                default:   Wait-to-be-Seated
                if-needed: IF plastic-orange-counter THEN Fast-Food,
                           IF stack-of-trays THEN Cafeteria,
                           IF wait-for-waitress-sign or reservations-made
                                   THEN Wait-To-Be-Seated,
                           OTHERWISE Seat-Yourself.
        Location:
                range:     an ADDRESS
                if-needed: (Look at the MENU)
        Name:
                if-needed: (Look at the MENU)
        Food-Style:
                range:     (Burgers, Chinese, American, Seafood, French)
                default:   American
                if-added:  (Update Alternatives of Restaurant)
```

```
Times-of-Operation:
      range:      a Time-of-Day
      default:    open evenings except Mondays
Payment-Form:
      range:      (Cash, CreditCard, Check, Washing-Dishes-Script)
Event-Sequence:
      default:    Eat-at-Restaurant Script
Alternatives:
      range:      all restaurants with same FoodStyle
      if-needed:  (Find all Restaurants with the same FoodStyle)
```

There are several different kinds of knowledge represented in this example. The Specialization-of slot is used to establish a *property inheritance hierarchy* among the frames, which in turn allows information about the parent frame to be *inherited* by its children, much like the ISA link in *semantic net* representations (see Article III.C3). Note that the Location slot has subslots of its own—slots can have a complex, frame-like structure in some systems. The contents of the Range slot in this generic restaurant example is an *expectation* about what kinds of things the Location of a restaurant might be. And the If-Needed slot contains an *attached procedure* that can be used to determine the slot's value if necessary (see discussion of procedural attachment below). Another important slot type is Default, which suggests a value for the slot unless there is contradictory evidence. Many other types of slots are used in the various frame systems, and the descriptions here are quite incomplete, but they will at least give an idea of the kinds of knowledge represented in frames.

As indicated in the Event-Sequence slot, knowledge about what typically happens at a restaurant might be represented in a script, like the one below:

```
EAT-AT-RESTAURANT Script

   Props:               (Restaurant, Money, Food, Menu, Tables, Chairs)
   Roles:               (Hungry-Persons, Wait-Persons, Chef-Persons)
   Point-of-View:       Hungry-Persons
   Time-of-Occurrence:  (Times-of-Operation of Restaurant)
   Place-of-Occurrence: (Location of Restaurant)
```

```
Event-Sequence:
    first:    Enter-Restaurant Script
    then:     if (Wait-To-Be-Seated-Sign or Reservations)
                  then Get-Maitre-d's-Attention Script
    then:     Please-Be-Seated Script
    then:     Order-Food-Script
    then:     Eat-Food-Script unless (Long-Wait) when
                  Exit-Restaurant-Angry Script
    then:     if (Food-Quality was better than Palatable)
                  then Compliments-To-The-Chef Script
    then:     Pay-For-It-Script
    finally:  Leave-Restaurant Script
```

This is a rough rendition in English of the type of Restaurant script described by Schank and Abelson (1977). The script specifies a normal or default sequence of events as well as exceptions and possible error situations. The script also requires the use of a few static descriptions such as Props and Roles that refer to other frames. Scripts are described more fully in Article IV.F6.

Procedural Knowledge in Frames and Scripts

Underlying the *declarative* structure of frames and scripts—the way that they organize the representation of static facts—is an important dynamic or *procedural* aspect of frame-based systems. In particular, procedures can be *attached* to slots to drive the reasoning or problem-solving behavior of the system. (See the general discussion of procedural representation of knowledge in Article III.C2.) In some frame-based systems, attached procedures are the principal mechanism for *directing* the reasoning process, being activated to fill in slots, If-Needed, or being triggered when a slot is filled (Bobrow et al., 1977).

Filling in slots. After a particular frame or script has been selected to represent the current context or situation, the primary process in a frame-based reasoning system is often just filling in the details called for by its slots. For example, after selecting the Generic Restaurant Frame above, one of the first things we might want the system to do is to determine the value of the Type slot. This could be accomplished in one of several ways. Sometimes the type is directly inherited, but in this case there are several alternatives. For instance, the *default* restaurant type can be used if there are no contraindications, or the attached If-Needed procedure can be used to decide.

Default and inherited values are relatively inexpensive methods of filling in slots; they don't require powerful reasoning processes. These methods account for a large part of the power of frames—any new frames interpreting the situation can make use of values determined by prior experience, without having to recompute them. When the needed information must be derived, attached procedures provide a means of specifying appropriate methods that can take advantage of the current context, namely, *slot-specific heuristics*. In other words, general problem-solving methods can be augmented by domain-specific knowledge about how to accomplish specific, slot-sized goals.

Besides directing the gathering of further information, filling in the slots provides confirmation that the frame or script is appropriate for understanding the scene or event. For example, Schank's script-based story-understander, SAM, can be said to have understood a written story when each slot in the appropriate script has been filled by an event in the story, either explicit in the text or implied (see Article IV.F6). Should the frame or script be found to be inappropriate, attached procedures can trigger transfer of control to other frames.

Triggers. Another frequently used form of procedural attachment is routines that are activated when the value of a slot is found or changed. These "trigger" procedures implement *event-* or *data-driven processing*, since they take over control only when certain events or data occur (see Article III.C4). For example, the If-Added procedure in the Food-Style slot of the Generic Restaurant Frame is used to modify the list of alternative restaurants once a particular cuisine is chosen.

In some systems, trigger procedures attached to special slots in the frame are used to decide what to do in the event that the frame is found not to match the current situation. For instance, if the Eat-at-Restaurant script were to discover a food line and a stack of trays, it might trigger the Eat-at-Cafeteria script as being more appropriate. This triggering procedure has been used in various frame-driven systems for medical diagnosis (Szolovitz, Hawkinson, and Martin, 1977; Aikins, 1979). Since a number of related diseases might share a core set of signs and symptoms, the ability to make a differential diagnosis depends strongly on the ability to detect those factors that rule out or confirm a particular diagnosis. Typically, in medicine, when one diagnosis is ruled out, a similar but more likely disease is indicated.

Current Research on Frames and Scripts

A number of experimental prototype systems have been implemented to explore the idea of frame-based processing introduced by Minsky (1975). The following descriptions are intended to give an indication of the domains and problems that researchers in this area address.

Bobrow and his associates (1977) have experimented with frame-based natural language understanding in their GUS system, and their article includes clear examples of how frames might be used to control a system's reasoning. Designed as a prototype of an automated airline reservation assistant, the system attempted to demonstrate how various aspects of dialogue understanding—such as handling mixed-initiative dialogues, indirect answers, and anaphoric references—could be facilitated by the ability to make expectations and defaults available with frames. This system was also used to explore procedural attachment issues.

Concurrently with the design of GUS, a frame-based programming and representation language called KRL (Knowledge Representation Language) was developed to explore frame-based processing (Bobrow and Winograd, 1977b). Many of the specific ideas about how frame-based systems might work were first suggested by the KRL research group. As part of their early design work, the KRL group implemented several AI systems in the first version of the language (Bobrow and Winograd, 1977a). The report details a number of difficulties and shortcomings they encountered, some of which are inherent in frame-based processing.

Other work with frame-based systems includes the NUDGE system, developed by Goldstein and Roberts (1977), which was used to understand incomplete and possibly inconsistent management-scheduling requests and to provide a complete specification for a conventional scheduling algorithm. Implemented in their FRL–0 language, the system also used a frame-based semantics to resolve anaphoric requests (Bullwinkle, 1977).

A program that solves physics problems stated in English was developed by Novak (1977). It used a set of canonical object frames, such as Point, Mass, and Pivot, to interpret the actual objects and their relations in a number of statics problems. These canonical object frames were used to construct a view of an actual object as an abstract object, thereby simplifying the problem representation.

The UNITS package, developed by Stefik (1980), is a useful implementation of a variety of ideas about frame systems in a transportable programming package. The UNITS package has been used to build working AI systems for scientific applications.

Finally, work on KLONE (Brachman, 1978) represents current research in the theory and design of frame-based systems.

Work on script-based processing in AI has for the most part been carried on by Schank and Abelson (1977) and their colleagues. They have used scripts to investigate the notions of causality and the understanding of sequences of events. In particular, the SAM program (Article IV.F6) attempts to understand short stories using a script to guide the interpretation of occurrences in the story. After establishing the appropriate script and filling some of its slots with information from the story, SAM can make inferences from script-based information about similar events.

Summary

Frames and scripts are recent attempts by AI researchers to provide a method for organizing the large amounts of knowledge needed to perform cognitive tasks. Much of the work in this area is quite conjectural, and there are many fundamental differences in approach among the researchers who have designed frame-based systems. The development of large-scale organizations of knowledge and the concomitant ability of these structures to provide direction for active cognitive processing are the current direction of AI research in knowledge representation. A number of serious problems must be solved before the conjectured benefits of frames will be realized.

References

Minsky (1975) coined the word *frame* and set off the recent flurry of AI work in the area. The clearest detailed descriptions of frame-based reasoning systems are Kuipers (1975) and Bobrow and Winograd (1977b). Fahlman (1975), Charniak (1978), and Brachman (1978) discuss some important current research issues in this area. Schank and Abelson (1977) provide an excellent discussion of AI research on scripts.

Chapter IV

Understanding Natural Language

CHAPTER IV: UNDERSTANDING NATURAL LANGUAGE

A. OVERVIEW

THE MOST COMMON WAY that people communicate is by speaking or writing in one of the "natural" languages, like English, French, or Chinese. Computer programming languages, on the other hand, seem awkward to humans. These "artificial" languages are designed so that sentences have a rigid format, or *syntax*, making it easier for compilers to *parse* the programs and convert them into the proper sequences of computer instructions. Besides being structurally simpler than natural languages, programming languages can express easily only those concepts that are important in programming: "Do this, then do that," "See whether such and such is true," and so forth. The things that can be meant by expressions in a language are referred to as the *semantics* of the language.

The research described in this chapter concerns the development of computer programs that try to deal with the full range of meaning in languages like English. If computers could understand what people mean when people type (or speak) English sentences, the systems would be easier to use and would fit more naturally into people's lives. Furthermore, AI researchers hope that learning how to build computers that can communicate as people do will extend our understanding of the nature of language and of the mind.

So far, programs have been written that are quite successful at processing somewhat constrained input: The user is limited in either the structural variation of his sentences (syntax constrained by an artificial *grammar*) or in the number of things he can mean (in domains with constrained semantics). Some of these systems are adequate for building English "front ends" for a variety of data processing tasks and are available commercially. But the fluent use of language typical of humans is still elusive, and understanding natural language (NL) is an active area of research in AI.

This article presents a brief sketch of the history of research in natural language processing and an idea of the state of the art in NL. The next article is a historical sketch of research on *machine translation* from one language to another, which was the subject of the very earliest ideas about processing language with computers. It is followed by several technical articles on some of the grammars and parsing techniques that AI researchers have used in their programs. Then, after an article on *text generation*, that is, the creation of sentences by a program to express what it wants to say, there are several articles describing the NL programs themselves: the early systems of the 1960s and the major research projects of the last decade, including Wilks's machine translation system, Winograd's SHRDLU, Woods's LUNAR, Schank's MARGIE, SAM, and PAM, and Hendrix's LIFER.

Two other chapters of the *Handbook* are especially relevant to NL research. Speech understanding research (Chap. V) attempts to build computer interfaces that understand *spoken* language. In the 1970s, research on speech and understanding natural language was often closely linked. Increasingly inseparable from NL research is the study of *knowledge representation* (Chap. III), because AI researchers have come to believe that a very large amount of knowledge about the world is needed to understand even simple dialogues. AI research in the representation of knowledge explores ways of making this *world knowledge* accessible to the computer program by building representational data structures in the machine's memory.

Early History

Research in *computational linguistics*, the use of computers in the study of language, started soon after computers became available in the 1940s (Bott, 1970). The machine's ability to manipulate symbols was readily applied to written text to compile word indexes (lists of word occurrences) and concordances (indexes that included a line of context for each occurrence). Such surface-level machine processing of text was of some value in linguistic research, but it soon became apparent that the computer could perform much more powerful linguistic functions than merely counting and rearranging data.

In 1949, Warren Weaver proposed that computers might be useful for "the solution of world-wide translation problems" (Weaver, 1955, p. 15). The resulting research, on what was called *machine translation*, attempted to simulate with a computer the presumed functions of a human translator: looking up each word in a bilingual dictionary, choosing an equivalent word in the output language, and, after processing each sentence in this way, arranging the resulting string of words to fit the output language's word order.

Despite the attractive simplicity of the idea, many unforeseen problems arose, both in selecting appropriate word equivalences and in arranging them to produce a sentence in the output language. (Article IV.B discusses the history, problems, and current state of research on machine translation.) The concept of translating by replacing words with their equivalents and then adjusting the word order was abandoned. In its place, eventually, *understanding* became the focus of

AI research in language—if the machine could actually "understand the meaning" of a sentence, it could presumably *paraphrase* it, *answer questions* about it, or translate it into another language. But the nature of understanding is itself a difficult problem. New AI approaches to natural language processing were influenced by many scientific developments of the 1960s, including high-level programming languages and *list processing*, vastly expanded computer power and memory capacity, and Chomsky's breakthroughs in linguistic theory.

In the 1960s, AI researchers developed a new group of computer programs, attempting to deal with some of the issues that had thwarted attempts at machine translation. These early natural language programs marked the beginning of AI work in understanding language. They began to view human language as a complex cognitive ability involving knowledge of different kinds: the structure of sentences, the meaning of words, a model of the listener, the rules of conversation, and an extensive, shared body of general information about the world. (Several of these programs are described briefly in Article IV.F1.) The general AI approach has been to model human language as a *knowledge-based system* for processing communications and to create computer programs that serve as working instantiations of those models (see Winograd, 1980b, however, for a discussion of some possible limitations of this approach to the study of language).

AI researchers in natural language processing expect their work to lead both to the development of practical, useful, language understanding systems and to a better understanding of language and the nature of intelligence. The computer, like the human mind, has the ability to manipulate symbols in complex processes, including processes that involve decision making based on stored knowledge. It is an assumption of the field that the human use of language is a cognitive process of this sort. By developing and testing computer-based models of language processing that approximate human performance, researchers hope to understand better how human language works.

Approaches to NL Processing

Natural language research projects have had diverse emphases and have employed diverse methods, making their classification difficult. One coherent scheme, borrowed from Winograd (1972), groups natural language programs according to how they represent and use knowledge of their subject matter. On this basis, natural language programs can be divided into four historical categories.

The earliest natural language programs sought to achieve only limited results in specific, constrained domains. These programs, like Green's BASEBALL, Lindsay's SAD–SAM, Bobrow's STUDENT, and Weizenbaum's ELIZA, used ad hoc data structures to store facts about a limited domain (see Article IV.F1). Input sentences were restricted to simple declarative and interrogative forms and were scanned by the programs for predeclared key words or patterns that indicated known objects and relationships. Domain-specific rules, called *heuristics*, were used to derive the required response from the key words in the sentence and the knowledge in the database. Because their domains of discourse were so restricted, these early systems were able to ignore many of the complexities of language and achieve sometimes impressive results in answering questions. (Weizenbaum, 1976, argues that to the extent the results were impressive, they were also misleading.)

Another early approach to NL processing was tried in PROTO-SYNTHEX–I (Simmons, Burger, and Long, 1966) and Semantic Memory (Quillian, 1968). These systems essentially stored a representation of the text itself in their databases, using a variety of clever indexing schemes to retrieve material containing specific words or phrases. In this *text-based* approach, the systems were not tied by their construction to a specific domain, since the textual database could cover any subject. However, they were still severely restricted in the sense that they could only respond with material that had been prestored explicitly. Though more general than their predecessors, these programs still failed to notice even obvious implications of the sentences in the database, because they did not deal with the *meaning* of the English language input—that is, they had no *deductive* powers.

To approach the problem of how to characterize and use the meaning of sentences, a third group of programs was developed during the mid–1960s. In these *limited-logic systems*, including SIR (Raphael, 1968), TLC (Quillian, 1969), DEACON (Thompson, 1966), and CONVERSE (Kellogg, 1968), the information in the database was stored in some formal notation, and mechanisms were provided for translating input sentences into this internal form (*semantic analysis*). The formal notation was an attempt to liberate the informational content of the input from the structure of English. The overall goal of these systems was to perform *inferences* on the database in order to find answers to questions that were not stored explicitly in the database. For instance, if a system has been told that *Fido is a collie* and that *All collies are dogs,* then it should be able to answer the question, *Is Fido a dog?* The systems of this period were limited in the sense that the deductions they could make were only a subset of the full range of logical inferences used in ordinary conversation.

The fourth group of natural language understanding programs might be called *knowledge-based systems;* their development is closely intertwined with AI research on the representation of knowledge (see Chap. III). These programs use a large amount of information about the domain under discussion to help understand sentences—knowledge that is stored within the program using some knowledge representation scheme like logic, procedural semantics, semantic networks, or frames. But before discussing these knowledge-based systems of the 1970s, we should first mention an important development in the study of language during the preceding decade that strongly influenced their design.

Grammars and Parsing

A *grammar* of a language is a scheme for specifying the sentences allowed in the language, indicating the syntactic rules for combining words into well-formed phrases and clauses. The theory of *generative grammar* introduced by Chomsky (1957) radically influenced all linguistic research, including AI work in computational linguistics. In natural language processing programs, the grammar is used in *parsing* to "pick apart" the sentences that were input to the program to help determine their meaning and thus an appropriate response. Several very different kinds of grammars have been used in NL programs, including phrase-structure grammars, transformational grammars, case grammars, systemic grammars (described in Sec. IV.C), and semantic grammars (see Article IX.C3, in Vol. II).

Parsing is the "delinearization" of linguistic input, that is, the use of grammatical rules and other sources of knowledge to determine the functions of the words in the input sentence (a linear string of words) in order to create a more complicated data structure, for example, a *derivation tree*. This structure depicts some of the relations between words in the sentence ("this adjective modifies that noun, which is the object of a prepositional phrase . . . ") and can be used to get at the "meaning" of the sentence. All natural-language-processing computer systems contain a parsing component of some sort, but those of the early NL programs were based on keywords expected in the input or were constrained to quite limited phrase structures. The practical application of grammars to the full range of natural language has proved difficult.

The design of a parser is a complex problem, in both theory and implementation. The first part of the design concerns the specification of the grammar to be used. The rest of the parsing system is concerned with the method of *use* of the grammar, that is, the manner in which strings of words are matched against patterns of the grammar. These considerations run into many of the general questions of computer science and Artificial Intelligence concerning process control and manipulation of representational data structures (see, e.g., recent work by Marcus, 1980, on the PARSIFAL system).

Knowledge-based Natural Language Systems

In the early 1970s, two systems were built that attempted to deal in a comprehensive way with both syntactic and semantic aspects of language processing. William Woods's LUNAR program answered questions about the samples of rock brought back from the moon, using a large database provided by the National Aeronautics and Space Agency (see Article IV.F3). It was one of the first programs to attack the problems of English grammar, by means of an *augmented transition network* parser (Article IV.D2). LUNAR utilized the notion of *procedural semantics* in which queries were first converted systematically into a "program" to be executed by the information retrieval component. The other system, Terry Winograd's SHRDLU, carried on a dialogue with a user in which the system simulated a robot manipulating a set of simple objects on a table top (see Article IV.F4). The naturalness of the dialogue, as well as SHRDLU's apparent reasoning ability, made it particularly influential in the development of AI ideas on natural language processing. These two systems integrated syntactic and semantic analysis with a body of world knowledge about a limited domain, allowing them to deal with more sophisticated aspects of language and discourse than had previously been possible.

Central to these two systems is the idea of representing knowledge about the world as procedures within the system. The meanings of words and sentences were expressed as programs in a computer language, and the execution of these programs corresponded to reasoning from the meanings. *Procedural representations* are often the most straightforward way to implement the specific reasoning steps needed for a natural language system. Most of the actual working systems that have been developed have made heavy use of specialized procedural representations, to fill in those places where the more *declarative* representation schemes—those where the "knowledge" is encoded in passive data structures that are interpreted by other procedures—are insufficient. (The *procedural-declarative controversy* was at one time an important focus in the development of AI; see Article III.A.)

Perhaps the most influential declarative representation schemes were *logic* and *semantic networks*. Semantic networks were first proposed by Quillian (1968) as a model for human associative memory. They applied the concepts of graph theory, representing words and meanings as a set

of linked nodes implemented as data structures in the computer program. By using a systematic set of link types, Quillian was able to
program simple operations (such as following chains of links) that corresponded to drawing *inferences*. The advantage of semantic networks
over standard logic as a representation scheme (see Article III.C1) is that
some selected set of inferences, of those that are possible, can be made
in a specialized and efficient way. If these correspond to the inferences
that people make naturally, then the system will be able to do a more
natural sort of reasoning than can be easily achieved by formal logical
deduction. Semantic networks have been the basis for representation of
the knowledge in a number of systems, including LIFER (Article IV.F7)
and many of the *speech understanding* systems (Chap. V). Recently
there has been a good deal of work on formalizing the network notions,
so that there is a clear correspondence between the graph operations
and the formal semantics of the statements represented (see Article III.C3
on semantic nets).

Case representations extend the basic notions of semantic nets with
the idea of a *case frame*, a cluster of the properties of an object or
event into a single concept (Article IV.C4). There have been several
variations on this idea, some of which remain close to the linguistic
forms. Others, such as *conceptual dependency*, are based on the notion
of *semantic primitives*, that is, the construction of all semantic notions
from a small set of elementary concepts (see Article III.C6). Conceptual
dependency theory was developed by Roger Schank and his colleagues
and used in their NL systems, MARGIE and SAM. (See Articles IV.F5
and IV.F6 and also Schank, 1980, which is a recent review of his work
in natural language understanding.)

As with semantic networks, the advantage of case representations
lies in their focus on grouping relevant sets of relationships into single
data structures. The idea of clustering structures in a coherent and efficient way has been carried much further in representation schemes based
on the notion of a *frame* (Minsky, 1975; see Article III.C7). Where case
representations deal primarily with single sentences or acts, frames are
applied to whole situations, complex objects, or series of events. In
analyzing a sentence, narrative, or dialogue, a frame-based language
understanding system tries to match the input to the prototypes of
objects and events in its domain that are stored in its database.

For example, Schank's SAM system makes use of frame-like data
structures called *scripts*, which represent stereotyped sequences of events,
to understand simple stories. It assumes that the events being described
will fit (roughly) into one of the scripts in its knowledge base, which it
then uses to fill in missing pieces in the story. The GUS system

(Bobrow et al., 1977) is an experimental, frame-based travel consultant, engaging in dialogue to help a person schedule an air trip.

The important common element in all of these systems is that the prototype frames make it possible to use *expectations* about the usual properties of known concepts and about what typically happens in a variety of familiar situations to help understand sentences about those objects and situations. When a sentence or phrase is input that is ambiguous or underspecified, it can be compared to a description of what would be expected based on the prototype. If there is a plausible match, assumptions can be made about what was meant. This *expectation-driven* processing seems to be an important aspect of the human use of language, where incomplete or ungrammatical sentences can be understood in appropriate contexts (see Article V.A).

Investigation of script- and frame-based systems is the most active area of AI research in natural language understanding at the present time. Recent systems expand the domain of expectations used in processing language beyond those involving typical objects and events to include those based on how people use plans to achieve goals (see, e.g., Schank and Abelson, 1977; Wilensky, 1978b) and on the rules people appear to follow in a dialogue (Cohen and Perrault, 1979; Kaplan, 1979; Grosz, 1980; Robinson et al., 1980). The state of the art in operational (nonexperimental) NL systems is exemplified by ROBOT (Harris, 1979), LIFER (Hendrix, 1977a), and PHLIQA1 (Landsbergen, 1976).

References

General discussions of natural-language-processing research in AI include those by Boden (1977), Charniak and Wilks (1976), Schank and Abelson (1977), and Winograd (in press). The recent review articles by Schank (1980) and Winograd (1980b) give interesting perspectives to the history of their NL research. Waltz (1977) contains more than 50 brief summaries of current projects and systems.

In addition, many historically important NL systems are described in Feigenbaum and Feldman (1963), Minsky (1968), and Rustin (1973). Bobrow and Collins (1975), COLING (1976), TINLAP-1 (1975), and TINLAP-2 (1978) are proceedings of conferences that describe current work in the field. Related AI work on speech understanding is described in the collection of articles edited by Lea (1980b).

B. MACHINE TRANSLATION

The concept of translation from one language to another by machine is older than the computer itself. According to Yehoshua Bar–Hillel, one of the early investigators in the field, the idea was conceived perhaps already in the early 1930s by P. P. Smirnov–Troyansky of the Soviet Union and G. B. Artsouni of France (see Bar–Hillel, 1964, p. 7). Their work apparently never received much attention, lying dormant until a decade later, when the climate was much more favorable because of the recent invention of the digital computer. In certain quarters of the scientific world, people imagined—with some justification—that computers would lead to many entirely new and far-reaching ideas about man and—perhaps less justifiably—that computers would help bring about a new world order. In short, there was tremendous excitement over the potential of these new *thinking machines*, as they were quickly dubbed. This was also the time when Claude Shannon was formulating his ideas on information theory, when Norbert Wiener was devising the concept of *cybernetics*, and when Pitts and McCullough were developing their ideas on neural nets and brain function. During the war, moreover, computing had just passed with flying colors its initial tests—in such strategic tasks as breaking codes and calculating complicated nuclear cross sections.

It would be well to bear in mind that when machine translation (MT) work began, programming was done by wiring boards and the only computer language available was machine language. Such concepts as arrays and subroutines were yet to appear—not to mention pushdown stacks, compiler languages, recursive procedures, and the like. Furthermore, no one had heard of *context-free* and *context-sensitive grammars*, or of *transformational grammars*, or of *augmented transition networks*. At the forefront of computational linguistics—the application of the computer to the study of language—were statistical experiments with language, such as compiling matrices of letter frequencies and of transition frequencies between successive letters. Such matrices could be used to produce interesting samples of *pseudo-language* by producing words from randomly generated letters with the same characteristics as English words. (See the related discussion of Yngve's *random text generation* system in Article IV.E.)

First Attempts

The real genesis of machine translation dates from a series of discussions between Warren Weaver and A. Donald Booth in 1946. Both men were familiar with the work on code breaking by computers, based on letter-frequency and word-frequency tables. It seemed to them that some of the same methods would be applicable to translation and that the principal obstacle would be incorporating a full dictionary of the two languages. Of course, they recognized that simply having a dictionary would not solve all problems. Some of the remaining problems would be the following: (a) Many words have several translations, depending upon context; (b) word orders vary from language to language; and (c) idiomatic expressions cannot be translated word for word but must be translated *in toto*. Nevertheless, it appeared plausible, at the time, that the major problem in translating between two languages was simply that of vocabulary—and so at least a large part of translation seemed mechanizable.

In 1947, Booth and D. H. V. Britten worked out a program for dictionary lookup. This was a full-form dictionary, in that each variant of any basic word (e.g., *love, loves, loving*) had to be carried as a separate entry in the dictionary. In 1948, R. H. Richens suggested the addition of rules concerning the inflections of words, so that the redundancy of the multiple dictionary entries could be eliminated.

In 1949, Weaver distributed a memorandum entitled "Translation" to about 200 of his acquaintances (see Weaver, 1955), and a considerable wave of interest ensued. In addition to the idea that all languages have many features in common, three other items from that memorandum are worth repeating. The first is the notion of a *window* through which one can view exactly $2N + 1$ words of text; Weaver suggests that when N is sufficiently large, one will be able to determine the unique, correct translation for the word that sits in the middle of the window. He then points out that N may be a function of the word, rather than a constant, and discusses the idea of choosing a value of N such that, say, 95% of all words would be correctly translated 98% of the time. The second is this intriguing statement: "When I look at an article in Russian, I say, *This is really written in English, but it has been coded in some strange symbols. I will now proceed to decode.*" This certainly carries to an extreme the concept that source text and translated text "say the same thing." In fact, it leads naturally to the third provocative idea of the memorandum that translating between languages A and B means going from A to an intermediate "universal language," or *interlingua*, that, supposedly, all humans share, and thence to B. This idea, of an intermediate representation of the *semantics* or meaning of an utterance, appears often in modern, natural language processing work in AI under the rubric *representation of knowledge* (see discussion in Article IV.A and in Chap. III).

After Weaver's memorandum, work began in several centers in the United States. Erwin Reifler conceived the idea of two auxiliary functions to be performed by human beings, those of *pre-editor* and *post-editor*. The pre-editor would prepare the input text to be as free as possible of ambiguities and other sources of difficulty; the post-editor would take the machine-translated text and turn it into grammatical, comprehensible prose.

A conference in 1952 produced recommendations to implement a dictionary-lookup program and to work towards the invention, or discovery, of the hypothetical universal language, called *Machinese*, which Weaver had proposed as an intermediate language for machine translation.

A. G. Oettinger was one of the first to design a program that carried out word-for-word translation of Russian text into English. A very high percentage of the Russian words had more than one possible translation, so all of them were listed in the output English text, enclosed in parentheses. Thus, a sample of English output text read as follows:

> (In, At, Into, To, For, On) (last, latter, new, latest, lowest, worst) (time, tense) for analysis and synthesis relay-contact electrical (circuit, diagram, scheme) parallel-(series, successive, consecutive, consistent) (connection, junction, combination) (with, from) (success, luck) (to be utilize, to be take advantage of) apparatus Boolean algebra. (Oettinger, 1955, p. 55)

A cleaned-up version of this sentence reads: "In recent times Boolean algebra has been successfully employed in the analysis of relay networks of the series-parallel type" (p. 58). Readers of the translated text were expected to discern from the jumble of synonyms what the cleaned-up text really should be. Clearly, there was still a long, long way to go toward mechanical translation.

In the next year or two, most of the effort was directed toward devising ways to handle different endings of inflected words and estimating the size of vocabulary needed for translations of varying degrees of quality. In 1954, a journal of mechanical translation was founded, called *MT*. Machine translation received considerable public attention when a group from IBM and Georgetown University made grand claims for a program that translated from Russian to English, although this program was not particularly advanced over any others. In any case, machine-translation research groups sprang up in many countries.

Problems Encountered

Early attempts focusing on syntactic information were able to produce only low-quality translation and led eventually to extreme pessimism about the possibility of the endeavor. It has since become clear that high-quality translation systems must in some sense *understand* the input text before they can reconstruct it in a second language. For the first time, it was becoming apparent that much "world knowledge" is applied implicitly when human beings translate from one language to another. Bar–Hillel gave as an example the pair of sentences, *The pen is in the box* and *The box is in the pen.* Of this example he said, "I now claim that no existing or imaginable program will enable an electronic computer to determine that the word *pen*" in the second sentence has the meaning "an enclosure where small children can play" (Bar–Hillel, 1960, p. 159). He goes on to remark that, to his amazement, no one had ever pointed out that in language understanding there is a world-modeling process going on in the mind of the listener and that people are constantly making use of this subconscious process to guide their understanding of what is being said. Bar–Hillel continues:

> A translation machine should not only be supplied with a dictionary but also with a universal encyclopedia. This is surely utterly chimerical and hardly deserves any further discussion. . . . We know . . . facts by inferences which we are able to perform . . . instantaneously, and it is clear that they are not, in any serious sense, stored in our memory. Though one could envisage that a machine would be capable of performing the same inferences, there exists so far no serious proposal for a scheme that would make a machine perform such inferences in the same or similar circumstances under which an intelligent human being would perform them. (pp. 160–161)

Bar–Hillel despaired of ever achieving satisfactory machine translation. His sentiments were not universally shared, but in 1966 they came to prevail officially in the so-called ALPAC report (National Research Council, 1966). This report, made to the National Research Council after a year of study by its Automatic Language Processing Advisory Committee, resulted in the discontinuance of funding for most machine translation projects. The report stated:

> "Machine Translation" presumably means going by algorithm from machine-readable source text to useful target text, without recourse to human translation or editing. In this context, there has been no machine translation of general scientific text, and none is in immediate prospect. (p. 19)

Examples of the output of several MT systems were included in the report; they showed little improvement from the results Oettinger had obtained 10 years before. Even with post-editing, the output was found to be generally of poorer quality, and sometimes slower and more expensive to obtain, than entirely human translation.

Current Status

The conclusions of the ALPAC report were directed only against funding for MT as a practical tool. Support for computational linguistics, evaluated in terms of its scientific worth rather than its immediate utility, was to be continued. It was also recognized that there had been fundamental changes in the study of linguistics, partly as a result of cross-fertilization with computational activities.

Both linguistics and computer science have made contributions relevant to the revival of MT research. A signal event was the publication in 1957 of Noam Chomsky's *Syntactic Structures,* in which *transformational grammars* were introduced. This book spurred many new developments in the analysis of syntax. Concurrently, new computer languages and new types of data structures were being explored by computer scientists, leading to the creation (in 1960) of both ALGOL and LISP, with their features of lists, recursion, and so forth. These languages were the first in a series of languages geared more toward symbol manipulation than toward "number crunching," as discussed in Chapter VI, in Volume II. In Artificial Intelligence, the 1960s saw considerable progress toward natural language understanding, such as the development of programs that carried on a dialogue of sorts with the user—BASEBALL, SAD-SAM, STUDENT, SIR, and the like—which are described in Article IV.F1.

The early 1970s saw some revival of interest in machine translation, partly because some progress had been made in the internal *representation of knowledge.* The programs of Wilks (Article IV.F2) and Schank (Articles IV.F5 and IV.F6) can perform translation tasks. They begin by translating input sentences into internal data structures based on *semantic primitives* that are intended to be language independent— that is, elements of meaning that are common to all natural languages. The internal representation can be manipulated relatively easily by procedures that carry out *inferences;* it forms in effect an internal language or *interlingua* for modeling the world.

It is difficult to evaluate the practicality of machine translation. In some applications it is worthwhile to have even a very bad translation, if it can be done by a computer in a much shorter time (or much more cheaply) than by humans. In others (such as the preparation of instruction manuals) it is possible to deal with input texts that use a specially restricted form of the language, thereby making translation easier. There is also the possibility of machine-human interactive translating, in which the output of the computer is used not by the ultimate reader but by someone engaged in producing the final translation. The computer can perform subtasks (like dictionary lookup) or can produce more or less complete translations that are then checked and polished by a human post-editor, who perhaps does not know the original language.

At the present time, computers are being used in these ways in a number of translation systems. There is also a renewed interest in fully automatic translation, based on some of the techniques developed for dealing with the meaning of sentences, as described in the articles that follow. However, it is not clear whether the goal of "fully automatic, high-quality translation" is yet realistic. Much current AI work on language is based on a belief that deep understanding of what is being said is vital to every use of language. Applied to translation, this means that an MT program must first understand a subject before it can translate material written about that subject. And the machine's ability to *understand* is, of course, the focus of current AI research in all areas.

References

A brief, popular review of current work in machine translation can be found in Wilks (1977d). For the earliest history, see the introduction to Locke and Booth (1955). Later surveys include Bar–Hillel (1960), Josselson (1971), and Hays and Mathias (1976).

See also Bar–Hillel (1964), Booth (1967), National Research Council (1966), Oettinger (1955), Schank (1975a), Weaver (1955), and Wilks (1973).

C. GRAMMARS

C1. Formal Grammars

A *grammar* of a language is a scheme for specifying the sentences allowed in the language, indicating the rules for combining words into phrases and clauses. In natural language processing programs, the grammar is used in *parsing*—"picking apart"—the sentences input to the program, in order to determine their meaning and thus an appropriate response. Several very different kinds of grammars have been used in NL programs and are described in the articles that follow.

One of the more important contributions to the study of language was the theory of *formal languages* introduced by Noam Chomsky in the 1950s. The theory has developed as a mathematical study, not a linguistic one, and has strongly influenced computer science in the design of computer programming languages (artificial languages). Nevertheless, it is useful in connection with *natural language* understanding systems, as both a theoretical and a practical tool.

Definitions

A *formal language* is defined as a (possibly infinite) set of strings of finite length formed from a finite vocabulary of symbols. (E.g., the strings might be sentences composed from a vocabulary of words.) The *grammar* of a formal language is specified in terms of the following concepts.

1. The *syntactic categories* (such as <SENTENCE> and <NOUN PHRASE>). These syntactic categories are referred to as *nonterminal symbols*, or *variables*. Notationally, the nonterminals of a grammar are often indicated by enclosing the category names in angle brackets, as above.

2. The *terminal symbols* of the language (e.g., the words in English). The terminal symbols are to be concatenated into strings called *sentences* (if the terminals are words). A language is then just a subset of the set of all the strings that can be formed by combining the terminal symbols in all possible ways. Exactly which subset is permitted in the language is specified by the rewrite rules, described next.

3. The *rewrite rules*, or *productions*, which specify the relations between certain strings of terminal and nonterminal symbols. Some examples of productions are:

```
⟨SENTENCE⟩ → ⟨NOUN PHRASE⟩ ⟨VERB PHRASE⟩
⟨NOUN PHRASE⟩ → the ⟨NOUN⟩
      ⟨NOUN⟩ → dog
      ⟨NOUN⟩ → cat
⟨VERB PHRASE⟩ → runs
```

The first production says that the nonterminal symbol <SENTENCE> may be "rewritten" as the symbol <NOUN PHRASE> followed by the symbol <VERB PHRASE>. The second permits <NOUN PHRASE> to be replaced by a string composed of the word *the,* which is a terminal symbol, followed by the nonterminal <NOUN>. The next two allow <NOUN> to be replaced by either *dog* or *cat.* Since there are sequences of productions permitting <NOUN PHRASE> to be replaced by *the dog* or *the cat,* the symbol <NOUN PHRASE> is said to *generate* these two terminal strings. Finally, <VERB PHRASE> can be replaced by the terminal *runs.*

4. The *start symbol.* One nonterminal is distinguished and called the "sentence" or "start" symbol, typically denoted <SENTENCE> or *S.* The set of strings of terminals that can be derived from this distinguished symbol, by applying sequences of productions, is called the *language generated by the grammar.* In the simple grammar of our example, exactly two sentences are generated:

```
The cat runs.
The dog runs.
```

The important aspect of defining languages formally, from the point of view of computational linguistics and natural language processing, is that if the structure of the sentences the system is to process is well understood, then a *parsing* algorithm for analyzing the input sentences will be relatively easy to write (see Article IV.D1).

The Four Types of Formal Grammars

Within the framework outlined above, Chomsky delineated four types of grammars and numbered them 0 through 3. The most general class of grammar is type 0, which has no restrictions on the form that rewrite rules can take. For successive grammar types, the form of the rewriting rules allowed is increasingly restricted, and the languages that are generated are correspondingly simpler. The simplest formal languages (types 2 and 3) are, as it turns out, inadequate for describing the complexities of human languages (see Article IV.C2 for a fuller discussion). On the other hand, the most general formal languages are difficult to handle computationally. There is an intimate and interesting connection between the theory of formal languages and the theory of computational complexity (see Hopcroft and Ullman, 1969). The following discussion gives a brief, formal account of the different restrictions applied in each of the four grammar types.

A grammar G is defined by a quadruple (VN, VT, P, S) representing the nonterminals, the terminals, the productions, and the start symbol, respectively. The symbol V, for *vocabulary*, represents the union of the sets VN and VT, which are assumed to have no elements in common. Each production in P is of the form

$$X \rightarrow Y ,$$

where X and Y are strings of elements in V, and X is not the empty string.

Type 0. A type 0 grammar is defined as above: a set of productions over a given vocabulary of symbols with no restrictions on the form of the productions. It has been shown that a language can be generated by a type 0 grammar if and only if it can be recognized by a Turing machine, that is, if we can build a Turing machine that will halt in an ACCEPT state for exactly those input sentences that can be generated by the language.

Type 1. A type 0 grammar is also of type 1 if the form of the rewrite rules is restricted so that, for each production $X \rightarrow Y$ of the grammar, the right-hand side, Y, contains at least as many symbols as the left-hand side, X. Type 1 grammars are also called *context-sensitive* grammars. An example of a context-sensitive grammar with start symbol S and terminals a, b, and c is the following:

$$S \rightarrow aSBC$$
$$S \rightarrow aBC$$
$$CB \rightarrow BC$$
$$aB \rightarrow ab$$
$$bB \rightarrow bb$$
$$bC \rightarrow bc$$
$$cC \rightarrow cc$$

The language generated by this grammar is the set of strings abc, $aabbcc$, $aaabbbccc$, ... This language, where each symbol must occur the same number of times and must appear in the proper position in the string, cannot be generated by any grammar of a more restricted type (i.e., type 2 or type 3).

An alternate (equivalent) definition for context-sensitive grammars is that the productions must be of the form

$$uXv \rightarrow uYv ,$$

where X is a single nonterminal symbol; u and v are arbitrary strings, possibly empty, of elements of V; and Y is a nonempty string over V. It can be shown that this restriction generates the same languages as the first restriction, but this latter definition clarifies the term *context-sensitive*: X may be rewritten as Y only in the context of u and v.

    Type 2. *Context-free grammars*, or type 2 grammars, are grammars in which each production must have only a single nonterminal symbol on its left-hand side. For example, a context-free grammar generating the sentences *ab, aabb, aaabbb*, ... is:

$$S \rightarrow aSb$$
$$S \rightarrow ab$$

Again, it is not possible to write a context-free grammar for the language composed of the sentences *abc, aabbcc, aaabbbccc,* ... ; having the same number of *c*'s at the end makes the language more complex. The simpler language here, in turn, cannot be generated by a more restricted (type 3) grammar.

    An example of a context-free grammar that might be used to generate some sentences in natural language is the following:

```
⟨SENTENCE⟩ → ⟨NOUN PHRASE⟩ ⟨VERB PHRASE⟩
⟨NOUN PHRASE⟩ → ⟨DETERMINER⟩ ⟨NOUN⟩
⟨NOUN PHRASE⟩ → ⟨NOUN⟩
⟨VERB PHRASE⟩ → ⟨VERB⟩ ⟨NOUN PHRASE⟩
⟨DETERMINER⟩ → the
⟨NOUN⟩ → boys
⟨NOUN⟩ → apples
⟨VERB⟩ → eat
```

In this example, *the, boys, apples,* and *eat* are the terminals in the language, and <SENTENCE> is the start symbol.

    An important property of context-free grammars in their use in NL programs is that every derivation can conveniently be represented as a tree, which can be thought of as displaying the structure of the derived sentence. Using the grammar above, the sentence *The boys eat apples* has the following *derivation tree:*

```
                        ⟨SENTENCE⟩
                       /          \
              ⟨NOUN PHRASE⟩      ⟨VERB PHRASE⟩
               /        \          /         \
      ⟨DETERMINER⟩    ⟨NOUN⟩   ⟨VERB⟩    ⟨NOUN PHRASE⟩
           |            |        |            |
          the         boys      eat        ⟨NOUN⟩
                                              |
                                            apples
```

Of course, *The apples eat boys* is also a legal sentence in this language. Derivation trees can also be used with context-sensitive (type 1) grammars, provided the productions have the alternate form $uXv \rightarrow uYv$, described above. For this reason, context-free and context-sensitive grammars are often called *phrase-structure grammars* (see Chomsky, 1959, pp. 143–144, and Lyons, 1968, p. 236).

Type 3. Finally, if every production is of the form

$$X \rightarrow aY \qquad \text{or} \qquad X \rightarrow a \ ,$$

where X and Y are single variables and a is a single terminal, the grammar is a type 3 or *regular grammar*. For example, a regular grammar can be given to generate the set of strings of one or more a's followed by one or more b's (but with no guarantee of an equal number of a's and b's):

$$S \rightarrow aS$$
$$S \rightarrow aT$$
$$T \rightarrow b$$
$$T \rightarrow bT$$

Discussion: Language and Computational Algorithms

Because of the increasingly restricted forms of productions in grammars of types 0, 1, 2, and 3, each type is a proper subset of the type above it in the hierarchy. A corresponding hierarchy exists for formal languages. A language is said to be of type i if it can be generated by a type i grammar. It can be shown that there are languages that are context free (type 2) but not regular (type 3), context sensitive (type 1) but not context free, and type 0 but not context sensitive. Examples of the first two have been given above.

For regular and context-free grammars, there are practical parsing algorithms to determine whether or not a given string is an element of the language and, if so, to assign to it a syntactic structure in the form of a derivation tree. Context-free grammars have considerable application to programming languages. Natural languages, however, are not generally context-free (Chomsky, 1963; Postal, 1964), and they also contain features that can be handled more conveniently, if not exclusively, by a more powerful grammar. An example is the requirement that the subject and verb of a sentence be both singular or both plural. Some of the types of grammars and parsing algorithms that have been explored as more suitable for natural language are discussed in the articles that follow.

References

For a general discussion of the theory of formal grammars and their relation to automata theory, see Hopcroft and Ullman (1969). Their use in NL research is discussed in Winograd (in press).

Also of interest are the works of Chomsky (especially 1956, 1957, and 1959), as well as Lyons (1968, 1970) and Postal (1964).

C2. Transformational Grammars

The term *transformational grammar* refers to a theory of language introduced by Noam Chomsky in *Syntactic Structures* (1957). In the theory, an utterance is characterized as the surface manifestation of a "deeper" structure representing the "meaning" of the sentence. The deep structure can undergo a variety of "transformations" of form (word order, endings, etc.) on its way up, while retaining its essential meaning. The theory assumes that an adequate grammar of a language like English must be a *generative grammar*, that is, that it must be a statement of finite length capable of (a) accounting for the infinite number of possible sentences in the language and (b) assigning to each a structural description that captures the underlying knowledge of the language held by an idealized native user. A *formal system of rules* is such a statement; it "can be viewed as a device of some sort for producing the sentences of the language under analysis" (Chomsky, 1957, p. 11). The operation of the device is not intended to reflect the processes by which people actually speak or understand sentences, just as a formal proof in mathematics does not purport to reflect the processes by which the proof was discovered. As a model of abstract knowledge and not of human behavior, generative grammar is said to be concerned with *competence*, as opposed to *performance*.

The Inadequacy of Phrase-structure Grammars

Given that a grammar is a generative rule-system, it becomes a central task of linguistic theory to discover what the rules should look like. In *Syntactic Structures* and elsewhere (Chomsky, 1957, 1963; Postal, 1964), it was shown that English is neither a *regular* nor a *context-free* language. The reason is that those restricted types of grammars (defined in Article IV.C1) cannot generate certain common constructions in everyday English, such as the one using *respectively:*

```
Arthur, Barry, Charles, and David are the husbands of
Jane, Joan, Jill, and Jennifer, respectively.
```

It was not determined whether a more powerful (i.e., context-sensitive) grammar could be written to generate precisely the sentences of English; rather, such a grammar was rejected for the following reasons.

1. It made the description of English unnecessarily clumsy and complex—for example, in the treatment required for conjunction, auxiliary verbs, and passive sentences.

2. It assigned identical structures (derivation trees) to sentences that are understood differently, as in the pair:

> The picture was painted by a new technique.
> The picture was painted by a new artist.

3. It provided no basis for identifying as similar the sentences that have different surface structures but much of their "meaning" in common:

> John ate an apple.
> Did John eat an apple?
> What did John eat?
> Who ate an apple?

The failure of phrase-structure grammar to explain such similarities and differences was taken to indicate the need for analysis on a higher level, which transformational grammar provides.

Transformational Rules

In *Syntactic Structures,* Chomsky proposed that grammars should have a tripartite organization. The first part was to be a phrase-structure grammar generating strings of morphemes representing simple, declarative, active sentences, each with an associated phrase marker or derivation tree. Second, there would be a sequence of *transformational rules* rearranging the strings and adding or deleting morphemes to form representations of the full variety of sentences. Finally, a sequence of morphophonemic rules would map each sentence representation to a string of phonemes. Although later work has changed this model of the grammar, as well as the content of the transformational rules, it provides a basis for a simple illustration.

Suppose the phrase-structure grammar is used to produce the following derivation tree:

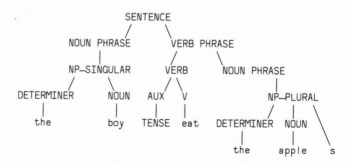

To generate *The boy ate the apples,* one would apply transformations mapping "TENSE + *eat*" to "*eat* + PAST"; a morphophonemic rule would then map "*eat* + PAST" to *ate.* To derive *The boy eats the apples,* the transformational rule used would select present tense and, because the verb follows a singular noun phrase, would map "TENSE + *eat*" to "*eat* + *s.*" It is noteworthy that the transformational rule must look at nonterminal nodes in the derivation tree to determine that *the boy* is in fact a singular noun phrase. This example illustrates one way in which transformational rules are broader than the rules of a phrase-structure grammar.

The transformations mentioned so far are examples of *obligatory transformations,* ensuring agreement in number of the subject and the verb. To obtain *The apples were eaten by the boy,* it would be necessary first to apply the optional *passive* transformation, changing a string analyzed as

NOUN-PHRASE-1 + AUX + V + NOUN-PHRASE-2

to

NOUN-PHRASE-2 + (AUX + be) + (en + V) + by + NOUN-PHRASE-1 .

In other words, this *optional transformation* changes "*The boy* TENSE *eat the apples*" to "*The apples* TENSE *be (en eat) by the boy,*" and then forces agreement of the auxiliary verb with the new plural subject. Further obligatory transformations would yield "*The apples be* PAST *eaten by the boy*" (where "*be* + PAST," as opposed to "*be* + *s* + PAST," is ultimately mapped to *were*). The *ordering* of transformational rules is thus an essential feature of the grammar.

Revisions to the Model

In *Aspects of the Theory of Syntax* (1965), Chomsky made several revisions to the model presented in *Syntactic Structures* (1957). The version outlined in the more recent book has been called the "standard theory" of generative grammar and has served as a common starting point for further discussion. In the standard theory (as summarized in Chomsky, 1971), sentence generation begins from a context-free grammar generating a sentence structure and is followed by a selection of words for the structure from a *lexicon.* The context-free grammar and lexicon are said to form the *base* of the grammar; their output is called a *deep structure.* A system of transformational rules maps deep structures to *surface structures;* together, the base and transformational parts of the grammar form its *syntactic component.* The sound of a sentence is determined by its surface structure, which is interpreted by the *phonological component* of the grammar; deep structure, interpreted by the *semantic component*, determines sentence meaning. It follows that the application of transformational rules to deep structures must preserve meaning: This was the Katz–Postal hypothesis, which required enlarging the generative capacity of the base and revising many of the transformational rules suggested earlier (Katz and Postal, 1964).

The place of the semantic component in the standard theory has been the major source of current issues. For example, the following pairs of sentences have different meanings, but their deep structures, in the standard theory, are the same.

```
Not many arrows hit the target.
Many arrows didn't hit the target.

Each of Mary's sons loves his brothers.
His brothers are loved by each of Mary's sons.
```

Chomsky's response was to revise the standard theory so that both the deep structure of a sentence and its subsequent transformations are input to the semantic component (Chomsky, 1971). He exemplifies the position of *interpretive semantics*, which keeps the syntactic component an autonomous system. The opposing view, called *generative semantics*, is that syntax and semantics cannot be sharply separated and, consequently, that a distinct level of syntactic deep structure does not exist. (This issue is discussed in Charniak and Wilks, 1976.)

There have been a number of developments within the theory of transformational grammar since the work reviewed here, and current debates have called into question many of the basic assumptions about the role of transformations in a grammar. For current discussions of these issues, see Culicover, Wasow, and Akmajian (1977) and Bresnan (1978).

References

The classic references here are, of course, Chomsky (1957) and Chomsky (1965). Chomsky (1971) is a shorter and more recent discussion. Culicover, Wasow, and Akmajian (1977) and Bresnan (1978) are the latest word on transformation theory.

Also see Akmajian and Heny (1975), Charniak and Wilks (1976), Chomsky (1956, 1959, 1963), Harman (1974), Katz and Postal (1964), Lyons (1968, 1970), Postal (1964), and Steinberg and Jakobovits (1971).

C3. Systemic Grammar

Systemic grammar, developed by Michael Halliday and others at the University of London, is a theory within which linguistic structure as related to the *function* or use of language, often termed *pragmatics*, is studied. According to Halliday (1961, p. 241), an account of linguistic structure that pays no attention to the functional demands made on language is lacking in perspicacity, since it offers no principles for explaining why the structure is organized one way rather than another. This viewpoint is in contrast to that of *transformational grammar*, which has been concerned with the syntactic structure of an utterance apart from its intended use.

The Functions of Language

Halliday distinguishes three general functions of language, all of which are ordinarily served by every act of speech.

The *ideational function* serves for the expression of content. It says something about the speaker's experience of the world. Analyzing a clause in terms of its ideational function involves asking questions like the following: What kind of process does the clause describe—an action, a mental process, or a relation? Who is the actor (the logical subject)? Are there other participants in the process, such as goal (direct object) or beneficiary (indirect object)? Are there adverbial phrases expressing circumstances like time and place? The organization of this set of questions is described by what Halliday calls the *transitivity system* of the grammar. (This is related to the ideas of *case grammars* discussed in Article IV.C4.)

The *interpersonal function* relates to the purpose of the utterance. The speaker may be asking a question, answering one, making a request, giving information, or expressing an opinion. The *mood system* of English grammar expresses these possibilities in terms of categories such as statement, question, command, and exclamation.

The *textual function* reflects the need for coherence in language use (e.g., how a given sentence is related to preceding ones). Concepts for analysis in textual terms include (a) the theme, that is, the element that the speaker chooses to put at the beginning of a clause, and (b) the distinction between what is new in a message and what is given—the latter being the point of contact with what the hearer already knows.

Categories of Systemic Grammar

The model of a grammar proposed by Halliday has four primitive categories:

1. *The units of language,* which form a hierarchy. In English, these are the sentence, clause, group, word, and morpheme. The rank of a unit refers to its position in the hierarchy.

2. *The structure of units.* Each unit is composed of one or more units at the rank below, and each of these components fills a particular role. The English clause, for example, is made up of four groups, which serve as subject, predicator, complement, and adjunct.

3. *The classification of units,* as determined by the roles to be filled at the level above. The classes of English groups, for instance, are the verbal, which serves as predicator; the nominal, which may be subject or complement; and the adverbial, which fills the adjunct function.

4. *The system.* A system is a list of choices representing the options available to the speaker. Since some sets of choices are available only if other choices have already been made, the relation between systems is shown by combining them into networks, as in the simple example below:

```
                                  | imperative
                  | independent →
                  |               | indicative →      | declarative
 clause →         |                              |→
                  | dependent ──────────────────│    | interrogative
```

The interpretation is that each clause is independent or dependent; if independent, it is either imperative or indicative; and if either indicative or dependent, then it is either declarative or interrogative. In general, system networks can be defined for units of any rank, and entry to a system of choices may be made to depend on any Boolean combination of previous choices.

Conclusion

Systemic grammar views the act of speech as a simultaneous selection from among a large number of interrelated options, which represent the "meaning potential" of the language. If system networks representing these options are suitably combined and carried to enough detail, they provide a way of writing a generative grammar quite distinct from that proposed by *transformational grammar* (see Hudson, 1971, 1976; McCord, 1975; Self, 1975). Furthermore, this formalism has been found more readily adaptable for use in natural language understanding programs in AI (see especially Winograd's SHRDLU system, Article IV.F4).

References

Halliday (1961) and Halliday (1970b) are the most general original references. Winograd (1972) discusses the application of systemic grammar in his famous SHRDLU system.

Also see Halliday (1967–68, 1970a), Hudson (1971, 1976), McCord (1975), McIntosh and Halliday (1966), and Self (1975).

C4. Case Grammars

Case systems, as used both in modern linguistics and in Artificial Intelligence, are descendants of the concept of *case* as it occurs in traditional grammar. Traditionally, the case of a noun was denoted by an inflectional ending indicating the noun's role in the sentence. Latin, for example, has at least six cases: nominative, accusative, genitive, dative, ablative, and vocative. The rules for case endings make the meaning of a Latin sentence almost independent of word order: The function of a noun depends on its inflection rather than on its position in the sentence. Some present-day languages, including Russian and German, have similar inflection systems, but English limits case forms mainly to the personal pronoun—as in *I, my, me*—and to the possessive ending " *'s*." Case functions for nouns are indicated in English by word order or by the choice of preposition to precede a noun phrase—as in "*of* the people, *by* the people, and *for* the people."

The examples above describe what have been called "surface" cases; they are aspects of the *surface structure* of the sentence. Case systems that have attracted more recent attention are "deep" cases, proposed by Fillmore (1968) in his paper "The Case for Case," as a revision to the framework of *transformational grammar*. The central idea is that the proposition embodied in a simple sentence has a deep structure consisting of a verb (the central component) and one or more noun phrases. Each noun phrase is associated with the verb in a particular relationship. These relationships, which Fillmore characterized as "semantically relevant syntactic relationships," are called *cases*. For example, in the sentence

```
John opened the door with the key.
```

John would be the AGENT of the verb *opened, the door* would be the OBJECT, and *the key* would be the INSTRUMENT. For the sentence

```
The door was opened by John with the key.
```

the case assignments would be the same, even though the surface structure has changed.

It was important to Fillmore's theory that the number of possible case relationships be small and fixed. Fillmore (1971b) proposed the following cases:

Agent	— the instigator of the event.
Counter-Agent	— the force or resistance against which the action is carried out.
Object	— the entity that moves or changes or whose position or existence is in consideration.
Result	— the entity that comes into existence as a result of the action.
Instrument	— the stimulus or immediate physical cause of an event.
Source	— the place from which something moves.
Goal	— the place to which something moves.
Experiencer	— the entity which receives or accepts or experiences or undergoes the effect of an action.

Still another proposal (Fillmore, 1971a) recognizes nine cases: Agent, Experiencer, Instrument, Object, Source, Goal, Location, Time, and Path.

Verbs were classified according to the cases that could occur with them. The cases for any particular verb formed an ordered set called a *case frame*. For example, the verb *open* was proposed to have the case frame

[OBJECT   (INSTRUMENT)   (AGENT)]

indicating that the object is obligatory in the deep structure of the sentence, whereas it is permissible to omit the instrument *(John opened the door)* or the agent *(The key opened the door),* or both *(The door opened).* Thus, verbs provide *templates* within which the remainder of the sentence can be understood.

The Case for Case

The following are some of the kinds of questions for which case analysis was intended to provide answers:

1. In a sentence that is to contain several noun phrases, what determines which noun phrase should be the subject in the surface structure? Cases are ordered, and the highest ranking case that is present becomes the subject.

2. Since one may say *Mother is baking* or *The pie is baking,* what is wrong with *Mother and the pie are baking?* Different cases may not be conjoined.

3. What is the precise relationship between pairs of words like *buy* and *sell* or *teach* and *learn?* They have the same basic meaning but different case frames.

One way of looking at deep cases is to view the verb as a predicate taking an appropriate array of arguments. Fillmore has extended the class of predicates to include other parts of speech, such as nouns and adjectives, as well as verbs. Viewing *warm* as a predicate, for example, enabled case distinctions to account for the differences among the following sentences:

```
I am warm.             [experiencer]
This jacket is warm.   [instrument]
Summer is warm.        [time]
The room is warm.      [location]
```

The Representation of Case Frames

In AI programs, such predicates and their arguments can readily be equated to nodes in *semantic networks;* and the case relations, to the types of links between them. Systems making such identifications include those of Hendrix (Article IV.F7), Schank (Articles IV.F5 and IV.F6), Simmons (Article IV.E), and Norman and Rumelhart (Article XI.E4, in Vol. III). Semantic nets and related work on *semantic primitives* and *frames* are discussed in Chapter III.

There are many other systems using case representations. As pointed out in an extensive survey by Bruce (1975), considerable variation is found in both the sets of cases adopted and the ways in which case representation is applied. The number of cases used varies from four or five (Schank) to over 30 (Martin). Bruce's proposal on criteria for choosing cases, which departs significantly from Fillmore's original goal of finding a small, fixed set of relationships, is that

> a case is a relation which is "important" for an event in the context in which it is described. (Bruce, 1975)

Case notation has been used to record various levels of sentence structure. As Fillmore introduced it, within the transformational grammar framework, deep cases were deep in the sense that *John opened the door* and *The door was opened by John* were given the same representation. They can also be viewed as relatively superficial, however, in that *John bought a car from Bill* and *Bill sold a car to John* could have distinct representations since they have different verbs. At this level, cases have been used in parsing (Taylor and Rosenberg, 1975; Wilks, 1976); in the representation of English sentences as opposed to their underlying meanings, as discussed above (Simmons, 1973); and in *text generation* (see Article IV.E).

Systems using case at the deepest level, on the other hand, may represent the meaning of sentences in a way that collapses *buy* and *sell,* for example, into a single predicate (Norman and Rumelhart, 1975; Schank, 1975a). A typical problem attacked by these systems is *paraphrasing,* in which identifying sentences with the same deep structure is the goal. Schank also requires that all cases be filled, even if the information required was not explicitly given in the input sentences (see Article IV.F5). Charniak (1975) suggests that the appropriate use of case at this level of representation is in drawing *inferences:* The "meaning" of a case would then be the set of inferences one could draw about an entity knowing only its case. In the view of some writers, however, the function of case in natural language understanding systems is usually only as a convenient notation (see Charniak, 1975; Welin, 1975).

References

Fillmore (1968) is the classic reference on case grammars. Bruce (1975) is a thorough review of different approaches to case grammar.

Also see Charniak (1975), Fillmore (1971a, 1971b), Norman and Rumelhart (1975), Samlowski (1976), Schank (1973b, 1975a), Schank and Abelson (1977), Simmons (1973), Taylor and Rosenberg (1975), Welin (1975), and Wilks (1976).

D. PARSING

D1. Overview of Parsing Techniques

Parsing is the "delinearization" of linguistic input, that is, the use of syntax and other sources of knowledge to determine the functions of the words in the input sentence in order to create a data structure, like a *derivation tree*, that can be used to get at the "meaning" of the sentence. A parser can be viewed as a *recursive pattern matcher* seeking to map a string of words onto a set of meaningful syntactic patterns. For example, the sentence *John kissed Mary* could be matched to the pattern:

```
            SENTENCE
            /      \
       SUBJECT    PREDICATE
                  /      \
               VERB     OBJECT
```

The set of syntactic patterns used is determined by the *grammar* of the input language. (Several types of grammars are described in the articles in Sec. IV.C.) In theory, by applying a comprehensive grammar, a parser can decide what is and what is not a grammatical sentence and can build up a data structure corresponding to the syntactic structure of any grammatical sentence it finds. All natural-language-processing computer systems contain a parsing component of some sort, but the practical application of grammars to natural language processing has proved difficult.

The design of a parser is a complex problem, in both theory and implementation. The first part of the design concerns the specification of the grammar to be employed. The rest of the parsing system is concerned with the method of *use* of the grammar, that is, the manner in which strings of words are matched against patterns of the grammar. These considerations run into many of the general questions of computer science and Artificial Intelligence concerning process control and manipulation of knowledge.

General Issues in Parser Design

The design considerations discussed below overlap; that is, a decision in one dimension affects other design decisions. Taken together, they present a picture of the variety of issues involved in parsing natural language.

Uniformity. Parsers may *represent* their knowledge about word meanings, grammar, and so forth, with a single scheme or with specialized structures for specific tasks. The representation scheme affects the complexity of the system and the application of that knowledge during parsing. If rules and processes are based on specialized knowledge of what the input to the parser will contain, it is possible to do things more quickly and efficiently. On the other hand, if one has a simple, uniform set of rules and a consistent algorithm for applying them, the job of writing and modifying the language understanding system is greatly simplified, since all the knowledge in the system is uniformly explicated. In general, there is a trade-off between efficiency and uniformity; an algorithm specially designed for only one language can perform more efficiently than one that could uniformly handle any language.

Multiple sources of knowledge. Parsing, as originally developed (and still used in compilers for programming languages), was based purely on syntactic knowledge—knowledge about the *form* of sentences allowed in the language. However, it is possible to design systems in which syntax-based parsing is intermixed with other levels of processing, such as word recognition and use of word meanings. Such methods can alleviate many of the problems of language complexity by bringing more information to bear. Present systems tend toward such intermixed structures, both for effective performance and for more psychologically valid modeling of human language understanding (see, e.g., Article IV.F4 on SHRDLU; the extensive discussion of multiple sources of knowledge in Article IX.C3, in Vol. II, on the SOPHIE system; and the *blackboard* model described in Chap. V).

Precision. Another major trade-off in parser design is *precision* versus *flexibility*. Humans are capable of understanding sentences that are not quite grammatical; even if a person knows that a sentence is "wrong" syntactically, he can often understand it, that is, assign a meaning to it. Some natural language processing systems, such as PARRY (Colby, Weber, and Hilf, 1971) and ELIZA (Article IV.F1), have been designed to incorporate this kind of flexibility. By looking for key words and applying loose grammatical criteria, these systems can accept far more sentences than would a precise parser. However, these "knowledge-poor," *flexible* parsers lose many benefits of the more complete analysis possible with a precise system, since they rely on vaguer notions of sentence meaning than a precise system does. While they reject less often, flexible systems tend to misinterpret more often. Many systems attempt to apply additional *knowledge sources*, especially domain-specific knowledge, to increase flexibility while retaining precision.

Type of structure returned. As mentioned, parsing is the process of assigning structures to sentences. The form of the structure can vary, from a representation that closely resembles the surface structure of the sentence to a deeper representation in which the surface structure has been extensively modified. Which form is chosen depends on the use to which the parse structure will be put. Currently, most work in natural language favors the deep structure approach.

These four issues—uniformity, multiple knowledge sources, precision, and level of representation—are very general questions and are dealt with in different ways by different systems. In implementing a parser, after settling such general design questions, natural-language programmers run up against another set of problems involving specific parsing *strategies.*

Parsing Strategies

Backtracking versus parallel processing. Unfortunately for computational linguists, the elements of natural languages do not always have unique meanings. For example, in going through a sentence, the parser might find a word that could be either a noun or a verb, like *can,* or pick up a prepositional phrase that might be modifying any of a number of the other parts of the sentence. These and many other ambiguities in natural languages force the parser to make choices between multiple alternatives as it proceeds through a sentence. Alternatives may be dealt with all at the same time, through *parallel processing,* or one at a time, using a form of *backtracking*—backing up to a previous choice-point in the computation and trying again. Both of these methods require a significant amount of bookkeeping to keep track of the multiple possibilities: all the ones being tried, in the case of parallel processing, or all the ones not yet tried, in the case of backtracking. Neither strategy can be said to be intrinsically superior, though the number of alternatives that are actually tried can be significantly reduced when backtracking is guided by "knowledge" about which of the choices are more likely to be correct—called *heuristic* knowledge (see Article II.A).

Top-down versus bottom-up processing. In deriving a syntactic structure, a parser can operate from the goals, that is, the set of possible sentence structures (*top-down processing*), or from the words actually in the sentence (*bottom-up processing*). A strictly top-down parser begins by looking at the rules for the desired top-level structure (sentence, clause, etc.); it then looks up rules for the constituents of the top-level structure and progresses until a complete sentence structure is built up. If this sentence matches the input data, the parse is successfully completed; otherwise, it starts back at the top again, generating another sentence structure. A bottom-up parser looks first for rules in the grammar to combine the words of the input sentence into constituents of larger structures (phrases and clauses) and continues to try to recombine these to show how all the input words form a legal sentence in the grammar. Theoretically, both of these strategies arrive at the same final analysis, but the kind of work required and the working structures employed are quite different. The interaction of top-down and bottom-up process control is a common theme in AI research (see, e.g., the extended discussion in Article V.B).

Choosing how to expand or combine. With either a top-down or a bottom-up technique, it is necessary to decide how words and constituents will be combined (bottom-up) or expanded (top-down). The two basic methods are to proceed systematically in one direction (normally left to right) or to start anywhere and systematically look at neighboring chunks of increasing size (this method is sometimes called *island driving*). Both these methods will eventually look at all possibilities, but the choice of how to proceed at this level can have a significant effect on the efficiency of the parser. This particular feature is especially relevant to language processing in the presence of input uncertainty, as occurs, for example, in the *speech understanding* systems.

Multiple knowledge sources. As mentioned above, another important design decision that was especially conspicuous in the speech understanding systems was the effective use of multiple sources of knowledge. Given that there are a number of possibly relevant sets of facts to be used by the parser (phonemic, lexical, syntactic, semantic, etc.), which does one use when?

The issues discussed here under parsing strategies are all questions of *efficiency*. They will not in general affect the final result if computational resources are unlimited, but they will affect the amount of resources expended to reach it.

Actual Parsing Systems

Every natural language processing program deals with these seven issues in its own fashion. Several types of parsers have developed as experience with natural language systems increases.

Template matching. Most of the early NL programs (e.g., SIR, STUDENT, ELIZA) performed parsing by matching their input against a series of predefined *templates*—binding the variables of the template to corresponding pieces of the input string (see Article IV.F1). This approach was successful, up to a point. Given a very limited topic of discussion, the form of many of the input sentences could be anticipated by the system's designer, who then incorporated appropriate templates. However, the method was inextensible, and template matching was soon abandoned in favor of more sophisticated methods.

Simple phrase-structure grammar parsers. These parsers make use of a type of *context-free grammar* with various combinations of the parsing techniques mentioned above. The advantage of a phrase-structure grammar is that the structures derived correspond directly to the grammar rules; thus, the subsequent semantic processing is simplified. By using large grammars and skirting linguistic issues that are outside their limitations (such as some types of agreement, see Article IV.C2), a phrase-structure grammar parser can deal with a moderately large subset of English. Phrase-structure grammars are used primarily to produce systems with useful performance on a limited domain, rather than to explore more difficult language-processing issues (see, e.g., the early SAD–SAM system, Article IV.F1).

Transformational grammar parsers. These parsers attempt to extend the notions of *transformational grammar* into a parsing system. Transformational grammar is a much more comprehensive system than phrase-structure grammar, but it loses phrase structure's direct, rule-to-structure correspondence. Moreover, methods that have been tried, such as analysis by synthesis (building up all possible sentences until one matches the input) and inverse transformations (looking for transformation rules that might have produced the input), have often failed because of *combinatorial explosion*—the proliferation of alternatives the system must examine—and other difficulties with reversing transformations. One of the major attempts to implement a transformational parser was that by Petrick (1973).

Extended grammar parsers. One of the most successful AI approaches to parsing yet developed has been to extend the concept of phrase-structure rules and derivations by adding mechanisms for more complex representations and manipulations of sentences. Methods such as *augmented transition net grammars* (ATNs) and *charts* provide additional resources for the parser to draw on beyond the simple phrase-structure approach (Articles IV.D2 and IV.D3, respectively). Some of these mechanisms have validity with respect to some linguistic theory, while others are merely computationally expedient. The very successful NL systems of Woods (1973a), Winograd (1972), and Kaplan (1973), as described in the articles in Section IV.F, use extended grammar parsers.

Semantic grammar parsers. Another very successful modification to the traditional phrase-structure-grammar approach involves changing the conception of grammatical classes from the traditional <NOUN>, <VERB>, and so forth, to classes that are motivated by concepts in the domain being discussed. For instance, such a *semantic grammar* for a system that talks about airline reservations might have grammatical classes like <DESTINATION>, <FLIGHT>, <FLIGHT-TIME>, and so on. The *rewrite rules* used by the parser would describe phrases and clauses in terms of these semantic categories (see Article V.B for a more complete discussion). The LIFER and SOPHIE systems (Articles IV.F7 and IX.C3 [Vol. II], respectively) use semantic-grammar-based parsers.

Grammarless parsers. Some NL system designers have abandoned totally the traditional use of grammars for linguistic analysis. Such systems are sometimes referred to as *ad hoc*, although they are typically based on some loose theory that happens to fall outside the scope of standard linguistics. These "grammarless" parsers opt for flexibility in the above-mentioned trade-off between precision and flexibility. They are based on special procedures (often centered on individual words rather than syntactic elements) that use semantics-based techniques to build up structures relevant to meaning, and these structures bear little resemblance to the normal structures that result from syntactic parsing. A good example of this approach can be found in the work of Riesbeck (1975; see Article IV.F5).

Conclusion

Recent research in parsing has been directed primarily towards two kinds of simplification: simplified systems for dealing with less than full English and simplified underlying mechanisms that bring the computer parsing techniques closer to being a theory of syntax. Systems such as LIFER (Article IV.F7) have been developed that use the basic mechanisms of augmented grammars in a clean and easily programmable way. Although they cannot deal with the more difficult problems of syntax, systems of this sort can be used to assemble specialized parsers relatively quickly and easily and are likely to be the basis for natural language "front ends" for simple applications.

At the same time, there has been a reevaluation of the fundamental notions of parsing and syntactic structure, viewed from the perspective of programs that understand natural language. Systems like PARSIFAL (Marcus, 1980) attempt to capture in their design the same kinds of generalizations that linguists and psycholinguists posit as theories of language structure and language use. Attention is being directed toward the interaction between the structural facts about syntax and the control structures for implementing the parsing process. The current trend is away from simple methods of applying grammars (as with phrase-structure grammars), toward more integrated approaches. In particular, the grammar-strategy dualism mentioned earlier in this article has been progressively weakened by the work of Winograd (1972) and Riesbeck (1975). It appears that any successful attempt to parse natural language must be based upon some more powerful approach than traditional syntactic analysis. Also, parsers are being called upon to handle more "natural" text, including discourse, conversation, and sentence fragments. These involve aspects of language that cannot be easily described in the conventional, grammar-based models.

References

Again, much of this discussion is based on Winograd (in press). Other general surveys include Charniak and Wilks (1976) and Grishman (1976). For examples of recent work, the proceedings of the TINLAP conferences (1975, 1978) are recommended.

D2. Augmented Transition Networks

Augmented transition networks (ATNs) were first developed by William Woods (1970) as a versatile representation of grammars for natural languages. The concept of an ATN evolved from that of a *finite-state transition diagram*, with the addition of tests and "side effect" actions to each arc, as described below. These additions resulted in the power needed for handling features of English like *embedding* and *agreement* that could not be conveniently captured by regular (or even context-free) grammars. An ATN can thus be viewed as either a grammar formalism or a machine.

Many current language processors use an ATN-like grammar; in some ways, it may be considered state of the art, at least for actual working systems.

Preliminary Theoretical Concepts

A finite-state transition diagram (FSTD) is a simple theoretical device consisting of a set of states (nodes) with arcs leading from one state to another. One state is designated the START state. The arcs of the FSTD are labeled with the terminals of the grammar (i.e., words of the language), indicating which words must be found in the input to allow the specified transition. A subset of the states is identified as FINAL; the device is said to *accept* a sequence of words if, starting from the START state at the beginning of the sentence, it can reach a FINAL state at the end of the input.

FSTDs can recognize only regular (type 3) languages (see the discussion of *formal languages* in Article IV.C1). To recognize a language, a machine must be able to tell whether an arbitrary sentence is part of the language or not. Regular grammars (those whose rewrite rules are restricted to the form $Y \rightarrow aX$ or $Y \rightarrow a$) are the simplest, and FSTDs are only powerful enough to recognize these languages. In other words, it is impossible to build an FSTD that can dependably distinguish the sentences in even a context-free language.

For example, the following FSTD, in which the start state is the left-most node and the final state is labeled **, will accept any sentence that begins with *the*, ends with a noun, and has an arbitrary number of adjectives in between (Fig. D2-1).

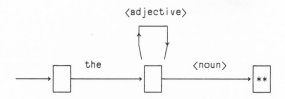

Figure D2-1.   A finite-state transition diagram.

Let's follow through the net with the input phrase *the pretty picture*. We start in the START state and proceed along the arc labeled *the,* because that is the left-most word in the input string. This leaves us in the middle box, with *pretty picture* left as our string to be parsed. After one loop around the *adjective* arc, we are again at middle node, but this time with the string *picture* remaining. Since this word is a noun, we proceed to the FINAL node, **, and arrive there with no words remaining to be processed. Thus, the parse is successful; in other words, our sample FSTD accepts this string.

However, regular grammars are inadequate for dealing with the complexity of natural language, as discussed in Article IV.C2. A natural extension to FSTDs, then, is to provide a recursion mechanism that increases their recognition power to handle the more inclusive set of context-free languages. These extended FSTDs are called *recursive transition networks* (RTNs). An RTN is a finite-state transition diagram in which labels of an arc may include not only terminal symbols but also nonterminal symbols that denote the name of another subnetwork to be given temporary control of the parsing process.

An RTN operates similarly to an FSTD. If the label on an arc is a terminal (word or word class), the arc may be taken, as in FSTDs, if the word being scanned matches the label. For example, the word *ball* would match an arc labeled <noun> but not one labeled <adjective>. Otherwise, if the arc is labeled with a nonterminal symbol, representing a syntactic construct (e.g., PREPOSITIONAL PHRASE) that corresponds to the name of another network, the current state of the parse is put on a stack and control is transferred to the corresponding named subnetwork, which continues to process the sentence, returning control when it finishes or fails.

Whenever an accepting state is reached, control is transferred to the node obtained by "popping the stack" (i.e., returning to the point from which the subnetwork was entered). If an attempt is made to pop an empty stack, and if the last input word was the cause of this attempt, the input string is accepted by the RTN; otherwise, it is rejected. The effect of arcs labeled with names of syntactic constructs is that an arc is followed only if a construction of the corresponding type follows as a phrase in the input string. Consider the following example of an RTN (Fig. D2-2):

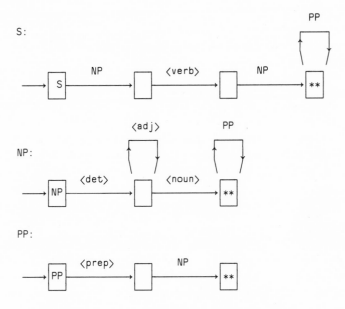

Figure D2-2.   A recursive transition network.

Here *NP* denotes a noun phrase; *PP*, a prepositional phrase; *det*, a determiner; *prep*, a preposition; and *adj*, an adjective. Accepting nodes are labeled **. If the input string is *The little boy in the swimsuit kicked the red ball,* the above network would parse it into the following phrases:

```
NP:    The little boy in the swimsuit
PP:    in the swimsuit
NP:    the swimsuit
Verb:  kicked
NP:    the red ball
```

Notice that any subnetwork of an RTN may call any other subnetwork, including itself; in the example above, for instance, the prepositional phrase contains a noun phrase. Also notice that an RTN may be nondeterministic in nature; that is, there may be more than one possible arc to be followed at a given point in a parse. Parsing algorithms handle nondeterminism by *parallel processing* of the various alternatives or by trying one and then *backtracking* if it fails. These general parsing issues are discussed in Article IV.D1.

Context-free grammars, however, are still insufficient to handle natural language. The RTNs, then, must be extended, to provide even more parsing power.

ATNs

An augmented transition network (ATN) is an RTN that has been extended in three ways:

1. A set of *registers* has been added; these can be used to store information, such as partially formed *derivation trees*, between jumps to different subnetworks.

2. Arcs, aside from being labeled by word classes or syntactic constructs, can have arbitrary *tests* associated with them that must be satisfied before the arc is taken.

3. Certain *actions* may be "attached" to an arc, to be executed whenever it is taken (usually to modify the data structure returned).

This addition of registers, tests, and actions to the RTNs extends their power to that of Turing machines, thus making ATNs theoretically powerful enough to recognize any language that might be recognized by a computer. ATNs offer a degree of expressiveness and naturalness not found in the Turing machine formalism and are a useful tool to apply to the analysis of natural language.

The operation of the ATN is similar to that of the RTN except that if an arc has a test, then the test is performed first and the arc is taken only if the test is successful. Also, if an arc has *actions* associated with it, then these operations are performed after following the arc. In this way, by permitting the parsing to be guided by the parse history (through tests on the registers) and by allowing for a rearrangement of the structure of the sentence during the parse (through the actions on the registers), ATNs are capable of building deep structure descriptions of a sentence in an efficient manner. For a well-developed and clear example, the reader is referred to Woods (1970).

Evaluation of ATNs and Results

ATNs serve as a computationally implementable and efficient solution to some of the problems of recognizing and generating natural language. Their computational power provides the capability of embedding different kinds of grammars, making them an effective testbed for new ideas (Woods, 1970, p. 602). Two of the features of ATNs, the test and the actions on the arcs, make them especially well suited to handling *transformational grammars*. The ability to place arbitrary conditions on the arcs provides context sensitivity, equivalent to the preconditions for applying transformational rules. The capability of rearranging the parse structure, by copying, adding, and deleting components, provides the full power of transformations (see Article IV.C2).

The ATN paradigm has been successfully applied to question answering in limited (closed) domains, such as the LUNAR program, which is described in Article IV.F3. Also, ATNs have been used effectively in a number of *text generation* systems (Article IV.E). In addition, the BBN *speech understanding* system, HWIM, used an ATN control structure (see Article V.C3).

There are limitations to the ATN approach; one, in particular, is that the heavy dependence on syntax restricts the ability to handle ungrammatical (although meaningful) utterances.

References

The principal references here are, of course, Woods (1970), Woods and Kaplan (1971), and Woods (1973a). Also see Bobrow and Fraser (1969), Conway (1963), Matuzceck (1972), and Winograd (1976).

D3. The General Syntactic Processor

Ronald Kaplan's (1973) General Syntactic Processor (GSP) is a versatile system for the parsing and generation of strings in natural language. Its data structures are intuitive and the control structures are conceptually straightforward and relatively easy to implement. Yet, by adjusting certain control parameters, GSP can directly emulate several other syntactic processors, including Woods's ATN grammar (Article IV.D2), Kay's MIND parser (Kay, 1973), and Friedman's *text generation* system (Article IV.E).

GSP represents an effort both to synthesize the formal characteristics of different parsing methods and to construct a unifying framework within which to compare them. In this respect, GSP is a meta-system—it is not in itself an approach to language processing, but rather it is a system in which various approaches can be described.

Data Structure: Charts

GSP gains much of its power through the use of a single, basic data structure—the *chart*—to represent both the grammar and the input sentence. A chart can be described as a modified *tree*, which, in turn, is usually defined as a set of nodes that can be partitioned into a root and a set of disjoint subtrees. A tree encodes two sorts of relations between nodes: DOMINANCE, the relation between a parent and daughter node, and PRECEDENCE, the relation between a node and its right-hand sister node. Figure D3-1 shows a tree representing a particular noun phrase.

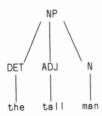

Figure D3-1. A tree for a noun phrase.

A chart is basically a tree that has been modified in two ways:

1. The arcs of the tree have been rearranged to produce a binary tree, that is, a tree in which each node has at most two

dangling nodes (this rearrangement is described by Knuth [1973, p. 333] as the "natural correspondence" between trees and binary trees).

2. The nodes and arcs have been interchanged; what were previously nodes are now arcs, and vice versa.

For example, Figure D3-2 is the chart representation for the tree of Figure D3-1:

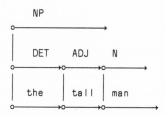

Figure D3-2. A chart for a noun phrase.

The chart representation has a number of advantages, including ease of access for certain purposes. For example, in Figure D3-1 there is no direct connection from *DET* to *ADJ*. In Figure D3-2 this connection has been made; that is, the PRECEDENCE relations have been made explicit, and the DOMINANCE ones have been removed. This explicit encoding of precedence can be helpful in language processing, where the concept of one element following another is a basic relation.

Also, the chart can be used to represent a "string of trees" or "forest"—that is, a set of disjoint trees. For example, Figure D3-3a shows a string of two disjoint trees, headed by *NP* and *V*. Note that these trees cannot be connected, except with a dummy parent node (labeled ?). In Figure D3-3b, the equivalent chart representation is shown.

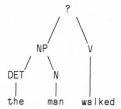
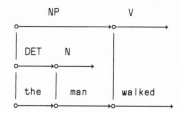

Figure D3-3a. Two disjoint trees.   Figure D3-3b. The equivalent chart.

Finally, the chart provides a representation for multiple interpretations of a given word or phrase, through the use of multiple *edges*. The arcs in a chart are called edges and are labeled with the names of words or grammatical constructs. For example, Figure D3-4 represents the set of trees for *I saw the log,* including the two interpretations for the word *saw.* The chart allows explicit representation of ambiguous phrases and clauses, as well as of words.

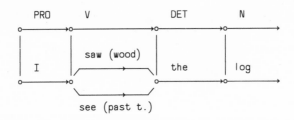

Figure D3-4. A chart showing multiple interpretations.

Note that ambiguity could also be represented by distinct trees, one for every possible interpretation of the sentence. However, this approach is inefficient, as it ignores the possibility that certain subparts may have the same meaning in all cases. With the chart representation, these common subparts can be merged.

As mentioned above, the arcs in a chart are called edges and are labeled with the names of words or grammatical constructs. The nodes are called *vertexes*. The chart can be accessed through various functions, which permit one to retrieve specific edges, sets of edges, or vertexes.

At any given moment during the processing of a sentence, the attention of the system is directed to a particular point in the chart called the CHART FOCUS. The focus is described by a set of global variables: EDGE (the current edge), VERTEX (the name of the node from which EDGE leaves), and CHART (the current subchart being considered by the processing strategy). GSP's attention is redirected by changing the values of these variables.

When the chart is initialized, each word in the sentence is represented by an edge in the chart for each category of speech the word can take. Figure D3-4 was an example of an initial chart configuration, preparatory to parsing. Each analysis procedure that shares the chart is restricted to adding edges, which makes it possible in later analyses to modify or ignore earlier possibilities without constraining future interpretations. In this way, the individual syntactic programs remain relatively independent while building on each other's work in a generally *bottom-up* way.

It should be emphasized that the chart is just a data structure and is not directly related to the grammar. It merely serves as the global *blackboard* upon which the various pieces of the grammar operate. We still must specify the sorts of operations that use the chart—that is, the form of the grammar itself.

Data Structure: Grammatical Rules

Grammars for syntactic processing of language can be understood in terms of a network model like Woods's ATN grammar. That is, a grammar is viewed as a series of *states*, with transitions between the states accomplished by following *arcs* (see Article IV.D2).

The grammars encoded by GSP fit this description. What gives GSP its power, however, is that a grammar can be represented in the same way as a chart. That is, we can use the chart manipulation mechanisms, already developed, to operate upon the grammar itself. There is a difference, of course. The chart is merely a passive data store; the grammar contains instructions for (a) acting on the chart—adding pieces and shifting attention—and (b) acting on the grammar—shifting attention (i.e., moving from one grammar state to another).

Control Structure

To handle the full complexity of grammars, GSP has some extra features. These include:

1. REGISTERS. As in ATNs, these are used as pointers to structures.

2. LEVELSTACK. This is a stack used to implement recursion. The chart focus, grammar focus (state), and register list are saved before a recursive call.

3. NDLIST (nondeterminism list). This is a list of choice points in the grammar. Whenever a choice is made, the user can optionally save the current configuration on NDLIST, to allow for backtracking.

4. PROCSTACK. This is a list of suspended processes. GSP allows a *co-routining* facility, under which processes can be suspended and resumed (ATNs have no equivalent to this).

Features like recursion, backtracking, and movement of the pointer through the input sentence must all be implemented by the user within the general framework provided. This approach can be beneficial, particularly with features such as backtracking: Automatic backtracking can be a less than desirable feature in a grammar (see the discussion in Chap. VI, Vol. II).

Using GSP

Note one facet of the approach outlined: All operations on the grammar and chart must be *explicitly* stated. Thus, GSP has placed much power in the hands of the grammar designer, with a corresponding cost in complexity.

GSP appears to be similar to an ATN, with three extensions:

1. The data structure used is a chart, instead of simply a string of words.

2. The grammar is encoded in the same manner as the chart; thus, it is accessible to the system.

3. Processes can be suspended and resumed.

ATNs do not fully demonstrate the power of GSP. Kaplan also used GSP to implement Kay's MIND parser (a context-free, bottom-up system) and Friedman's transformational-grammar text-generation system. The last two made more extensive use of GSP's capabilities, in particular: (a) the possibilities of multiple levels in the chart, (b) the ability to suspend and restart processes, and (c) the ability to rearrange the chart, changing it as necessary. The Kay algorithm, in particular, made extensive use of the ability to modify the chart "on the fly," adding sections as required.

Conclusions and Observations

GSP provides a simple framework within which many language processing systems can be described. It is not intended to be a high-level system that will do many things for the user; rather, it provides a "machine language" for the user to specify whatever operations he wants. GSP's small set of primitive operations appears to be sufficient for representing most of the desirable features of syntax-based parsing. The clean, uniform structure allows GSP to be used as a tool for comparison (and possibly evaluation) of different systems.

The chart seems to be an effective data structure for representing the syntax of natural language sentences. It provides convenient merging of common subparts (i.e., to prevent scanning known components again), while permitting representation of various forms of ambiguity. As Kay explained, the function of the chart is to "record hypotheses about the phraseological status of parts of the sentence so that they will be available for use in constructing hypotheses about larger parts at some later time" (Kay, 1973, p. 167).

References

Kaplan (1973) is the principal reference.

E. TEXT GENERATION

Computer text generation is the process of constructing text (phrases, sentences, paragraphs) in a natural language—in a sense, it is the opposite of natural language understanding by machine. Although this problem has been investigated for 15 years, few coherent principles have emerged, and the approaches have varied widely. Attempts at generating text have been made with two general research goals: (a) generating random sentences to test a grammar or grammatical theory and (b) converting information from an internal representation into a natural language.

Random Generation

This approach, the random generation of text constrained by the rules of a test grammar, is of limited interest to workers in Artificial Intelligence, since it is oriented more toward theoretical linguistics than toward functional natural-language-processing systems. The objective of implementing a generation system of this sort is to test the descriptive adequacy of the test grammar, as illustrated by the following two systems.

Victor Yngve (1962) was one of the first researchers to attempt English text generation; the work was seen as preliminary to a full program for machine translation (see Article IV.B). Yngve used a generative *context-free grammar* and a random-number generator to produce "grammatical" sentences: The system randomly selected one production from among those that were applicable at each point in the generation process, starting from those productions that "produced" <SENTENCE> and finally randomly selecting words to fill in the <NOUN>, <VERB>, and other like positions. This is an example of the text produced by the system:

```
The water under the wheels in oiled whistles and its polished shiny
big and big trains is black.
```

Joyce Friedman's (1969, 1971) system was designed to test the effectiveness of *transformational grammars* (Article IV.C2). It operated by generating *phrase markers* (derivation trees) and by performing transformations on them until a *surface structure* was generated. The generation was random, but the user could specify an input phrase marker and semantic restrictions between various terminals in order to test specific rules for grammatical validity.

These two systems, while relevant to work in linguistics, are only peripherally related to recent work in Artificial Intelligence. The fundamental emphasis in AI text-generation work has been on the meaning, as opposed to the syntactic form, of language.

Surface Realization of Meaning

The general goal of text-generation programs in the AI paradigm is to take some internal representation of the "meaning" of a sentence and convert it to *surface-structure* form, that is, into an appropriate string of words. There has been considerable variety among such systems, reflecting differences both in the type of internal representation used and in the overall purpose for which the text is generated. Representation schemes have included largely syntactic dependency trees, stored generation patterns of different degrees of complexity, and several versions of *semantic nets* (see Chap. III). Purposes have included automatic *paraphrasing* or *machine translation* of an input text, providing natural-sounding communication with the user of an interactive program, and simply testing the adequacy of the internal representation.

Sheldon Klein (1965) made a first step beyond the random generation of sentences, by means of a program that attempted to generate a *paraphrase* of a paragraph of text through an internal representation of that text (see also Klein and Simmons, 1963). The program used a type of grammar called *dependency grammar*, a context-free grammar with word-dependency information attached to each production. That is, the right-hand side of each rule in the grammar has a "distinguished symbol"; the "head" of the phrase associated with that rule is the head of the phrase that is associated with the distinguished symbol. All other words that are part of the phrase associated with the production are said to *depend* on this head.

For instance, given the following simple dependency grammar and the sentence *The fierce tigers in India eat meat,* Klein's parser would produce both an ordinary phrase-structure derivation tree (see Article IV.C1) and also the dependency tree shown below (Fig. E-1):

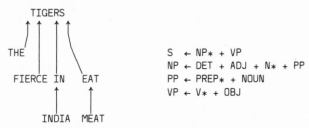

Figure E-1.   A dependency tree.

The symbols followed by * are the distinguished symbols in the productions. The dependency trees from the individual sentences of the input paragraph were bound together with "two-way dependency" links between similar nouns. For example, the input paragraph

```
The man rides a bicycle.  The man is tall.  A bicycle
is a vehicle with wheels.
```

would yield the dependency structure shown in Figure E-2. One paraphrase generated from the given paragraph was *The tall man rides a vehicle with wheels.*

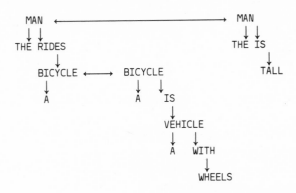

Figure E-2. Multiple dependency trees.

The grammar used in generating the paraphrases was similar to the one used for analysis. Rule selection was random (as in Yngve's method) but with the added constraint that all dependencies among the words that were generated must be derivable from the initial dependency trees. In the example above, *vehicle* could be generated as the object of *rides* because *vehicle* depends on *is*, *is* on *bicycle*, and *bicycle* on *rides*. Two restrictions were imposed on the transitivity of dependency relations: Dependency did not cross verbs other than *be* or prepositions other than *of*. Thus, *The man rides wheels* could not be generated.

The use of dependency trees was expected to ensure that the output sentences would "reflect the meaning of the source text" (Klein, 1965, p. 74). A difficulty, however, was that the trees encoded only the crudest of the semantic relations present in the paragraph. In fact, the dependency relation between words only indicates that some semantic relation exists between them without really specifying the nature of the relation.

Ross Quillian (1968), in contrast, emphasized the expression of semantic relationships almost to the exclusion of concern for syntactic

well-formedness.   Quillian did pioneering work in the representation of
knowledge (see Chap. III) and was also one of the first to deal with the
problems of text generation.   His system employed a *semantic net* to
represent the relations between words, which can be interpreted as their
meaning.   The task the system was then to perform was to compare
two words, that is, find some semantic relation between them, and then
to express the comparison in "understandable, though not necessarily
grammatically perfect, sentences" (p. 247).   For example:

```
Compare:   Plant, Live

Answer:    PLANT IS A LIVE STRUCTURE.
```

This relation between the two words was discovered as a path in the
net between the nodes that represented the words.   Although this was a
primitive semantic net scheme, many fundamental issues were first raised
by Quillian's system.

One important point was that paths in the semantic net did not
necessarily correspond to input sentences. Instead, the discovery of paths
between two nodes amounted to making *inferences* on the knowledge in
memory.   For example, another relation the system found between *plant*
and *live* was:

```
PLANT IS STRUCTURE WHICH GET-FOOD FROM AIR.  THIS FOOD
IS THING WHICH BEING HAS-TO TAKE INTO ITSELF TO KEEP LIVE.
```

In order to have found this connection, the system had to discover a
connection between PLANT and LIVE, by way of FOOD, that was not
directly input.

Although Quillian's semantic net system was limited, it strongly influenced much of the later work in NL and the representation of knowledge in AI.   This influence reflected Quillian's stress on the importance
of the semantic versus the surface components of language:

> As a theory, the program implies that a person first has something
> to say, expressed somehow in his own conceptual terms (which is
> what a "path" is to the program), and that all his decisions about
> the syntactic form that a generated sentence is to take are then
> made *in the service of* this intention. (Quillian, 1968, p. 255)

This is a strong statement about language, and this view, of a cognitive
process manipulating an internal representation, is perhaps the essence of
the AI perspective.

Terry Winograd's *blocks world* program, SHRDLU (1972), contained
several text-generation devices.   Their function was to allow the system, which is described in Article IV.F4, to answer questions about the
state of its tabletop domain and certain of the system's internal states.

The basic text-generation techniques used were "fill in the blank" and stored response patterns. For example, if an unfamiliar word was used, SHRDLU responded, "I don't know the word . . . " More complex responses were called for by questions asking why or how an action had been done. For *why*, the system answered with "because <event>" or "in order to <event>," where <event> referred to a goal that the program had had when the action was taken. For example, "Why did you clear off that cube?" might be answered by "To put it on a large green cube." The program retrieved the appropriate event from its history list and then used a generation pattern associated with events of that type. For an event of the type "(PUTON OBJ1 OBJ2)," the pattern would be:

```
(<correct form of to put>, <NP for OBJ1>, ON, <NP for OBJ2>)
```

Noun phrases in the pattern were generated by associating an English word with every known object; adjectives and relative clauses were added until a unique object (within the domain of discourse) was described.

The stilted text generated by this scheme was moderated by the (heuristic) use of pronouns for noun phrases. For example, if the referent of a noun phrase had been mentioned in the same answer or in the previous one, an appropriate pronoun could be selected for it. SHRDLU's limited domain of discourse allowed it to exhibit surprisingly natural dialogue with such simple techniques.

Simmons and Slocum (1972) developed a natural language system that generated sentences from a *semantic network* representation of knowledge, based on a *case grammar* (see Article IV.C4). The program produced surface structure from the network by means of an *augmented transition net* (ATN), adapted for the purpose of generation rather than parsing (see Article IV.D2). The object of the work was to substantiate the claim that "the semantic network adequately represents some important aspect of the meaning of discourse"; if the claim were true, then "the very least requirement" was that "the nets be able to preserve enough information to allow regeneration of the sentences—and some of their syntactic paraphrases—from which the nets were derived" (p. 903).

An illustration of the capabilities of the system is given by the paragraph below, which was initially hand-coded into semantic network notation. (For a later version of the program in which the parsing was done automatically, see Simmons, 1973.)

John saw Mary wrestling with a bottle at the liquor bar. He went over to help her with it. He drew the cork and they drank champagne together.

The network notation, in simplified form, is indicated by the following representation of *John saw Mary wrestling:*

```
C1    TOKEN   (see)          C3    TOKEN   (wrestle)
      TIME    PAST                 TIME    PROGRESSIVE PAST
      DATIVE  C2                   AGENT   C4
      OBJECT  C3

C2    TOKEN   (John)         C4    TOKEN   (Mary)
      NUMBER  SINGULAR             NUMBER  SINGULAR
```

Here C1, C2, C3, and C4 are nodes in the network representing concepts that are tokens of meanings of *see, wrestle, John,* and *Mary.* PAST and SINGULAR are also nodes. TOKEN, TIME, OBJECT, and the like are types of arcs, or relations.

The representation shown was augmented by other relations, attached to verb nodes, such as MOOD (indicative or interrogative), VOICE (active or passive), and information about the relative times of events. Using this representation, the system was able to reconstruct several versions of the original paragraph. One read:

> John saw Mary wrestling with a bottle at the liquor bar. John went over to help her with it before he drew the cork. John and Mary together drank the champagne.

The actual generation was accomplished by an ATN in which the arcs were labeled with the names of relations that might occur in the semantic net. The actual path followed through the ATN—and thus the exact text generated—depended both on which relations were actually present and on which node or nodes were chosen as a starting point.

Wong (1975) has extended this approach, incorporating features to handle extended discourse.

Neil Goldman's (1975) program generates surface structure from a database of *conceptual dependency* networks, as the text-generation part of the MARGIE system, described in Article IV.F5. The conceptual dependency (CD) knowledge representation scheme is based on language-independent *semantic primitives*, so the actual word selection for output must be performed by Goldman's text-generation subsystem, called BABEL. This is accomplished by means of a *discrimination net* (a kind of binary decision tree—see Article XI.D, in Vol. III) that operates on a CD network that is to be verbalized. This discrimination net is used to select an appropriate *verb sense* to represent the event specified by the CD. (A verb sense is a meaning of the verb—DRINK, for example, has two senses, to drink a fluid and to drink alcohol.) Essentially, there are only a few verbs that can represent the event, and a set of predicates determines which one to use. For instance, the primitive INGEST can be expressed as *eat, drink,* or *breathe,* depending on the nature of the substance ingested:

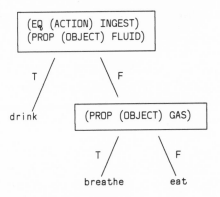

Figure 1. A sample discrimination net from MARGIE. (Goldman, 1975, p. 331)

Once a verb sense has been selected, an associated framework is used to generate a case-oriented syntax net, which is a structure similar to the semantic net of Simmons and Slocum. These frameworks include information concerning the form of the net and where in the conceptualization the necessary information is located. After the framework has been filled out, other language-specific functions operate on the syntax net to complete it syntactically with respect to such things as tense, form, mood, and voice. Finally, an ATN is used to generate the surface structure, as in the Simmons and Slocum program.

Yorick Wilks (1973) has developed a program that generates French from a semantic base of *templates* and *paraplates.* This is part of his *machine translation* system described in Article IV.F2.

Discussion

In computer text generation, as the richness and completeness of the underlying semantic representation of the information has increased, the quality of the resulting paraphrase has improved. Like other areas of AI, the basic problem is to determine exactly what the salient points to be discussed are and to obtain a good representation of them. Future work in text generation will also have to address areas such as *extended discourse* and *stylistics.* In this direction, Clippinger (1975) has looked at psychological mechanisms underlying discourse production, and Cohen

(1978) has studied the planning of *speech acts* for communication in context.

References

Recent research in text generation is described by Appelt (1980), McDonald (1980), McKeown (1980), and Mann and Moore (1980).

F. NATURAL LANGUAGE PROCESSING SYSTEMS

F1. Early Natural Language Systems

Early work on machine processing of natural language assumed that the syntactic information in the sentence, along with the meaning of a finite set of words, was sufficient to perform certain language tasks—in particular, to answer questions posed in English. Several of these early natural language programs are reviewed here—their techniques, their successes, and their shortcomings. These programs were limited to dialogues about restricted domains in simple English and ignored the difficult grammatical problems of complex constructions found in unrestricted English. Through work with programs of this genre, it became apparent that people constantly apply extensive world-knowledge in processing language and that a computer could not hope to be a competent language user without "understanding." These programs bridge the gap between the early *machine translation* attempts of the 1950s and current, semantics-based natural language systems (see Article IV.A).

SAD-SAM

SAD-SAM (Syntactic Appraiser and Diagrammer—Semantic Analyzing Machine) was programmed by Robert Lindsay (1963a) at Carnegie Institute of Technology in the IPL-V list-processing language. The program accepts English sentences about kinship relations, builds a database, and answers questions about the facts it has stored.

It accepts a vocabulary of Basic English (about 1,700 words) and follows a simple *context-free grammar*. The SAD module parses the input from left to right, builds a derivation tree structure, and passes this structure on to SAM, which extracts the semantically relevant (kinship-related) information to build the family trees and find answers to questions.

Though the subset of English processed by SAD is quite impressive in extent and in complexity of structure, only kinship relations are considered by SAM; all other semantic information is ignored. SAM does not depend on the order of the input for building the family trees; if a first input assigns offspring B and C to X, and offspring D and E to Y, two "family units" will be constructed, but they will be collapsed into one if we learn later that E and C are siblings. (Multiple marriages are illegal.) However, SAM cannot handle certain ambiguities; the sentence *Joe plays in his Aunt Jane's yard* indicates that Jane is either the sister or sister-in-law of Joe's father, but SAM assigns one and only one connection at a time and therefore cannot use the ambiguous information: The structure of the model permits storing definite links but not possible *inferences*.

BASEBALL

Also in the early 1960s, Bert Green and his colleagues at Lincoln Laboratories wrote a program called BASEBALL (Green et al., 1963), again using the IPL–V programming language. BASEBALL is essentially an *information retrieval* program, since its database of facts about all of the American League games during one year is not modified by the program. Acceptable input questions from the user must have only one clause, no logical connectives (*and, or, not*), no comparatives (*higher, longer*), and no facts about sequences of events; also, most words must be recognized by the extensive dictionary.

The parsing system uses 14 categories of parts of speech and *right to left* scanning to structure the input question into functional phrases. Using this structure and the *keywords* found in the question, the input is transformed into a specification list that is the *canonical expression* for the meaning of the question. For example, the question *How many games did the Yankees play in July?* becomes:

```
TEAM                = YANKEES
MONTH               = JULY
GAMES (number of) = ?
```

The answer is found by searching the database for data items matching the specification list, storing them on a "found" list, and eventually processing and outputting them.

The size of the dictionary and the *heuristics* for resolving syntactic ambiguities (*score* can be a verb or a noun; *Boston*, a place or the name of a team) make it possible for BASEBALL to answer most reasonable English questions about the games stored in the database. However, BASEBALL does not return to the user for clarification of semantic ambiguities. It simply fails to parse the sentence and asks for a rephrasing of the question. Though the database is not modified by the program, BASEBALL exhibits deductive abilities in parsing questions and processing the found-list.

SIR

SIR (Semantic Information Retrieval) was written in LISP by Bertram Raphael (1968) as part of his thesis research at M.I.T. It is a prototype "understanding" machine, since it can accumulate facts and then make deductions about them in order to answer questions.

SIR accepts a restricted subset of English. It matches sentences against 24 matching patterns of the following sort:

```
* is *
* is part of *
Is * * ?
How many * does * have ?
What is the * of * ?
```

where the elements matched against * are nouns, possibly modified by a "quantifier" such as *a, the, every, each,* or a number. The match with a pattern triggers the appropriate action in the program. A sample conversation might look like this:

```
Every boy is a person
I UNDERSTAND

A finger is part of a hand
I UNDERSTAND

There are two hands on each person
I UNDERSTAND

How many fingers does John have ?
THE ABOVE SENTENCE IS AMBIGUOUS BUT I ASSUME (has) MEANS
    (has as parts)
I DON'T KNOW WHETHER FINGER IS PART OF JOHN

John is a boy
I UNDERSTAND

How many fingers does John have ?
THE ABOVE SENTENCE IS AMBIGUOUS BUT I ASSUME (has) MEANS
    (has as parts)
HOW MANY FINGERS PER HAND ?

Every hand has 5 fingers
THE ABOVE SENTENCE IS AMBIGUOUS BUT I ASSUME (has) MEANS
    (has as parts)
THE ANSWER IS 10

Who is President of the United States ?
STATEMENT FORM NOT RECOGNIZED
```

SIR's world is concerned with only a small group of relations between objects, as specified by the 24 matching patterns. Declarative input statements are used to build the model, and the patterns have been chosen to express concepts that commonly occur in human conversation: set inclusion, spatial relationship, and the like. The program has certain built-in knowledge (like transitivity of set inclusion) that allows it to answer questions about some facts not explicitly stated during input. SIR can also interact with the user to gather more information or to resolve ambiguities.

STUDENT

STUDENT is another pattern-matching natural language program, written by Daniel Bobrow (1968) as his doctoral research project at M.I.T. STUDENT can read and solve high-school-level algebra story problems like the following:

> If the number of customers Tom gets is twice the square of 20 per cent of the number of advertisements he runs, and the number of advertisements he runs is 45, what is the number of customers Tom gets?

The entire subset of English recognized by STUDENT is derived from the following set of basic patterns:

```
(WHAT ARE * AND *)              (FIND * AND *)
(WHAT IS *)                     (* IS MULTIPLIED BY *)
(HOW MANY *1 IS *)             (* IS DIVIDED BY *)
(HOW MANY * DO * HAVE)         (* IS *)
(HOW MANY * DOES * HAVE)       (* (*1/VERB) *1 *)
(FIND *)
(* (*1/VERB) * AS MANY * AS * (*1/VERB) *)
```

The * sign indicates a string of words of any length, *1 indicates one word, and (*1/VERB) means the matching element must be recognized as a verb by the dictionary.

To construct the algebraic equations that will lead to the solution, the problem statement is scanned, first for linguistic forms associated with the equality relation (such as [* IS *]), then for algebraic operators. STUDENT then builds a list of the answers required, the units involved in the problem, and a list of all the variables in the equations. Then STUDENT invokes the SOLVE module with the set of equations and the desired unknowns.

If SOLVE fails, STUDENT applies *heuristics* such as expanding idioms, identifying two previously "slightly different" variables, or invoking the REMEMBER module that contains special facts like:

```
(FEET IS THE PLURAL OF FOOT)
(ONE HALF ALWAYS MEANS .5)
(SUCCESSFUL CANDIDATES SOMETIMES MEANS STUDENTS WHO
   PASSED THE ADMISSIONS TEST)
(DISTANCE EQUALS SPEED TIMES TIME)
(ONE FOOT EQUALS 12 INCHES)
```

If all else fails, STUDENT can request more information from the user. Each time a heuristic succeeds in finding a new equation, the augmented set is sent to SOLVE. STUDENT finally prints the solution (using the pattern "variable IS value") or reports its inability to solve the problem. In this example, STUDENT would print

```
(THE NUMBER OF CUSTOMERS TOM GETS IS 162)
```

STUDENT's simple pattern-matching scheme, combined with its small set of well-chosen heuristics, does an impressive job of parsing typical high-school-algebra word problems. The program can be tricked easily (*Bill has 3 apples, 2 pears, and one dog* would be parsed into two clauses); but as implemented, it solved the problems submitted as fast as humans could (in one case, several times faster than an M.I.T. graduate student who was not using the special "age problem" heuristics). A slightly modified version was found to be a good model for *human problem solving*, in a study conducted by Paige and Simon (1966).

ELIZA

Perhaps the most famous of these "pattern-matching" natural language programs was ELIZA, written by Joseph Weizenbaum (1966) at M.I.T. This program assumes the role of a Rogerian, or "nondirective," therapist in its dialogue with the user. Although ELIZA's dialogue with the user appears surprisingly realistic, the program uses no more intelligent mechanisms than those described above. Rather, the nature of therapist-patient dialogue lends itself to simulation in this manner. A sample dialogue might look like this (with ELIZA's response in caps):

```
Men are all alike.
IN WHAT WAYS

They're always bugging us about something or other.
CAN YOU THINK OF A SPECIFIC EXAMPLE

Well, my boyfriend made me come here.
YOUR BOYFRIEND MADE YOU COME HERE

He says I'm depressed much of the time.
I AM SORRY TO HEAR THAT YOU ARE DEPRESSED
```

It's true. I'm unhappy.
DO YOU THINK COMING HERE WILL HELP YOU NOT TO BE UNHAPPY

I need some help, that much seems certain.
WHAT WOULD IT MEAN TO YOU IF YOU GOT SOME HELP

Perhaps I could learn to get along with my mother.
TELL ME MORE ABOUT YOUR FAMILY
  . . .

WHAT ELSE COMES TO MIND WHEN YOU THINK OF YOUR FATHER

Bullies.
DOES THAT HAVE ANYTHING TO DO WITH THE FACT THAT YOUR
     BOYFRIEND MADE YOU COME HERE
  . . .

ELIZA is programmed in the SLIP language (Symmetric List Processor), developed by Weizenbaum (1963). An off-line *script* composed of *key lists* specifies the nature of the input language by specifying for each keyword a set of patterns to look for and the possible transformations associated with each pattern. For example, assuming the keyword is *me*, a pattern used for matching might be

(0 YOU 0 ME)

and one of the transformation rules associated with this pattern might be

(WHAT MAKES YOU THINK I 3 YOU)

where 0 in the pattern matches any string of words, and 3 in the transformation rule designates the third element matched (in this case, everything between YOU and ME). The input is scanned from left to right for a keyword; a systematic *hashing* procedure very quickly eliminates words that cannot be keywords. ELIZA deletes the part of text preceding a punctuation delimiter if no keyword has been found; otherwise, the part following it (ensuring thus that the transformation will be applied to one single phrase or sentence). If several keywords are found, they are stored in turn in a "key stack" according to the rank of precedence associated with each of them; then the input is matched against each decomposition rule in turn. These patterns can be ordered in the key list so that the more complex ones are tried first; for example, the pattern

(0 I 0 DEPRESSED 0)

for the keyword *I* is hard to match, but if a match is achieved, the answer can be more spectacular than the transformations for the "general match" pattern for *I*,

(0 I 0) .

When a match is found, ELIZA generates a response, cyclically using the reassembly rules associated with the appropriate decomposition rule. If no decomposition rule matches for a given keyword, the key stack is popped and the pattern-matching procedure is repeated for the new keyword. If the key stack is empty, a response like "Please go on," "I see," or "Very interesting" will always do.

Several other tricks—like substituting for keywords in its response, associating keywords with a class or situation (*Mother* implies *family*), and remembering these keyword affiliates over the course of the conversation—help enhance the illusion of intelligent dialogue.

Conclusions

None of these early natural language systems dealt with the syntax of language in any sophisticated way. In these programs, the semantic knowledge needed to respond to the user was implicit in the patterns and the ad hoc rules used for parsing. More recent natural language programs maintain large databases of explicit world-knowledge that they use to assist in parsing the sentence as well as in interpreting it.

References

For general reference, see Boden (1977), in which there are lucid discussions of several of these systems; see also Simmons (1965, 1970) and Winograd (1974). The collections edited by Feigenbaum and Feldman (1963) and by Minsky (1968) contain much of the original material.

F2. Wilks's Machine Translation System

Current work in machine translation of languages is exemplified by Yorick Wilks's system (1973), which can produce good French from small English paragraphs. The system stresses semantics-based processing over conventional syntactic analysis in both the analysis and the generation stages. The input English text is first converted to a semantic representation and then to the final translated text. (The use of an intermediate representation bears some similarity to Weaver's idea of *interlingua*, discussed in Article IV.B.) Wilks stresses that his semantic representation is designed for machine translation and may not be appropriate for other NL tasks like question answering. The rationale for this is that an explicit representation of all of the logical implications of a sentence, which is necessary for some tasks, may be mostly unnecessary for translation: If the two languages are similar, an appropriate target sentence with the *same* implications can often be found in a more straightforward way.

Wilks's system first fragments the input text into substrings of words; it then replaces each word in the text fragments with the internal *formulas* representing the word's meanings and matches the resulting string of formulas against a set of standard forms called *bare templates*. The output of this stage is a first approximation to a semantic representation of each of these fragments. The system then tries to tie together these representations to produce a more densely connected representation for the complete text. When this process has been completed, the generation of the output text is accomplished by unwinding the interlingual representation using functions that interpret it in the target language.

The interlingual representation is based on *semantic primitives* that Wilks calls *elements*. Elements express the *basic* entities, states, qualities, and actions about which humans communicate. In the system as reported in Wilks (1973), there were 60 of these elements, which fell into five classes. For example, the class ENTITIES contains elements like MAN and STUFF, and the class ACTIONS includes CAUSE and FLOW. (See Article III.C6 for a thorough dicussion of the status of semantic primitives in Wilks's research.)

The elements are used to build up *formulas*—each formula represents the sense of a word and is composed of elements combined into a binarily bracketed list-data structure. For example, the sense of the word *drink* when used as a verb is represented by the following formula:

```
((*ANI SUBJ)
 (((FLOW STUFF) OBJE)
  ((*ANI IN) (((THIS (*ANI (THRU PART))) TO) (BE CAUSE)))))
```

In other words, the word *drink* is an action, (BE CAUSE), done by animate subjects, (*ANI SUBJ), to liquids, ((FLOW STUFF) OBJE). It causes the liquid to be in the animate object, (*ANI IN), through a particular aperture of the animate object, ((THIS (*ANI (THRU PART))) TO).

Wilks and Herskovits (1973) point out that the formulas represent information about a word, or one sense of a word, not knowledge about the thing that the word stands for. In particular, the formulas represent the *preferences* a word has for being used in sentences with certain other kinds of words. For example, in analyzing the sentence *John drank a whole pitcher,* it is the preference of *drink* for a liquid object that would help select the formula representing the *container-of-liquid* sense of *pitcher* rather than the *baseball-player* sense. And these are preferences, not requirements, since in understanding the metaphorical sentence *My car drinks gasoline,* the preference of *drink* for an animate subject must be overlooked.

The system's dictionary contains formulas for all the word senses paired with *stereotypes* for producing the translated words in the target language. The following is an example of two stereotypes for the word *advise* (into French):

```
(ADVISE (CONSEILLER A (FN1 FOLK MAN))
        (CONSEILLER (FN2 ACT STATE STUFF)))
```

The two functions FN1 and FN2 are used to distinguish the two possible constructions in French for the object of *conseiller*: *conseiller à* . . . and simply *conseiller* . . . The first would be used in translating *I advise John to have patience;* the second, for *I advise patience.* Functions like these in stereotypes are evaluated by the generation routines. Each function evaluates either to NIL, in which case the stereotype fails, or to words that will appear in the output text. The stereotypes serve the purpose of a *text generation* grammar, providing complex, context-sensitive rules for overriding defaults where required, without search of a large store of such rules. This is an example of *procedural representation of knowledge* (see Article III.C2).

Analysis of an English sentence by the system proceeds in several stages. First, as mentioned above, the text is broken into fragments (at punctuation marks, conjunctions, prepositions, etc.), and each fragment is replaced by a sequence of formulas, one formula for each word in the fragment. Now, the dictionary may contain several formulas for a word, representing its different senses, so there may be several alternative sequences of formulas that could represent a given fragment.

To select the right formula sequence, each sequence is reduced to the sequence of elements that form the *heads* of its formulas. For example, the sentence *Small men sometimes father big sons* would produce the following head-element sequences:

```
(KIND MAN HOW MAN KIND MAN)
(KIND MAN HOW CAUSE KIND MAN)
```

which reflect the two senses of *father,* noun and verb, respectively. These sequences of head elements are matched against the *bare templates,* a built-in set of element triples in actor-action-object format. Examples of such triples are MAN-CAUSE-MAN (which happens to match the second interpretation above) and MAN-DO-THING. The system interprets a sentence fragment on the basis of one of the bare templates that matches one of the alternative sequences of formula headers. It is assumed that it is possible to build up a finite inventory of bare templates that would be adequate for the analysis of ordinary language. The inventory for the system has been determined empirically and is easily modified. Special forms of templates are available to match fragments like prepositional phrases.

At the initial stage of bare-template matching, some senses of the words in the fragment can be rejected because they produce head-element sequences that fail to match any bare template (as does the first interpretation of *father* above). However, more than one candidate template may remain. For example, if the fragment is *The policeman interrogated the crook,* there will still be two possible bare templates, MAN-FORCE-MAN and MAN-FORCE-THING, that match the fragment when *crook* is taken to be a person and a shepherd's staff, respectively. At the next stage of the analysis, called *expansion,* a more detailed matching algorithm is used. The principle followed is that the final *template* representation chosen for a fragment is the one in which the most preferences are satisfied. In this example, the preference of *interrogate* for a *human* object is decisive. The result of this stage is a full template—a network of formulas—for each fragment, in which semantic dependencies among the formulas (indicating satisfied preferences) have been noted. The overall goal of *semantic density*—that is, of maximizing the interdependence of formulas—is one of the key ideas in Wilks's work and produces a good solution to many problems of ambiguity.

In the succeeding stage of analysis, the templates for individual fragments are tied together with higher level dependencies, expressed in terms of *paraplates*, or patterns that span two templates. The use of paraplates is to resolve prepositional or *case* ambiguities (see Article IV.C4). For example, the fragments *he ran the mile* and *in four minutes* would be tied together by a paraplate for the TIMELOCATION case; had the second fragment been *in a plastic bag,* a CONTAINMENT case paraplate would have matched instead. A similar technique is used to resolve simple problems of pronoun reference, as in *I bought the wine, sat on a rock, and drank it.* In both cases, the chief preference of the system is for semantic density.

Finally, the system applies some commonsense *inference* rules to deal with situations in which, to resolve pronoun references, more explicit world-knowledge is required than formulas, templates, and paraplates provide. At the completion of this analysis, the input text has been replaced by an interlingual representation with suitable markers, and other information is used by the *text generation* routines in a relatively straightforward manner to produce the final output text.

References

This description of Wilks's work is based primarily on Wilks (1973) and Wilks and Herskovits (1973). Other descriptions include Wilks (1975a, 1975b, 1975c, 1977b, 1978).

Also of interest: Charniak and Wilks (1976) and Schank (1975a).

F3. LUNAR

LUNAR is an experimental, natural-language, *information retrieval* system designed by William Woods at BBN (Woods, Kaplan, and Nash–Webber, 1972; Woods, 1973b) to help geologists access, compare, and evaluate chemical-analysis data on moon rock and soil composition obtained from the Apollo–11 mission. The primary goal of the designers was research on the problems involved in building a man-machine interface that would allow communication in ordinary English. A "real world" application was chosen for two reasons: First, it tends to focus effort on the problems really in need of solution (sometimes this is implicitly avoided in "toy" problems) and, second, the possibility of producing a system capable of performing a worthwhile task lends additional impetus to the work.

LUNAR operates by translating a question entered in English into an expression in a formal *query language* (Codd, 1974). The translation is done with an *augmented transition network* (ATN) parser coupled with a rule-driven semantic interpretation procedure, which guides the analysis of the question. The "query" that results from this analysis is then applied to the database to produce the answer to the request. The query language is a generalization of the *predicate calculus* (Article III.C1). Its central feature is a quantifier function that is able to express, in a simple manner, the restrictions placed on a database-retrieval request by the user. This function is used in concert with special enumeration functions for classes of database objects, freeing the quantifier function from explicit dependence on the structure of the database. LUNAR also served as a foundation for the early work on *speech understanding* at BBN (see Article V.C3).

Detailed Description

The following list of requests is indicative of the kinds of English constructions that can be handled by LUNAR (shown as they would actually be presented to the system):

1. (WHAT IS THE AVERAGE CONCENTRATION OF ALUMINUM IN
       HIGH ALKALI ROCKS?)
2. (WHAT SAMPLES CONTAIN P205?)
3. (GIVE ME THE MODAL ANALYSES OF P205 IN THOSE SAMPLES)
4. (GIVE ME EU DETERMINATIONS IN SAMPLES WHICH CONTAIN ILM)

LUNAR processes these requests in the following three steps:

Syntactic analysis using an augmented transition network parser and *heuristic* information (including semantics) to produce the most likely *derivation tree* for the request;

Semantic interpretation to produce a representation of the meaning of the request in a formal query language;

Execution of the query language expression on the database to produce the answer to the request.

LUNAR's language processor contains an ATN grammar for a large subset of English, the semantic rules for interpreting database requests, and a dictionary of approximately 3,500 words. As an indication of the capabilities of the processor, it is able to deal with tense and modality, some anaphoric references and comparatives, restrictive relative clauses, certain adjective modifiers (some of which alter the range of quantification or interpretation of a noun phrase), and embedded complement constructions. Some problems do arise in parsing conjunctive constructions and in resolving ambiguity in the scope of quantifiers. Emphasis has been placed on the types of English constructions actually used by geologists, so that the system knows how geologists habitually refer to the objects in its database.

The Query Language

The formal query language contains three types of objects: *designators*, which name classes of objects in the database (including functionally defined objects); *propositions*, which are formed from predicates with designators as arguments; and *commands*, which initiate actions. Thus, if S10046 is a designator for a particular sample, OLIV is a designator for the mineral olivine, CONTAIN is a predicate, and TEST is a truth-value-testing command, then "(TEST (CONTAIN S10046 OLIV))" is a sample expression in the query language. The primary function in the language is the quantifier function FOR, which is used in expressions of the following type:

$$(\text{FOR QUANT } X \text{ / CLASS : } PX \text{ ; } QX)$$

where QUANT is a quantifier like *each* or *every*, or a numerical or comparative quantifier, X is a variable of quantification, CLASS determines the class of objects over which the quantification is to range, PX specifies a restriction on the range, and QX is the proposition or command being quantified. FOR is used with enumeration functions that can access the database. Thus, FOR itself is independent of the database structure. As an example (taken from Woods, 1973b), if SEQ is an enumeration function for enumerating a precomputed list, and if

PRINTOUT is a command that prints a representation for the designator given as its argument, then

```
( FOR EVERY X1 / (SEQ TYPECS) : T ; (PRINTOUT X1) )
```

prints the sample numbers for all type C samples. In this case, there is no restriction on the range of quantification in that $PX = T$.

A fuller example of the operation of LUNAR (simplified slightly from the same source) is shown below.

```
Request:
     (DO ANY SAMPLES HAVE GREATER THAN 13 PERCENT ALUMINUM)
Query Language Translation (after parsing):
     (TEST (FOR SOME X1 / (SEQ SAMPLES) : T ; (CONTAIN X1
          (NPR* X2 / 'AL2O3) (GREATERTHAN 13 PCT))))
Response:
     YES
```

LUNAR is perhaps the best operational example of a finely tuned ATN parsing system applied to a real-world problem. Since the system does have limited performance goals (in that facilitating database inquiry is not as demanding as, say, holding an interesting conversation), some of the complications inherent in understanding natural language dialogues are avoided.

References

See Woods (1973b), Woods and Kaplan (1971), and Woods, Kaplan, and Nash–Webber (1972).

F4. SHRDLU

The natural language processing system SHRDLU was written by Terry Winograd (1972) as his doctoral research project at M.I.T.   It was written in LISP and MICRO-PLANNER, a LISP-based programming language.   The design of the system was based on the belief that to understand language, a program must deal in an integrated way with syntax, semantics, and reasoning. The basic viewpoint guiding its implementation was that meanings (of words, phrases, and sentences) can be embodied in procedural structures and that language is a way of activating appropriate procedures within the hearer.   Thus, instead of representing knowledge about syntax and meaning as rules in a grammar or as patterns to be matched against the input, Winograd embodied the knowledge in SHRDLU in pieces of executable computer code.   For example, the context-free rule saying that a sentence is composed of a noun phrase and a verb phrase,

$$S \rightarrow NP \ VP \ ,$$

is embodied in the MICRO-PLANNER procedure:

```
(PDEFINE SENTENCE
    (((PARSE NP) NIL FAIL)
     ((PARSE VP) FAIL FAIL RETURN)))
```

When called, this program, named SENTENCE, uses independent procedures for parsing a noun phrase followed by a verb phrase.   These, in turn, can call other procedures.   The process FAILs if the required constituents are not found.   With such special *procedural representations* for syntactic, semantic, and reasoning knowledge, SHRDLU was able to achieve unprecedented performance levels.

SHRDLU operates within a small "toy" domain so that it can have an extensive model of the structures and processes allowed in the domain.   The program simulates the operation of a robot arm that manipulates toy blocks on a table.   The system maintains an interactive dialogue with the user: It can accept statements and commands as well as answer questions about the state of its world and the reasons for its actions.   The implemented system consists of four basic elements: a parser, a recognition grammar for English, programs for semantic analysis (to change a sentence into a sequence of commands to the robot or into a query of the database), and a problem solver (which knows about how to accomplish tasks in the blocks world).

Each procedure can make any checks on the sentence being parsed, perform any actions, or call on other procedures that may be required to accomplish its goal. For example, the VERB PHRASE procedure called above contains calls to functions that establish verb-subject agreement by searching through the entire derivation tree for other constituents while still in the middle of parsing the *VP*. SHRDLU's knowledge base includes a detailed model of the blocks world it manipulates, as well as a simple model of its own reasoning processes, so that it can explain its actions.

Reasoning in SHRDLU

SHRDLU's model of the world and reasoning about it are done in the MICRO-PLANNER programming language, which facilitates the representation of problem-solving procedures, allowing the user to specify his own heuristics and strategies for a particular domain. (The philosophy and implementation of PLANNER are described in Article VI.C2, in Vol. II—the brief discussion here will illustrate its use in SHRDLU.) Knowledge about the state of the world is translated into MICRO-PLANNER assertions, and manipulative and reasoning knowledge is embodied in MICRO-PLANNER programs. For example, the input sentence *The pyramid is on the table* might be translated into an assertion of the form:

```
(ON PYRAMID TABLE)
```

SHRDLU's problem solver consists of a group of "theorems" about the robot's environment and actions, represented as MICRO-PLANNER procedures. In operation, the theorem prover manipulates the state of the domain by running MICRO-PLANNER programs that perform the actions requested by the user.

The main idea of PLANNER is to solve problems by means of specific procedures built into the problem statements themselves, as well as by applying general problem-solving rules. The advantage of these problem-specific rules, or *heuristics*, is that they can radically increase the efficiency of the process. Furthermore, the problem statements are programs and thus can carry out actions in the problem-solving process. Thus, to put one block on another, there might be a MICRO-PLANNER program of the form:

```
(THGOAL (ON ?X ?Y)
        (OR (ON—TOP ?X ?Y)
            (AND (CLEAR—TOP ?X)
                 (CLEAR—TOP ?Y)
                 (PUT—ON ?X ?Y))))
```

This means that, if X is not already on Y, such a state can be achieved by clearing off everything that is stacked on top of X (so that the robot can move X), clearing off Y (so that X can be placed on top of Y), and then putting X on Y. The procedure resembles a *predicate calculus* theorem, but there are important differences. The PLANNER procedure is a program, and its operators carry out actions. The THGOAL procedure finds an assertion in the database or proves it with other procedures. AND and OR are logical connectives. The crucial element is that though PLANNER may end up doing a proof, it does so only after checking some conditions that may make the proof trivial, or impossible, and it only performs the proof on relevant arguments, rather than checking all entities in the database as a blind theorem prover might. Moreover, no sharp distinction is drawn between proof by showing that a desired assertion is already true and proof by finding a sequence of actions (manipulating blocks) that will make the assertion true.

Grammar, Syntax, and Semantics

SHRDLU's grammar is based on the notion of *systemic grammar*, a system of choice networks that specifies the features of a syntactic unit, how the unit functions, and how it influences other units (as described in Article IV.C3). Thus, a systemic grammar contains not only the constituent elements of a syntactic group but also higher level features such as mood, tense, and voice.

To facilitate the analysis, the parsing process looks for syntactic units that play a major role in meaning, and the semantic programs are organized into groups of procedures that are applicable to a certain type of syntactic unit. In addition, the database definitions contain *semantic markers* that can be used by the syntactic programs to rule out grammatical but semantically incorrect sentences such as *The table picks up blocks*. These markers are calls to semantic procedures that check for restrictions, for example, that only animate objects pick up things. These semantic programs can also examine the context of discourse to clarify meanings, establish pronoun referents, and initiate other semantically guided parsing functions.

Parsing

To write SHRDLU's parser, Winograd first wrote a programming language, embedded in LISP, which he called PROGRAMMAR. This language supplies primitive functions for building systemically described syntactic structures. The theory behind the language is that basic programming methods, such as procedures, iteration, and recursion, are also basic to the cognitive process. Thus, a grammar can be implemented without additional programming paraphernalia; special syntactic items (such as conjunctions) are dealt with through calls to special procedures. PROGRAMMAR operates basically in a top-down, left-to-right fashion but uses neither a *parallel processing* nor a *backtracking* strategy in dealing with multiple alternatives (see Article IV.D1). It finds one parsing rather directly, since decisions at choice points are guided by the semantic procedures. By functionally integrating its knowledge of syntax and semantics, SHRDLU can avoid exploring alternative choices in an ambiguous situation. If the choice does fail, PROGRAMMAR has primitives for returning to the choice point with the reasons for the failure and informing the parser of the next best choice based on these reasons. This "directed backup" is far different from PLANNER's automatic backtracking in that the design philosophy of the parser is oriented toward making an original correct choice rather than establishing exhaustive backtracking.

The key to the system's successful operation is the interaction of PLANNER reasoning procedures, semantic analysis, and PROGRAMMAR. All three of these elements examine the input and help direct the parsing process. By making use of this *multiple-source* knowledge and programmed-in "hints" (heuristics), SHRDLU successfully dealt with language issues such as pronouns and referents. The reader is referred to Winograd's *Understanding Natural Language* (1972), pages 8–15, for an illustrative sample dialogue with SHRDLU.

Discussion

SHRDLU constituted a significant step forward in natural language processing research because of its attempts to combine models of human linguistic and reasoning methods in the language understanding process. Before SHRDLU, most AI language programs were linguistically simple; they used keyword and pattern-oriented grammars. Furthermore, even the more powerful grammar models used by linguists made little use of inference methods and semantic knowledge in the analysis of sentence structure. A union of these two techniques gives SHRDLU impressive results and makes it a more viable theoretical model of human language processing.

SHRDLU does have its problems, however. Like most existing natural language systems, SHRDLU cannot handle many of the more complex features of English. Some of the problem areas are agreement, dealing with hypotheses, and handling words like *the* and *and*.

Wilks (1974) has argued that SHRDLU's power does not come from linguistic analysis but from the use of problem-solving methods in a simple, logical, and closed domain (blocks world), thus eliminating the need to face some of the more difficult language issues. It seems doubtful that if SHRDLU were extended to a larger domain, it would be able to deal with these problems. Further, the level at which SHRDLU seeks to simulate the intermixing of knowledge sources typical of human reasoning is embedded in its processes rather than made explicit in its control structure, where it would be most powerful. Lastly, its problem solving is still highly oriented toward predicate calculus and limited in its use of inferential and heuristic data (Winograd, 1974, pp. 46–48).

References

Winograd (1972) is the principal reference on SHRDLU. A convenient summary is given in Winograd (1973). Boden (1977) also presents a clear and concise discussion of the system. Winograd (1980b) reviews SHRDLU and subsequent directions of his research into understanding language.

Also of interest are the MICRO-PLANNER manual (Sussman, Winograd, and Charniak, 1970) and Wilks (1974), Winograd (1974), and Winograd (in press).

F5. MARGIE

MARGIE (Meaning Analysis, Response Generation, and Inference on English) was a program developed by Roger Schank and his students at the Stanford AI Laboratory (see Schank, 1975a). Its intent was to provide an intuitive model of the process of natural language understanding. More recent work by Schank and his colleagues at Yale University on *script-based story understanding* in their SAM and PAM systems is described in Article IV.F6.

Conceptual Dependency Theory

Schank (1973b) developed conceptual dependency (CD) as a representation for the meaning of phrases and sentences. The "basic axiom" of conceptual dependency theory is:

> For any two sentences that are identical in meaning, regardless of language, there should be only one representation of that meaning in CD. (Schank and Abelson, 1977, p. 11)

Schank thus allies himself with the early machine translation concept of *interlingua*, or intermediate language (see Article IV.B), and has in fact done some *machine translation* research in conjunction with the *story understanding* project, SAM.

A second important idea is that conceptual dependency representations are made up of a very small number of *semantic primitives*, which include primitive acts and primitive states (with associated attribute values). Examples of *primitive acts* are:

```
PTRANS   The transfer of the physical location of an
         object. For one to "go" is to PTRANS oneself.
         "Putting" an object somewhere is to PTRANS it
         to that place.

PROPEL   The application of physical force to an object.

ATRANS   The transfer of an abstract relationship. To
         "give" is to ATRANS the relationship of possession
         or ownership.

MTRANS   The transfer of mental information between people
         or within a person. "Telling" is an MTRANS between
         people; "seeing" is an MTRANS within a person.

MBUILD   The construction of new information from old.
         "Imagining," "inferring," and "deciding" are MBUILDs.
```

In the most recent version of CD theory (1977), Schank and Abelson included 11 of these primitive acts. Relations among concepts are called *dependencies*, and there is a fixed number of these, each represented graphically by a special kind of arrow. For example, the canonical representation of the sentence *John gives Mary a book* is the graph:

```
                          o        R  ┌──→ Mary
         John <===> ATRANS ←── book ←──┤
                                       └──← John
```

where *John*, *book*, and *Mary* are concept nodes, and the ATRANS node represents one of the primitive acts. The complicated, three-pointed arrow labeled "R" indicates a recipient-donor dependency between Mary and John and the book, since Mary got the book from John. The arrow labeled "o" indicates an "objective" dependency; that is, the book is the object of the ATRANS, since it is the thing being given. Dependency links may link concepts or other conceptual dependency networks.

Examples of *primitive states* in conceptual dependency theory include:

```
STATES:
       Mary HEALTH(-10)              Mary is dead.
       John MENTAL STATE(+10)        John is ecstatic.
       Vase PHYSICAL STATE(-10)      The vase is broken.
```

The number of primitive states is much larger than the number of primitive actions. States and actions can be combined; for example, the sentence *John told Mary that Bill was happy* can be represented (in a newer, arrowless representation) as

```
John MTRANS (Bill BE MENTAL-STATE(5)) to Mary.
```

An important class of sentences involves *causal chains*, and Schank and Abelson and their colleagues have worked out some rules about causality that apply to conceptual dependency theory. Five important rules are:

1. Actions can result in state changes.
2. States can enable actions.
3. States can disable actions.
4. States (or acts) can initiate mental events.
5. Mental events can be reasons for actions.

These are fundamental pieces of knowledge about the world, and CD includes a shorthand representation of each (and combinations of some) called *causal links*.

The third important idea in conceptual dependency theory is:

Any information in a sentence that is implicit must be made explicit in the representation of the meaning of that sentence. (Schank and Abelson, 1977, p. 11)

This idea is the basis for much of the sophisticated inferential ability of MARGIE and the later systems. It can be illustrated by the CD representation of the sentence *John eats the ice cream with a spoon:*

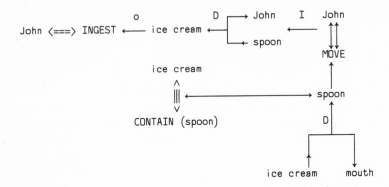

where the *D* and *I* arrows indicate *direction* and *instrument* dependencies, respectively. Note that in this example, *mouth* has entered the diagram as part of the conceptualization, even though it was not in the original sentence. This is a fundamental difference between conceptual dependency networks and the *derivation tree* that is produced in *parsing* a sentence. John's mouth as the recipient of the ice cream is inherent in the meaning of the sentence, whether it is expressed or not. In fact, the diagram can never be finished, because we could add such details as "John INGESTed the ice cream by TRANSing the ice cream on a spoon to his mouth, by TRANSing the spoon to the ice cream, by GRASPing the spoon, by MOVing his hand to the spoon, by MOVing his hand muscles," and so on. Such an analysis is known to both the speaker and the hearer of the sentence and normally would not need to be expanded.

For some tasks, like *paraphrasing* and *question answering*, CD representation has a number of advantages over more surface-oriented systems. In particular, sentences like

```
Shakespeare wrote Hamlet.
```

and

```
The author of Hamlet was Shakespeare.
```

which in some sense have the same meaning, map into the same CD structure. Another important aspect of conceptual dependency theory is its independence from syntax; in contrast with earlier work in the paradigms of *transformational grammar* or *phrase-structure grammar*, a "parse" of a sentence in conceptual dependency bears little relation to the syntactic structure. Schank (1975a) also claims that conceptual dependency has a certain amount of psychological validity, in that it reflects intuitive notions of human cognition. The status of semantic primitives in conceptual dependency theory is discussed further in Article III.C6.

MARGIE

The MARGIE system, programmed in LISP 1.6, was divided into three components. The first, written by Christopher Riesbeck, was a *conceptual analyzer*, which took English sentences and converted them into an internal conceptual-dependency representation. This was done through a system of "requests," which are similar to *demons* or *productions* (see Article III.C4). A request is essentially a piece of code that looks for some surface linguistic construct and takes a specific action if it is found. It consists of a test condition, to be searched for in the input, and an action, to be executed if the test is successful. The test might be as specific as a particular word or as general as an entire conceptualization. The action might contain information about (a) what to look for next in the input, (b) what to do with the input just found, and (c) how to organize the representation. The flexibility of this formalism allows the system to function without depending heavily on syntax, although it is otherwise quite similar to the tests and actions that make ATNs such a powerful parsing mechanism.

The middle phase of the system, written by Charles Rieger, was an inferencer designed to accept a proposition (stated in conceptual dependency) and deduce a large number of facts from the proposition in the current context of the system's memory. The reason behind this component was the assumption that humans understand far more from a sentence than is actually stated. Sixteen types of inferences were identified, including cause, effect, specification, and function. The inference knowledge was represented in memory in a modified *semantic net*. Inferences were organized into "molecules," for the purpose of applying them. An example of this process might be:

```
John hit Mary.
```

from which the system might infer (among many other things):

```
John was angry with Mary.
Mary might hit John back.
Mary might get hurt.
```

The module does relatively unrestricted forward inferencing, which tended to produce large numbers of inferences for any given input.

The last part of the system was a *text generation* module written by Neil Goldman. This took an internal conceptual-dependency representation and converted it into English-like output, in a two-part process:

1. A *discrimination net* was used to distinguish between different word-senses. This permitted the system to use English-specific contextual criteria for selecting words (especially verbs) to "name" conceptual patterns.

2. An ATN was used to linearize the conceptual dependency representation into a surface-like structure.

The text generation module is also discussed in Article IV.E.

MARGIE ran in two modes: *inference* mode and *paraphrase* mode. In inference mode, it would accept a sentence and attempt to make inferences from that sentence, as described above. In paraphrase mode, it would attempt to restate the sentence in as many equivalent ways as possible. For example, given the input

```
John killed Mary by choking her.
```

it might produce the paraphrases

```
John strangled Mary.
John choked Mary and she died because she was unable to breathe.
```

Discussion

Of particular interest in MARGIE, an experimental system that provided a foundation for Schank's further work in *computational linguistics*, was the use of conceptual dependency as an *interlingua*, a language-independent representation scheme for encoding the meaning of sentences. Once the sentence was processed, the surface structure was dropped and all further work was done using the conceptual dependency notation. The existence of a canonical representation for all sentences with the same meaning facilitates tasks like paraphrasing and question answering.

References

Conceptual dependency theory and all three parts of the MARGIE system are described in detail in Schank (1975a). Since then, the theory has evolved considerably, and several new systems have been built using the CD formalisms, all described very well in Schank and Abelson (1977). Other references for MARGIE include Schank (1973b) and Schank et al. (1973). The review article by Schank (1980) is a very interesting discussion of the development of his ideas about natural language.

F6.   SAM and PAM

Story Understanding

SAM (Script Applier Mechanism) and PAM (Plan Applier Mechanism) are computer programs developed by Roger Schank, Robert Abelson, and their students at Yale University to demonstrate the use of *scripts* and *plans* in understanding simple stories (Schank et al., 1975; Schank and Abelson, 1977). Most work in natural language understanding prior to 1973 involved parsing individual sentences in isolation; it was thought that text composed of paragraphs could be understood simply as collections of sentences. But just as sentences are not unconstrained collections of words, so paragraphs and stories are not without structure. The structures of stories have been analyzed (Propp, 1968; Rumelhart, 1975; Thorndyke, 1977), and it is clear that the context provided by these structures facilitates sentence comprehension, just as the context provided by sentence structure facilitates word comprehension. For example, if we have been told in a story that John is very poor, we can expect later sentences to deal with the consequences of John's poverty or with the steps he takes to alleviate it.

Different researchers have very different ideas about what constitutes the structure of a story. Some *story grammars* are rather syntactic; that is, they describe a story as a collection of parts like setting, characters, goal introduction, and plans, determined by their sequential position in the story rather than by their meaning. The work of Schank and Abelson reported here has a more semantic orientation. They propose an underlying representation of each phrase in a story that is based on a knowledge representation formalism called *conceptual dependency* theory (CD; described in Article IV.F5). Conceptual dependency, which creates, from a set of *semantic primitives*, unique representations for all sentences with the same meaning, is the theoretical basis for more complex story structures such as *scripts*, *plans*, *goals*, and *themes*. The SAM and PAM programs understand stories using these higher level structures.

Conceptual dependency representation is, then, the interlingua that is produced when SAM or PAM parses sentences. The parser for these programs is an extension of the one developed by Christopher Riesbeck (1975) for the MARGIE system (Article IV.F5). Further processing in SAM and PAM involves the manipulation of CD structures and of higher level structures built on them—scripts, plans, goals, and themes.

Scripts

A script is a standardized sequence of events that describes some stereotypical human activity, such as going to a restaurant or visiting a doctor. Schank and Abelson's assumption is that people know many such scripts and use them to establish the context of events. A script is functionally similar to a *frame* (Minsky, 1975) or a *schema* (Bartlett, 1932; Rumelhart, 1975), in the sense that it can be used to *anticipate* aspects of the events it represents. For example, the RESTAURANT script (see Fig. F6-1) involves going to a restaurant, being seated, consulting the menu, and so on. People who are presented with an abbreviated description of this activity, for example, the sentence *John went out to dinner,* infer from their own knowledge about restaurants that John ordered, ate, and paid for food. Moreover, they anticipate from a sentence that fills part of the script (e.g., *John was given a menu*) what sort of sentences are likely to follow (e.g., *John ordered the lamb*). Scripts attempt to capture the kind of knowledge that people apply to make these inferences. (Article III.C7 discusses scripts, frames, and representation schemes.)

```
Players:       customer, server, cashier

Props:         restaurant, table, menu, food, check, payment, tip

Events:

          1. customer goes to restaurant
          2. customer goes to table
          3. server brings menu
          4. customer orders food
          5. server brings food
          6. customer eats food
          7. server brings check
          8. customer leaves tip for server
          9. customer gives payment to cashier
         10. customer leaves restaurant

Header:        event 1

Main concept:  event 6
```

Figure F6-1.   Restaurant script.

Two components of scripts are of special importance. We will discuss later how the first component, the *script header*, is used by SAM to match scripts to parsed sentences. The second important component is the *main concept*, or *goal*, of the script. In the restaurant script, the goal is to eat food.

The scripts in SAM grew out of Abelson's (1973) notion of scripts as networks of causal connections. However, they do not depend on explicit causal connections between their events. In hearing or observing events that fit a standard script, one need not analyze the sequence of events in terms of causes, since they can be anticipated just on the basis of knowing what typically happens in situations in which the script applies. The identification of events as filling their slots in the script gives us the intuition of "understanding what happened."

Scripts describe everyday events, but frequently these events (or our relating of them) do not run to completion. For example:

```
I went to the restaurant.  I had a hamburger.
Then I bought some groceries.
```

This story presents several problems for a system like SAM that matches scripts to input sentences. One problem is that the restaurant script is "left dangling" by the introduction of the last sentence. It is not clear to the system whether the restaurant script (a) has terminated and a new (grocery shopping) script has started, (b) has been distracted by a "fleeting" (one sentence) grocery script, or (c) is interacting with a new grocery script (e.g., buying groceries in the restaurant). Another thing that can happen to everyday scripts is that they can be thwarted, as in:

```
I went to the gas station to fill up my car.
But the owner said he was out of gas.
```

This is called an *obstacle*.

Scripts describe rather specific events, and although it is assumed that adults know thousands of them, story comprehension cannot be simply a matter of finding a script to match a story. There are just too many possible stories. Moreover, there are clear cases in which people comprehend a story even though it does not give enough information to cause a program to invoke a script, as in

```
John needed money.  He got a gun and went to a liquor store.
```

Schank and Abelson point out that even if the program had a script for Robbery, this story offers no basis for invoking it. Nonetheless, people understand John's goals and his intended actions.

There must be relevant knowledge available to tie together sentences that otherwise have no obvious connection. . . . The
problem is that there are a great many stories where the
connection cannot be made by the techniques of causal chaining
nor by reference to a script. Yet they are obviously connectable.
Their connectability comes from these stories' implicit reference to
plans. (Schank and Abelson, 1977, p. 75)

Plans

Schank and Abelson introduce *plans* as the means by which goals
are accomplished, and they state that understanding *plan-based* stories
involves discerning the goals of the actor and the methods by which the
actor chooses to fulfill those goals.   The distinction between script-based
and plan-based stories is very simple: In a script-based story, parts or
all of the story correspond to one or more scripts available to the story
understander; in a plan-based story, the understander must discern the
goals of the main actor and the actions that accomplish those goals.
An understander might process the same story by matching it with a
script or scripts or by figuring out the plans that are represented in the
story. The difference is that the first method is very specialized since a
script refers to a specific sequence of actions, while plans can be very
general since the goals they accomplish are general.   For example, in

        John wanted to go to a movie. He walked to the bus stop.

we understand that John's *immediate* goal (called a *delta goal* or D-goal
because it brings about a change necessary for accomplishment of the
ultimate goal) is to get to the movie theater.   *Going somewhere* is a
very general goal and does not apply just to going to the movies.   In
Schank and Abelson's theory, this goal has associated with it a set of
plan boxes, which are standard ways of accomplishing the goal.   Plan
boxes for *going somewhere* include riding an animal, taking public
transportation, driving a car, and so forth.
    Obviously, a story understander might have a "Go to the movies"
script in its repertoire, so that analysis of John's goals would be
unnecessary—the system would just "recognize" the situation and retrieve the script.   This script can be thought of as the standardized
intersection of a number of more or less general goals and their associated plan boxes.   It would be a "routinized plan" made up of a set of
general subplans: Go to somewhere (the theater), Purchase something (a
ticket), Purchase something (some popcorn), and so forth.

A routinized plan can become a script, at least from the planner's personal point of view.

Thus, plans are where scripts come from. They compete for the same role in the understanding process, namely as explanations of sequences of actions that are intended to achieve a goal. (Schank and Abelson, 1977, p. 72)

The process of understanding plan-based stories involves determining the actor's goal, establishing the subgoals (D-goals) that will lead to the main goal, and matching the actor's actions with plan boxes associated with the D-goals. For example, in

```
John was very thirsty.  He hunted for a glass.
```

we recognize the D-goal of PTRANSing liquid and the lower level goal (specified in the plan box for PTRANSing liquid) of finding a container to do it with.

Goals and Themes

In story comprehension, goals and subgoals may arise from a number of sources. For example, they may be stated explicitly, as in

```
John wanted to eat.
```

they may be nested in a plan box, or they may arise from *themes*. For example, if a LOVE theme holds between John and Mary, it is reasonable to expect the implicit, mutual goal of protecting each other from harm: "Themes, in other words, contain the background information upon which we base our predictions that an individual will have a certain goal" (Schank and Abelson, 1977, p. 132).

Themes are rather like production systems in their situation-action nature. A theme specifies a set of actors, the situations they may be in, and the actions that will resolve the situation in a way consistent with the theme. The goals of a theme are to accomplish these actions. Schank and Abelson have proposed seven types of goals; we have already considered D-goals. Other examples are:

```
A- or Achievement-goals:    To desire wealth is to have an
                            A-Money goal.
P- or Preservation-goal:    To protect someone may be a P-Health
                            or P-Mental State goal.
C- or Crisis-goal:          A special case of P-goals, when action
                            is immediately necessary.
```

The LOVE theme can be stated in terms of some of these goals:

```
X is the lover; Y is the loved one; Z is another person.

    SITUATION                              ACTION

    Z cause Y harm                 A-Health(Y) and possibly
                                   cause Z harm
                            or     C-Health(Y)


    not-Love(Y,X)                  A-Love(Y,X)

    General goals:                 A-Respect(Y)
                                   A-Marry(Y)
                                   A-Approval(Y)
```

To summarize the knowledge structures we have discussed, we note their interrelationships:

1. Themes give rise to goals.

2. A plan is understood when its goals are identified and its actions are consistent with the accomplishment of those goals.

3. Scripts are standardized models of events.

4. Scripts are specific; plans are general.

5. Plans originate from scripts.

6. Plans are ways of representing a person's goals. These goals are implicit in scripts, which represent only the actions.

7. A script has a header, which is pattern-matched to an input sentence. Plans do not have headers, but each plan is subsumed under a goal.

SAM

Both SAM and PAM accept stories as input; both use an English-to-CD parser to produce an internal representation of the story (in conceptual dependency). Both can paraphrase the story and make intelligent inferences from it. They differ with respect to the processing that goes on after the CD representation has been built.

SAM understands stories by fitting them into one or more scripts. After this match is completed, it makes summaries of the stories. The process of fitting a story into a script has three parts—a PARSER, a memory module (MEMTOK), and the script applier (APPLY). These modules work together: The parser generates a CD representation of each sentence, but APPLY gives it a set of Verb-senses to use once a script has been identified. For example, once the restaurant script has been established, APPLY tells the parser that the appropriate sense of the verb *to serve* is *to serve food* rather than, for example, *to serve in the army*.

The parser does not make many inferences; thus, it does not realize that *it* refers to the hot dog in *The hot dog was burned. It tasted awful.* This task is left to MEMTOK. This module takes references to people, places, things, and so forth and fills in information about them. It recognizes that the *it* in the sentence above refers to the hot dog, and "instantiates" the *it* node in the CD representation of the second sentence with the "hot dog" node from the first sentence. Similarly, in a story about John, MEMTOK would replace *he* with *John* where appropriate, and would continually update the *John* data structure as more information became available about him.

The APPLY module has three functions. First, it takes a sentence from the parser and checks whether it matches the current script, a concurrent (interacting) script, or *any* script in the database. If this matching is successful, it makes a set of predictions about likely inputs to follow. Its third task is to instantiate any steps in the current script that were "skipped over" in the story. For example, if the first sentence of a story is *John went to a restaurant,* APPLY finds a match with the *script header* of the restaurant script in its database (refer back to Fig. F6-1). APPLY then sets up predictions for seeing the other *events* listed in the restaurant script in the input. If the next sentence is *John had a hamburger,* then APPLY successfully matches this sentence to the restaurant script (event 6). It then assumes that events 2–5 happened, and instantiates structures in its CD representation of the story to this effect. Events 7–10 remain as predictions.

When the whole story has been mapped into a CD representation in this manner, the SAM program can produce a summary of the story or answer questions about it. (See Schank and Abelson, 1977, pp. 190–204, for an annotated sample protocol.) Consistent with the idea of an interlingua, SAM can produce summaries in English, Chinese, Russian, Dutch, and Spanish. An example of a SAM paraphrase follows; note the powerful inferences made by instantiating intermediate script steps:

ORIGINAL: John went to a restaurant. He sat down. He got mad.
                 He left.

PARAPHRASE: JOHN WAS HUNGRY. HE DECIDED TO GO TO A RESTAURANT.
                 HE WENT TO ONE. HE SAT DOWN IN A CHAIR. A WAITER
                 DID NOT GO TO THE TABLE. JOHN BECAME UPSET. HE
                 DECIDED HE WAS GOING TO LEAVE THE RESTAURANT. HE
                 LEFT IT.

SAM inferred that John left the restaurant because he did not get any service. The basis for this inference is that in the restaurant script, event 3 represents the waiter coming over to the table after the main actor has been seated. SAM knows that people can get mad if their expectations are not fulfilled and infers that John's anger results from the nonoccurrence of event 3.

PAM

Wilensky's (1978a) PAM system understands stories by determining the goals that are to be achieved in the story and attempting to match the actions of the story with the methods that it knows will achieve the goals. More formally:

The process of understanding plan-based stories is as follows:

a) Determine the goal,

b) Determine the D-goals that will satisfy that goal,

c) Analyze input conceptualizations for their potential realization of one of the planboxes that are called by one of the determined D-goals. (Schank and Abelson, 1977, p. 75)

PAM utilizes two kinds of knowledge structures in understanding goals: *named plans* and *themes*. A named plan is a set of actions and sub-goals for accomplishing a main goal. It is not very different from a script, although the emphasis in named plans is on goals and the means to accomplish them. For example, a script for rescuing a person from a dragon would involve riding to the dragon's lair and slaying it—a sequence of actions—but a named plan would be a list of subgoals (find some way of getting to the lair, find some way of killing the dragon, etc.) and their associated plan boxes. When PAM encounters a goal in a story for which it has a named plan, it can make predictions about the D-goals and the actions that will follow. It will look for these D-goals and actions in subsequent inputs. Finding them is equivalent to understanding the story.

Themes provide another source of goals for PAM. Consider the sentences:

1. John wanted to rescue Mary from the dragon.
2. John loves Mary. Mary was stolen away by a dragon.

In both of these cases, PAM will expect John to take actions that are consistent with the goal of rescuing Mary from the dragon, even though this goal was not explicitly mentioned in sentence 2. The source of this goal in sentence 2 is, of course, the LOVE theme mentioned above—if another actor tries to cause harm to a loved one, the main actor sets up the goal of Achieving-Health of the loved one and possibly harming the evil party. (It is assumed that the dragon stole Mary in order to hurt her.)

PAM determines the goals of an actor by (a) noting their explicit mention in the text of the story, (b) establishing them as D-goals for some known goal, or (c) inferring them from a theme mentioned in the story. To understand a story is to "keep track of the goals of each of the characters in a story and to interpret their actions as means of achieving those goals" (Schank and Abelson, 1977, p. 217). The program begins with written English text, converts it into CD representation, and then interprets each sentence in terms of goals (predicting D-goals and actions to accomplish them) or actions themselves (marking the D-goals as accomplished). When this process is completed, PAM can summarize the story and answer questions about the goals and actions of the characters.

Summary

Scripts, plans, goals, and themes are knowledge structures built upon conceptual dependency theory. SAM is a program for understanding script-based stories. It matches the input sentences of a story to events in one or more of the scripts in its database. As such, it processes input based on *expectations* it has built up from the scripts. PAM understands plan-based stories by determining the goals of the characters of the story and by interpreting subsequent actions in terms of those goals or subgoals that will achieve them. A great deal of inference can be required of PAM simply to establish the goals and subgoals of the story from the input text.

Schank and Abelson argue that human story-understanding is a mixture of applying known scripts and inferring goals (where no script is available or of obvious applicability). They are experimenting with interactions of SAM and PAM, particularly with using SAM to handle script-based substories under the control of PAM.

References

The recent book by Schank and Abelson (1977) is the most complete and readable source on both of these systems and on the current state of conceptual dependency theory. For a thorough treatment of PAM, see the doctoral dissertation by Wilensky (1978a). Schank (1980) reviews the development of his ideas about natural language processing and his work on these NL systems.

Also of interest: Abelson (1973), Bartlett (1932), Minsky (1975), Propp (1968), Riesbeck (1975), Rumelhart (1975), Schank (1973b), Schank et al. (1975), Thorndyke (1977), and Wilensky (1978b).

F7. LIFER

The natural language systems described in the preceding articles fall into two categories: those built to study natural language processing issues in general and those built with a particular task domain in mind. In contrast, LIFER, built by Gary Hendrix (1977a) as part of the internal research and development program of SRI International, is designed to be an off-the-shelf utility for building "natural language front-ends" for applications in any domain.   In other words, LIFER can be used by systems designers to create a program that interprets English input and produces the appropriate sequence of commands for their system—for example, formal queries for an information retrieval system.   The front-end designers can augment LIFER to fit their particular applications, and even the eventual users can tailor the LIFER-supported front-end to meet their individual styles and needs.

Language Specification and Parsing

The LIFER system has two major components: (a) a set of interactive functions for specifying a language and (b) a parser.   Initially it contains neither a grammar nor the semantics of any language domain. An interface builder uses the language specification functions to define an *application language*, which is a subset of English that is appropriate for interacting with his or her application system.   The LIFER system then uses this language specification to *interpret* natural language inputs as commands for the application system.

The interface builder specifies the language primarily in terms of grammatical *rewrite rules* (see Article IV.C1). LIFER automatically translates these into transition trees, which are a simplified form of augmented transition networks (Article IV.D2).   Using the transition tree, the parser interprets inputs in the application language.   The result is an interpretation in terms of the appropriate routines from the applications system, as specified by the interface builder.   The parser attempts to parse an input string from the top down and left to right by nondeterministically tracing down the transition tree whose root node is the start symbol (known as <L.T.G.> for "LIFER top grammar"). For example, suppose the interface builder has specified the following three production rules as part of the application language:

```
<L.T.G.>  →  WHAT IS THE <ATTRIBUTE> OF <PERSON>  |  e1
<L.T.G.>  →  WHAT IS <PERSON> <ATTRIBUTE>  |  e2
<L.T.G.>  →  HOW <ATTRIBUTE> IS <PERSON>  |  e3
```

If an input matches one of these patterns, the corresponding expression (e_1, e_2, or e_3) is evaluated—these are the appropriate *interpretations* that the system is to make for the corresponding input. The transition tree built by the language specification functions would look like this:

```
                              /—THE—<ATTRIBUTE> OF <PERSON>  | e1
                  — WHAT IS /
                         /     \—<PERSON> <ATTRIBUTE>  | e2
      <L.T.G.> /
                 \
                  \— HOW <ATTRIBUTE> IS <PERSON>  | e3
```

Sentences such as:

```
What is the age of Mary's sister?
How old is Mary's sister?
What is John's height?
How tall is John?
```

might be parsed with this simple transition tree, depending on how the *nonterminal* symbols or meta-symbols, <ATTRIBUTE> and <PERSON>, are defined. (The interface builder can supply a preprocessing function that is applied to the input string before LIFER attempts to parse it. Typically, the preprocessor strips trailing apostrophes and *s*'s, so that LIFER sees *John's* as *John*.)

During parsing, LIFER starts at the symbol <L.T.G.> and attempts to move toward the expressions to be evaluated at the right. The parser follows a branch only if some portion at the left of the remaining input string can be matched to the first symbol on the branch. Actual words (such as *what* or *of* in the above example) can be matched only by themselves. Meta-symbols (such as <ATTRIBUTE> or <PERSON>) can be matched in a number of ways, depending on how the interface builder has defined them:

1. As a simple set (e.g., <PERSON> = the set {Mary, John, Bill});

2. As a predicate that is applied to the string to test for satisfaction (e.g., some meta-symbol used in a piece of grammar to recognize dates might test whether the next string of characters is a string of digits, and thus a number); or

3. By another transition tree that has this meta-symbol as its root node.

The above example is typical: A large amount of semantic information is embedded in the syntactic description of the application language. JOHN and HEIGHT are not defined as instances of the single meta-symbol <NOUN> as they would be in a more formal grammar, but rather are separated into the semantic categories indicated by the meta-symbols <PERSON> and <ATTRIBUTE>. The technique of embedding such semantic information in the syntax has been referred to as *semantic grammar* (Burton, 1976), and it greatly increases the performance of LIFER's automatic spelling correction, ellipsis, and paraphrase facilities, described below.

Applications

LIFER has been used to build a number of natural language interfaces, including a medical database, a task scheduling and resource allocation system, and a computer-based expert system. The most complex system built with a LIFER interface involved a few man-months of development of the natural language front-end: The LADDER system (Language Access to Distributed Data with Error Recovery) developed at SRI, which provides real-time natural language access to a very large database spread over many smaller databases in computers scattered throughout the United States (Sacerdoti, 1977; Hendrix et al., 1978). Users of the system need have no knowledge of how the data are organized nor where they are stored. More important from the point of view of this article is that users do not need to know a data query language: They use English, or rather a subset that is "natural" for the domain of discourse and that is usually understood by the LIFER front-end. The output of LIFER is a translation into a general database query language, which the rest of the LADDER system converts to a query of the appropriate databases on the appropriate computers.

Another interesting system to use a LIFER front-end was the HAWKEYE system (Barrow et al., 1977), also developed at SRI. This is an integrated interactive system for cartography or surveillance, which combines aerial photographs and generic descriptions of objects and situations with the topographical and cultural information found in traditional maps. The user queries the database and invokes image-processing tasks through a LIFER natural language interface. A unique feature of this interface is the combination of natural language and nontextual forms of input. For instance, using a cursor to point to places within an image, the user can ask questions such as "What is this?" and "What is the distance between here and here?" The interpretation of such expressions results in requests for coordinates from the subsystem providing graphical input, which are then handed to other subsystems that have access to the coordinates-to-object correspondences.

Human Engineering

LIFER is intended as a system that facilitates, for interface builders, the describing of an appropriate subset of a language and its interpretation in their system and also helps nonexpert users to communicate with the application system in whatever language has been defined. For this reason, close attention was paid to the human engineering aspects of LIFER. Experience with the system has shown that, for some applications, users previously unfamiliar with LIFER have been able to create usable natural language interfaces to their systems in a few days. The resulting systems have been directly usable by people whose field of expertise is not computer science.

The interface builder. Unlike Winograd's PROGRAMMAR language (in SHRDLU, Article IV.F4), there is no compilation phase during which the language specification is converted into a program. Instead, changes are made incrementally every time a call to the language specification functions is made. Furthermore, it is easy (by typing a prefix character) to intermix statements to be interpreted by the specification functions, statements to be parsed with the partially specified grammar, and statements to be evaluated in the underlying implementation language of LIFER, namely, INTERLISP. Thus, the interface builder can define a new rewrite rule for the grammar or write a predicate for some metasymbol and test it immediately, which leads to a highly interactive style of language definition and debugging. A *grammar editor* facilitates fixing mistakes. The ability to intermix language definition with parsing allows the interface user to extend the interface language to personal needs or taste during a session using the application system. This extension can be done either by directly invoking the language specification functions, or, if the interface builder has provided the facility, by typing natural language sentences whose interpretations invoke the same language specification functions.

The interface user. LIFER provides many features to ease the task of the user as he or she types in sentences to be understood by the system. Interactions with the user are numbered, and the user can refer back to a previous question and specify some substitution to be made. For instance:

12.   How many minority students took 20 or more units of credit
        last quarter?

PARSED!
    87

```
13.    Use women for minority in 12
PARSED!
     156
```

(Note the "PARSED!" printed by LIFER to indicate parsing success.) This facility can be used to save typing (and more errors), both when similar questions are being asked and when errors in previous inputs are being corrected. The user can simply specify synonyms to be used. For instance:

```
28.    Define Bill like William
```

will cause LIFER to treat the word BILL the same as WILLIAM. LIFER also allows for easy inspection of the language definition, which is useful for both interface builders and sophisticated users.

There are three additional features implemented in LIFER to make interactions easier for the user—the spelling correction, ellipsis, and paraphrase mechanisms. Spelling correction is attempted when LIFER fails to parse an input. The INTERLISP spelling-correction facility is used to find candidate words that closely match the spelling of the suspect word. The use of a *semantic grammar* with its semantically significant (and small) syntactic categories (e.g., <PERSON> instead of <NOUN>) greatly restricts the number of alternatives that must be checked.

While interacting with an applications system, the user may want to carry out many similar tasks (e.g., in a database query system, one often asks several questions about the same object). The LIFER system automatically allows the user to type incomplete input fragments and attempts to interpret them in the context of the previous input. For instance, the following three questions might be entered successively and understood by LIFER:

```
42.    What is the height of John
43.    the weight
44.    age of Mary's sister
```

If an input fails normal parsing, and if spelling correction doesn't help, LIFER tries elliptic processing. Again, because languages defined in LIFER tend to encode semantic information in the syntax definition, similar syntactic structures tend to have similar semantics. Therefore LIFER accepts any input string that is syntactically analogous to any contiguous substring of words in the last input that parsed without ellipsis. The analogies do not have to be in terms of complete subtrees of the syntactic tree, but they do have to correspond to contiguous words in the previous input. The elliptical processing facilitates quite natural interactions.

The paraphrase facility allows users to define new syntactic structures in terms of old structures. The user gives an example of the structure and interpretation desired, and the system builds the most general, new syntactic rule allowed by the syntactic rules already known. The similarity between the semantics and syntax is usually sufficient to ensure that a usable syntax rule is generated. The following example assumes that the interface builder has included a rule to interpret the construction shown to invoke a call to the language specification function PARAPHRASE with appropriately bound arguments. After typing

```
63.    Let "Describe John" be a paraphrase of "Print the
       height, weight and age of John"
```

the user could expect the system to understand the requests

```
64.    Describe Mary
65.    Describe the tallest person
66.    Describe Mary's sister
```

even with a fairly simply designed LIFER grammar.

Conclusions

Although grammars constructed with LIFER may not be as powerful as specially constructed grammars, LIFER demonstrates that useful natural language systems for a wide variety of domains can be built simply and routinely without a large-scale programming effort. Human engineering features and the ability of the naive user to extend the system's capabilities are important issues in the usefulness of the system.

References

Hendrix (1977a), Hendrix (1977b), and the LIFER manual (Hendrix, 1977c) all describe the LIFER system. The LADDER information retrieval application is described in Hendrix et al. (1978) and Sacerdoti (1977). Barrow et al. (1977) describe the HAWKEYE system.

Chapter V

Understanding Spoken Language

CHAPTER V: UNDERSTANDING SPOKEN LANGUAGE

A. OVERVIEW

A MAJOR OBJECTIVE of current work in computer science and engineering is to achieve more comfortable, natural, and efficient interfaces between people and their computers. Since speech is our most natural form of communication, using spoken language to access computers has become an important research goal.

There are several specific advantages to speech as an input medium. With speech as the means of accessing the computer, even casual users need relatively little training before interacting with a complex system. Interactions in such a case can be quick, since speech is our fastest mode of communication (about twice the speed the average typist can type), and the computer user's hands are free to point, manipulate the display, and so forth. This capability is especially important in environments that place many simultaneous demands on the user, as in aircraft or space flight operations (see Lea, 1980c).

The Problem: Understanding Connected Speech

Work on *isolated-word recognition* systems in the 1960s preceded the development of *speech understanding* systems. The technique of the isolated-word systems is to compare the incoming speech signal with an internal representation of the acoustical pattern of each word in a relatively small vocabulary and to select the best match, using some "distance" metric (Vincens, 1969). In doing this, several troublesome characteristics of the speech signal must be overcome. One problem is that the microphone and background noise introduce interference into the recording of the spoken utterance. Another is that a given speaker does not pronounce the same words quite the same way every time he or she speaks, and even if the program is tuned to one speaker, the matching process between the acoustical pattern of the vocabulary words (the templates) and the actual utterance is inherently inexact. If the system must recognize words spoken by more than one speaker, the task is that much more difficult:

> Sizable vocabularies (more than a hundred words) can be realistically utilized with speaker-dependent templates. Smaller vocabularies (on the order of one or two dozen words) can be reliably utilized in talker-independent systems. (Flanagan et al., 1980, p. 442)

Until quite recently, these isolated-word recognition systems cost in the tens of thousands of dollars and offered about 95% accuracy on a small vocabulary. This methodology has recently been refined to produce a range of commercially available, isolated-word recognizers of varying capabilities at prices from $200 to $80,000. The top-of-the-line systems are said to recognize isolated words from vocabularies of up to 120 words with accuracy as high as 99.5% (Lea, 1980a, pp. 75–76).

Unfortunately, *connected speech* signals—utterances containing whole phrases or sentences—cannot be handled by simply matching each word in the signal against the stored patterns for vocabulary words. For one thing, the pronunciation of individual words changes when the words are juxtaposed to form a sentence—sometimes whole syllables are dropped, or "swallowed," at word boundaries. In fact, finding the boundaries between words in a connected-speech signal is itself a difficult part of the speech understanding process. In short, the connected acoustic signal, which is the foundation for the rest of the processing, does not look at all like the concatenation of the signals of the individual words.

The difficulties introduced in attempting to recognize connected speech required a new outlook on the methodology. Researchers speculated that there was more information available to the hearer than just the acoustic signal and that *expectations* about the content of the utterance could be gleaned from additional knowledge about the allowed *forms* of utterances and about the subject being discussed (see, e.g., Nash–Webber, 1975). For example, in many situations there are rules about word order (called the *grammar*) that can be applied to predict which words may legally follow an already recognized word. The use of *syntactic and semantic knowledge* to constrain a system's expectations in other areas of AI research is discussed in Articles III.A and IV.A.

This change of perspective in speech research—from that of matching acoustic patterns to one of *interpretation* of acoustic signals in light of *knowledge* about syllables, words, and sentences, about the rules of conversation, and about the subject under discussion—is often referred to as the change from *speech recognition* to *speech understanding*. One of the key focuses of recent AI research has indeed been the problem of organizing and manipulating these large and diverse *sources of knowledge*.

Current experimental systems for understanding connected speech can be viewed in terms of a "bottom end" and a "top end" (Klatt, 1977). The task of the bottom end in such a system is to use knowledge about the variable phonetic composition of the words in the vocabulary (lexicon) to interpret pieces of the speech signal by comparing the signal with prestored patterns. The top end, then, aids in recognition by *building expectations* about which words the speaker is likely to have said, applying syntactic, semantic, and pragmatic constraints. (See Article V.B on the architecture of speech understanding systems.) In some systems, the top end is also responsible for deciding what the utterance *means*, once it is recognized, and for responding appropriately. Top-down processing, based on predicting what the utterance must mean (from the context and from the words that have already been recognized), is an important feature of some systems that are actually capable of responding without recognizing every word that was said, as people often do.

The ARPA Speech Understanding Research Program

In the early 1970s, the Advanced Research Projects Agency of the U.S. Department of Defense (ARPA), a major sponsor of AI research, funded a five-year program in speech understanding research. At that time, a few isolated-word recognition systems existed, but none that was capable of recognizing continuous speech. These early systems worked only with small vocabularies under ideal acoustic conditions. Knowledge about the phonemic and phonological structure of speech was scattered through the linguistics literature and had not been applied to the engineering of speech understanding systems. There was little or no literature dealing with semantics, prosodics, or pragmatics, and the parsers that were available were not designed to parse sentences in which the component words might have been incorrectly identified.

A study group met in 1971 to set guidelines for the ARPA speech understanding research (SUR) project, with the goal of achieving a breakthrough in connected-speech understanding capability (Newell et al., 1973). This group of scientists set specific performance criteria for each dimension of system inputs and outputs: The systems to be designed and built were to accept normally spoken sentences (connected speech) in a constrained domain with a 1,000–word vocabulary and were to respond reasonably fast with less than 10% error.

Some of the goals established for the ARPA SUR project were intentionally flexible. In particular, they specified a lexicon of 1,000 words, but not *which* words; they allowed for an artificial syntax, but did not say how simple or complicated the syntactic structure of the language could be; they specified a constraining task, but not *which* task. The various ARPA SUR projects, therefore, had considerable freedom in the choice of the semantics, syntax, and lexicon handled by their systems, and, as we shall see later, final performance was difficult to compare.

This was one of the few times that AI programs had had any design objectives specified before they were developed. Setting these standards was important, since they approximated the minimum performance requirements for a practical, connected-speech understanding system in a highly constrained domain (although producing a practical system was notably not a goal of the ARPA program).

ARPA funded five speech projects and several subcontracts for developing parts of speech-systems. Some of the major ARPA contractors produced multiple systems during the five-year period: Work at Bolt, Beranek and Newman, Inc. (BBN) produced first SPEECHLIS and then HWIM (Hear What I Mean), building on earlier BBN research on understanding natural language (see Article IV.F3). Carnegie–Mellon University (C.M.U.) produced the HEARSAY-I and DRAGON systems in the early development phase (1971–1973) and the HARPY and HEARSAY-II programs by 1976. SRI International also developed a speech understanding program, partly in collaboration with Systems Development Corporation (SDC). Although these systems were all built for the same purpose, they emphasized different problems in speech understanding research and systems design.

The Status of Speech Understanding Research

The differences in emphasis among the experimental SUR systems complicated comparison of their performance at the termination of the ARPA project (in September 1976). Since the systems operated in different task domains, they could not be compared on a standard set of utterances. These different task domains—document retrieval (HARPY, HEARSAY-II), answering questions from a database (the SRI system and BBN's HWIM), and voice chess (HEARSAY-I)—had considerably different levels of difficulty. If one measures a task's difficulty by the average of the number of words that might come next after each word in each legal sentence, called the *average branching factor* (ABF), then HARPY's document-retrieval task had a difficulty of only 33 compared to an ABF of 196 for HWIM's database-retrieval task. Furthermore, little effort was made to exclude words from HWIM's vocabulary that sounded alike, making recognition still harder. Although restrictions on the vocabulary and sentences to simplify the understanding task were within the ARPA guidelines, it has been argued that they were carried to extremes and that the HARPY system in particular was too restricted:

> This grammar . . . characterizes a non-habitable, finite set of sentences, with virtually no "near-miss" sentence pairs included. . . .
> The grammar permits sentences of the form "We wish to get the

latest forty articles on <topic>," but one cannot say a similar
sentence with "I" for "we," "want" for "wish," "see" for "get,"
"a" for "the," "thirty" for "forty," or any similar deviation from
exactly the word sequence given above. (Wolf and Woods, 1980,
p. 334)

The systems also varied in the number of speakers and amount of room
noise that could be accommodated and in the amount of tuning required
for each new speaker.

Illustrating the effect of the task domain on performance, the
DRAGON system, developed at C.M.U. during the first phase of the
ARPA-sponsored research, was tested on different tasks. The system's
performance on recognizing the words ranged from 63% to 94%, and
varied from 17% to 68% on recognition of complete utterances. This
variation of results across domains demonstrates the difficulty of specifying how well a system performs. The number of words in the lexicon
alone is an inadequate measure of the complexity of the understanding
task. For example, DRAGON's performance was better with a particular
194-word vocabulary than with another 37-word vocabulary (consisting of
just the alphabet plus numbers), since the similiarity in phonemic structure of the 26 letters gave the latter a much higher average branching
factor.

With the proviso about comparing the performance of the systems,
HARPY demonstrated the most convincing success at the end of the
ARPA program. The performance requirements established by the work-
ing committee and the final results of the HARPY, HEARSAY-II, and
HWIM systems are compared in Figure A-1. (HWIM was not quite com-
pleted at the time of the evaluation.)

Since the ARPA-funded research work, new systems have been
developed at IBM, Bell Laboratories, and Lincoln Laboratories, and subsystems have been designed at the University of California at Berkeley,
Haskins Laboratories, Speech Communications Research Laboratory, and
Sperry Univac (Lea and Shoup, 1980). The IBM system, which represents
the state of the art in connected-speech understanding, utilizes the dynamic programming approach explored in the DRAGON system and is
the most active speech understanding project since the termination of
the ARPA program (see Bahl et al., 1978).

GOAL (November 1971)	HARPY	HEARSAY-II	HWIM
Accept connected speech	Yes	Yes	Yes
from many speakers	3 male 2 female	1 male	3 male
in a quiet room using a good microphone	Computer terminal room Close-talking microphone		
with a few training sentences for each speaker	20-30	60	no training
accepting 1,000 words	1,011	1,011	1,097
using an artificial syntax	finite-state BF = 33	language BF = 33, 46	restricted ATN BF = 196
in a constraining task	Document retrieval	Document retrieval	Travel management
yielding < 10% error	5%	9%, 26%	56%
in a few times real time (on a very fast computer)	Yes	Yes, slower than HARPY	Not quite

Figure A-1.   Comparison of ARPA SUR systems (after Klatt, 1977, and Lea and Shoup, 1980).

Summary

Considerable progress toward practical speech-understanding systems was made in the 1970s. In addition to meeting performance goals, the ARPA SUR projects developed important ideas in systems design that influenced AI research in natural language understanding, knowledge representation, search, vision, and control strategies (see the corresponding chapters of the *Handbook*, as well as Article V.B). At the level of phonetics, all the systems developed representations of words that accounted for different pronunciations, and they all incorporated between-word *juncture rules* to account for contextual effects. *Network representations* for phonetic knowledge were developed, including SDC's spelling graphs, HEARSAY's pronunciation graphs, HWIM's segmented lattices, and HARPY's integrated network.

Much was learned during the ARPA SUR work about the architecture and control of large AI systems. One of the most flexible frameworks to have emerged is HEARSAY's *blackboard* organization for representing hypotheses at different levels, which has been applied in several domains besides speech. At the other end of the spectrum, HARPY's precompiled knowledge structure makes it hard to modify but results in very high performance.

The following is the summary of the conclusions in 1976 of the same study group that had established the requirements for the ARPA project five years earlier:

> The gains go beyond empirical knowledge and engineering technique to basic scientific questions and analyses. A few examples: Network representations for speech knowledge at several levels have been created that have substantial generality. A uniform network representation for the recognition process has been developed. Rule schemes have been created to express certain phonological and acoustic-phonetic regularities. . . . Techniques have been found for measuring the difficulty and complexity of the recognition task. The problem of parsing (syntactic analysis) with unreliable or possibly missing words (so that one cannot rely on parsing left-to-right, but must be able to parse in either direction or middle-out from good word matches) has been successfully analyzed. New paradigms have been developed for many of the component analysis tasks and for the control structure of intelligent systems. Substantial progress has been made on understanding how to score performance in a multi-component system, how to combine those scores, and how to order search priorities. (ARPA SUR Steering Committee, 1977, pp. 313–314)

The next article in this chapter discusses the important issues in the design of AI systems that emerged during the ARPA SUR projects. It is followed by short articles outlining the main features of each of the ARPA systems.

References

The recent book edited by Lea (1980b) contains the best comparative overview of the ARPA speech systems, as well as detailed articles on the systems themselves written by their designers. The *Computing Surveys* article by Erman et al. (1980) is a good, brief account of the HEARSAY system, illuminating many of the issues in speech understanding research. For an excellent popular account of the ambiguities inherent in the phonetic description of an utterance, see Cole (1979). And for descriptions of early speech research and the goals of the ARPA program, see Newell (1975) and Reddy (1975).

B. SYSTEMS ARCHITECTURE

During the ARPA–funded research on speech understanding, different system designs were explored that varied both in their organization of the knowledge applied to the task and in the way the reasoning process was controlled. In a typical system, the speech understanding process begins with a series of transformations that are applied to the original speech *signal*, resulting in a compact digital encoding of the utterance. Further processing of the digitized signal by the different systems can be viewed as the *interpretation* of this signal in light of different kinds of knowledge about the vocabulary and grammar allowed and about the subject under discussion.

What Knowledge Can Be Applied to Understanding Speech?

The types of knowledge at various "levels" that are used in processing spoken language include (from the signal level up):

1. *Phonetics*—representations of the physical characteristics of the sounds in all of the words in the vocabulary;

2. *Phonemics*—rules describing variations in pronunciation that appear when words are spoken together in sentences (coarticulation across word boundaries, "swallowing" of syllables, etc.);

3. *Morphemics*—rules describing how morphemes (units of meaning) are combined to form words (formation of plurals, conjugations of verbs, etc.);

4. *Prosodics*—rules describing fluctuation in stress and intonation across a sentence;

5. *Syntax*—the *grammar* or rules of sentence formation, resulting in important constraints on the number of sentences (not all combinations of words in the vocabulary are legal sentences);

6. *Semantics*—the "meaning" of words and sentences, which can also be viewed as a constraint on the speech understander (not all grammatically legal sentences have a meaning—e.g., *The snow was loud*); and, finally,

7. *Pragmatics*—rules of conversation (in a dialogue, a speaker's response must not only be a meaningful sentence but also be a reasonable reply to what was said to him). For instance, it is pragmatic knowledge that tells us that the question *Can you tell me what time it is?* requires more than just a *Yes* or *No* response.

Phonetic knowledge was used in the early isolated-word recognition systems in the form of *word templates*, representations of the acoustic signal produced by a speaker uttering a single word, which were matched against the signal to be recognized. However, when words are spoken in a sentence, the acoustic characteristics of the sounds within the words vary, so that it is necessary to choose a representation of the speech signal that includes elementary speech sounds as basic units. Two kinds of basic unit are the *allophone* and the *phoneme*. Allophones are representations of sounds as they actually occur in words. Phonemes are more abstract representations that capture the common characteristics of a class of allophones.

For example, the phoneme /t/ is known to have four allophones in English, corresponding to four different ways in which it occurs. (Two of the allophones of /t/ are the "hard" *t* at the beginning the word *top* and the "flap" *t* in the middle of the word *rattle*.) The major advantage of using phonemes as the basic unit for representing spoken words is that there are relatively few to recognize, which simplifies the higher levels of the speech understanding task. The disadvantage is that phonemes are abstract units that are not actually found in spoken utterances. To map from the allophones that can be identified in the speech signal (like the two kinds of /t/ above) to abstract phonemes requires a sophisticated understanding of how the speech context determines the allophones of a phoneme. Contextual rules of this kind are the domain of *phonemics*. There has been only limited success in applying phonemic rules in speech understanding systems (see Shoup, 1980, p. 125).

A third possible "basic unit" of speech is the *syllable*. The syllable is a difficult unit to define, but it can be recognized with some success by following the stress patterns in speech. One advantage of using the syllable as the basic recognition unit is that the subtle transitional phenomena are subsumed in one syllabic unit. Two problems in doing so are that it is difficult to decide where one syllable ends and another begins in the speech signal and that there are a great many more syllables in a language than there are phonemes.

The *lexicon*, or vocabulary, allowed by each speech understanding system was represented internally in terms of the pronunciations of all of the words. (Some systems encoded all of the multiple pronunciations of each word that could arise from context effects.) In general, the *morphemic* level of analysis of traditional linguistics (e.g., determining number or tense by looking for word endings) is not used in speech understanding research; the words in the lexicon are taken as basic units of recognition, even though they may contain more than one morpheme. One exception to this is the lexical knowledge used in the SDC speech system (see Barnett et al., 1980, p. 272).

Prosody, the pattern of *stress* and *intonation* in spoken language, provides extensive information about the meaning of an utterance: At the lower levels of analysis, prosody can help identify syllable and word boundaries; at a syntactic level, it helps to identify phrases within a sentence; and at the semantic level, it helps to differentiate questions from declarations and can be a cue to subtle speech acts like irony and sarcasm. However, prosodic analysis has not yet been used in AI speech understanding systems.

Syntax and Semantics: Top-down Processing

The most dramatic use of knowledge in speech processing focused on the application of syntax and semantics to the generation of *expectations* about the speech signal. The bottom-end knowledge about phonemes and words described in the previous section was used to construct hypotheses about what words were present in the signal being analyzed. As mentioned in Article V.A, top-end knowledge about what things would be said at certain points in the dialogue and about what form they might take was used to help identify the words in the speech signal. The types of knowledge used in this way include *syntax, semantics,* and *pragmatics.*

For example, consider the HEARSAY-I speech system that played *voice chess* with a human by responding to the moves that he spoke into the microphone, using a *chess program* (see Article II.C5c) to figure out its best response. Not only did HEARSAY-I apply syntactic knowledge about the specific format of chess moves (e.g., "Pawn to King-4") to anticipate the form of incoming utterances, but it also used the *legal-move generator* of its chess program to suggest moves that were most likely to be tried by the opponent and then examined the incoming speech signal for evidence of those particular moves.

The importance of top-down or *expectation-driven* processing has also been pointed out by workers in natural language understanding. In their research on systems that respond to typed-in input, rather than to spoken sentences, recognition of individual words is not a problem, as it is in speech understanding. Nevertheless, determining the meaning of the input, so that an appropriate response is evoked, requires the use of much knowledge about the world to predict what the input might be (see Chap. IV, especially Articles IV.F5 and IV.F6).

Similarly, in AI research on *vision,* where the computer must interpret a visual scene supplied by a TV camera, a strong model of the physical world, as well as knowledge about what things the camera is likely to find, is typically used to help figure out what is in the scene (see Chap. XIII, in Vol. III). It is generally agreed that this *constraining knowledge* is necessary for adequate performance in tasks like speech understanding: Without expectations about what to look for in the input, the task of identifying what is there is impossible. Recent AI research on knowledge representation using *frames* and *scripts* has stressed this *predictive* use of knowledge (see Articles III.A and III.C7).

"Experiments" with several systems demonstrated the effect of removing the constraints on signal interpretation supplied by syntactic and semantic knowledge. The HARPY system, which combined all of the phonetic, syntactic, and semantic knowledge into one integrated network, was 97% accurate in actually identifying the words in the utterance, even though it showed only 42% accuracy in phonetic segmentation of the utterance. In other words, because of top-end knowledge about what sequences of words were allowed in utterances, HARPY could often guess the right words even when it didn't have an accurate phonetic interpretation of the signal.

In the HEARSAY-I system, where the phonetic, syntactic, semantic, and other knowledge was separated into independent *knowledge sources*, a more convincing kind of experiment, called *ablation studies* by Newell (1975), could be performed: The system was designed so that it could run with only some of the knowledge sources "plugged in." Compared with its performance with just the phonetics and lexicon knowledge sources operating, the performance of HEARSAY-I improved by 25% with the addition of its syntax knowledge source and by another 25% with the addition of the semantics knowledge source (Lea, 1980a).

Generality versus power. The way that top-down processing is used to constrain the expected content of sentences reflects an important, universal issue in AI systems design—the trade-off between generality and power. The top end of the speech systems contains knowledge about a *specific* language and a specific domain of discourse. In the development of all of the speech understanding systems, the use of general grammatical knowledge gave way to grammars that were very specific to the task requirements (called *semantic* or *performance grammars*). By incorporating the structure of the typical phrases used in a particular task domain, these grammars combined syntactic, semantic, and sometimes pragmatic knowledge (see Articles V.C3 and V.C4). Repeatedly in AI research, general methods for problem solving have proved inadequate until supplemented with large amounts of knowledge and *heuristics* specific to the problem at hand (see Article II.A).

Knowledge Sources

Given all of the knowledge needed during the processing of the speech signal, much AI research focused on finding ways of organizing this knowledge within the system. One influential approach, used by the HEARSAY systems, involves separating the different types of knowledge into coherent modules, called *knowledge sources* (KSs). For example, there might be a prosodics knowledge source that examines the speech signal for intonation and stress patterns and makes hypotheses about syllable, word, and phrase boundaries. The knowledge sources were viewed as independent modules of expertise that cooperated in analyzing the speech signal. This modular organization of the knowledge in the system should be contrasted with the other principal architecture used in the ARPA SUR projects, the *precompiled network,* which represents all possible pronunciations of all possible sentences in one data structure (see below).

In the HEARSAY model, the independent knowledge sources for phonetics, syntax, semantics, and the like were, in theory, to know nothing about each other, not even of each other's existence. They were thought of as independent processes that looked at the speech signal and *posted hypotheses* about likely syllables, words, phrases, and so forth on the *blackboard*—a global data-structure accessed by all of the KSs through an established protocol. Hypotheses generated by the lower level knowledge sources (about syllables and words) would be examined for feasibility by the syntactic and semantic KSs; these, in turn, could make suggestions about what words might be *expected* and post them on the blackboard.

The advantages of this organization are those generally associated with *modularization* of knowledge (see Article III.A): Adding, modifying, or removing a knowledge source could theoretically be accomplished without changing the other knowledge sources. Also, in a distributed-processing implementation, where the different knowledge sources are running as processes on different machines, a modular system would be less sensitive to transient failures of processors and communication links, exhibiting *graceful degradation,* as it is called (see Erman et al., 1976; Lesser and Erman, in press). The blackboard organization for representing multiple types of knowledge has been used in several domains besides speech understanding, including crystallography (Article VII.C3, in Vol. II), signal interpretation (Nii and Feigenbaum, 1978), vision (Hanson and Riseman, 1978b; Levine, 1978), and psychological modeling (Rumelhart, 1976; Hayes–Roth and Hayes–Roth, 1979).

Compiled Knowledge

The other principal kind of system architecture explored in the ARPA SUR projects is one in which the knowledge about all of the sentences that are legal or meaningful in the task domain are *precompiled* into one decision-tree-like network. The nodes in the network are *allophonic* templates, representing the different sounds in the language, to be matched against the voice signal. The links in the network are used to control the matching process: After a successful match at node N, only the nodes that are linked in the net to node N need be tried next—no other sounds are "legal" at that point. The processing of the input signal matches some node in the net to a portion of the utterance and proceeds left to right through the network, trying to find the best match according to some comparison metric. Since all of the alternative sound sequences are already in the network and are not "hypothesized" on the fly as in the blackboard model, precompiled network systems are relatively efficient and fast. Deciding which alternatives are in fact present at each instant of the utterance is the essence of the processing performed by systems like DRAGON and HARPY and can be viewed as a form of *search.* (See the discussions of *island driving* and *beam search* below.)

The HARPY system is distinguished by its integration of phonemic, lexical, and syntactic knowledge into a single network; other systems also adopted network representations, usually for one knowledge source only. In particular, the SDC system used network-like *spelling graphs* to represent the different pronunciations possible for a word. Similarly, the HWIM system used a *segmented lattice* representation of different pronunciations and embedded the lattices in a tree-like dictionary that had the important property that any two words that could be spoken in sequence were linked by an arc representing any contextual effect on pronunciation. The phonemic and lexical knowledge sources in HWIM are thus integrated in a manner similar to HARPY, although its other knowledge sources are not.

Precompiling the alternatives has some disadvantages. For one, every time the knowledge base is changed—for example, when a new pronunciation of some word is added—the entire network must be reconstructed (which took 13 *hours* of PDP–10 processing time for one of HARPY's vocabularies). A second disadvantage is that, to fit into present-day computers, the language recognized by the speech system must be quite constrained syntactically. In general, only subsets of English that can be represented by a *finite-state grammar* can be compiled into a network of finite size (see Article IV.C1). Finally, the strategies that *control* the network-based understanding process may tend to be more sensitive to errors, like getting off on a wrong track, than are the more flexible, blackboard-like systems.

With the exception of HARPY, the ARPA SUR systems implemented independent, modular organizations for their knowledge bases (although only in HEARSAY was their independence a theoretical issue). The way that knowledge sources interact, and the strategy for applying the knowledge to the understanding process, is, as always, the complement to knowledge-base organization in any discussion of system architecture.

Control Strategies: Hypotheses and Agendas

How do the different speech understanding systems go about interpreting an utterance? Where do they start? What are the steps of the process? How do they decide what to *focus* on next? The different knowledge organizations reflect different ideas about how the process of interpreting the speech signal is to be carried out, and each of the speech understanding systems has its own complicated algorithm. But the basic ideas involve the concepts of *agenda* and *search*.

In the preceding discussions of *knowledge sources* and *top-down processing*, the idea of a knowledge source *posting* a hypothesis on a global data structure was introduced. The hypotheses indicate that the knowledge source has either (a) found evidence (in the signal or already posted on the blackboard) for a certain phoneme, word, or phrase or (b) predicts, based on what has already been posted, that certain words or phrases will be found at certain points in the utterance.

The question of control arises here because, somehow, this process of hypothesis posting has to be coordinated. Will all of the knowledge sources make hypotheses simultaneously? Or will lower level sources be used to confirm the guesses of higher sources? Or will it be the other way around, with phonemic and lexical sources proposing words and syntactic and semantic sources checking the likelihood of these proposals? How much effort should be focused on the different hypotheses that are "active," and which alternative hypothesis should be tried first? These issues of *top-down versus bottom-up processing* and *focus of attention* find their expression within the systems in an agenda-like mechanism—every time the processor (or one of the processors if there are several) is free, it must decide, based on some *control strategy*, what to do next.

In different systems, this strategy is more or less involved and more or less explicit. In the HEARSAY systems, *all* knowledge sources post hypotheses on the blackboard, and the lower level knowledge sources look for evidence in the speech signal supporting these hypotheses. In the SRI system, explicit procedures were incorporated to identify the *phrases* that were the focus of the discourse, and to process tasks on the agenda in light of this knowledge. In the HWIM system, the interaction of knowledge sources is governed by one of many *control processes*, controlling the interaction of *procedural* (subroutine-like) knowledge sources. In HARPY, where the posting of hypotheses is all done implicitly when the network is compiled, the control strategy takes the form of a *search* through a space of alternatives in the network.

Speech Understanding as Search

In systems like HARPY, in which all or part of the knowledge is in the form of a precompiled network with "sounds" at each node connected to all of the sounds that can follow it in any of the legal sentences in the language, interpreting an utterance corresponds to finding a path through the network representing a sequence of sounds that most closely matches the sounds in the utterance. Finding such a path can be thought of in terms of the important AI paradigm of *search* (see Chap. II). The *goal* is the optimal path, and the *search space* consists of *nodes* representing partially completed paths and *branches* representing each alternative continuation from the partial paths. The strategy problem is then rephrased in terms of anchor points or *islands*, keeping track of *alternatives, backtracking,* and *beam width.*

Island driving. The first question that arises when a speech system is given a sentence to understand is where to start. It turns out that starting with the first word in the sentence is not necessarily the most efficient strategy, just as a purely bottom-up interaction of knowledge sources was not always optimal. This left-to-right strategy was, however, used in HARPY and works well with the precompiled network representation. The disadvantage of this strategy is that if the first word is not identified correctly, or is not identifiable, understanding of the rest of the sentence is retarded.

A *middle-out strategy* was used in HEARSAY and the SRI speech systems: Find whatever words can be immediately identified, then expand out to either side of all of them. It is called *island driving*, because it establishes islands of relatively certain hypotheses and pushes out from these islands into the rest of the sentence. One problem with the strategy is that the number of hypothesized extensions of islands can be very large, and this *combinatorial* problem is compounded by having many islands, especially if the islands are not really reliable hypotheses and will soon be abandoned.

A strategy explored in the HWIM system is a *hybrid* between island driving and the left-to-right strategy. The problem of not being able to understand reliably the first word in the sentence is overcome by trying to understand any of the first three or four words. Then the expansion of this word is in one direction at a time: first back to the beginning of the sentence, and then on to the end. This dramatically reduces the number of extension hypotheses that must be considered at one time.

Scoring of alternative hypotheses. The sound templates stored in the system's database never exactly match segments of the acoustic signal, so that the hypotheses about individual speech sounds must be "scored." Briefly, the internal template representation of the proposed sound (phoneme, or allophone, or syllable) is compared with a segment of the actual speech signal, and the similarities and differences are noted and a number is calculated representing the likelihood that the proposed sound exists at that point in the signal.

Above the level of individual speech sounds, the scoring of hypotheses is handled differently by different systems. In HARPY, which searches through its net of individually scored allophones, scoring can be regarded as simple cumulation of the allophone scores along a path. The score given to a hypothesized allophone depends on how closely it matches the speech signal and also on the score of the preceding allophone in the path. HARPY expands several paths at once, but the scoring system guarantees that the highest scoring allophone in the net is the last allophone in the best available interpretation of the sentence, up to that point in the sentence.

In the other systems, where the knowledge sources remain separate, each hypothesis can be evaluated by several of the knowledge sources. A hypothesis that has the support of several knowledge sources is given a score that is a linear combination of the individual scores contributed by each knowledge source. The relative weights of the different KSs are determined by trial and error in the HEARSAY systems. However, the designers of HWIM put a great deal of effort into devloping a *uniform scoring policy* for hypotheses.

Focus of attention. One important issue in the control of the recognition process is determining which hypotheses about the contents of the signal should be attended to at each instant. In the HEARSAY and SDC systems, hypotheses are ordered by their score and the highest scoring alternative is examined first. Thus, all hypotheses *compete* in these systems.

In HWIM, hypotheses are not ordered by their scores alone, because it is recognized that all hypotheses should not necessarily compete. In particular, two hypotheses about different parts of the utterance should both be examined and a "bridge" formed between them if possible. An ordering metric called the *shortfall density* was developed for HWIM based on these considerations. (This was, in addition, an *admissible* strategy—see Article V.C3.) In HARPY, if the score of an allophone falls below a certain threshold, the entire path leading up to that allophone is discarded. HARPY applies a heuristic technique called *beam search* that involves expanding a small number of the highest scoring allophones, the *beam width* (Article V.C2).

Backtracking. Typically in the speech understanding process, a system will have an interpretation for some of the words in a sentence that gets disconfirmed. For example, it may propose that the third word in the sentence is *elephant*, only to learn from its syntactic knowledge source that the third word in the sentence must be a verb. In cases like this, the system must revise its interpretation; it must *backtrack* to some point at which it was sure of its interpretation and start again from there. The choice of control strategy, including the scoring mechanism, beam width, and so on, can make backtracking unnecessary, easy, or very expensive.

Summary

In many respects, the systems discussed here are quite similar. All employ *multiple sources of knowledge* and apply *constraining knowledge* about what utterances are likely to be made to help figure out what was said. However, the systems reflect different design philosophies. The HARPY system is noted for its use of a precompiled-network knowledge representation; HWIM and HEARSAY-II use similar modular knowledge sources. However, the systems differ in the control of speech processing. Specifically, control strategies are regarded as a major variable affecting the success or failure of HWIM, while in HEARSAY, emphasis is put on the organization—the *architecture*—of the speech system.

The differences in the final systems produced by the ARPA SUR projects reflect a difference in emphasis in the research. At the outset of the HWIM project, a technique called *incremental simulation* was employed to explore the process of speech understanding. Individuals simulated the not-yet-developed components of the system, and their interactions were analyzed. In experiments with humans interpreting speech spectrograms, a number of knowledge sources were identified, but, in addition, it was obvious that the spectrogram readers were making use of an additional ability that was considerably less overt. By some criteria, they were making decisions about which fragmentary hypotheses to rule out, which ones to pursue further by trying to find compatible interpretations of adjacent portions of the utterance, and when to return to a previously rejected hypothesis in light of new information. These decisions imply the existence of a *control strategy for speech understanding,* and from the beginning, our speech understanding system has been designed to facilitate the discovery and exploration of such strategies. (Wolf and Woods, 1980, p. 317)

Control strategies certainly were not ignored by the HARPY or HEARSAY designers. The emphasis, however, in both systems, has been on knowledge representation and organization:

Much of . . . Harpy's success is the result of solving the difficult technical problems associated with forcing all the diverse KSs into a unified framework. (Lowerre and Reddy, 1980, p. 346)

The Hearsay II architecture is based on the view that the inherently errorful nature of processing connected speech can be handled only through the effective and efficient cooperation of multiple, diverse sources of knowledge. Additionally, the experimental approach needed for system development requires the ability to add and replace sources of knowledge and to explore different control strategies. . . . The major focus of the design of the Hearsay II system was the development of a framework for experimenting with the representation of and cooperation among these diverse sources of knowledge. (Erman and Lesser, 1980, p. 362)

Many of the issues of system design and language processing discussed here are also important in *natural language understanding* research (see especially Article IV.D1). The remaining articles in this chapter describe the main features of the HEARSAY, HARPY, HWIM, and SRI/SDC systems in more detail.

C. THE ARPA SUR PROJECTS

C1. HEARSAY

The HEARSAY speech understanding system, developed as part of the ARPA-funded speech understanding research project, has been one of the most influential of all AI programs over the years. The importance of HEARSAY lies not in how well the system understands speech, but in the way that it is constructed—the idea of independent *knowledge sources* cooperatively solving a problem by posting hypotheses on a global *blackboard* data structure. This *modular* architecture—the knowledge sources don't address each other directly—proved to allow great flexibility as the system evolved and different combinations of knowledge sources and *control strategies* were tried (see Article III.A for a discussion of modularity in *knowledge representation*).

In problem domains characterized by a large *search space*, by the need to combine different kinds of knowledge, and by ambiguous or noisy data, HEARSAY's architecture has proved especially well suited for the design of a problem-solving system. It has been incorporated into AI systems for solving diverse tasks in crystallography (Article VII.C3, in Vol. II), signal interpretation (Nii and Feigenbaum, 1978), vision (Hanson and Riseman, 1978b; Levine, 1978), and psychological modeling (Rumelhart, 1976; Hayes-Roth and Hayes-Roth, 1979). A considerable number of articles about the HEARSAY architecture and its applications have been written. In this short description of the system, we introduce the technical terms used in the descriptions of it in the literature.

HEARSAY-I

HEARSAY went through two major stages in its development at Carnegie-Mellon University. The first implementation of the system, called HEARSAY-I, was already based on the idea of cooperating, independent knowledge sources (Reddy et al., 1976). The three knowledge sources in HEARSAY-I represented knowledge about—

1. Acoustics and phonetics (the features in the speech signal that are evidence for each type of *syllable*), including ways the signal may change because of different speakers and noise in the environment;

2. The *syntax* of legal utterances; and

3. The *semantics* of the domain.

The domain was *voice chess*, which pits the computer against a person (who makes his moves by speaking into a microphone). The fact that only particular phrases make sense in the world of chess was utilized to limit the searching required by the program. (As discussed in Article V.B, the use of *constraining knowledge* about what utterances can be *expected* is a central idea in all successful speech understanding research.)

Consider the possible ways that knowledge about chess could be used to help identify a spoken chess move. For example, in trying to understand an incomplete utterance like "Pawn to King *[missing word]*," prior knowledge about the *form*, or *syntax*, of spoken chess moves would lead to the conclusion that the missing word is a small number corresponding to one of the rows of the chess board. Moreover, if knowing the current positions of all the pieces and the rules for making moves would further narrow the possibilities to one of the places a pawn could move to in the King's file and if a person who knew something about chess strategy saw that this was the first move of the game, he or she could guess that it was very likely that this was one of the standard opening moves—for example, "Pawn to King–four." HEARSAY–I was tied directly into the *legal-move generator* of a chess-playing program for its knowledge about likely moves.

Despite the obvious simplifications inherent in this domain, it is certainly possible that speech understanding systems that could handle domains of equal complexity might find tremendous utility in specialized areas, like air traffic control. At any rate, HEARSAY–I was the first system to demonstrate recognition of nontrivial, connected speech. This system marked a radical departure in both knowledge representation and control structure from previous AI systems. *Top-down processing*—the use of expectations generated by syntactic and semantic knowledge sources to help judge the relevance of words hypothesized by bottom-end acoustic processing—proved to be a widely useful idea. In fact, it is believed that had current acoustic processing techniques been available in the early 1970s, HEARSAY–I might have met the 1976 ARPA speech goals in the voice chess domain (Lea and Shoup, 1980). Many of the concepts applied in this system were incorporated into the HEARSAY–II and HARPY systems developed later at C.M.U.

Changes to Knowledge Sources and the Blackboard

The modifications that resulted in the final implementation of HEARSAY included the development of many specialized knowledge sources—12 were used in the final version of the system. The blackboard was divided into a number of *levels* corresponding to a hierarchical breakdown of speech into units such as segments, syllables, words, and phrases (see Fig. C1-1). Hypotheses about these sentence units are posted at the appropriate level, along with a *time frame* that indicates when the unit is hypothesized to occur in the utterance.

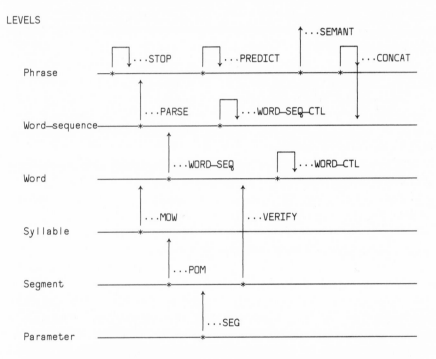

Figure C1-1. Knowledge sources and blackboard configuration for final version (C2) of HEARSAY-II (from Erman et al., 1980, p. 366).

The horizontal lines in Figure C1-1 represent the levels of the blackboard. Each knowledge source looks at hypotheses posted on one level, called its *stimulus frame* (indicated by *), and in turn posts hypotheses on one or more levels, possibly the same one (the *response frame*). For example, the PREDICT knowledge source illustrated in Figure C1-1 works completely within the phrase level on the blackboard, predicting the words that might extend a phrase. In contrast, the

VERIFY knowledge source looks for acoustic evidence in the signal for hypotheses at the word level.

The knowledge sources shown in Figure C1-1 were those used in the C2 configuration of HEARSAY–II, the version that was evaluated at the end of the ARPA SUR project in 1976. The bottom-end processing was accomplished by the acoustic segmentation (SEG) and word-spotting (POM, MOW, and WORD–CTL) knowledge sources. The SEG knowledge source abstracts a string of allophones from the acoustic signal (actually the same allophones recognized by HARPY). These are assigned to *syllable classes* by the POM knowledge source, and the syllable classes are used by the MOW knowledge source to hypothesize words. (HEARSAY's *lexicon* is organized by syllable classes; each section of the lexicon contains pronunciations of all the words that make up one syllable-class.) The number of hypotheses that MOW makes is controlled by the WORD–CTL knowledge source. The WIZARD procedure *scores* the hypothesized words by comparing their acoustic characteristics to stored representations of the pronunciations of the words. (This representation is similar in structure to the integrated network used to represent all knowledge in the HARPY system.)

The top-end processing in HEARSAY–II involved predicting, testing, and concatenating multiple-word sequences, one or more of which will eventually account for all of the words spoken. The WORD–SEQ and WORD–SEQ–CTL knowledge sources extend those words recognized by the bottom end into a small number of *islands* of one or more words, using a data structure that contains all legal pairings of words. Islands can be extended recursively in this manner—by hypothesizing extensions of the newly hypothesized words. However, the *syntax* of islands longer than three words must be checked, because the island was generated from legal *pairs* of words and therefore the longer island may not be syntactically correct. The PARSE knowledge source checks the syntax.

When a number of multiple-word islands are developed, the VERIFY knowledge source tries to check each word against the segmented acoustic signal in the context of its island. The PREDICT and CONCAT knowledge sources are also used to extend hypothesized word sequences. PREDICT generates all the words that can immediately precede or follow a word sequence, while CONCAT tries to join word sequences together to form longer ones. Finally, the STOP knowledge source is used to terminate processing of the speech signal, either because the best interpretation of the sentence has been found or because too much processing time has been used. The SEMANT knowledge source generates machine instructions to carry out the spoken command (in the case of HEARSAY–II, answering a question about a database on AI publications).

Control in HEARSAY–II

The majority of the hypotheses contributed by knowledge sources at any level do not find their way into the final interpretation of the sentence. It is important that the system *focus* its limited computational resources on expanding the best word hypotheses into word sequences and that only the best of these get verified, expanded, and concatenated into larger phrases. This is accomplished by *scoring the response frame* of each knowledge source on the hypothesis—that is, estimating the expected result of operating on the hypothesis with the relevant knowledge sources—and using a *scheduling* routine to expand high-scoring hypotheses before lower scoring ones.

In theory, the blackboard framework permits autonomous and asynchronous activation of knowledge sources, meaning that, at any time, any knowledge source can post hypotheses on the blackboard. In practice, some constraints were placed on the order in which knowledge sources were activated. In HEARSAY–I the bottom-end knowledge sources propagated hypotheses to higher levels in an asynchronous order, but it was found that these hypotheses were not accurate enough to be reliably expanded. As a result, processing at the bottom end of HEARSAY–II is strictly bottom-up: The SEG, POM, and MOW knowledge sources are activated in that order, and the processing done by one is completed before another is activated.

Some effort was made in HEARSAY to separate the operation of knowledge sources from the control of their operation. Two knowledge sources, WORD–CTL and WORD–SEQ–CTL, have been included specifically to control the MOW and WORD–SEQ knowledge sources, respectively.

Summary

The HEARSAY–II speech understanding system achieved the performance goals of the five-year ARPA SUR program in the same document-retrieval task used to evaluate HARPY. The system has also been used in other conversational domains. More important is that its architecture has been useful in the design of AI systems unrelated to speech understanding. The design ideas of HEARSAY can be summarized along the following lines:

Separate, independent, anonymous knowledge sources. Isolating the knowledge along functional lines allows efficient modification of the problem-solving structure of the program, by allowing a free substitution of modular *knowledge sources.* Substitution is possible since each knowledge source is not dependent on the methodology behind, or even the existence of, any other.

Self-activating, asynchronous, parallel processes. The knowledge sources can be viewed as individual knowledge-based programs that respond to patterns in the blackboard database autonomously. No temporal relationship between their execution is explicitly required (although, as described above, this condition was sometimes relaxed in the interest of efficiency). A parallel-processor version of portions of the HEARSAY design has been built to exploit these features (see Fox, in press; Lesser and Erman, in press).

Globally accessed database. The blackboard acts as a structure on which the hypotheses and their support criteria can be stored. The data structure is fixed for each information level on the blackboard. This feature allows the creation of kernel-accessing routines, used in common by each KS for manipulating the global store at each level. A snapshot of the blackboard during HEARSAY execution reveals a partial analysis of the utterance as a three-dimensional network consisting of the levels of representation, time, and the possible alternatives—with the contextual and structural support for each alternative explicitly marked in the network.

Data-directed knowledge invocation. The knowledge sources react to changes in the blackboard and criticize or create hypotheses wherever practical. This procedure sets up a new pattern over the blackboard, to which other KSs may be able to respond. This activity continues until no knowledge source can respond or until the time and space limits of the program are exceeded.

References

Erman et al. (1980) is an excellent introduction to HEARSAY. Several articles in the recent book edited by Lea (1980b) are of interest, especially Erman and Lesser (1980). Also of interest is C.M.U. Speech Group (1977).

C2. HARPY

The HARPY speech understanding system was developed at Carnegie-Mellon University after extensive evaluation of two earlier systems, HEARSAY–I (Article V.C1) and DRAGON (Baker, 1975). HARPY's most important characteristic is its use of a single, *precompiled*, network knowledge structure (Lowerre and Reddy, 1980). The network contains knowledge at all levels: acoustic, phonemic, lexical, syntactic, and semantic. It stores acoustic representations of every possible pronunciation of the words in all of the sentences that HARPY recognizes. The alternative sentences are represented as paths through the network, and each node in the network is a template of *allophones*. The paths through the network can be thought of as "sentence templates," much like the *word templates* in *isolated-word recognition* (see Article V.A). HARPY's integration of diverse forms of knowledge into a single network representation is its principal contribution.

The Knowledge Compiler

The program that actually builds the network is called the *knowledge compiler*. Its task is to generate allophonic representations of all possible sentences, given HARPY's syntax and lexicon. The first step in this process is to substitute words from the lexicon into the *grammar* in order to generate all possible sentences. For example, if the syntax was defined by the rules:

```
Sentence ← ⟨ss⟩
    ⟨ss⟩   ← please help ⟨m⟩
           ← please show ⟨m⟩ ⟨q⟩
    ⟨q⟩    ← everything
           ← something
    ⟨m⟩    ← me
           ← us
```

then the possible meaningful sentences are:

```
Please help me
Please help us
Please show me everything
Please show us everything
Please show me something
Please show us something
```

The sentences are put into a network structure (see Fig. C2-1) that eliminates much of the redundancy involved in representing sentences individually but has the effect of introducing grammatical sentences that are not meaningful, namely, *Please help me everything* and *Please help me something.* (See the discussion of transition-network representations for grammars in Article IV.D2.)

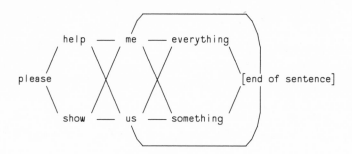

Figure C2-1. HARPY's sentence network.

The next step in compiling the network is to substitute phonetic representations of words for the words themselves. In the event that there is more than one pronunciation for a word, all pronunciations are put into the network. For example, if two pronunciations of *show* are known, then both would be alternative paths following the phonetic representation of *please.* In this way, the network is expanded to contain all possible pronunciations of all possible sentences.

The last step is to embed *juncture phenomena* in the network. These are descriptions of the effect of context on the allophones at word boundaries. For example, in *please show,* the *z* sound at the end of *please* is sometimes dropped, although it is not dropped in *please tell.* For the 1976 version of HARPY, the juncture rules were hand-tailored to the words in the lexicon. This was a very time-consuming process, but the phonemic rules available at the time were not sufficiently powerful or complete to capture the necessary range of juncture phenomena.

This discussion of the knowledge compiler is highly abbreviated. In fact, the process is considerably more complicated and consumes a great deal of computer processing time: It required 13 hours of PDP-10 time to generate a network of 15,000 allophonic templates for HARPY's 1,011-word vocabulary.

Control in HARPY

HARPY utilizes a heuristic search method called *beam search.* Briefly stated, it proceeds left to right through the network, matching spoken sounds to allophonic states. The first sounds spoken are matched to all of the starting states in the network (in the example above, this would correspond to all possible pronunciations of *please*). HARPY assigns scores to all of these, and it prunes away the paths that do not score well (see the discussion of *scoring* in Article V.B). The few that score best are kept as alternative interpretations of the sentence. These constitute the "beam" of hypotheses that HARPY will examine. It is an important characteristic of beam search that the paths included in the beam are the best interpretations of the sentence that HARPY has found. Thus, it need never *backtrack*, but need only extend the paths in its beam as long as they retain sufficiently high scores.

Beam search is an approximate *heuristic* method that does not guarantee that the interpretation of a sentence is the best possible interpretation. Nevertheless, in its trial domains of chess and document retrieval, HARPY was the most efficient and accurate performer of all of the ARPA SUR systems (see Article V.A).

Summary

A case study of two dissimilar early speech understanding systems, DRAGON and HEARSAY-I, led to a first in system design: a system that met the 1976 goals of the speech understanding research community. This objective was accomplished by combining DRAGON's *dynamic programming techniques* with useful heuristics for search, such as *beam search*. The main ideas incorporated into HARPY are the following.

Precompiled network. HARPY creates a large network comprised of all phonetic "spellings" for each syntactic path in the grammar. This network includes word junction phenomena, which are the adjustments made in the pronunciations of words due to the words preceding and following them in continuous speech.

Beam search. The best paths in the recognition network are selected for further evaluation. This pruning is determined by the comparison of the likelihood of success with a variable threshold. This strategy eliminates evaluation of possible sentences that start correctly but contain one or more incorrect words. HARPY keeps about 1% of the states at each step in the evaluation of the network. Experiments showed that neither a fixed number nor a fixed fraction worked well for this process. Finally, a fixed range of likelihood from the best state was settled upon (Newell, 1978).

Processing segmented speech. The decision to use a flexible division of the acoustic signal according to acoustic events, rather than according to a fixed time interval, allows for a single acoustic template per phone. However, since the network is composed of a sequential phonetic representation, the system is very sensitive to missing or poorly labeled segments.

Heuristics to limit search time and size of network. The computation time of the program is drastically reduced by the compilation of the speech recognition knowledge into the network representation. The network is condensed by removing redundant states or by recognizing common groupings of states. The number of states is slightly increased, but the number of connections (i.e., pointers) can be markedly decreased, by introducing special states at common intersections in the network.

The extension of HARPY's design to handle much larger vocabularies must be examined in future research work, since the explicit creation of the network of possibilities can have a large memory and processing requirement. Also, the design of the current system cannot easily accommodate the pragmatics of the utterance, which other systems use to constrain search. HARPY's algorithm is also relatively sensitive to missing acoustical segments and missing words.

References

See Lowerre and Reddy (1980). Also of interest is C.M.U. Speech Group (1977).

C3. HWIM

The HWIM ("Hear What I Mean") speech understanding system was developed between 1974 and 1976 at BBN (Wolf and Woods, 1980). HWIM was the successor to BBN's earlier SPEECHLIS speech understanding system (Woods, 1975a) and to the BBN work on natural language understanding (see Article IV.F3 on the LUNAR system).

> The BBN speech understanding system has evolved within a general framework for viewing perceptual processes. Central to this framework is an entity called a *theory*. A theory represents a particular hypothesis about some or all of the sensory stimuli that are present. Perception is viewed as the process of forming a believable, coherent theory that can account for all of the stimuli. In our framework, this is achieved by successive refinement and extension of partial theories until a best complete theory is found. (Wolf and Woods, 1980, p. 318)

In the speech setting, a typical theory is a set of compatible word hypotheses, with possible gaps between words, and partial syntactic and semantic interpretations.

HWIM was used to answer questions in the role of a travel budget manager, using a database of facts about trips and expenses. This was the most demanding task in any of the ARPA SUR projects, and the resulting system shows concern with some issues of language and of systems design that were not considered by the other SUR projects.

System Organization

In the HWIM system, all processing passes through its *control strategy* component; in fact, this component uses the *knowledge sources* as subroutines. This is in contrast to the HEARSAY model, in which knowledge sources are autonomous and don't call each other. (Of course, knowledge sources in HEARSAY can attempt to control processing by what they *post* on the *blackboard;* see Article V.C1.) HWIM's organization permits more direct experimentation with control strategies—manipulating, for example, how many *word islands* are generated, the direction in which they are expanded, and the interactions of system components (see Article V.B).

The lower level system components of HWIM (see Fig. C3-1) are responsible for digitizing the speech signal (RTIME) and generating a parametric representation of it (PSA), as well as segmenting and labeling the parametric representation (APR) and lexical retrieval. The APR component produces a *segmented lattice* by segmenting the output of the PSA component at phoneme boundaries, then generating one or more possible phoneme labels for each segment, and finally ranking the alternative interpretations of each segment. The final segmented lattice is a graph that is read from left to right, and is divided into time segments each of which has one or more ranked phonetic interpretations. (See related discussion of *charts* in Article IV.D3.) This lattice is matched against a dictionary of word pronunciations by the lexical retrieval component, which generates word hypotheses.

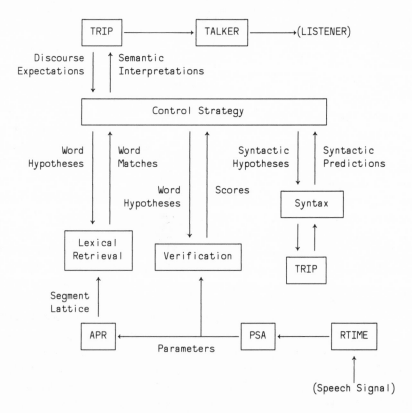

Figure C3-1.   The structure of HWIM (after Wolf and Woods, 1980, p. 321).

The structure of the dictionary is interesting for several reasons. First, it is a network with phonemes for nodes. Nodes can be shared by different words; for example, *list* and *like* share the /l/ phoneme. Another important characteristic of the dictionary is its implementation of *juncture rules*. The words *like, list,* and *some* are all included in the network represented in Figure C3-2, but, in addition, the phrase *list some* is represented as it is actually pronounced: "lissum."

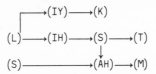

Figure C3-2.   Network of phonemes.

The dictionary is generated semiautomatically by applying phonological rules to the base set of words. The initial vocabulary of 1,138 words is increased to a list of 1,363 possible pronunciations by accounting for inflection patterns, then to 3,371 by the application of within-word phonological rules, and then to 8,642 pronunciations by the application of across-word juncture rules.

The higher levels of the HWIM system include word verification, syntax, and the TRIP semantic component (Fig. C3-1). The verification component takes a word pronunciation and the available context and generates a synthesized acoustic signal for words that are hypothesized by other knowledge sources. The actual acoustic signal is compared to this synthesized signal and the hypothesis is *scored.* This method, which was found to be rather expensive computationally, allows an independent verification of hypothesized words, since all other methods use the same acoustic source as a basis for making conclusions.

The syntactic component is used to judge whether proposed word-sequences are grammatical or not and to predict grammatical extensions of existing word-sequences. The parser used by this component is built around an ATN grammar (Article IV.D2). It is a *performance grammar;* that is, the parts of speech in the grammar are tailored specifically to the trip-planning task domain, rather than being the usual parts of speech: noun, verb, adjective, and so on. (See related discussion of *semantic grammars* in Article IX.C3, in Vol. II.) The TRIP component uses a *semantic network* representation of all the facts and relations relevant to this task domain. It supplies top-down discourse expectations, interprets the sentences passed to it, and carries out the spoken instructions when they are finally interpreted.

Control Strategy

HWIM was designed to have a flexible control structure. However, there is a basic form common to all control strategies in the system that involves bottom-up word theories that are extended top-down by the syntactic component until an entire sentence is achieved. More specifically, the following algorithm is followed:

1. Form the segmented lattice. Generate a set of words that match the lattice well and rate these *seed* matches for their goodness of fit to the segmented lattice. Put the seed matches on an *event queue* ordered by their ratings.

2. Take the event at the top of the queue and send it to the parser, which will reject it, find that it constitutes a whole sentence, or propose words or categories of words that can extend the event.

3. Use the lexical retrieval component to predict between-word context effects for each of the proposals made by the parser. Rate the proposals and put them on the event list.

4. Before selecting the highest rating event from the event list for further expansion, some additional processing is needed. One task is to check the event list for islands of words that have proposed the same word as an extension. If the proposed word forms a bridge between the islands, then a *collision event* that includes both islands is added to the event list. Another process is used to check for the possibility that a proposed extension exhausts the words in the sentence. This is called an *end event.*

5. Unless the resources allowed to HWIM for this sentence have been exhausted, return to (2).

The HWIM system allows for many variations on this control strategy. In particular, some search strategies were designed to be *admissible*, which means that any solution they find is guaranteed to be the best possible solution (see Article II.C3b). In general, admissible strategies require more processing time than *approximate* methods that do not guarantee the best possible solution (e.g., the *heuristic beam search* used in HARPY). One powerful admissible strategy, a middle-out control strategy using the *shortfall density* metric for *scoring* alternative theories, was discovered to be not much more expensive than approximate methods, although it was still not used in the final tests of HWIM because of time limitations (see Wolf and Woods, 1980, p. 327).

A *hybrid* strategy for focus of attention is used in HWIM. Rather than processing words in strictly left-to-right order (as in HARPY) or by expanding islands wherever they are found (as in HEARSAY), HWIM was most successful when it was configured to find an island in the first part of the sentence, expand it backwards to the beginning of the sentence, and then continue to the end of the sentence. This method overcame the problem of identifying incorrectly the first word in a left-to-right strategy and the combinatorial problems of following alternative extensions of multiple islands (see Article V.B).

In most speech systems, it is assumed that the order in which hypotheses are expanded is a function of their scores. High-scoring hypotheses are expanded before lower scoring ones. In HWIM, much effort went into designing scoring and scheduling policies for theories. One result of this was that the intuitive scheduling algorithm mentioned above is not optimal in HWIM. Used instead is the *shortfall density strategy*, which involves the difference between a theory's score and its *ideal* score divided by the length of the theory in segments.

References

See Wolf and Woods (1980) and the earlier report by the BBN speech group (Woods et al., 1976).

C4. The SRI/SDC Speech Systems

One of the ARPA speech understanding projects was to be undertaken jointly by SRI International and Systems Development Corporation (SDC). The low-end portions of the system—signal-processing, acoustics, and phonetics—were developed at SDC from earlier work done there on speech recognition systems. SRI was to provide the top-end of the system—parsing, syntax, semantics, pragmatics, and discourse-analysis. Unfortunately, the two components were never actually merged. The SDC research stressed the bottom-end processing involved in speech understanding—encoding and analysis of the speech waveform (although a top-end processor was eventually developed to make testing and evaluation possible). Several interesting aspects of the SDC system are described in Barnett et al. (1980).

The SRI speech understanding research extended earlier work in natural language understanding and knowledge representation. The top-end system was developed and tested with simulated output from the SDC bottom-end. The important features of the SRI speech understanding research included concern with the nature of real man-machine discourse, a language definition system for specifying the input language to be understood, techniques for focusing the system's attention on certain aspects of the dialogue, top-down process control stressing phrase-level hypothesizing, knowledge representation using partitioned semantic networks, and experimental evaluation of system design parameters.

Discourse

The SRI research stressed understanding spoken utterances in a "natural" environment—a situation that might realistically involve a person talking to a computer-based assistant. In particular, the two tasks explored in the SRI work were an information retrieval task and an assembly task (in which the computer acted as a consultant in a maintainence work-station setting). The novelty of the SRI approach to understanding dialogues in these domains was the concern with the nature of the actual discourse: In realistic conversations focused on a particular goal, partial utterances (words and phrases) and implicit references to previous statements are common and present special problems for the understanding system.

For example, the two questions *What is the depth of the Ethan Allen?* and *What is its speed?* both refer to the ship *Ethan Allen*. In order to disambiguate such *anaphoric references* (pronoun reference to previous phrases), the system must use information gleaned from previous utterances. Similarly, *elliptic references* require filling out incomplete phrases using terms already mentioned. For example, the utterances *What is the depth of the Ethan Allen? ... The Lafayette?* seek the depth of both ships. *Discourse analysis* is also used to predict what kinds of questions might be expected in subsequent utterances.

Language Definition System

The complete specification of the portion of the English language to be accepted by the system is provided in the language definition system. The lexicon is divided along semantic boundaries into categories for ships, countries, and so on (a *semantic* or *performance grammar;* see Robinson, 1975). The language definition contains rules for combining words and phrases into larger phrases. Associated with each phrase-rule are procedures for calculating attributes of member words (like mood, number, meaning representation, and acoustic form) and a procedure for evaluating the acceptability of the phrase hypothesis in context. These rules also specify which attributes can be assigned to the new phrase; for example, they determine the focus of the phrase or relate the semantics of a particular word to the whole phrase. *Prosodic* information is also included, such as the expected change in pitch at the end of an interrogative utterance.

Process Control and Focus of Attention

Perhaps because it never really had a bottom end to work with, the SRI system stressed top-down processing in its control strategy. Top-down control allows the semantic information to guide the search through potentially ambiguous acoustic information. The system is controlled from the parsing mechanism that tries to form phrases to match the acoustic signal. The parser uses the language definition system to integrate all sources of knowledge in a coherent way. Thus, the main program representation is at the *phrase* level, a relatively large linguistic unit, with the meaning and ramifications (e.g., likelihood) of each phrase recorded. Semantic nets encode the relations between concepts, both in the static knowledge base and in the representations of the contents of previous utterances. Pragmatic information is used to *predict* likely utterances based on previous utterances.

The main data structure for the parser is the *parse net*, which represents phrases generated by the language definition system. The parse net is made up of nodes representing the phrases that have been generated and the predictions to be examined (usually against acoustic data). Predictions are of the form: "Look for a word of category X at location Y in the utterance." The nodes are linked by connections between unverified phrases and the predictions they spawn. The parse net also contains attribute information such as the expected start and stop time of the candidate phrases. False steps are avoided in the parsing process by storing past mistakes, but the generated mistaken phrases can be used again if they are recognized as appropriate in another context.

A *task queue* holds a selection of operations waiting to be performed to expand the parse net (e.g., requests for checking the acoustic information for a specific word or phrase). Tasks in the queue are scheduled to run according to priorities determined by the language definition system—a *best-first* approach. To help coordinate the choice of which phrases to expand next, a particular part of the parse net is singled out as being the *focus of attention* and this decision biases future decisions until another area looks more promising. By considering the topics of most recent interest, focusing attention not only can affect the amount of processing needed but also can be used to disambiguate utterances with multiple meanings. The parse is completed when the task queue is empty or when limits on resources are exceeded.

Knowledge Representation

The system's knowledge representation scheme was based on the partitioned semantic-net formalism (see Article IV.F7 on SRI's LIFER system). The scheme was used both to encode the concepts of the subject domain and to represent the meaning of previous utterances. The mechanism of partitioning the network into spaces is used to handle *quantification*, to distinguish real and hypothetical worlds, and to distinguish different levels of abstractions. The semantic processor, for example, contains a series of functions that map between the surface and the deep case structures; these functions facilitate suggestions as to which surface features to examine, based on semantic knowledge. There are also functions that *generate text* (e.g., answers) corresponding to a given semantic net representation of the intended meaning (see Article IV.E).

Performance Evaluation

The SRI research group made a serious effort to evaluate systematically their speech understanding program. In particular, they attempted to determine the effect on the system's performance of changes in several design parameters—for example, whether to consider the current context when setting priorities, whether to match all possible words to pick the best versus taking the first one above a certain criterion, whether to process out from known points in the signal (*island driving*) versus strictly left-to-right activity, and whether to identify and use a focus of attention in assigning processing priorities (see Paxton, 1976).

Summary

The SRI system stressed the natural language understanding aspects of the speech recognition problem. Detailed symbolic models of the domain of discourse were available for assisting in the interpretation and response phases of the program.

References

See the summary article by Walker (1980) or the extended discussion of the system in the book edited by Walker (1978).

Bibliography

List of Abbreviations

Journals, Technical Reports, and Conference Proceedings

AAAI	Conferences of the American Association for AI
ACM	Journal of the Association for Computing Machinery
AFIPS	American Federation of Information Processing Societies
AISB	European Society for AI and the Simulation of Behavior
CACM	Communications of the Association for Computing Machinery
IEEE	Institute for Electrical and Electronic Engineers
IFIPS	International Federation of Information Processing Societies
IJCAI	International Joint Conferences on AI
SIGART	Newsletter of the ACM Special Interest Group on AI
TINLAP	Workshops on Theoretical Issues in Natural Language Processing

Abelson, R. 1973. The structure of belief systems. In Schank and Colby, 287–339.

Adelson–Velskiy, G. M., Arlazarov, V. L., and Donskoy, M. V. 1975. Some methods of controlling the tree search in chess programs. *Artificial Intelligence* 6:361–371.

Aho, A. V., Hopcroft, J. E., and Ullman, J. D. 1974. *The design and analysis of computer algorithms.* Reading, Mass.: Addison-Wesley.

Aikins, J. S. 1979. Prototypes and production rules: An approach to knowledge representation for hypothesis formation. *IJCAI 6*, 1–3.

Akmajian, A., and Heny, F. 1975. *An introduction to the principles of transformational syntax.* Cambridge, Mass.: MIT Press.

Allen, J. 1978. *Anatomy of LISP.* New York: McGraw-Hill.

Amarel, S. 1968. On representations of problems of reasoning about actions. In D. Michie (Ed.), *Machine intelligence 3.* New York: American Elsevier, 131–171.

Anderson, J. 1976. *Language, memory, and thought.* Hillsdale, N.J.: Lawrence Erlbaum.

Anderson, J., and Bower, G. 1973. *Human associative memory.* Washington, D.C.: Winston.

Anderson, J., Kline, P., and Beasley, C. 1979. A general learning theory and its application to schema abstraction. In G. H. Bower (Ed.), *The psychology of learning and motivation* (Vol. 13). New York: Academic Press, 277–318.

Appelt, D. 1980. Problem solving applied to natural language generation. *Proceedings of the Association of Computational Linguistics, Philadelphia*, 59–63.

ARPA SUR Steering Committee. 1977. Speech understanding systems: Report of a steering committee. *Artificial Intelligence* 9:307–316.

Bahl, L. R., Baker, J. K., Cohen, P. S., Cole, A. G., Jelinek, F., Lewis, B. L., and Mercer, R. L. 1978. Automatic recognition of continuously spoken sentences from a finite state grammar. *Proceedings of the 1978 IEEE International Conference on Acoustics, Speech, and Signal Processing, Tulsa, Oklahoma*, 418–421.

Baker, J. K. 1975. The DRAGON system: An overview. *IEEE Transactions on Acoustics, Speech, and Signal Processing* ASSP–23(1), 24–29.

Baker, R. 1973. A spatially-oriented information processor which simulates the motions of rigid objects. *Artificial Intelligence* 4:29–40.

Bar–Hillel, Y. 1960. The present status of automatic translation of languages. In F. L. Alt (Ed.), *Advances in computers* (Vol. 1). New York: Academic Press, 91–163.

Bar–Hillel, Y. 1964. *Language and information.* Reading, Mass.: Addison-Wesley.

Barnett, J., Bernstein, M., Gillman, R., and Kameny, I. 1980. The SDC speech understanding system. In Lea, *Trends,* 272–293.

Barrow, H. G., Bolles, R. C., Garvey, T. D., Kremers, J. H., Lantz, K., Tenenbaum, J. M., and Wolf, H. C. 1977. Interactive aids for cartography and photo interpretation. In L. S. Baumann (Ed.), Image understanding: Proceedings of a workshop held at Palo Alto, California, October 20–21, 1977. Rep. No. SAI–78–656–WA, Science Applications, Inc., Sunnyvale, Calif., 111–127.

Barstow, D. R. 1979. *Knowledge-based program construction.* New York: American Elsevier.

Bartlett, F. C. 1932. *Remembering: A study in experimental and social psychology.* Cambridge, England: Cambridge University Press. Reprinted in 1977.

Baudet, G. M. 1978. On the branching factor of the alpha-beta pruning algorithm. *Artificial Intelligence* 10:173–199.

Berliner, H. J. 1973. Some necessary conditions for a master chess program. *IJCAI 3,* 77–85.

Berliner, H. J. 1974. Chess as problem solving: The development of a tactics analyzer. Dept. of Computer Science, Carnegie-Mellon University.

Berliner, H. J. 1977a. Experiences in evaluation with BKG—A program that plays backgammon. *IJCAI 5,* 428–433.

Berliner, H. J. 1977b. A representation and some mechanisms for a problem-solving chess program. In M. R. B. Clarke (Ed.), *Advances in computer chess 1.* Edinburgh: Edinburgh University Press, 7–29.

Berliner, H. J. 1977c. Search and knowledge. *IJCAI 5,* 975–979.

Berliner, H. J. 1978a. The B^* search algorithm: A best-first proof procedure. Rep. No. CMU–CS–78–112, Dept. of Computer Science, Carnegie-Mellon University.

Berliner, H. J. 1978b. A chronology of computer chess and its literature. *Artificial Intelligence* 10:201–214.

Bernstein, A., Arbuckle, T., Roberts, M. de V., and Belsky, M. A. 1959. A chess playing program for the IBM 704. In *Proceedings of the Western Joint Computer Conference, 1958.* New York: American Institute of Electrical Engineers, 157–159.

Bernstein, M. I. 1977. Knowledge-based systems: A tutorial. Rep. No. TM–(L)–5903/000/00A, Systems Development Corporation, Santa Monica, Calif.

Bobrow, D. G. 1968. Natural language input for a computer problem-solving system. In Minsky, 146–226.

Bobrow, D. G. 1975. Dimensions of representation. In Bobrow and Collins, 1–34.

Bobrow, D. G., and Collins, A. (Eds.). 1975. *Representation and understanding: Studies in cognitive science.* New York: Academic Press.

Bobrow, D. G., and Fraser, B. 1969. An augmented state transition network analysis procedure. *IJCAI 1,* 557–567.

Bobrow, D. G., Kaplan, R. M., Kay, M., Norman, D. A., Thompson, H., and Winograd, T. 1977. GUS, a frame-driven dialog system. *Artificial Intelligence* 8:155–173.

Bobrow, D. G., and Winograd, T. 1977a. Experience with KRL–0, one cycle of a knowledge representation language. *IJCAI 5,* 213–222.

Bobrow, D. G., and Winograd, T. 1977b. An overview of KRL, a knowledge representation language. *Cognitive Science* 1:3–46.

Boden, M. 1977. *Artificial intelligence and natural man.* New York: Basic Books.

Booth, A. D. (Ed.). 1967. *Machine translation.* Amsterdam: North-Holland.

Bott, M. F. 1970. Computational linguistics. In J. Lyons (Ed.), *New horizons in linguistics.* Harmondsworth, England: Penguin Books, 215–228.

Brachman, R. J. 1978. A structural paradigm for representing knowledge. Rep. No. 3605, Bolt Beranek and Newman, Inc., Cambridge, Mass.

Brachman, R. J. 1979. What's in a concept: Structural foundations for semantic networks. In Findler, 3–50.

Brachman, R. J., and Smith, B. C. 1980. *SIGART Newsletter* 70 (special issue on knowledge representation).

Bratko, I., Kopec, D., and Michie, D. 1978. Pattern-based representation of chess end-game knowledge. *Computer J.* 21:149–153.

Bresnan, J. 1978. A realistic transformational grammar. In M. Halle, J. Bresnan, and G. A. Miller (Eds.), *Linguistic theory and psychological reality.* Cambridge, Mass.: MIT Press, 1–59.

Brooks, R. 1977. Production systems as control structures for programming languages. *SIGART Newsletter* 63:33–37.

Bruce, B. 1975. Case systems for natural language. *Artificial Intelligence* 6:327–360.

Bullwinkle, C. 1977. Levels of complexity in discourse for anaphora disambiguation and speech act interpretation. *IJCAI 5,* 43–49.

Burton, R. R. 1976. Semantic grammar: An engineering technique for constructing natural language understanding systems. BBN Rep. No. 3453, Bolt Beranek and Newman, Inc., Cambridge, Mass.

Burton, R. R., and Brown, J. S. 1979. Toward a natural-language capability for computer-assisted instruction. In H. O'Neil (Ed.), *Procedures for instructional systems development.* New York: Academic Press, 273–313.

Bibliography

368

Bibliography

Carbonell, J. R. 1970. AI in CAI: An artificial intelligence approach to computer-assisted instruction. *IEEE Transactions on Man–Machine Systems* MMS–11:190–202.

Carbonell, J. R., and Collins, A. M. 1974. Natural semantics in AI. *IJCAI 3*, 344–351.

Chafe, W. L. 1972. Discourse structure and human knowledge. In R. O. Freedle and J. B. Carroll (Eds.), *Language comprehension and the acquisition of knowledge.* Washington, D.C.: Winston, 41–69.

Chang, C. L., and Slagle, J. R. 1971. An admissible and optimal algorithm for searching AND/OR graphs. *Artificial Intelligence* 2:117–128.

Charness, N. 1977. Human chess skill. In Frey, 34–53.

Charniak, E. 1972. Toward a model of children's story comprehension. Rep. No. TR–266, AI Laboratory, Massachusetts Institute of Technology.

Charniak, E. 1975. A brief on case. Rep. No. 22, Institute for Semantic and Cognitive Studies, Castagnola, Switzerland.

Charniak, E. 1978. With spoon in hand this must be the Eating frame. *TINLAP-2*, 187–193.

Charniak, E., Riesbeck, C. K., and McDermott, D. V. 1980. *Artificial intelligence programming.* Hillsdale, N.J.: Lawrence Erlbaum.

Charniak, E., and Wilks, Y. 1976. *Computational semantics: An introduction to artificial intelligence and natural language comprehension.* Amsterdam: North-Holland.

Chomsky, N. 1956. Three models for the description of language. *IRE Transactions on Information Theory* 2:113–124. (Also in R. D. Luce, R. Bush, and E. Galanter, Eds., *Readings in mathematical psychology.* New York: Wiley, 1965, 105–124.)

Chomsky, N. 1957. *Syntactic structures.* The Hague: Mouton.

Chomsky, N. 1959. On certain formal properties of grammars. *Information and Control* 2:137–167. (Also in R. D. Luce, R. Bush, and E. Galanter, Eds., *Readings in mathematical psychology.* New York: Wiley, 1965, 125–155.)

Chomsky, N. 1965. *Aspects of the theory of syntax.* Cambridge, Mass.: MIT Press.

Chomsky, N. 1963. Formal properties of grammars. In R. D. Luce, R. Bush, and E. Galanter (Eds.), *Handbook of mathematical psychology* (Vol. 2). New York: Wiley, 323–418.

Chomsky, N. 1971. Deep structure, surface structure, and semantic interpretation. In Steinberg and Jakobovits, 183–216.

Clippinger, J. H., Jr. 1975. Speaking with many tongues: Some problems in modeling speakers of actual discourse. *TINLAP-1*, 78–83.

C.M.U. Speech Group. 1977. Speech understanding systems: Summary of results of the five-year research effort at Carnegie-Mellon University. Computer Science Dept. Tech. Report, Carnegie-Mellon University.

Codd, E. F. 1974. Seven steps to rendezvous with the casual user. In J. W. Klimbie and K. L. Koffeman (Eds.), *Data base management.* Amsterdam: North-Holland, 179–200.

Cohen, P. R. 1978. On knowing what to say: Planning speech acts. Tech. Rep. 118, Dept. of Computer Science, University of Toronto.

Cohen, P. R., and Perrault, C. R. 1979. Elements of a plan-based theory of speech acts. *Cognitive Science* 3:177–212.

Colby, K., Weber, S., and Hilf, F. 1971. Artificial paranoia. *Artificial Intelligence* 2:1–25.

Cole, R. A. 1979. Navigating the slippery stream of speech. *Psychology Today* (12):11, 77–87.

COLING76. 1976. *Preprints of the 6th International Conference on Computational Linguistics, Ottawa, Ontario, Canada, June 1976.*

Conway, M. E. 1963. Design of a separable transition-diagram compiler. *CACM* 6:396–408.

Culicover, P. W., Wasow, T., and Akmajian, A. 1977. *Formal syntax.* New York: Academic Press.

Davies, D. J. M. 1972. POPLER: A POP-2 Planner. Rep. No. MIP–89, School of AI, University of Edinburgh.

Davis, R. In press. The application of meta-level knowledge to the construction, maintenance, and use of large knowledge bases. In Davis and Lenat.

Davis, R., and Buchanan, B. G. 1977. Meta-level knowledge: Overview and applications. *IJCAI 5,* 920–927.

Davis, R., Buchanan, B. G., and Shortliffe, E. H. 1977. Production rules as a representation for a knowledge-based consultation system. *Artificial Intelligence* 8:15–45.

Davis, R., and King, J. J. 1977. An overview of production systems. In E. Elcock and D. Michie (Eds.), *Machine intelligence 8.* Chichester, England: Ellis Horwood, 300–332.

Davis, R., and Lenat, D. B. In press. *Knowledge-based systems in artificial intelligence.* New York: McGraw-Hill.

de Champeaux, D., and Sint, L. 1977. An improved bi-directional heuristic search algorithm. *J. ACM* 24:177–191.

Dijkstra, E. W. 1959. A note on two problems in connection with graphs. *Numerische Mathematik* 1:269–271.

Doran, J. E. 1967. An approach to automatic problem-solving. In N. L. Collins and D. Michie (Eds.), *Machine intelligence 1.* New York: American Elsevier, 105–123.

Doran, J. E., and Michie, D. 1966. Experiments with the graph traverser program. *Proceedings of the Royal Society of London* (Series A) 294:235–259.

Dreyfus, H. L. 1972. *What computers can't do.* New York: Harper and Row.

Duda, R. O., Hart, P. E., Nilsson, N. J., and Sutherland, G. L. 1978. Semantic network representations in rule-based inference systems. In Waterman and Hayes–Roth, 203–221.

Eastman, C. M. 1970. Representations for space planning. *CACM* 13:242–250.

Eastman, C. M. 1973. Automated space planning. *Artificial Intelligence* 4:41–64.

Elcock, E. W. 1977. Representation of knowledge in a geometry machine. In E. W. Elcock and D. Michie (Eds.), *Machine intelligence 8*. New York: Wiley, 11–29.

Erman, L. D., Fennell, R. D., Lesser, V. R., and Reddy, D. R. 1976. System organizations for speech understanding: Implications of network and multiprocessor computer architectures for AI. *IEEE Transactions on Computers* C–25(4):414–421.

Erman, L. D., Hayes–Roth, F., Lesser, V. R., and Reddy, D. R. 1980. The HEARSAY–II speech understanding system: Integrating knowledge to resolve uncertainty. *Computing Surveys* 12(2):213–253.

Erman, L. D., and Lesser, V. R. 1975. A multi-level organization for problem solving using many diverse, cooperating sources of knowledge. *IJCAI 4*, 483–490.

Erman, L. D., and Lesser, V. R. 1980. The HEARSAY–II speech understanding system: A tutorial. In Lea, *Trends*, 361–381.

Ernst, G., and Newell, A. 1969. *GPS: A case study in generality and problem solving*. New York: Academic Press.

Fahlman, S. E. 1974. A planning system for robot construction tasks. *Artificial Intelligence* 5:1–49.

Fahlman, S. E. 1975. Symbol-mapping and frames. *SIGART Newsletter* 53:7–8.

Feigenbaum, E. A. 1969. Artificial intelligence: Themes in the second decade. In A. J. H. Morrell (Ed.), *Information processing 68: Proceedings IFIP Congress 1968* (Vol. 2). Amsterdam: North-Holland, 1008–1024.

Feigenbaum, E. A. 1977. The art of artificial intelligence: Themes and case studies of knowledge engineering. *IJCAI 5*, 1014–1029.

Feigenbaum, E. A., and Feldman, J. (Eds.). 1963. *Computers and thought*. New York: McGraw-Hill.

Fikes, R. E., Hart, P., and Nilsson, N. J. 1972. Learning and executing generalized robot plans. *Artificial Intelligence* 3:251–288.

Fikes, R. E., and Hendrix, G. 1977. A Network-based knowledge representation and its natural deduction system. *IJCAI 5*, 235–246.

Fikes, R. E., and Nilsson, N. J. 1971. STRIPS: A new approach to the application of theorem proving to problem solving. *Artificial Intelligence* 2:189–208.

Fillmore, C. 1968. The case for case. In E. Bach and R. Harms (Eds.), *Universals in linguistic theory*. New York: Holt, Rinehart, and Winston, 1–88.

Fillmore, C. 1971a. Some problems for case grammar. In R. J. O'Brien (Ed.), *Report of the twenty-second annual round table meeting on linguistics and language studies.* (Monograph Series on Languages and Linguistics, No. 24.) Washington, D.C.: Georgetown University Press, 35–56.

Fillmore, C. 1971b. Types of lexical information. In Steinberg and Jakobovits, 370–392.

Filman, R. E. 1979. The interaction of observation and inference in a formal representation system. *IJCAI 6,* 269–274.

Filman, R. E., and Weyhrauch, R. W. 1976. An FOL primer. Memo 288, AI Laboratory, Stanford University.

Findler, N. V. (Ed.). 1979. *Associative networks: The representation and use of knowledge by computers.* New York: Academic Press.

Flanagan, J., Levinson, S., Rabiner, L., and Rosenberg, A. 1980. Techniques for expanding the capabilities of practical speech recognizers. In Lea, *Trends,* 425–444.

Flavell, J. H. 1977. *Cognitive development.* Englewood Cliffs, N.J.: Prentice-Hall.

Flavell, J. H. 1979. Metacognition and cognitive monitoring: A new area for cognitive-developmental inquiry. *American Psychologist* 34:906–911.

Forgy, C., and McDermott, J. 1977. OPS, a domain-independent production system language. *IJCAI 5,* 933–939.

Fox, M. In press. An organizational view of distributed systems. *IEEE Transactions on Systems, Man, and Cybernetics.*

Frey, P. W. (Ed.). 1977. *Chess skill in man and machine.* New York: Springer-Verlag.

Friedman, J. 1969. Directed random generation of sentences. *CACM* 12:40–46.

Friedman, J. 1971. *A computer model of transformational grammar.* New York: American Elsevier.

Fuller, S. H., Gaschnig, J. G., and Gillogly, J. J. 1973. Analysis of the alpha-beta pruning algorithm. Dept. of Computer Science, Carnegie-Mellon University.

Funt, B. V. 1976. WHISPER: A computer implementation using analogs in reasoning. Rep. No. 76–09, Computer Science Dept., University of British Columbia.

Funt, B. V. 1977. WHISPER: A problem-solving system utilizing diagrams and aparallel processing retina. *IJCAI 5,* 459–464.

Garvey, T., and Kling, R. 1969. User's guide to QA3.5 question-answering system. Tech. Note 15, AI Group, Stanford Research Institute, Menlo Park, Calif.

Gaschnig, J. 1977. Exactly how good are heuristics? Toward a realistic predictive theory of best-first search. *IJCAI 5,* 434–441.

Gelernter, H. 1959. A note on syntactic symmetry and the manipulation of formal systems by machine. *Information and Control* 2:80–89.

Gelernter, H. 1963. Realization of a geometry-theorem proving machine. In Feigenbaum and Feldman, 134–152.

Gelernter, H., Hansen, J. R., and Gerberich, C. L. 1960. A FORTRAN-compiled list processing language. *J. ACM* 7:87–101.

Gelernter, H., Hansen, J. R., and Loveland, D. W. 1963. Empirical explorations of the geometry-theorem proving machine. In Feigenbaum and Feldman, 153–163.

Gelernter, H., and Rochester, N. 1958. Intelligent behavior in problem-solving machines. *IBM J. Research and Development* 2:336–345.

Gelperin, D. 1977. On the optimality of A^*. *Artificial Intelligence* 8:69–76.

Gentner, D., and Collins, A. M. In press. Knowing about knowing: Effects of meta-knowledge on inference. In *Memory and Cognition*.

Gillogly, J. J. 1972. The technology chess program. *Artificial Intelligence* 3:145–163.

Gilmore, P. C. 1970. An examination of the geometry theorem machine. *Artificial Intelligence* 2:171–187.

Goldman, N. 1975. Conceptual generation. In Schank, 289–371.

Goldstein, I. P., and Roberts, R. B. 1977. NUDGE, a knowledge-based scheduling program. *IJCAI 5*, 257–263.

Good, I. J. 1968. A five-year plan for automatic chess. In E. Dale and D. Michie (Eds.), *Machine intelligence 2*. New York: American Elsevier, 89–118.

Green, B. F., Jr., Wolf, A. K., Chomsky, C., and Laughery, K. 1963. BASEBALL: An automatic question answerer. In Feigenbaum and Feldman, 207–216.

Green, C. C. 1969. The application of theorem-proving to question-answering systems. *IJCAI 1*, 219–237.

Greenblatt, R. D., Eastlake, D. E., and Crocker, S. D. 1967. The Greenblatt chess program. In *AFIPS Conference Proceedings, Fall Joint Computer Conference, 1967.* Washington, D.C.: Thompson, 801–810.

Griffith, A. K. 1974. A comparison and evaluation of three machine learning procedures as applied to the game of checkers. *Artificial Intelligence* 5:137–148.

Grishman, R. 1976. A survey of syntactic analysis procedures for natural language. *American Journal of Computational Linguistics*, Microfiche 47.

Grosz, B. J. 1980. Utterance and objective: Issues in natural language communication. *AI Magazine* 1:11–20.

Hall, P. A. V. 1971. Branch-and-bound and beyond. *IJCAI 2*, 641–650.

Halliday, M. A. K. 1961. Categories of the theory of grammar. *Word* 17:241–292.

Halliday, M. A. K. 1967–68. Notes on transitivity and theme in English. *Journal of Linguistics* 3:37–81, 199–244; 4:179–215.

Halliday, M. A. K. 1970a. Functional diversity in language as seen from a consideration of modality and mood in English. *Foundations of Language* 6:322–361.

Halliday, M. A. K. 1970b. Language structure and language function. In J. Lyons (Ed.), *New horizons in linguistics.* Harmondsworth, England: Penguin Books, 140–165.

Hanson, A. R., and Riseman, E. M. (Eds.). 1978a. *Computer vision systems.* New York: Academic Press.

Hanson, A. R., and Riseman, E. M. 1978b. VISIONS: A computer system for interpreting scenes. In Hanson and Riseman, 303–333.

Harman, G. (Ed.). 1974. *On Noam Chomsky: Critical essays.* Garden City, N.Y.: Anchor Books.

Harris, L. R. 1973. The bandwidth heuristic search. *IJCAI 3*, 23–29.

Harris, L. R. 1974. The heuristic search under conditions of error. *Artificial Intelligence* 5:217–234.

Harris, L. R. 1975. The heuristic search and the game of chess: A study of quiescence, sacrifices, and plan oriented play. *IJCAI 4*, 334–339.

Harris, L. R. 1977a. The heuristic search: An alternative to the alpha-beta minimax procedure. In Frey, 157–166.

Harris, L. R. 1977b. ROBOT: A high performance natural language processor for data base query. *SIGART Newsletter* 61:39–40.

Harris, L. 1979. Experience with ROBOT in twelve commercial natural language data base query applications. *IJCAI 6*, 365–368.

Hart, P. E., Nilsson, N. J., and Raphael, B. 1968. A formal basis for the heuristic determination of minimum cost paths. *IEEE Transactions on SSC* SSC–4:100–107.

Hart, P. E., Nilsson, N. J., and Raphael, B. 1972. Correction to 'A formal basis for the heuristic determination of minimum cost paths.' *SIGART Newsletter* 37:28–29.

Hayes, P. J. 1973. Computation and deduction. *Symposium on mathematical foundations of computer science, Czechslovakia Academy of Science.*

Hayes, P. J. 1974. Some problems and non-problems in representation theory. *British Computer Society, AI and Simulation of Behavior Group summer conference, University of Sussex,* 63–79.

Hayes, P. J. 1977a. In defence of logic. *IJCAI 5*, 559–565.

Hayes, P. J. 1977b. On semantic nets, frames, and associations. *IJCAI 5*, 99–107.

Hayes-Roth, B., and Hayes-Roth, F. 1979. A cognitive model of planning. *Cognitive Science* 3:275–310.

Hays, D. G., and Mathias, J. (Eds.). 1976. FBIS seminar on machine translation. *American Journal of Computational Linguistics*, Microfiche 46.

Hearst, E. 1977. Man and machine: Chess achievements and chess thinking. In Frey, 167–200.

Hedrick, C. 1976. Learning production systems from examples. *Artificial Intelligence* 7:21–49.

Heidorn, G. E. 1976. Automatic programming through natural language dialogue: A survey. *IBM J. Research and Development* 20:302–313.

Hendrix, G. G. 1976. Expanding the utility of semantic networks through partitioning. *Artificial Intelligence* 7:21–49.

Hendrix, G. G. 1977a. Human engineering for applied natural language processing. *IJCAI 5*, 183–191.

Hendrix, G. G. 1977b. LIFER: A natural language interface facility. *SIGART Newsletter* 61:25–26.

Hendrix, G. G. 1977c. The LIFER manual: A guide to building practical natural language interfaces. Tech. Note 138, Artificial Intelligence Center, SRI International, Inc., Menlo Park, Calif.

Hendrix, G. G., Sacerdoti, E. D., Sagalowicz, D., and Slocum, J. 1978. Developing a natural language interface to complex data. *ACM Transactions on Database Systems* 3:105–147.

Hendrix, G. G., Thompson, C., and Slocum, J. 1973. Language processing via canonical verbs and semantic models. *IJCAI 3*, 262–269.

Heuristic Programming Project—1980. 1980. Computer Science Department, Stanford University.

Hewitt, C. 1972. Description and theoretical analysis (using schemata) of PLANNER, a language for proving theorems and manipulating models in a robot. Rep. No. TR-258, AI Laboratory, Massachusetts Institute of Technology.

Hewitt, C. 1975. How to use what you know. *IJCAI 4*, 189–198.

Hillier, F. S., and Lieberman, G. J. 1974. *Operations research* (2nd ed.). San Francisco: Holden-Day.

Hofstadter, D. 1979. *Gödel, Escher, Bach: an eternal golden braid.* New York: Basic Books.

Hopcroft, J. E., and Ullman, J. D. 1969. *Formal languages and their relation to automata.* Reading, Mass.: Addison-Wesley.

Hudson, R. A. 1971. *English complex sentences: An introduction to systemic grammar.* Amsterdam: North-Holland.

Hudson, R. A. 1976. *Arguments for a non-transformational grammar.* Chicago: University of Chicago Press.

Jackendoff, R. 1975. A system of semantic primitives. *TINLAP-1*, 28–33.

Jackendoff, R. 1976. Toward an explanatory semantic representation. *Linguistic Inquiry* 7:89–150.

Jackson, P. C. 1974. *Introduction to artificial intelligence.* New York: Petrocelli.

Josselson, H. H. 1971. Automatic translation of languages since 1960: A linguist's view. In M. C. Yovits (Ed.), *Advances in computers* (Vol. 11). New York: Academic Press, 1–58.

Kaplan, R. M. 1973. A general syntactic processor. In Rustin, 193–241.

Kaplan, S. J. 1979. *Cooperative responses from a portable natural language data base query system.* Doctoral dissertation, Dept. of Computer and Information Science, University of Pennsylvania.

Karp, R. M. 1972. Reducibility among combinatorial problems. In R. E. Miller and J. W. Thatcher (Eds.), *Complexity of computer computations.* New York: Plenum Press, 85–103.

Katz, J., and Postal, P. 1964. *An integrated theory of linguistic descriptions.* Cambridge, Mass.: MIT Press.

Kay, M. 1973. The MIND system. In Rustin, 155–188.

Kellogg, C. 1968. A natural language compiler for on-line data management. *AFIPS Conference Proceedings 33, 1968 Fall Joint Computer Conference.* Washington, D.C.: Thompson, 473–492.

Kister, J., Stein, P., Ulam, S., Walden, W., and Wells, M. 1957. Experiments in chess. *J. ACM* 4:174–177.

Klatt, D. H. 1977. Review of the ARPA speech understanding project. *Journal of the Acoustical Society of America* 62:1345–1366.

Klein, S. 1965. Automatic paraphrasing in essay format. *Mechanical Translation* 88:68–83.

Klein, S., and Simmons, R. F. 1963. Syntactic dependence and the computer generation of coherent discourse. *Mechanical Translation* 7:50–61.

Knuth, D. 1973. *The art of computer programming: Fundamental algorithms* (Vol. 1, 2nd ed.). Reading, Mass.: Addison-Wesley.

Knuth, D. 1979. *TEX and Metafont: New directions in typesetting.* Providence, R.I.: American Mathematical Society and Bedford, Mass.: Digital Press.

Knuth, D. E., and Moore, R. W. 1975. An analysis of alpha-beta pruning. *Artificial intelligence* 6:293–326.

Kotok, A. 1962. A chess playing program. RLE and MIT Computation Center Memo 41, Artificial Intelligence Project, Massachusetts Institute of Technology.

Kowalski, R. 1972. And-or graphs, theorem-proving graphs, and bi-directional search. In B. Meltzer and D. Michie (Eds.), *Machine intelligence 7.* New York: Wiley, 167–194.

Kowalski, R. 1974. Predicate logic as a programming language. *IFIP 74.* Amsterdam: North-Holland, 569–574.

Kuipers, B. 1975. A frame for frames: Representing knowledge for recognition. In Bobrow and Collins, 151–184.

Landsbergen, S. P. J. 1976. Syntax and formal semantics of English in PHLIQA1. In L. Steels (Ed.), *Advances in natural language processing*. Antwerp, Belgium: University of Antwerp.

Lawler, E. W., and Wood, D. E. 1966. Branch-and-bound methods: A survey. *Operations Research* 14:699–719.

Lea, W. 1980a. Speech recognition: Past, present, and future. In Lea, *Trends*, 39–89.

Lea, W. (Ed.). 1980b. *Trends in speech recognition*. Englewood Cliffs, N.J.: Prentice-Hall.

Lea, W. 1980c. The value of speech recognition systems. In Lea, *Trends*, 3–18.

Lea, W., and Shoup, J. 1980. Specific contributions of the ARPA SUR project. In Lea, *Trends*, 382–421.

Lehnert, W. C. 1978. *The process of question answering: A computer simulation of cognition*. Hillsdale, N.J.: Lawrence Erlbaum.

Lenat, D. B. In press. AM: An AI approach to discovery in mathematics. In Davis and Lenat.

Lenat, D. B., and McDermott, J. 1977. Less than general production system architectures. *IJCAI 5*, 928–932.

Lesser, V. R., and Erman, L. D. In press. Distributed interpretation: A model and experiment. In *IEEE Transactions on Computers*.

Levi, G., and Sirovich, F. 1975. A problem reduction model for non-independent subproblems. *IJCAI 4*, 340–344.

Levi, G., and Sirovich, F. 1976. Generalized AND/OR graphs. *Artificial Intelligence* 7:243–259.

Levine, M. D. 1978. A knowledge-based computer vision system. In A. Hanson and E. Riseman (Eds.), *Computer vision systems*. New York: Academic Press, 335–352.

Levy, D. 1979. The computer chess revolution. *Chess Life and Review* (February):84–85.

Lindsay, R. K. 1963a. Inferential memory as the basis of machines which understand natural language. In Feigenbaum and Feldman, 217–233.

Lindsay, R. K. 1963b. A program for parsing sentences and making inferences about kinship relations. In A. C. Hoggatt and F. E. Balderston (Eds.), *Symposium on simulation models: Methodology and applications to the behavioral sciences*. Cincinnati: South-Western Publishing, 111–138.

Lindsay, R. K., Buchanan, B. G., Feigenbaum, E. A., and Lederberg, J. 1980. *Applications of Artificial Intelligence for Chemical Inference: The DENDRAL Project*. New York: McGraw-Hill.

Locke, W. N., and Booth, A. D. (Eds.). 1955. *Machine translation of languages*. New York: Technology Press of MIT and Wiley.

Lowerre, B., and Reddy, R. 1980. The HARPY speech understanding system. In Lea, *Trends*, 340–360.

Lyons, J. 1968. *Introduction to theoretical linguistics.* London: Cambridge University Press.

Lyons, J. 1970. *Noam Chomsky.* New York: Viking Press.

Mann, W., and Moore, J. 1980. Computer as author—Results and prospects. Tech. Rep. RR–79–82, Information Science Institute, Marina del Rey, Calif.

Manna, Z. 1973. *Introduction to the mathematical theory of computation.* New York: McGraw-Hill.

Manove, M., Bloom, S., and Engelman, E. 1968. Rational functions in MATHLAB. In D. G. Bobrow (Ed.), *Symbol manipulation languages and techniques.* Amsterdam: North-Holland, 86–102.

Marcus, M. P. 1980. *A theory of syntactic recognition for natural language.* Cambridge, Mass.: MIT Press.

Martelli, A. 1977. On the complexity of admissible search algorithms. *Artificial Intelligence* 8:1–13.

Martelli, A., and Montanari, U. 1973. Additive AND/OR graphs. *IJCAI 3*, 1–11.

Matuzceck, D. 1972. An implementation of the augmented transition network system of Woods (as revised by J. Slocum). Dept. of Computer Sciences and CAI Laboratory, University of Texas, Austin.

McCarthy, J. 1977. Epistmological problems of artificial intelligence. *IJCAI 5*, 1038–1044.

McCarthy, J., and Hayes, P. J. 1969. Some philosophical problems from the standpoint of artificial intelligence. In D. Michie and B. Meltzer (Eds.), *Machine intelligence 4.* Edinburgh: Edinburgh University Press, 463–502.

McCord, M. 1975. On the form of a systemic grammar. *Journal of Linguistics* 11:195–212.

McCorduck, P. 1979. *Machines who think.* San Francisco: Freeman.

McDermott, D. 1974. Assimilation of new information by a natural language-understanding system. Rep. No. TR–291, AI Laboratory, Massachusetts Institute of Technology.

McDermott, D. 1976. Artificial intelligence meets natural stupidity. *SIGART Newsletter* 57:4–9.

McDermott, D., and Doyle, J. In press. Non-monotonic logic—I. *Artificial Intelligence* 13.

McDermott, J., and Forgy, C. 1978. Production system conflict resolution strategies. In Waterman and Hayes–Roth, 177–199.

McDermott, J., Newell, A., and Moore, J. 1978. The efficiency of certain production system implementations. In Waterman and Hayes–Roth, 155–176.

McDonald, D. 1980. *Natural language production as a process of decision making under constraint.* Doctoral dissertation, Laboratory for Computer Science, Massachusetts Institute of Technology.

McIntosh, A., and Halliday, M. A. K. 1966. *Patterns of language.* Bloomington: Indiana University Press.

McKeown, K. 1980. Generating relevant explanation: Natural language responses to questions about database structure. *Proceedings of the AAAI,* 306–309.

Michie, D. 1967. Strategy building with the graph traverser. In N. L. Collins and D. Michie (Eds.), *Machine intelligence 1.* New York: American Elsevier, 135–152.

Michie, D. 1977. A theory of advice. In E. W. Elcock and D. Michie (Eds.), *Machine intelligence 8.* New York: Wiley, 151–168.

Michie, D., and Bratko, I. 1978. Advice table representations of chess endgame knowledge. In *Proceedings of the AISB/GI Conference on Artificial Intelligence,* 194–200.

Michie, D., and Ross, R. 1970. Experiments with the adaptive graph traverser. In B. Meltzer and D. Michie (Eds.), *Machine intelligence 5.* New York: American Elsevier, 301–318.

Miller, G. A. 1975. Comments on lexical analysis. *TINLAP-1,* 34–37.

Miller, G. A., and Johnson–Laird, P. N. 1976. *Language and perception.* Cambridge, Mass.: Harvard University Press.

Minsky, M. 1963. Steps toward artificial intelligence. In Feigenbaum and Feldman, 406–450.

Minsky, M. (Ed.). 1968. *Semantic information processing.* Cambridge, Mass.: MIT Press.

Minsky, M. 1975. A framework for representing knowledge. In P. Winston (Ed.), *The psychology of computer vision.* New York: McGraw-Hill, 211–277.

Mittman, B. 1977. A brief history of the computer chess tournaments: 1970–1975. In Frey, 1–33.

Moore, E. F. 1959. The shortest path through a maze. In *Proceedings of an International Symposium on the Theory of Switching, Part II.* Cambridge, Mass.: Harvard University Press, 285–292.

Moore, R. C. 1975. Reasoning from incomplete knowledge in a procedural deductive system. Rep. No. TR–347, AI Laboratory, Massachusetts Institute of Technology.

Moses, J. 1967. Symbolic integration. Rep. No. MAC–TR–47, Project MAC, Massachusetts Institute of Technology.

Myopolous, J., Cohen, P., Borgida, A., and Sugar, L. 1975. Semantic networks and the generation of context. *IJCAI 4,* 134–142.

Nash–Webber, B. 1974. Semantics and speech understanding. BBN Rep. No. 2896, Bolt Beranek and Newman, Inc., Cambridge, Mass.

Nash–Webber, B. L. 1975. The role of semantics in automatic speech understanding. In Bobrow and Collins, 351–382.

National Research Council, Automatic Language Processing Advisory Committee. 1966. Language and machines: Computers in translation and linguistics. Publication 1416, National Academy of Sciences, National Research Council, Washington, D.C.

Newborn, M. 1975. *Computer chess.* New York: Academic Press.

Newborn, M. 1977. The efficiency of the alpha-beta search on trees with branch-dependent terminal node scores. *Artificial Intelligence* 8:137–153.

Newborn, M. 1978. Computers and chess news: Recent tournaments. *SIGART Newsletter* 65:11.

Newell, A. 1973a. Artificial intelligence and the concept of mind. In Schank and Colby, 1–60.

Newell, A. 1973b. Production systems: Models of control structure. In W. Chase (Ed.), *Visual information processing.* New York: Academic Press, 463–526.

Newell, A. 1975. A tutorial on speech understanding systems. In D. R. Reddy (Ed.), *Speech recognition: Invited papers presented at the 1974 IEEE symposium.* New York: Academic Press, 3–54.

Newell, A. 1978. HARPY: Production systems and human cognition. Rep. CMU–CS–78–140, Dept. of Computer Science, Carnegie-Mellon University.

Newell, A., Barnett, J., Forgie, J., Green, C., Klatt, D. H., Licklider, J. C. R., Munson, J., Reddy, D. R., and Woods, W. A. 1973. *Speech understanding systems: Final report of a study group.* Amsterdam: North-Holland.

Newell, A., and Ernst, G. 1965. The search for generality. In W. A. Kalenich (Ed.), *Information processing 65: Proceedings IFIP Congress 1965.* Washington, D.C.: Spartan Books, 17–24.

Newell, A., Shaw, J. C., and Simon, H. A. 1960. A variety of intelligent learning in a general problem-solver. In M. C. Yovits and S. Cameron (Eds.), *Self-organizing systems.* New York: Pergamon Press, 153–189.

Newell, A., Shaw, J. C., and Simon, H. A. 1963a. Chess-playing programs and the problem of complexity. In Feigenbaum and Feldman, 39–70.

Newell, A., Shaw, J. C., and Simon, H. A. 1963b. Empirical explorations with the logic theory machine: A case history in heuristics. In Feigenbaum and Feldman, 109–133.

Newell, A., and Simon, H. A. 1963. GPS, a program that simulates human thought. In Feigenbaum and Feldman, 279–293.

Newell, A., and Simon, H. A. 1972. *Human problem solving.* Englewood Cliffs, N.J.: Prentice-Hall.

Newell, A., and Simon, H. A. 1976. Computer science as empirical inquiry: Symbols and search. (The 1976 ACM Turing Lecture.) *CACM* 19:113–126.

Nii, H. P., and Feigenbaum, E. A. 1978. Rule-based understanding of signals. In Waterman and Hayes–Roth, 483–501.

Nilsson, N. J. 1969. Searching problem-solving and game-playing trees for minimal cost solutions. In A. J. H. Morrell (Ed.), *Information processing 68: Proceedings IFIP Congress 1968* (Vol. 2). Amsterdam: North-Holland, 1556–1562.

Nilsson, N. J. 1971. *Problem-solving methods in artificial intelligence.* New York: McGraw-Hill.

Nilsson, N. J. 1974. Artificial intelligence. In J. L. Rosenfeld (Ed.), *Information processing 74: Proceedings IFIP Congress 1974.* Amsterdam: North-Holland, 778–801.

Nilsson, N. J. 1980. *Principles of artificial intelligence.* Palo Alto, Calif.: Tioga.

Norman, D. A., Rumelhart, D. E., and the LNR Research Group. 1975. *Explorations in cognition.* San Francisco: Freeman.

Novak, G. S. 1977. Representation of knowledge in a program for solving physics problems. *IJCAI 5*, 286–291.

Oettinger, A. G. 1955. The design of an automatic Russian–English technical dictionary. In Locke and Booth, 47–65.

Paige, J. M., and Simon, H. A. 1966. Cognitive processes in solving algebra word problems. In B. Kleinmuntz (Ed.), *Problem solving.* New York: Wiley, 51–119.

Paxton, W. H. 1976. A framework for language understanding. SRI Tech. Note 131, AI Center, SRI International, Inc., Menlo Park, Calif.

Petrick, S. R. 1973. Transformational analysis. In Rustin, 27–41.

Pitrat, J. 1977. A chess combination program which uses plans. *Artificial Intelligence* 8:275–321.

Plath, W. 1976. REQUEST: A natural language question-answering system. *IBM J. Research and Development* 20:326–335.

Pohl, I. 1969. Bi-directional and heuristic search in path problems. SLAC Rep. No. 104, Stanford Linear Accelerator Center, Stanford, Calif.

Pohl, I. 1970a. First results on the effect of error in heuristic search. In B. Meltzer and D. Michie (Eds.), *Machine intelligence 5.* New York: American Elsevier, 219–236.

Pohl, I. 1970b. Heuristic search viewed as path finding in a graph. *Artificial Intelligence* 1:193–204.

Pohl, I. 1971. Bi-directional search. In B. Meltzer and D. Michie (Eds.), *Machine intelligence 6.* New York: American Elsevier, 127–140.

Pohl, I. 1973. The avoidance of (relative) catastrophe, heuristic competence, genuine dynamic weighting and computational issues in heuristic problem solving. *IJCAI 3*, 12–17.

Pohl, I. 1977. Practical and theoretical considerations in heuristic search algorithms. In E. W. Elcock and D. Michie (Eds.), *Machine intelligence 8.* New York: Wiley, 55–72.

Polya, G. 1957. *How to solve it* (2nd ed.). New York: Doubleday Anchor.

Post, E. 1943. Formal reductions of the general combinatorial problem. *American Journal of Mathematics* 65:197–268.

Postal, P. 1964. Limitations of phrase structure grammars. In J. A. Fodor and J. J. Katz, *The structure of language*. Englewood Cliffs, N.J.: Prentice-Hall, 137–151.

Prawitz, D. 1965. *Natural deduction: A proof-theoretical study*. Stockholm: Almqvist and Wiksell.

Propp, V. 1968. *Morphology of the folktale* (2nd. ed., transl. L. Scott). Austin: University of Texas Press.

Pylyshyn, Z. 1973. What the mind's eye tells the mind's brain: A critique of mental imagery. *Psychological Bulletin* 13:1–24.

Pylyshyn, Z. 1975. Do we need images and analogs? *TINLAP-1*, 174–177.

Pylyshyn, Z. 1978. Imagery and artificial intelligence. In C. W. Savage (Ed.), *Perception and cognition: Issues in the foundations of psychology*. Minneapolis: University of Minnesota Press.

Quillian, M. R. 1968. Semantic memory. In Minsky, 227–270.

Quillian, M. R. 1969. The teachable language comprehender: A simulation program and the theory of language. *CACM* 12:459–476.

Raphael, B. 1968. SIR: A computer program for semantic information retrieval. In Minsky, 33–145.

Raphael, B. 1976. *The thinking computer*. San Francisco: Freeman.

Reboh, R., Sacerdoti, E., Fikes, R. E., Sagalowicz, D., Waldinger, R. J., and Wilber, M. 1976. QLISP: A language for the interactive development of complex systems. Rep. No. TN-120, AI Center, SRI International, Inc., Menlo Park, Calif.

Reddy, R. (Ed.). 1975. *Speech recognition: Invited papers of the IEEE symposium*. New York: Academic Press.

Reddy, R., Erman, L., Fennell, R., and Neely, R. 1976. The HEARSAY speech understanding system: An example of the recognition process. *IEEE Transactions on Computers* C-25:427–431.

Reingold, E. M., Nievergelt, J., and Deo, N. 1977. *Combinatorial algorithms: Theory and practice*. Englewood Cliffs, N.J.: Prentice-Hall.

Reiter, R. 1978. On reasoning by default. *TINLAP-2*, 210–218.

Rieger, C. 1975. Conceptual memory and inference. In Schank, 157–288.

Riesbeck, C. K. 1975. Conceptual analysis. In Schank, 83–156.

Robinson, A. E., Appelt, D. E., Grosz, B. J., Hendrix, G. G., and Robinson, J. J. 1980. Interpreting natural-language utterances in dialogs about tasks. Tech. Note 210, Artificial Intelligence Center, SRI International, Inc., Menlo Park, Calif.

Robinson, J. J. 1975. Performance grammars. In Reddy, 401–427.

Rulifson, J., Derkson, J. A., and Waldinger, R. J. 1972. QA4: A procedural calculus for intuitive reasoning. Rep. No. TN–83, AI Center, SRI International, Inc.

Rumelhart, D. 1975. Notes on a schema for stories. In Bobrow and Collins, 211–236.

Rumelhart, D. 1976. Toward an interactive model of reading. Tech. Rep. 56, Center for Human Information Processing, Univ. of California, San Diego.

Russell, S. W. 1972. Semantic categories of nominals for conceptual dependency analysis of natural language. Memo 172, AI Laboratory, Stanford University.

Rustin, R. (Ed.). 1973. *Natural language processing.* New York: Algorithmics Press.

Rychener, M. D. 1976. Production systems as a programming language for artificial intelligence applications. Computer Science Dept., Carnegie-Mellon University.

Rychener, M. D. 1977. Control requirements for the design of production system architectures. *ACM symposium on artificial intelligence and programming languages, Rochester, N.Y.,* 37–44.

Sacerdoti, E. D. 1974. Planning in a hierarchy of abstraction spaces. *Artificial Intelligence* 5:115–135.

Sacerdoti, E. D. 1977. Language access to distributed data with error recovery. *IJCAI 5,* 196–202.

Samlowski, W. 1976. Case grammar. In Charniak and Wilks, 55–72.

Samuel, A. L. 1963. Some studies in machine learning using the game of checkers. In Feigenbaum and Feldman, 71–105.

Samuel, A. L. 1967. Some studies in machine learning using the game of checkers. II—Recent progress. *IBM J. Research and Development* 11:601–617.

Sandewall, E. J. 1971. Heuristic search: Concepts and methods. In N. V. Findler and B. Meltzer (Eds.), *Artificial intelligence and heuristic programming.* New York: American Elsevier, 81–100.

Scha, R. J. H. 1976. A formal language for semantic representation. In L. Steels (Ed.), *Advances in natural language processing.* Antwerp, Belgium: University of Antwerp.

Schank, R. C. 1972. Conceptual dependency: A theory of natural language understanding. *Cognitive Psychology* 3:552–631.

Schank, R. C. 1973a. The fourteen primitive actions and their inferences. Memo 183, AI Laboratory, Stanford University.

Schank, R. C. 1973b. Identification of conceptualizations underlying natural language. In Schank and Colby, 187–247.

Schank, R. C. 1975a. *Conceptual information processing.* New York: North-Holland.

Schank, R. C. 1975b. The primitive ACTs of conceptual dependency. *TINLAP-1*, 38–41.

Schank, R. C. 1975c. The structure of episodes in memory. In Bobrow and Collins, 237–272.

Schank, R. C. 1980. Language and memory. *Cognitive Science* 4:243–284.

Schank, R. C., and Abelson, R. P. 1977. *Scripts, plans, goals, and understanding.* Hillsdale, N.J.: Lawrence Erlbaum.

Schank, R. C., and Colby, K. M. (Eds.). 1973. *Computer models of thought and language.* San Francisco: Freeman.

Schank, R., Goldman, N., Rieger, C., and Riesbeck, C. 1973. MARGIE: Memory, analysis, response generation, and inference on English. *IJCAI 3*, 255–261.

Schank, R., and Yale AI Project. 1975. SAM—A story understander. Research Rep. 43, Dept. of Computer Science, Yale University.

Schubert, L. K. 1975. Extending the expressive power of semantic networks. *IJCAI 4*, 158–164.

Searle, J. 1969. *Speech acts.* Cambridge, England: Cambridge University Press.

Searle, J. R. 1980. Mind, brains, and programs. *Behavioral and Brain Sciences* 3:417–457.

Self, J. 1975. Computer generation of sentences by systemic grammar. *American Journal of Computational Linguistics*, Microfiche 29.

Shannon, C. E. 1950. Programming a computer for playing chess. *Philosophical Magazine* (Series 7) 41:256–275.

Shannon, C. E. 1956. A chess-playing machine. In J. R. Newman (Ed.), *The world of mathematics* (Vol. 4). New York: Simon and Schuster, 2124–2133.

Shortliffe, E. H. 1976. *Computer-based medical consultations: MYCIN.* New York: North-Holland.

Shoup, J. 1980. Phonological aspects of speech recognition. In Lea, *Trends*, 125–138.

Siklossy, L. 1976. *Let's talk LISP.* Englewood Cliffs, N.J.: Prentice-Hall.

Simmons, R. F. 1965. Answering English questions by computer: A survey. *CACM* 8:53–70.

Simmons, R. F. 1966. Storage and retrieval of aspects of meaning in directed graph structures. *CACM* 9:211–214.

Simmons, R. F. 1970. Natural language question-answering systems: 1969. *CACM* 13:15–30.

Simmons, R. F. 1973. Semantic networks: Their computation and use for understanding English sentences. In Schank and Colby, 63–113.

Simmons, R. F., Burger, J. F., and Long, R. E. 1966. An approach toward answering English questions from text. *AFIPS Conference Proceedings 29, 1966 Fall Joint Computer Conference.* Washington, D.C.: Spartan Books, 357–363.

Bibliography

Simmons, R. F., Burger, J. F., and Schwarcz, R. M. 1968. A computational model of verbal understanding. *AFIPS Conference Proceedings 33, 1968 Fall Joint Computer Conference*. Washington, D.C.: Thompson, 441–456.

Simmons, R. F., Klein, S., and McConlogue, K. 1964. Indexing and dependency logic for answering English questions. *American Documentation* 15:196–204.

Simmons, R. F., and Slocum, J. 1972. Generating English discourse from semantic networks. *CACM* 15:891–905.

Simon, H. A. 1969. *The sciences of the artificial.* Cambridge, Mass.: MIT Press.

Simon, H. A., and Kadane, J. B. 1975. Optimal problem-solving search: All-or-none solutions. *Artificial Intelligence* 6:235–247.

Slagle, J. R. 1961. A heuristic program that solves symbolic integration problems in freshman calculus: Symbolic Automatic Integrator (SAINT). Rep. No. 5G–0001, Lincoln Laboratory, Massachusetts Institute of Technology.

Slagle, J. R. 1963. A heuristic program that solves symbolic integration problems in freshman calculus. In Feigenbaum and Feldman, 191–203. (Also in *J. ACM* 10:507–520 [1963].)

Slagle, J. R. 1971. *Artificial intelligence: The heuristic programming approach.* New York: McGraw-Hill.

Slagle, J. R., and Dixon, J. K. 1969. Experiments with some programs that search game trees. *J. ACM* 16:189–207.

Slagle, J. R., and Dixon, J. K. 1970. Experiments with the M and N tree-searching program. *CACM* 13:147–154.

Slate, D. J., and Atkin, L. R. 1977. CHESS 4.5—The Northwestern University chess program. In Frey, 82–118.

Sloman, A. 1971. Interactions between philosophy and AI: The role of intuition and non-logical reasoning in intelligence. *Artificial Intelligence* 2:209–225.

Sloman, A. 1975. Afterthoughts on analogical representations. *TINLAP-1*, 178–182.

Stefik, M. 1980. Planning with constraints. Rep. No. 784, Computer Science Dept., Stanford University.

Steinberg, D., and Jakobovits, L. 1971. *Semantics.* Cambridge, England: Cambridge University Press.

Suppes, P. 1957. *Introduction to logic.* New York: Van Nostrand Reinhold.

Sussman, G., and McDermott, D. V. 1972. CONNIVER reference manual. Memo 259, AI Laboratory, Massachusetts Institute of Technology.

Sussman, G., Winograd, T., and Charniak, E. 1970. MICRO–PLANNER reference manual. AI Memo 203, AI Laboratory, Massachusetts Institute of Technology.

Szolovitz, P., Hawkinson, L. B., and Martin, W. A. 1977. An overview of OWL, a language for knowledge representation. Rep. No. TM–86, Laboratory for Computer Science, Massachusetts Institute of Technology.

Taylor, B., and Rosenberg, R. S. 1975. A case-driven parser for natural language. *American Journal of Computational Linguistics*, Microfiche 31.

Thompson, F. B. 1966. English for the computer. *AFIPS Conference Proceedings 29, 1966 Fall Joint Computer Conference.* Washington, D.C.: Spartan Books, 349–356.

Thorndyke, P. W. 1977. Cognitive structures in comprehension and memory of narrative discourse. *Cognitive Psychology* 9:77–110.

Thorp, E., and Walden, W. E. 1970. A computer-assisted study of Go on $m \times n$ boards. In R. B. Banerji and M. D. Mesarovic (Eds.), *Theoretical approaches to non-numerical problem solving.* Berlin: Springer-Verlag, 303–343.

TINLAP-1 (Schank, R., and Nash–Webber, B., Eds.). 1975. *Theoretical issues in natural language processing: An interdisciplinary workshop in computational linguistics, psychology, linguistics, and artificial intelligence, June 1975.*

TINLAP-2 (Waltz, D. L., Ed.). 1978. *Theoretical issues in natural language processing—2.* New York: Association for Computing Machinery.

Turing, A. M., et al. 1953. Digital computers applied to games. In B. V. Bowden (Ed.), *Faster than thought.* London: Pitman, 286–310.

Vanderbrug, G., and Minker, J. 1975. State-space, problem-reduction, and theorem proving—Some relationships. *CACM* 18:107–115.

Vere, S. A. 1977. Relational production systems. *Artificial Intelligence* 8:47–68.

Vincens, P. 1969. *Aspects of speech recognition by computer.* Doctoral dissertation, Computer Science Dept., Stanford University.

Walker, D. E. (Ed.). 1976. *Speech understanding research.* New York: North-Holland.

Walker, D. E. (Ed.). 1978. *Understanding spoken language.* New York: North-Holland.

Walker, D. E. 1980. SRI research on speech understanding. In Lea, *Trends,* 294–315.

Waltz, D. L. 1977. Natural language interfaces. *SIGART Newsletter* 61:16–64.

Waltz, D. L. In press. An English language question answering system for a large relational data base.

Waterman, D. A. 1970. Generalization learning techniques for automating the learning of heuristics. *Artificial Intelligence* 1:121–170.

Waterman, D. A., and Hayes–Roth, F. (Eds.). 1978. *Pattern-directed inference systems.* New York: Academic Press.

Weaver, W. 1955. Translation. In Locke and Booth, 15–23. (Originally published, 1949.)

Weizenbaum, J. 1963. Symmetric list processor. *CACM* 6:524–544.

Weizenbaum, J. 1966. ELIZA—A computer program for the study of natural language communication between man and machine. *CACM* 9:36–45.

Weizenbaum, J. 1976. *Computer power and human reason: From judgment to calculation.* San Francisco: Freeman.

Welin, C. W. 1975. Semantic networks and case grammar. Publication 29, Institute of Linguistics, University of Stockholm.

Weyhrauch, R. W. 1978. Prolegomena to a theory of mechanized formal reasoning. Memo 315, AI Laboratory, Stanford University.

Whitehead, A. N., and Russell, B. 1925. *Principia mathematica* (2nd ed., Vol. 1). Cambridge, England: University Press.

Wilensky, R. 1978a. Understanding goal-based stories. Research Rep. No. 140, Dept. of Computer Science, Yale University.

Wilensky, R. 1978b. Why John married Mary: Understanding stories involving recurring goals. *Cognitive Science* 2:235–266.

Wilkins, D. 1979. Using plans in chess. *IJCAI 6.*

Wilks, Y. A. 1973. An artificial intelligence approach to machine translation. In Schank and Colby, 114–151.

Wilks, Y. A. 1974. Natural language understanding systems within the AI paradigm: A survey and some comparisons. AI Memo 237, AI Laboratory, Stanford University. (Also in A. Zampolli, Ed., *Linguistic structures processing.* Amsterdam: North-Holland, 1977, 341–398.)

Wilks, Y. A. 1975a. An intelligent analyzer and understander of English. *CACM* 18:264–274.

Wilks, Y. A. 1975b. Preference semantics. In E. L. Keenan (Ed.), *Formal semantics of natural language.* Cambridge, England: Cambridge University Press, 329–348.

Wilks, Y. A. 1975c. A preferential, pattern-seeking semantics for natural language inference. *Artificial Intelligence* 6:53–74.

Wilks, Y. A. 1975d. Primitives and words. *TINLAP-2*, 42–45.

Wilks, Y. A. 1976. Processing case. *American Journal of Computational Linguistics*, Microfiche 56.

Wilks, Y. A. 1977a. Good and bad arguments about semantic primitives. Research Rep. 42, Dept. of Artificial Intelligence, University of Edinburgh.

Wilks, Y. A. 1977b. Knowledge structures and language boundaries. *IJCAI 5*, 151–157.

Wilks, Y. A. 1977c. Methodological questions about artificial intelligence: Approaches to understanding natural language. *Journal of Pragmatics* 1:69–84.

Wilks, Y. A. 1977d. Time flies like an arrow. *New Scientist* 76:696–698.

Wilks, Y. A. 1977e. What sort of taxonomy of causation do we need for language understanding? *Cognitive Science* 1:235–264.

Wilks, Y. A. 1978. Making preferences more active. *Artificial Intelligence* 11:197–223.

Wilks, Y. A., and Herskovits, A. 1973. An intelligent analyser and generator for natural language. *Proceedings of the international conference on computational linguistics, Pisa, Italy.*

Winograd, T. 1972. *Understanding natural language.* New York: Academic Press.

Winograd, T. 1973. A procedural model of language understanding. In Schank and Colby, 152–186.

Winograd, T. 1974. Five lectures on artificial intelligence. AI Memo 246, AI Laboratory, Stanford University. (Also in A. Zampolli, Ed., *Linguistic structures processing.* Amsterdam: North-Holland, 1977, 399–520.)

Winograd, T. 1975. Frame representations and the declarative/procedural controversy. In Bobrow and Collins, 185–210.

Winograd, T. 1976. Parsing natural language via recursive transition net. In R. Yeh (Ed.), *Applied computation theory: Analysis, design, modeling.* Englewood Cliffs, N.J.: Prentice-Hall, 451–467.

Winograd, T. 1978. On primitives, prototypes, and other semantic anomalies. *TINLAP-2,* 25–32.

Winograd, T. 1979. Beyond programming languages. *CACM* 22(7):391–401.

Winograd, T. 1980a. Extended inference modes in reasoning by computer systems. *Artificial Intelligence* 13:5–26.

Winograd, T. 1980b. What does it mean to understand language? *Cognitive Science* 4:209–241.

Winograd, T. In press. *Language as a cognitive process.* Reading, Mass.: Addison-Wesley.

Winston, P. H. (Ed.). 1975. *The psychology of computer vision.* New York: McGraw-Hill.

Winston, P. H. 1977. *Artificial intelligence.* Reading, Mass.: Addison-Wesley.

Winston, P. H., and Brown, R. H. (Eds.). 1979. *Artificial intelligence: An MIT perspective.* Cambridge, Mass.: MIT Press.

Wolf, J., and Woods, W. 1980. The HWIM speech understanding system. In Lea, *Trends,* 316–339.

Wong, H. K. 1975. Generating English sentences from semantic structures. Tech. Rep. 84, Dept. of Computer Science, University of Toronto.

Woods, W. A. 1968. Procedural semantics for a question-answering machine. *Fall Joint Computer Conference* 33:457–471.

Woods, W. A. 1970. Transition network grammars for natural language analysis. *CACM* 13:591–606.

Woods, W. A. 1973a. An experimental parsing system for transition network grammars. In Rustin, 111–154.

Woods, W. A. 1973b. Progress in natural language understanding: An application to lunar geology. *AFIPS Conference Proceedings 42, 1973 National Computer Conference.* Montvale, N.J.: AFIPS Press, 441–450.

Woods, W. A. 1975a. SPEECHLIS: An experimental prototype for speech understanding research. *IEEE Transactions on Acoustics, Speech, and Signal Processing* 23(1):2–10.

Woods, W. A. 1975b. What's in a link: Foundations for semantic networks. In Bobrow and Collins, 35–82.

Woods, W. A., et al. 1976. Speech understanding systems: Final report. Rep. No. 3438, Bolt Beranek and Newman, Inc., Cambridge, Mass.

Woods, W. A., and Kaplan, R. 1971. The lunar sciences natural language information system. BBN Rep. No. 2265, Bolt Beranek and Newman, Inc., Cambridge, Mass.

Woods, W. A., Kaplan, R., and Nash–Webber, B. 1972. The lunar sciences natural language information system: Final report. BBN Rep. No. 2378, Bolt Beranek and Newman, Inc., Cambridge, Mass.

Yngve, V. 1962. Random generation of English sentences. *1961 international conference on machine translation of languages and applied language analysis.* (National Physical Laboratory, Symposium No. 13.) London: Her Majesty's Stationery Office, 66–80.

Indexes

NAME INDEX

Pages where the work is discussed are italicized.

SUBJECT INDEX

by SHRDLU's PROGRAMMAR,
297–298
in speech understanding, 327, 359
template matching, 260
with a transformational grammar, 260
Partial development, in search, 59, 114
Partial expansion. *See* Partial develop-
ment.
Partial functions, operators viewed as, 33
Partitioned semantic network, 186, 360
Pattern matching, 123, 256, 260, 283–287.
See also Matching.
Perceptual primitives, in WHISPER, 204
Performance evaluation, of speech systems, 329
Performance grammar, 261, 335, 349, 355,
359. *See also* Semantic grammar.
PHLIQA1, 232
Phonemics
in speech understanding, 327, 332–333
in transformational grammar, 246
Phonetics, 327, 332–333, 343
Phonological component of a transformational grammar, 248
Phrase marker, in a transformational
grammar, 246, 273
Phrase-structure grammar, 240–246
compared with transformation grammar,
245
definition of, 243
in parsing, 260, 262
Plan
in problem solving, 107, 128, 131, 137
in story understanding, 306, 309–310
PLANNER, 151, 155, 171, 175–178,
295–297
Planning, 22, 28, 169. *See also* Problem
solving; Reasoning.
constraint-structured, 203
hierarchical, in ABSTRIPS, 135
generalized, in STRIPS, 131–134
Plausible-move generation, in game-tree
search, 104
Plausible reasoning, 177
Ply, in game trees, 99
POPLER, 176
Potential solution, in heuristic search,
77–79, 80, 82
Pragmatics, in discourse, 249, 327, 332,
334, 359
Preconditions, of an operator
in ABSTRIPS, 136
in STRIPS, 128, 131, 135

Predicate calculus, 128, 163, 200, 292,
297, 299. *See also* Logic.
Predicate, in logic, 163, 182
Preference semantics, 208, 279, 288–291
Primitive problem, 36, 38, 74, 121
Primitives
perceptual, in WHISPER, 204
semantic, 148–149, 183, 198, 207–215,
231, 237, 278, 288–291, 300–303, 306
Problem reduction, 7, 114, 119, 201
Problem-reduction representation, 25,
36–42, 54, 74, 113
Problem representation, 8, 22–28, 32–45
game tree, 25, 43–45, 84
AND/OR graph, 26, 38–40, 43, 74,
113, 119, 124
problem-reduction, 25, 36–42, 54, 74,
113
state space, 26, 33, 195
theorem-proving, 25
Problem solving, 7, 21, 58, 74, 109, 113,
119, 123, 128, 135, 153, 284, 296.
See also Planning; Problem representation; Reasoning; Theorem proving.
generate-and-test, 30
human, 285
interdependent subproblems, 56, 81–83
means-ends analysis, 24, 59, 113, 117,
126, 129, 135, 169
operators, 22, 32, 36, 74, 110, 113, 119,
123, 128, 135
optimal solution, 28, 62, 74
primitive problem, 36, 38, 74, 121
problem reduction, 7, 114, 119, 201
for robots, 22, 128–139
solution, 33
state-space search, 30, 35, 46–53, 55,
58–73, 77, 80, 111, 153, 195
Problem space. *See* State space.
Procedural attachment, 156, 158, 179,
218–221
Procedural-declarative controversy, 151,
230
Procedural knowledge, 193, 198, 219
Procedural knowledge representation, 146,
149–150, 155–156, 172–179, 219–220,
230, 289, 295–297
Procedural semantics, 229–230
Process control. *See* Control strategy.
Production rule, 157, 190, 239, 303
Production system, 157, 190–199
adaptive, 195
conflict resolution in, 192, 197